SPORTS AND ATHLETICS PREPARATION, PERFORMANCE, AND PSYCHOLOGY

# INNOVATIVE WRITINGS IN SPORT AND EXERCISE PSYCHOLOGY

# SPORTS AND ATHLETICS PREPARATION, PERFORMANCE, AND PSYCHOLOGY

Additional books in this series can be found on Nova's website
under the Series tab.

Additional e-books in this series can be found on Nova's website
under the e-book tab.

Sports and Athletics Preparation, Performance, and Psychology

# Innovative Writings in Sport and Exercise Psychology

**Robert Schinke**
Editor

Copyright © 2014 by Nova Science Publishers, Inc.

**All rights reserved.** No part of this book may be reproduced, stored in a retrieval system or transmitted in any form or by any means: electronic, electrostatic, magnetic, tape, mechanical photocopying, recording or otherwise without the written permission of the Publisher.

For permission to use material from this book please contact us:
Telephone 631-231-7269; Fax 631-231-8175
Web Site: http://www.novapublishers.com

**NOTICE TO THE READER**

The Publisher has taken reasonable care in the preparation of this book, but makes no expressed or implied warranty of any kind and assumes no responsibility for any errors or omissions. No liability is assumed for incidental or consequential damages in connection with or arising out of information contained in this book. The Publisher shall not be liable for any special, consequential, or exemplary damages resulting, in whole or in part, from the readers' use of, or reliance upon, this material. Any parts of this book based on government reports are so indicated and copyright is claimed for those parts to the extent applicable to compilations of such works.

Independent verification should be sought for any data, advice or recommendations contained in this book. In addition, no responsibility is assumed by the publisher for any injury and/or damage to persons or property arising from any methods, products, instructions, ideas or otherwise contained in this publication.

This publication is designed to provide accurate and authoritative information with regard to the subject matter covered herein. It is sold with the clear understanding that the Publisher is not engaged in rendering legal or any other professional services. If legal or any other expert assistance is required, the services of a competent person should be sought. FROM A DECLARATION OF PARTICIPANTS JOINTLY ADOPTED BY A COMMITTEE OF THE AMERICAN BAR ASSOCIATION AND A COMMITTEE OF PUBLISHERS.

Additional color graphics may be available in the e-book version of this book.

**Library of Congress Cataloging-in-Publication Data**

ISBN: 978-1-62948-881-3

*Published by Nova Science Publishers, Inc. † New York*

# CONTENTS

**Introduction to the Compendium**      vii

**Chapter 1**    Personality Traits among Junior Elite Athletes in Norway, and a Comparison with Their Non-Athletic Counterparts    1
*Lars Bauger, Martin Eisemann and Hans Christian Vangberg*

**Chapter 2**    Exploring the Motivations Underpinning Track and Field Officials' Decisions to Volunteer    19
*Casey E. Gray and Philip M. Wilson*

**Chapter 3**    Psychological and Instructional Aspects of Serving in Tennis and Badminton –A Review and Implications for Coaching    37
*Ronnie Lidor and Gal Ziv*

**Chapter 4**    A Phenomenological Examination of Depression in Female Collegiate Athletes    51
*Alyson L. Jones, Ted M. Butryn, David M. Furst and Tamar Z. Semerjian*

**Chapter 5**    Subjective Beliefs among Sport Coaches about Communication during Coach-Athlete Conversations    71
*Frode Moen and Ragnvald Kvalsund*

**Chapter 6**    The Relationship between Athletic Identity and Physical Activity among Former College Athletes    93
*Erin J. Reifsteck, Diane L. Gill and DeAnne L. Brooks*

**Chapter 7**    Networking As an American Sport Psychology Doctoral Student: Creating and Marketing Your Personal Brand    107
*Scott Barnicle and Damon Burton*

**Chapter 8**    Common Features in Overtrained Athletes and Individuals with Professional Burnout: Implications for Sports Medical Practice    117
*Harri Selänne, Tatiana V. Ryba and Juhani Leppäluoto*

| | | |
|---|---|---|
| **Chapter 9** | Fans' Identification and Commitment to a Sport Team: The Impact of Self-Selection versus Socialization Processes<br>*Katrina Koch and Daniel L. Wann* | **131** |
| **Chapter 10** | Coaches' Perceptions of the Use of Chronological and Biological Age in the Identification and Development of Talented Athletes<br>*Matthew F. Fiander, Martin I. Jones and John K. Parker* | **147** |
| **Chapter 11** | Psychological Approaches to Enhancing Fair Play<br>*John L. Perry, Peter J. Clough and Lee Crust* | **165** |
| **Chapter 12** | Shared Deliberate Practice: A Case Study of Elite Handball Team Training<br>*Ole Lund, Peter Musaeus and Mette Krogh Christensen* | **179** |
| **Chapter 13** | A Longitudinal Qualitative Exploration of Elite Korean Tennis Players' Career Transition Experiences<br>*Sunghee Park, David Lavallee and David Tod* | **197** |
| **Chapter 14** | Psychological Skills Training and Self-Efficacy: The UNIFORM Approach with College-Age Swim Exercisers<br>*Brittany A. Glynn, Jenelle N. Gilbert and Dawn K. Lewis* | **225** |
| **Chapter 15** | Motivations and Perceived Benefits of Marathoning: An Exploratory Study<br>*Mary Jo Loughran, Deanna Hamilton and Meredith McGinley* | **245** |
| **Chapter 16** | Age and Gender-Related Changes in Exercise Motivation among Highly Active Individuals<br>*Matthew A. Stults-Kolehmainen, Joseph T. Ciccolo, John B. Bartholomew, John Seifert and Robert S. Portman* | **261** |
| **Chapter 17** | Examining the Superstitions of Sport Fans: Types of Superstitions, Perceptions of Impact, and Relationship with Team Identification<br>*Daniel L. Wann, Frederick G. Grieve, Ryan K. Zapalac, Christian End, Jason R. Lanter, Dale G. Pease, Brandy Fellows, Kelly Oliver and Allison Wallace* | **281** |
| **Chapter 18** | "Everything Was Different": A Qualitative Study of US Professional Basketball Players' Experiences Overseas<br>*Rainer J. Meisterjahn and Craig A. Wrisberg* | **305** |
| **Index** | | **325** |

# INTRODUCTION TO THE COMPENDIUM

The present compilation marks the fifth consecutive year that *Athletic Insight* has teamed with Nova Science on the development of a compendium of writings from the journal. This year's contributions feature a series of international scholars from Canada, the United States, Norway, Finland, Denmark, the United Kingdom, South Korea, Norway, and Israel. Upon review of these submissions, one also finds an interesting turn on the part of the journal – that more than half of the submissions are from outside of North America. More broadly speaking, submissions were received form five continents, excluding the Arctic and Antarctica. Dissect the submissions further and you will recognize several senior authors within these submissions, including Ronnie Lidor, Craig Wrisberg, Diane Gill, David Lavallee, Theodore Butryn, Tatiana Ryba, and several more.

Personally, I am quite excited by the series of authors and diversity in topic matter found in this compendium. I dare say that this year's compendium is the strongest offered by Athletic Insight to date. On behalf of the publisher and the editorial staff, I hope you enjoy the chapters that follow. What follows is a brief review of the contributions found in this compendium and then the accepted publications from 2013.

## BRIEF OVERVIEW OF THE CONTENT

The compendium begins with "Psychological and Instructional Aspects of Serving in Tennis and Badminton – A Review and Implications for Coaching', written by Ronnie Lidor and Gal Ziv from the Wingate Institute and the university of Haifa, respectively. The purpose of this article was to review a series of studies ($n = 16$) on psychological and instructional aspects of serving in two racquet sports – tennis and badminton. The main findings of this review were that (a) imagery and self-talk can help players improve their serves in tennis and badminton; (b) task-pertinent learning strategies which are introduced at the beginning of the learning process, or at some time after some knowledge of the serve was acquired, can enhance serving performances of beginning learners; (c) although there are not enough data to indicate what type of feedback benefit serving performances, instructional feedback based on the correct movement of the server should be useful in practicing the serve; (d) contextual variety appears to improve the learning of the badminton serve.

The second paper, titled "Subjective Beliefs among Sport Coaches about Communication during Coach-Athlete Conversations" was authored by Frode Moen and Ragnvald Kvalsund, from the Norwegian University of Science and Technology. The purpose in their project was to explore subjective beliefs among coaches in elite sports about what they think are effective communication during performance appraisals with their athletes. A Q-sample of 36 different opinions about different underlying aims for communication, and how this affects athletes' abilities to understand better (knowing), to perform better (doing), and/ or improve their focus, were presented to sport coaches from different top level sports. A sample of statements drawn from the actual concourse of communication was presented to 19 elite coaches who were asked to consider and rank-order the statements regarding performance appraisals through Q-sorting procedure.

Rainer J. Meisterjahn From Cardinal Stritch University and Craig A. Wrisberg from the University of Tennessee authored the third accepted submission, titled "Everything Was Different: A Qualitative Study of US Professional Basketball Players' Experiences Overseas. In their submission, the authors found that research on international labor migration in professional sports (e.g., Magee & Sugden, 2002) suggests that the experiences of athletes in foreign cultures are often diverse and entail numerous pressures. In order to examine such experiences in greater depth, existential phenomenological interviews (Thomas & Pollio, 2002) were conducted with ten current and former professional basketball players, ages 24 to 55, from the US. Thematic analysis of the interview transcripts produced eight major themes that clearly characterized participants' experiences: Learning the Local Mentality, Experiencing Isolation, Connecting with Others, Exploring the Physical Environment, Dealing with the Business, Adjusting to Team Resources, Managing Team Dynamics, and Playing the Game. Taken together, the results suggest that while playing overseas required participants to manage a variety of cultural and sport-related stressors, it also afforded them opportunities for personal and professional development.

Erin J. Reifsteck and Diane L. Gill from the University of North Carolina at Greensboro authored "The Relationship between Athletic Identity and Physical Activity among Former College Athletes". The purpose of this study was to examine the relationship between athletic identity and physical activity among former college athletes. The relationship was first examined with former Division I athletes ($N$=56) and then in a second sample of former Division III athletes (N=18) and non-athletes (N=31) from a small college. All participants (N=105) completed the Athletic Identity Measurement Scale (AIMS), the Godin Leisure Time Exercise Questionnaire, and the Stage of Exercise Behavior Change measure. The AIMS was a positive predictor of physical activity, and this relationship was stronger for alumni who had participated in college athletics. While former college athletes had higher AIMS scores, they were not more active than alumni who did not participate in college athletics. Former athletes were also more likely than non-athletes to report a decrease in physical activity after college. Substantial decreases in physical activity after the conclusion of a collegiate athletic career have important health implications for former college athletes, which warrant the development of transitional programs that promote lifelong physical activity participation among NCAA student-athletes.

Scott Barnicle and Damon Burton from the University of Idaho authored "Networking as an American Sport Psychology Doctoral Student: Creating and Marketing Your Personal Brand". The authors recognized that the field of applied sport and performance psychology is booming. More graduate education programs are emerging, attracting increasing numbers of qualified students, and growing the exposure and knowledge base of the field (Quinn, 2011). Coupled with a strong theoretical and research foundation, applied sport psychology consulting experiences are vital to developing well-rounded professionals in the field (Balague, 2011). Guided by the three fundamentals of positive relationships, exchange relationships, and positive self-efficacy, Network Theory (Turnbull, Ford, & Cunningham, 1996) can provide graduate students with the opportunities and experiences in which to practice their applied sport psychology skills. Future applied sport psychology consultants will need to mesh their academic foundation with solid business, marketing, advertising, and branding skills and techniques to grow their personal consulting brand as well as the field of sport psychology. This chapter provides theory-driven practical applications of Network Theory for sport psychology students whose goal is to enhance their depth of knowledge through applied sport psychology consulting experiences.

Harri Selänne, Tatiana V. Ryba, and Juhani Leppäluoto from LIKES Research Center, Jyväskylä, Finland, the Department of Public Health, Aarhus University, Denmark, and the Department of Physiology, University of Oulu, Finland, respectively contributed "Common Features in Overtrained Athletes and Individuals with Professional Burnout: Implications for Sports Medical Practice". In this paper, the authors discuss the symptoms of overtraining and burnout— two syndromes in which the etiology, after the decades of research, is still poorly understood. Overtraining is caused by an imbalance between exercise and rest, and often triggered by increased neuromuscular loading. There are no reliable diagnostic tests for overtraining. The neurological mechanisms underpinning burnout are similarly not known; however, it is generally accepted that the main cause is mental overloading. Both conditions are stress-related developmental processes suggesting malfunction of adrenal cortex and hypothalamus, mainly the pituitary. The two syndromes are also related to a variety of individual, environmental, and organizational factors. Based on the first author's extensive practical experience of working with overtrained athletes and individuals with occupational burnout, the authors draw on both literatures to offer invaluable insights into a medical assessment and treatment of athletes suffering from overtraining.

Katrina Koch and Daniel L. Wann from Murray State University added "Fans' Identification and Commitment to a Sport Team: The Impact of Self-Selection versus Socialization Processes as chapter seven. These authors proposed that team fandom origin, self-selected or socialized, should play an important role in one's level of team identification with and commitment to a favorite team. It was hypothesized that fans who self-selected their favorite team would report higher levels of team identification on three dimensions of team commitment: personal identity, affective commitment, and calculative commitment. Fans who were socialized to prefer a team were expected to report higher levels of two dimensions of team commitment: social obligation and regional tribalism. Participants completed the Sport Spectator Identification Scale, the Scale of Commitment to Sport Teams, and assessments of team fandom origin. It was found that socialized fans reported higher levels of social obligation and regional tribalism to their teams than self-selected fans. Additional findings include: Male fans reported higher levels of team identification, personal identity, affective commitment, calculative commitment, and social obligation than female fans; older fans reported more self-selection than younger fans; and female fans reported more socialization than male fans.

Lars Bauger, Martin Eisemann and Hans Christian Vangberg from the University of Tromsø, Norway authored "Personality traits among Junior Elite Athletes in Norway, and a comparison with their non-athletic counterparts". The authors explored personality dimensions, as measured by the Junior Temperament and Character Inventory, passion and self-esteem among junior elite athletes. In addition, the athletes were compared with non-athletic peers to investigate if they had a personality profile which could be viewed as beneficial for the athlete. Female athletes scored significantly higher on the personality dimensions Reward Dependence and Cooperativeness, and significantly lower on Self-esteem than their male counterparts. In addition, the athlete sample scored significantly higher on Persistence and Self-Directedness and lower on Harm Avoidance than non-athletes. The use of the J-TCI as a measure of personality yielded significant differences between groups, which should be relevant for the sport psychology community and increase our understanding of personality dimensions among aspiring elite athletes.

Casey E. Gray from the University of Western Ontario and Philip M. Wilson from Brock University in Canada, authored chapter nine, "Exploring the Motivations Underpinning Track and Field Officials' Decisions to Volunteer". The authors found that little is known about the factors that promote behavioural persistence among volunteer track and field officials. This preliminary qualitative study examined the explanations a sample of Canadian officials offered for their initial and continued involvement in track and field over time. Certified track and field officials ($N = 79$) responded to 3 open-ended survey items exploring their reasons for initial, current, and future involvement in officiating. Content analysis indicated a varied and dynamic pattern of motivations that informed decisions to volunteer in the sport. Among them, intrapersonal factors were often cited as reasons for initial and current motivations for officiating, while a combination of intra- and interpersonal reasons appeared salient reasons for anticipated future involvement. Overall, the current findings also support the important role played by satisfying the basic psychological needs outlined within Self-Determination Theory (Deci & Ryan, 2002) with respect to current involvement.

Matthew Fiander, Martin I. Jones, and John K. Parker from the University of Gloucestershire, UK contributed chapter ten, "Coaches' perceptions of the use of chronological and biological age in the identification and development of talented athletes". The authors posited that coaches and practitioners recognize that talent identification and development have a crucial role in the pursuit of excellence. National governing bodies routinely allocate youth participants, irrespective of biological age, to chronological age categories in an effort to ensure developmentally fair competition and opportunity. However, differences in the timing and tempo of maturation provide evidence to exclude chronological age and can lead to the misclassification of children in relation to their biological maturity. The purpose of this study was to explore coaches' perceptions of how they use chronological age and biological age in coaching practice, and the importance they place on the measurement and utilization of biological age to develop young athletes. The authors conducted semi-structured interviews with six coaches and analyzed data using a qualitative description methodology. The results revealed three main themes relating to the delivery of the long-term athlete development model, the limited or lack of knowledge of all aspects of the long-term athlete development model, and a desire for a different model. Results provide scholars and practitioners with a greater understanding of coaches' perspectives of the use of chronological and biological age in the identification and development of talented athletes.

John L. Perry, Peter J. Clough and Lee Crust, from Leeds Trinity University, the University of Hull, and the University of Lincoln, respectively added "Psychological Approaches to Enhancing Fair Play" as chapter eleven. These authors reviewed approaches to studying sportspersonship, moral behavior in sport and broader morality theory to offer practical strategies to enhance fair play. By identifying stages and levels of morality and reviewing research supporting the relationship between goal orientations and moral behavior, we propose five practical strategies. Namely, we suggest that developing a mastery climate, developing a moral community, role taking, reflection and power transfer can be effectively used to progress performers from pre-conventional to a conventional level of morality and ultimately, establish principled morality in sport.

Ole Lund, Peter Musaeus and Mette Krogh Christensen from the Institute of Sports Science and Clinical Biomechanics, University of Southern Denmark, and the Center for Medical Education, INCUBA Science Park – Skejby, Aarhus University, authored "Shared Deliberate Practice: A Case Study of Elite Handball Team Training", chapter twelve. In this case study of a Danish elite handball team, the authors explore team learning processes in order to examine to what extent team members' development of expertise is a shared deliberate practice. By drawing from theoretical frameworks on expertise and deliberate practice (Ericsson, 2006) and team cognition (Salas, Fiore, & Letsky, 2012), we aim to answer what characterizes efficient and successful handball team training. The case study involved participant observation and interviews, and it included the female first team in a Danish handball club Randers HK. The team is amongst the best three teams in Denmark. In particular, the case study found that important factors for shared deliberate practice are concentration, feedback and role modeling. There are four theoretical findings. 1. Deliberate practice in team sport is a shared activity. 2. Both structured tactical training and match training are deliberate practices. 3. Concentration mediates team cognitive skills. 4. Feedback and role modeling mediate team cognitive skills. From an applied perspective, this study points to the value of seeing team sport as necessitating shared deliberate practice. Team players need to train shared understanding and learn how to negotiate the coach's orchestration of the game plan. Specifically, the results may lead experienced coaches in high performance team sports to use experienced athletes to engage in verbal feedback and being explicit role models to less experienced players.

Alyson L. Jones, Ted M. Butryn, David M. Furst, and Tamar Z. Semerjian, from San José State University in the United States authored "A Phenomenological Examination Of Depression In Female Collegiate Athletes" as chapter thirteen. They proposed that despite the well-known mental health benefits of exercise, collegiate athletes may be at an increased risk of depression due to the number of stressors they face (Gill, 2008; Yang et al., 2007), and this risk may be even greater for female athletes (Donohue et al., 2004; Storch, Storch, Killikany, & Roberti, 2005). It has been suggested that a greater understanding of personal experiences would be helpful in increasing awareness and improving treatment. Therefore, the purpose of the current study was to explore the lived experience of depression in female collegiate athletes. In-depth, unstructured interviews were conducted with 10 current and former female collegiate athletes. The interviews were recorded, transcribed, and analyzed using phenomenological research methods (Dale, 1996, 2000). Thematic analysis revealed one ground (the role of sport) and four general categories (weariness, self-doubt, out of control, and nowhere to go). Practical implications and recommendations are made for athletes and coaches.

Sunghee Park, David Lavallee, and David Tod, from Kookmin University in South Korea, the University of Stirling, and Aberystwyth University, UK contributed "A Longitudinal Qualitative Exploration of Elite Korean Tennis Players' Career Transition Experiences" as chapter fourteen. The purpose of this study was to explore elite Korean tennis players' career transition experiences, focusing on psychological components (i.e., self-identity, life skills development, and coping strategies) and socio-cultural influences through the process. A longitudinal qualitative method was employed, and Korean tennis players ($N = 5$; two males and three females; mean age 29.8 ± 5.54 years) who were considering retirement participated in the current study. Data were analyzed by interpretative phenomenological analysis and resulted in three super-ordinate themes: (a) sense of self and process of identity shift, (b) available resources during the career transition process, and (c) decision-making processes and consequences of decisions. These results provided practical implications for supporting athletes' career transitions (e.g., developing a balanced self-identity and life skill during their athletic careers, providing proactive intervention) and future research directions (e.g., examining athletes' retirement decision-making process, the need of cross-cultural research).

Brittany A. Glynn, Jenelle N. Gilbert, and Dawn K. Lewis from the University of Ottawa, Canada, and California State University, Fresno in the United States provided "Psychological Skills Training and Self-efficacy: The UNIFORM Approach with College-Age Swim Exercisers" as chapter fifteen. In their project, thirty-nine college students enrolled in a swimming class participated in a psychological skills training program (PST) called UNIFORM (Gilbert, 2011). The self-efficacy based program examined the relationships between the participants' use of psychological skills, self-efficacy, swim conditioning and techniques. Results demonstrated greater use of the psychological skills of relaxation and self talk. Improvements in swim conditioning and technique, as well as increases in swim conditioning and technique efficacy, and the efficacy to swim in the future were also acknowledged. Imagery, self-talk, goal-setting, emotional control and attentional control were positively associated with swim conditioning and swim technique self-efficacy and future swim self-efficacy. Furthermore, swim conditioning and swim technique self efficacy, as well as future swim self-efficacy, were related to swim performance with results demonstrating swim technique self-efficacy to be the greatest predictor of swim performance. Therefore, PST interventions act as moderators to self-efficacy, while self-efficacy mediates students' performances and subsequent perceptions to swim for exercise in the future. Thus, PST interventions based in self-efficacy may help college-age students improve their swim self-efficacy, conditioning, skills, and efficacy to exercise in the future.

Mary Jo Loughran, Deanna Hamilton, and Meredith McGinley from Chatham University authored chapter sixteen, "Motivations and Perceived Benefits of Marathoning: An Exploratory Study". The authors found that the relationship between motivations for running a marathon and the benefits derived from its completion has not been systematically explored in the sport psychology literature. This study investigated motivations and perceived benefits of marathon participation in a non-elite population of runners. Ninety-nine runners completed questionnaires examining motivations and perceived benefits of marathon participation immediately after the event. Confirmatory factor analysis of a scale designed for the present study confirmed that the perceived benefits of marathon participation can be categorized as Psychological, Physical, and Relational. As expected, marathoners' motivations for running were predictive of perceived benefits along similar categories. Interestingly, participants also experienced perceived benefits that extended beyond their original motivations for running the marathon. The results of this study add to the body of evidence suggesting that marathon running enhances physical, psychological, and relational health.

Matthew A. Stults-Kolehmainen from Yale University Medical School, New Haven, CT and Northern Illinois University, Joseph T. Ciccolo from Brown Medical School and the Miriam Hospital, John B. Bartholomew from the University of Texas, John Seifert from Montana State University, and Robert S. Portman from Signal Nutrition, all from the United States contributed chapter seventeen "Age and Gender-related Changes in Exercise Motivation among Highly Active Individuals". The purpose of this investigation was to determine differences in exercise motivation across age groups and gender of recreational endurance athletes (N = 2756), ages 18-64. Participants selected their top 3 motives from a list of 10 intrinsic and extrinsic factors, which across all individuals were enjoyment (57.1%), performance (53.3%), and health (51.9%). Performance motivation was endorsed by 79.7% of those aged 18-24 years vs. 37.8% of those aged 55-64 years. Women selected weight maintenance (26.8% vs. 17.4%) and appearance (15.7% vs. 7.0%) to a greater degree than men. Men endorsed improving performance (54.6% vs. 47.1%), living longer (18.5% vs. 9.7%) and feeling better (26.0% vs. 20.3%) as a primary motives more than women. There was a non-significant ($p = 0.049$) age and gender interaction for weight maintenance with gender differences apparent in younger age groups but not in older ages.

Chapter eighteen features the writing of Daniel L. Wann from Murray State and his colleagues, relating to the "Examining the Superstitions of Sport Fans: Types of Superstitions, Perceptions of Impact, and Relationship with Team Identification". This work examined the superstitious behaviors of sport fans. A sample of 1661 college students completed a questionnaire packet assessing demographics, team identification, sport fandom, superstitions, perceptions of superstition impact and importance, and why they engaged in the superstitions. A total of 675 persons reported at least one superstition. Higher levels of sport fandom and higher levels of team identification correlated with a greater number of superstitions listed. Further, persons with higher levels of team identification reported greater perceptions of the impact and importance of their superstitions. The categorization of the superstitions revealed that apparel superstitions were most prominent. Other prominent superstitions included vocalizations, consumption of food/drink (nonalcoholic), watching or not watching the action, and good luck charms/superstitious rituals.

In closing, on behalf of the journal's editorial board and publisher, we strongly hope you find this resource helpful and revealing of current and future trends in sport and exercise psychology scholarship. We believe that these works feature some of the most innovative thinking within the field at present.

Robert Schinke, EdD, Editor of *Athletic Insight*
Canada Research Chair in Multicultural Sport and Physical Activity

In: Innovative Writings in Sport and Exercise Psychology
Editor: Robert Schinke

ISBN: 978-1-62948-881-3
© 2014 Nova Science Publishers, Inc.

*Chapter 1*

# PERSONALITY TRAITS AMONG JUNIOR ELITE ATHLETES IN NORWAY, AND A COMPARISON WITH THEIR NON-ATHLETIC COUNTERPARTS

## *Lars Bauger\*, Martin Eisemann and Hans Christian Vangberg*
University of Tromsø, Tromsø, Norway

### ABSTRACT

The present study explored personality dimensions, as measured by the Junior Temperament and Character Inventory, passion and self-esteem among junior elite athletes. In addition, the athletes were compared with non-athletic peers to investigate if they had a personality profile which could be viewed as beneficial for the athlete. Female athletes scored significantly higher on the personality dimensions Reward Dependence and Cooperativeness, and significantly lower on Self-esteem than their male counterparts. In addition, the athlete sample scored significantly higher on Persistence and Self-Directedness and lower on Harm Avoidance than non-athletes. The use of the J-TCI as a measure of personality yielded significant differences between groups, which should be relevant for the sport psychology community and increase our understanding of personality dimensions among aspiring elite athletes.

**Keywords:** Personality, passion, self-esteem, sport psychology, junior athletes, elite athletes

### PERSONALITY

Personality research in sport psychology has since the 1990s been almost nonexistent due to a view that the previous personality research often had been poorly conducted with the lack of substantiated conclusions. This has lead personality to be a dirty word in sport psychology (Auweele, Nys, Rzewnicki, and Van Mele, 2001). According to Cashmore (2002) personality

---

\* Correspondence concerning this article should be addressed to Lars Bauger, Tromsø, Norway. E-mail: larsbauger@gmail.com.

research in sport has almost exclusively been based on the Minnesota Multiphasic Personality Inventory (MMPI). The MMPI is a long true-false inventory which was developed as a measure of abnormality (Carver and Scheier, 2004; Cashmore, 2002). The MMPI has been the inventory of choice in research since it was assumed that the personality traits measured by the MMPI were best at differentiating successful and unsuccessful athletes. Almost all studies that are based on MMPI as an assessment have used the original version, developed in the 1930$^s$. This is problematic since the original MMPI was developed with a sample that was limited both ethnically and geographically, a fact that compromises the interpretation of scores from other populations.

Another widely used inventory in sport psychology has been the Profile of Mood States (POMS). Results from POMS studies showed that athletes, in general, exhibited what Morgan (1980) called an "iceberg profile" reflecting lower scores on tension, fatigue, depression and confusion and higher scores on vigor of the five "mood states" compared with non-athletes. Results also show that successful athletes have a more positive mood profile, i.e., lower scores on the four states mentioned above, than unsuccessful athletes. However, these differences are regarded as too small and hence not reliable in predicting performance among athletes (Hirschhorn, 2006). To a lesser extent, the 16 Personality Factor Inventory (16PF) (Cattell, Eber, and Tatsuoka, 1970) have been used as a measure of personality in sport psychology. The 16PF was developed using factor analysis of trait terms derived from lexical criterion of importance (Carver and Scheier, 2004).

Comparisons on personality traits between athletes and non-athletes seem to be inconclusive or diffuse. Where some researchers have found no difference (Fuchs and Zaichkowsky, 1983; Schurr, Ashley, and Joy, 1977), while others have found that competitive athletes have a higher emotional stability, self-confidence and mental resilience compared to non-athletes and unique scores for extraversion and neuroticism (Bara Filho, Ribeiro, and García, 2005; Morgan, 1980; Saint-Phard, Van Dorsten, Marx, and York, 1999). Although significant differences between athletes and non-athletes have emerged concerning various personality aspects, no specific personality profile could be delineated (Morris, 2000). When using MMPI and Cattel's 16PF some difference between amateur and professional athletes concerning conscientiousness, self control, intelligence and anxiety were found (Jarvis, 2006). When Dowd and Innes (1981) compared results on the 16PF scales between athletes ranked as top 15 in squash and volleyball, with athletes of lower ranking, the results showed that the former scored higher on intelligence and lower on anxiety. According to these results performance can be linked to extraversion and emotional stability, but they do not allow to assume a causal relationship (Eysenck, Nias, and Cox, 1982). Possibly, athletes performing on a high level are less anxious since they more often win their matches. When using a five-factor model of personality to predict performance in female college soccer players, neuroticism and conscientiousness were the only personality factors significantly related to performance, with lower scores on neuroticism related to higher scores on performance (Piedmont, Hill, and Blanco, 1999). On the other hand, conscientiousness was positively correlated with performance, which would be expected since this factor includes the individuals` will to achieve.

Although some research has found that personality traits have some use in predicting longitudinal athletic success (Aidman, 2007; Gee, Marshall, and King, 2010), most researchers agree that coaches should refrain from using personality as a basis for team or program selection (Singer, 1988; Weinberg and Gould, 2011). Rather, personality should be one of several psychological measures that can guide coaches and sport psychology consultants in their approach to develop good psychological skills training program. For example, if an athlete's personality indicates an anxious individual, he or she could be introduced to anxiety reduction techniques to avoid excess anxiety in competitive settings.

When athletes involved in team sports are compared with athletes in individual sports, the former score, not surprisingly, higher on extraversion than athletes competing in individual sports (Booth, 1958). There are also differences between athletes within the same sport. In the sport of track and field, sprinters and throwers are more extraverted than middle distance runners. One study even showed that as the distance increases the level of extraversion decreases, and long distance runners turned out to be more introverted (Clitsome and Kostrubala, 1977). There was also a tendency for the better runners being more introverted.

## SELF-ESTEEM

Self-esteem is now a household concept where high self-esteem is regarded as something that causes positive outcome in life in general (Baumeister, Campbell, Krueger, and Vohs, 2003) and in specific situations (Di Paula and Campbell, 2002). Self-esteem as a construct has had many varying definitions and ways of measuring. In this article it refers to a person's global evaluation of his or her overall worthiness (Rosenberg, 1979) by reflecting how you feel about own skills, abilities, and social relationships (Coatsworth and Conroy, 2006). The assumption that higher self-esteem causes positive outcomes has been investigated through several studies in academic (Bachman and Omalley, 1977; Rosenberg, Schooler, and Schoenbach, 1989; Skaalvik and Hagtvet, 1990) and work settings (Campbell and Fairey, 1985; Di Paula and Campbell, 2002; Judge and Bono, 2001). Baumeister and colleagues (2003) found little evidence for a positive effect of self-esteem on academic outcomes in their meta-analysis. On the contrary they found that some of the students with low grades actually performed worse after interventions aimed at increasing self-esteem. They did however find that higher self-esteem can help individuals to persist longer at a task in the face of failure (Baumeister et al., 2003). This could be viewed as beneficial for athletes since most sports require some form of tedious practice on the road to mastery. Although there is little evidence of a causal relationship between performance outcomes and self-esteem, studies have shown that these factors are in some way connected (Baumeister et al., 2003; Coatsworth and Conroy, 2006), and many researchers assume that self-esteem influences affect and behavior of individuals (Harter, 2001).

Researchers have also investigated self-esteem in relation to sport and empirical evidence has emerged supporting a link between participation in sport and higher levels of self-esteem (Deianey and Lee, 1995; Marsh and Kleitman, 2003). Deianey and Lee (1995) argued that highly active individuals score higher on self-esteem than low-active respondents. However, it is difficult to determine if it is the athletic participation per se or other factors that affect self-esteem.

## PASSION

An interesting aspect that has been shown to have an effect on athletes is the passion they have for their sport (Vallerand et al., 2008). Vallerand et al. (2003) proposed a dualistic model of passion, where they defined passion as a strong inclination toward an activity that people like, that they find important and something they invest time and energy. Therefore they would have to spend time on the activity and like the activity, for it to be defined as a passion. Vallerand et al. (2003) proposed two types of passion, one being harmonious and the other being obsessive. The difference between obsessive and harmonious passion consists in how the passionate activity is internalized into an individual's core identity. Obsessive passion is a result of a controlled internalization of the activity, which originates from pressure from some contingency attached to the activity. This can be social acceptance or self-esteem, or because the excitement from the activity becomes uncontrollable. It is important to mention that individuals with an obsessive passion for an activity still like to exert their activity, but they might feel a compulsion for their activity even when they should not. Vallerand et al. (2007) states that obsessive passion is expected to lead to a rigid form of Persistence, since it occurs even when there are personal costs, such as damage to relationships and failed work commitments.

On the other hand, harmonious passion is a result of an autonomous internalization of the activity into the individual identity, this happens when the individual has freely chosen that the activity is important to them, without any contingencies attached to it (Donahue, Rip, and Vallerand, 2009; Mageau et al., 2009; Vallerand, 2008; Vallerand et al., 2003; Vallerand et al., 2008; Vallerand et al., 2007). The activity is still occupying a significant space in the individual identity, but it is not an overpowering force and is in harmony with other aspects of the individual. Vallerand et al. (2007) hypothesized that harmonious passion will lead to greater positive affect, such as higher well-being, and less negative affect than obsessive passion.

## PURPOSE OF THE STUDY

Although personality research in the sport community has been non-existent in recent years, due to its checkered past with poor assessment tools and unsubstantiated conclusions, we believe that personality still has a role to play along with other psychological factors in sport psychology research.

The purpose of this study was, firstly, to investigate personality characteristics, with well-developed and validated instruments of personality, among junior elite athletes, secondly, to investigate the relationship between personality, demographic variables, and other psychological factors, such as passion for the sport and self-esteem. Finally, to test for differences in personality dimensions between those who attend sport-specific high schools with those attending general high schools in Norway.

When we regard personality as an important aspect of performance (Morgan, 1980), it would be interesting to explore this in the framework of Cloninger et al. (1993) biosocial model of personality. This model accounts for both temperament and character dimensions of personality. Where the dimensions novelty seeking, harm avoidance, reward dependence and persistence form the temperament which are independently heritable and manifest early in life. While the dimensions self-directedness, cooperation and self-transcendence form the character which matures in adulthood and influence personal and social effectiveness.

We hypothesize that the character dimension persistence, characterized by being hard-working, industrious and ambitious, should be higher among athletes than non-athletes. The rationale here are the inherent qualities of persistence would represent a prerequisite for a successful athlete. Further, we regard harm avoidance as an important personality dimension for athletes since low scorers are described as relaxed, bold, outgoing and vigorous whereas high scorers are described as worrying, fearful, shy and fatigable. Persistence, which is a temperament dimension, and self-directedness, a character dimension are assumed to be positively correlated, since individuals with high scores on self-directedness are described as mature, responsible, purposeful and self-accepted (Cloninger et al., 1993).

# METHOD

## Recruitment

To recruit participants to the study we contacted senior high schools in Norway that fulfilled our inclusion criteria of being a sport-specific high school. Out of the five schools contacted, three were willing to participate. The three schools, located in different parts of Norway, were non-profit private schools, where the curriculum is adjusted to the needs of athletes. These schools are in close collaboration with the national sport council and national Olympic committee. The participating schools had both Olympic medal winners and national champions among their alumni. Sport programs the schools were providing included: alpine skiing, football, track and field, handball, cross-country skiing, rifle shooting, swimming, cycling and biathlon.

Available data from an ongoing mental health study among adolescents on the J-TCI were used for comparison. This study had collected responses from 1290 participants in the same school grades as our study with an age range from 15 to 19 years (M = 16.79, SD = 1.18).

## Participants

Of the 175 participants who entered the present study, 139 (79.43 %) completed the questionnaire. The questionnaires were collected during the fall of 2010. The age among participants ranged from 15 to 19 years (M = 16.76, SD = .88). 69 (49.3 %) women and 70 (50.4 %) men participated. 90 (64.7 %) of the participants competed in individual sports and 49 (35.3 %) competed in team sports. The participants' competitive level in their sport differed: 8 (5.8 %) competed at the local level, 34 (24.5 %) at the regional level, 82 (59 %) at the national level and 15 (10.8 %) at an international level.

## Procedure

All students from the respective schools were invited to participate. They were briefed on the study orally by a researcher in the classroom at the beginning of a lesson. Students were informed about the voluntary character of participation and the possibility to withdraw from the study at any time. The students were also guaranteed anonymity. In addition to the oral briefing, all students obtained written information about the study. All the participating schools were visited within a two week period during autumn 2010, and all potential participants were briefed on the study as well as how to access the web-based questionnaire. The time limit for participation in the study was set to two weeks after briefing of the last school. A week before the given deadline, schools were sent a reminder per e-mail.

## Measures

The questionnaire was made available, together with information about the study and a link, to the students via the schools web-based learning management system "class fronter". The web-link directed the students to the study which was distributed through the internet-based survey tool "Survey Monkey". The study included demographic characteristics, such as age, gender, type of sport, level of competition, self-reported skill level and a set of questionnaires comprising four areas.

*Passion.* The Passion Scale (Vallerand et al., 2003) is comprised of two 6-item subscales: harmonious passion (e.g., "This activity is in harmony with the other activities in my life") and obsessive passion (e.g., "I have difficulties controlling my urge to do my activity"). Responses are given on a 1 (Do not agree at all) to 7 (Very strongly agree) scale. The Passion Scale also includes a four-item criterion subscale that measures whether participants were passionate about their own activity. Psychometric properties of the Passion Scale have been assessed in previous studies which supported its validity and reliability (Vallerand, 2008; Vallerand et al., 2003). The scale was translated into Norwegian by a native speaker while a bilingual colleague with no knowledge of the original scale back translated it to English. No discrepancies between the two versions emerged. Cronbach alpha coefficients of the different subscales for the Passion Scale were deemed acceptable (table 1).

### Table 1. Descriptives of the major study variables

| Variable | n | M | SD | α | Range | Skew |
|---|---|---|---|---|---|---|
| WHO-5 | 139 | 16.81 | 4.27 | 0.85 | 1-25 | -1.01 |
| Obsessive passion | 139 | 24.17 | 6.45 | 0.69 | 9-42 | -0.01 |
| Harmonious passion | 139 | 33.24 | 5.72 | 0.84 | 17-42 | -0.62 |
| Novelty Seeking | 139 | 29.94 | 7.41 | 0.69 | 14-54 | 0.72 |
| Harm Avoidance | 139 | 23.56 | 8.40 | 0.84 | 3-45 | 0.14 |
| Reward Dependence | 139 | 38.93 | 8.73 | 0.79 | 14-61 | 0.02 |
| Persistence | 139 | 36.94 | 7.25 | 0.79 | 20-52 | -0.12 |
| Self-Directedness | 139 | 37.86 | 9.39 | 0.86 | 13-57 | -0.31 |
| Cooperativeness | 139 | 46.97 | 8.19 | 0.80 | 27-67 | -0.16 |
| Self-Transcendence | 139 | 16.27 | 7.24 | 0.81 | 4-37 | 0.51 |
| RSES | 139 | 19.28 | 4.82 | 0.87 | 8-28 | -0.16 |

*Personality.* The junior version of the Temperament and Character Inventory (TCI) (Cloninger et al., 1993) was used as a measure of personality. We are not aware of any other study that has used the J-TCI to explore athletes' personality. Personality was assessed by the Norwegian version of the Junior Temperament and Character Inventory (J-TCI) (Vangberg, Eisemann, and Richter, 2011). The J-TCI contains 103 questions for assessing personality by means of four temperament and three character scales. The psychometric properties of the scale have been confirmed in previous research (Luby, Svrakic, McCallum, Przybeck, and Cloninger, 1999; Lyoo et al., 2004). A total of 60 items comprise the temperament scales: Novelty Seeking (15 items), Harm Avoidance (13 items), Reward Dependence (18 items), and Persistence (14 items), while 43 items comprise the character scales: Self-Directedness (15 items), Cooperativeness (18 items) and Self-Transcendence (10 items). The items have to be rated on a scale from 0 (totally agree) to 4 (totally disagree). Sample items are: "I always do my best" and "Most of the time I only do what I really have to do". Cronbach alpha coefficients for the subscales were satisfactory, ranging from .69 to .86 (table 1).

*Self-esteem.* Self-esteem was measured by the Norwegian validated version of Rosenberg's self-esteem scale (RSES) (Von Soest, 2005). The scale includes ten items measuring global self-esteem. Five of the items are positively worded and the remaining five negatively. Sample item: "I wish I had more respect for myself". The response format is from 1 (Strongly agree) to 4 (strongly disagree). Cronbach alpha for RSES was good (table 1).

*Well-being.* Well-being was measured using the Norwegian version of World Health Organization WHO-5 scale (Bakke, 2004) which allows brief assessment of emotional well-being over a 14 day period. The scale has demonstrated good internal consistency and validity (McDowell, 2010).

This five-item inventory covers the respondents' general well-being. Sample item: "The last two weeks I have been happy and in a good mood". Responses are given on a six-point rating scale from 0 (never) to 5 (all the time). Cronbach alpha for WHO-5 were good (table 1).

## Analysis

The data received from Survey Monkey were organized in Microsoft Office Excel 2007 and entered into SPSS 16.0 for the further analysis.

Skewness and kurtosis for the study variables were assessed. Values within the range of +/- 2 for skewness and +/-7 for kurtosis are considered as normally distributed (West, Finch, and Curran, 1995). All of the study variables fulfilled these criteria. A significance level of $\alpha$ = .05 was set for all of the subsequent analysis.

## RESULTS

Means, standard deviations, and correlation among the variables in the study are presented in Table 2. It shows that many of the personality variables in this study are significantly inter-correlated. The reported skill level was only significantly correlated with harmonious passion.

**Table 2. Means, SDs and correlations for the study variables among the study group (n=139)**

| Variable | Mean | SD | Age | Skill | WHO-5 | OP | HP | NS | HA | RD | PE | SD | CO | ST | RSES |
|---|---|---|---|---|---|---|---|---|---|---|---|---|---|---|---|
| Age | 16.76 | 0.89 | 1 | | | | | | | | | | | | |
| Skill | 7.13 | 1.33 | -.24** | 1 | | | | | | | | | | | |
| WHO-5 | 16.81 | 4.27 | .08 | .01 | 1 | | | | | | | | | | |
| Obsessive passion | 24.17 | 6.45 | -.12 | .13 | .13 | 1 | | | | | | | | | |
| Harmonious passion | 33.24 | 5.72 | -.07 | .18* | .42** | .55** | 1 | | | | | | | | |
| Novelty Seeking | 29.94 | 7.41 | .13 | -.01 | -.18* | -.06 | -.23** | 1 | | | | | | | |
| Harm Avoidance | 23.56 | 8.40 | -.11 | .05 | -.52** | -.09 | -.27** | .20** | 1 | | | | | | |
| Reward Dependence | 38.93 | 8.73 | -.10 | .06 | .16 | .07 | .06 | .08 | -.15 | 1 | | | | | |
| Persistence | 36.94 | 7.25 | -.20* | -.03 | .34** | .30** | .37** | -.30** | -.51** | .22** | 1 | | | | |
| Self-Directedness | 37.86 | 9.39 | -.03 | -.06 | .61** | .06 | .38** | -.31** | -.75** | .16 | .58** | 1 | | | |
| Cooperativeness | 46.97 | 8.19 | -.18 | .00 | .19* | .15 | .23** | -.28** | -.13 | .39** | .46** | .27** | 1 | | |
| Self-Transcendence | 16.27 | 7.24 | -.30** | .02 | -.09 | .04 | -.11 | .26** | .35** | .25** | -.10 | -.26** | .11 | 1 | |
| RSES | 19.28 | 4.82 | .09 | .03 | .63** | -.01 | .34** | -.10 | -.55** | .02 | .29** | .70** | -.03 | -.12 | 1 |

Note. SD = Standard Deviation, WHO-5 = Well-being, OP = Obsessive passion, HP = Harmonious passion, NS = Novelty Seeking, HA = Harm Avoidance, RD = Reward Dependence, PE = Persistence, SD = Self-Directedness, CO = Cooperativeness, ST = Self-Transcendence, RSES = Self-esteem, * $p < .05$, ** $p < .01$.

On the other hand, harmonious passion was positively correlated with WHO-5, RSES, self-directedness and persistence. In addition, harmonious passion was negatively correlated with novelty seeking and harm avoidance. Obsessive passion only showed significant correlations with harmonious passion and persistence. Further, self-esteem was positively correlated with WHO-5, self-directedness and negatively correlated with harm avoidance.

## Gender Differences

A one-way multivariate analysis of variance (MANOVA) was performed to investigate gender differences in the variables examined (Table 3). Eleven dependent variables were used: seven personality variables from the J-TCI, harmonious passion, obsessive passion, RSES and WHO-5.

The independent variable was gender. Preliminary assumption testing was conducted to check for normality, linearity, univariate and multivariate outliers, homogeneity of variance-covariance matrices, and multicollinearity, with no serious violations noted. There was a statistically significant difference between males and females on the combined dependent variables, $F (11,127) = 5.57, p < .001$; Wilks' Lambda = .67; partial $eta$ squared = .32. When the results for the dependent variables were considered separately, three differences reached statistical significance (see Table 3), using a Bonferroni adjusted alpha level of .005. Those were Reward Dependence, $F (1, 137) = 15.72, p < .001$, partial $eta$ squared = .10. Cooperativeness, $F (1, 137) = 17.09, p < .001$, partial $eta$ squared = .11. RSES, $F (1, 137) = 13.33, p < .001$, partial $eta$ squared = .09. An inspection of the mean scores indicated that females scored higher on the temperament trait reward dependence than males. On the character trait cooperativeness females had higher values than males.

Lastly females had lower values on Rosenberg's self-esteem scale than males. The significant differences in mean values between the groups were all moderate to large according to Cohen's (1977) guide to interpreting effect size. Cohen's $d$ for these differences in reward dependence, cooperativeness, and RSES were 0.68, 0.71, and - 0.62, respectively.

**Table 3. Mean scores for male and female on variables under investigation**

| Variable | Female (n=69) | | Male (n=70) | | F | p | Cohen's d |
|---|---|---|---|---|---|---|---|
| | Mean | SD | Mean | SD | | | |
| WHO-5 | 16.97 | 3.95 | 16.64 | 4.59 | 0.20 | .65 | 0.08 |
| Harmonious Passion | 33.42 | 5.31 | 33.06 | 6.12 | 0.14 | .71 | 0.06 |
| Obsessive Passion | 23.72 | 6.22 | 24.60 | 6.67 | 0.50 | .48 | -0.14 |
| Novelty Seeking | 29.49 | 6.61 | 30.38 | 8.15 | 0.76 | .38 | -0.12 |
| Harm Avoidance | 24.18 | 6.99 | 22.95 | 9.60 | 1.69 | .20 | 0.15 |
| Reward Dependence | 41.74 | 8.39 | 36.15 | 8.20 | 15.72 | < .001 | 0.68 |
| Persistence | 37.74 | 7.00 | 36.14 | 7.46 | 0.58 | .45 | 0.22 |
| Self Directedness | 38.25 | 8.85 | 38.46 | 9.91 | 1.56 | .21 | -0.02 |
| Cooperativeness | 49.71 | 7.09 | 44.27 | 8.36 | 17.09 | < .001 | 0.71 |
| Self Transcendence | 17.04 | 7.15 | 15.51 | 7.29 | 1.56 | .21 | 0.21 |
| RSES | 17.84 | 4.44 | 20.70 | 4.78 | 13.33 | < .001 | -0.62 |

## Team Sports versus Individual Sports

To investigate differences between athletes competing in team sports and those competing in individual sports, a MANOVA was conducted which yielded no significant differences between the two groups.

## Athletes versus Non-athletes

To investigate if our athlete population yielded significant different mean scores on the J-TCI compared to non-athletes, a MANOVA was performed with J-TCI subscales as dependent variables.

Results from the MANOVA are presented in Table 4. On the combined dependent variables there emerged significant differences between the two groups, $F (7, 1422) = 8.31, p < .001$; Pillai's Trace = .04; partial $eta$ squared = .04. Pillai's Trace is reported since it is more robust when there are unequal $N$ values. Since there were seven variables used in the analysis, a Bonferroni adjusted alpha level of .007 was set.

When the results were investigated separately, the following difference in personality dimension emerged as significant: Harm Avoidance, Persistence and Self-Directedness (see Table 4).

When inspecting the mean scores for harm avoidance we see that the athlete population has significantly lower mean values on this temperament trait than non-athlete. According to Cohen (1977) guideline for interpreting effect size, the difference in mean scores represents a small effect.

As concerns persistence, the athletes had significantly higher mean scores than the non-athletes, representing a moderate to strong effect. Self-directedness was the only character dimension of the J-TCI with significant inter-group differences in mean scores. Athletes revealed higher means for this dimension than non-athletes, reflecting a small effect.

### Table 4. Mean scores of athletes vs. non-athletes on J-TCI

| Variable | Athletes (n=139) | | Non-athletes (n =1291) | | F(1428) | p | Cohen's d |
|---|---|---|---|---|---|---|---|
| | M | SD | M | SD | | | |
| Age | 16.71 | 0.91 | 16.79 | 1.18 | 0.86 | .391 | -0.07 |
| Novelty Seeking | 29.94 | 7.41 | 31.69 | 8.13 | 5.87 | .016 | 0.22 |
| Harm Avoidance | 23.56 | 8.40 | 25.82 | 8.99 | 7.99 | .005 | -0.25 |
| Reward Dependence | 38.93 | 8.73 | 40.43 | 9.36 | 3.27 | .071 | -0.16 |
| Persistence | 36.94 | 7.25 | 32.41 | 7.68 | 44.00 | <.001 | 0.59 |
| Self-Directedness | 37.86 | 9.39 | 35.50 | 9.54 | 7.69 | .006 | 0.25 |
| Cooperativeness | 46.97 | 8.19 | 46.43 | 8.50 | 0.51 | .476 | 0.06 |
| Self-Transcendence | 16.27 | 7.24 | 17.25 | 7.26 | 2.28 | .131 | -0.14 |

## DISCUSSION

This study investigated personality characteristics, self-esteem and passion among junior elite athletes, and investigated differences in personality between athletes and non-athletes. Both harmonious and obsessive passions were positively correlated with the personality trait persistence. This is somewhat surprising since previous research had only found obsessive passion related with persistence and an autonomously regulated passion such as harmonious passion was not (Rip, Fortin, and Vallerand, 2006; Vallerand et al., 2003). This could be a result of a different measure of persistence in the previous research, and that persistence measured by the J-TCI does not entail what Mageau et al. (2009) described as unhealthy and hazardous persistence.

As concerns the other personality measures, we did not find any significant relationship with obsessive passion, while harmonious passion was significantly correlated with five of the seven personality measures. We found harmonious passion positively associated with the personality dimension of self-directedness and negatively associated with harm avoidance. This is understandable as low scores on harm avoidance indicate a more relaxed, optimistic, vigorous and outgoing personality (Cloninger et al., 1993), which is in line with the qualities of harmonious passion and not with obsessive passion. Higher scores on the personality dimension self-directedness reflect a more responsible, resourceful and self-accepted personality, which should be compatible with higher harmonious passion. To our knowledge, passion has not been investigated in relation to personality traits earlier, and therefore our result facilitate the understanding of the dualistic model of passion, and help to distinguish the different qualities of the two forms of passion, where harmonious seems to be the desirable form of passion (Vallerand et al., 2008).

Harm avoidance was negatively associated with both self-esteem and well-being. This makes sense since it is unlikely that individuals with a higher level of harm avoidance (reflecting a shy, pessimistic and fearful individual), should score higher on self-esteem and well-being. In accordance with previous research on both the TCI and J-TCI, harm avoidance was negatively correlated with the character dimension of self-directedness (Cloninger et al., 1993; Luby et al., 1999; Schmeck, Goth, Poustka, and Cloninger, 2001), which was even more pronounced in our sample. Harm avoidance in our sample was significantly negatively correlated with persistence. This might reflect that individuals with higher scores on harm avoidance are less likely to be hard-working, ambitious and diligent as indicated by higher values on persistence and on self-directedness characterizing purposeful, resourceful and effective individuals.

Our finding of a positive relationship between self-directedness, self-esteem and well-being, support previous results (Smith, Duffy, Stewart, Muir, and Blackwood, 2005). We regard this as reasonable as self-directedness represents one's concept of the self as an autonomous individual.

Both well-being and self-esteem should be better among individuals who can be described as responsible and reliable, self-accepted and resourceful. The strength of our correlation could also indicate that self-directedness represents some of the same constructs as both self-esteem and well-being.

## Gender Differences

We found significant gender differences for self-esteem, reward dependence and cooperativeness. Our results support previous research on gender differences in self-esteem (Blascovich and Tomaka, 1991; Feingold, 1994; Kling, Hyde, Showers, and Buswell, 1999), although our study found an even larger effect size disfavoring females. A gender difference in self-esteem has previously been explained by gender roles (Ruble, 1983), peer interaction (Maccoby, 1990), schools (Sadker, 1994), emphasis on physical appearance (Allgood-Merten, Lewinsohn, and Hops, 1990), violence against girls (Koss, 1990) and athletic participation (Deianey and Lee, 1995; Marsh and Kleitman, 2003).

As both our male and female participants are involved in large amounts of physical activity it is unlikely that this could explain the differences in mean scores among male and female participants. Kling et al. (1999) argued that females engage in several activities that protect their own self-esteem, and therefore the effect sizes of gender differences remain small. However, our result is challenging this argument since we yielded a moderate to large effect size (Cohen, 1977).

Females had significant higher mean values than males on the temperament dimension reward dependence and on the character dimension cooperativeness, which is in line with previous research into gender differences on the adult TCI version (Pelissolo et al., 2005; Snopek, Hublova, Porubanova, and Blatny, 2011) and the Korean J-TCI (Lyoo et al., 2004). Previous research has found significant lower mean values among females on novelty seeking compared to their male counterparts (Lyoo et al., 2004), and higher on self-directedness (Luby et al., 1999) which could not be confirmed in our sample.

According to Luby et al. (1999), gender differences "may suggest either significant sex differences in personality development during this period of development or alternatively significant differences in the ways girls and boys conceptualize and describe their own characteristics" (p.1136).

We theorize that females have higher mean values on reward dependence and cooperativeness, since these scales depict a more sentimental, warm, dependent, helpful, and compassionate personality, which may be favored by being female.

## Team Sports vs. Individual Sports

Surprisingly, we did not find significant differences between team athletes and individual athletes on the character dimension cooperativeness. This dimension accounts for identification and acceptance of other people (Kose, 2003) and could be viewed as more important for team athletes. Although mean differences on two personality dimensions were observed, neither reward dependence nor cooperativeness scores were significantly different between the two groups.

This could be a result of our participating team-sport athletes. Those competing in team sports were more homogeneous than those competing in individual sports, since there were only two types of team sport in our sample: football and handball. In addition, all the football players came from the same school and most likely played in the same team. This was also the case for the handball players.

## Athletes vs. Non-athletes

Our results showed that the athletes in our study obtained significantly different mean values on three of the seven personality dimensions, than a comparable non-athlete sample. It is however important to note that the comparison group might include participants competing in sports on varying levels, without attending a sport-specific high school. Athletes scored higher on persistence and self-directedness, and lower on harm avoidance. Although we expected athletes to have higher mean values on the personality dimension persistence, we did not expect the effect size to be as substantial as it was. We view persistence as an important aspect of an athlete's personality since this dimension is a measure of how ambitious, hard-working, industrious and perseverant an individual is. We theorize that our athlete group attained higher scores, than non-athlete, on this dimension since they have had to practice for longer periods of time with high quality, to be admitted to the sport-specific high school they now attend. It is also likely that those individuals scoring lower on Persistence would not have continued with their sport when this requires a more organized form, both in competition and training, in the ages of 12 years and older in Norway (Norges Idrettsforbund, 2007).

The athlete group's higher mean values on the character trait self-directedness seem reasonable, as higher values indicate a more mature, purposeful, resourceful and effective personality. We assume that higher scores on self-directedness could be important for athletes indicating that their habits are congruent with long term goals. Knowing that deliberate practice is a vital aspect of expert performance (Ericsson and Charness, 1994), it is reasonable to assume that individuals whose habits are in accordance with their goals would be more fitted as athletes. Even though the effect size of this mean difference has to be considered as small, higher self-directedness could be viewed as beneficial for athletes.

The athletes in our study had significantly lower mean scores on the dimension harm avoidance as compared to non-athletes. Lower scores on this temperament dimension indicate a more relaxed and optimistic, bold and confident, outgoing and vigorous personality. This supports earlier research which has found, with other personality measures, that athletes are more outgoing than the non-athlete population (Eysenck et al., 1982; Hirschhorn, 2006). We argue that low scores on harm avoidance would allow athletes to perform better in highly stressful situations such as competitions, while high scores on harm avoidance could in the same situations be inhibited by being too cautious and apprehensive.

## Limitations

The present research has some limitations. Firstly, the study relied exclusively on self-reported measures, which might compromise the reliability of our results, which further might be confounded by response biases such as social desirability.

Secondly, our sample was recruited from the same non-profit private athletic school organization, although the schools were from different locations in Norway, which delimits the generalization of our results to a broader student athlete population. We cannot exclude that the participating schools have organizational guidelines for admission, teaching, curricula, training, etc. Future research should therefore include such variables in addition to demographic ones (e.g., social background).

Thirdly, our team athletes was not as diverse with athletes from football and handball, additionally both football and handball players came from the same school and most likely played for the same team. This is in contrast to our individual athletes who were from a greater variety of sports and sport clubs from around the country.

Lastly, our study did not have an optimal performance variable, which might have indicated which psychological characteristics affect performance and would be more desirable for athletes. Future research should include an external measure of either skill level or performance, e.g., in terms of a rating by a coach who does not have a day to day interaction with the athletes, but has a firm knowledge of the skill level needed in the actual sport.

## CONCLUSION

Summing up, this study has explored psychological characteristics, such as personality, passion, self-esteem and well-being among junior elite athletes. In addition, it has revealed significant differences among athletes in self-esteem and personality dimensions. This is of importance as it may help coaches to individualize schedules to most optimally suit the athlete and improve performance. The obvious dedication to a sport is a phenomenon that deserves further investigation. The results from the Junior Temperament and Character Inventory (J-TCI) have revealed specific personality profiles and their relationships with other factors such as passion and self-esteem, and suggest that it could become a useful instrument in sport psychology for the assessment of personality traits among young athletes. In particular, the possible predictive power of specific personality traits for performance in different sports warrants further investigation.

## REFERENCES

Aidman, E. V. (2007). Attribute-based selection for sucess: The role of personality attributes in long-term predictions of acheivement in sport. *The Journal of the American Board of Sport Psychology, 1*, 1-18.

Allgood-Merten, B., Lewinsohn, P. M., and Hops, H. (1990). Sex differences and adolescent depression. *Journal of Abnormal Psychology, 99*, 55-63. doi: 10.1037/0021-843x.99.1.55

Auweele, Y. V., Nys, K., Rzewnicki, R., and Van Mele, V. (2001). Personality and the athlete. In R. N. Singer, H. A. Hausenblas and C. M. Janelle (Eds.), *Handbook of sport psychology* (2 ed., pp. 239-268). New York: John Wiley and Sons, Inc.

Bachman, J. G., and Omalley, P. M. (1977). Self-esteem in young men: A longitudinal analysis of the impact of educational and occupational attainment. [Article]. *Journal of Personality and Social Psychology, 35*, 365-380. doi: 10.1037//0022-3514.35.6.365

Bakke, O. (2004). WHO-5: 5 spørsmål om trivsel og velvære 1.1. Retrieved August 10, 2011, from http://www.cure4you.dk/354/WHO-5_Norwegian.pdf

Bara Filho, M. G., Ribeiro, L. C. S., and García, F. G. (2005). Comparison of personality characteristics between high-level Brazilian athletes and non-athletes. *Revista Brasileira de Medicina do Esporte, 11*, 115-120. Retrieved from http://www.scielo.br/scielo.php?script=sci_arttextandpid=S1517-86922005000200004andnrm=iso

Baumeister, R. F., Campbell, J. D., Krueger, J. I., and Vohs, K. D. (2003). Does High Self-Esteem Cause Better Performance, Interpersonal Success, Happiness, or Healthier Lifestyles? *Psychological Science in the Public Interest, 4*, 1-44. doi: 10.1111/1529-1006.01431.

Blascovich, J., and Tomaka, J. (1991). Measures of self-esteem. In J. P. Robinson, P. R. Shaver and L. S. Wrightman (Eds.), *Measures of personality and social psychological attitudes.* (pp. 115-160). San Diego, CA: Academic Press.

Booth, E., G. (1958). Personality traits of athletes as measured by the MMPI. *Research Quarterly 29*, 127-138.

Campbell, J. D., and Fairey, P. (1985). Effects of self-esteem, hypothetical explanations, and verbalization of expectancies on future performance. *Journal of Personality and Social Psychology, 48*, 1097-1111. doi: 10.1037/0022-3514.48.5.1097.

Carver, C. S., and Scheier, M. (2004). *Perspectives on personality.* Boston: Pearson Allyn and Bacon.

Cashmore, E. (2002). *Sport psychology: The key concepts.* London: Routledge.

Cattell, R. B., Eber, H. W., and Tatsuoka, M. M. (1970). *Handbook for the sixteen personality factor questionnaire(16 PF).* Champaign, IL.: Institute for Personality and Ability Testing.

Clitsome, T., and Kostrubala, T. (1977). A psychological study of 100 marathoners using the Myers-Briggs type indicator and demographic data. *Annals of the New York Academy of Sciences, 301*, 1010-1019. doi: 10.1111/j.1749-6632.1977.tb38265.x

Cloninger, C. R., Svrakic, D. M., and Przybeck, T. R. (1993). A psychobiological model of temperament and character. *Archives of General Psychiatry, 50*, 975-990. Retrieved from http://archpsyc.ama-assn.org/

Coatsworth, J., and Conroy, D. E. (2006). Enhancing the self-esteem of youth swimmers through coach training: Gender and age effects. *Psychology of Sport and Exercise, 7*, 173-192. doi: 10.1016/j.psychsport.2005.08.005

Cohen, J. (1977). *Statistical power analysis for the behavioral sciences.* New York: Academic Press.

Deianey, W., and Lee, C. (1995). Self-esteem and sex roles among male and female high school students: Their relationship to physical activity. *Australian Psychologist, 30*, 84 - 87. doi: 10.1080/00050069508258908.

Di Paula, A., and Campbell, J. D. (2002). Self-esteem and persistence in the face of failure. *Journal of Personality and Social Psychology, 83*, 711-724. doi: 10.1037/0022-3514.83.3.711.

Donahue, E. G., Rip, B., and Vallerand, R. J. (2009). When winning is everything: on passion, identity, and agression in sport. *Psychology of Sport and Exercise, 10*, 526-534. doi: 10.1016/j.psychsport.2009.02.002

Dowd, R., and Innes, J. M. (1981). Sport and personality: Effects of type of sport and elite level of competition. *Perceptual and Motor Skills, 53*, 79-89. Retrieved from http://www.ammonsscientific.com/AmSci/

Ericsson, K. A., and Charness, N. (1994). Expert performance: Its structure and acquisition. *American Psychologist, 49*, 71-76. doi: 10.1037/0003-066X.50.9.803.

Eysenck, H. J., Nias, D. K. B., and Cox, D. N. (1982). Sport and personality. *Advances in Behaviour Research and Therapy, 4*, 1-56.

Feingold, A. (1994). Gender differences in personality: A meta-analysis. *Psychological Bulletin, 116*, 429-456. doi: 10.1037/0033-2909.116.3.429.

Fuchs, C. Z., and Zaichkowsky, L. D. (1983). Psychological characteristics of male and female bodybuilders: The iceberg profile. *Journal of Sport Behavior, 6*, 136-145.

Gee, C., Marshall, J. C., and King, J. F. (2010). Should coaches use personality assessments in the talent identification process? A 15 year predictive study on professional hockey players. *International Journal of Coaching Science, 4*, 25-34.

Harter, S. (2001). *The construction of the self: A developmental perspective.* New York: Guilford Press.

Hirschhorn, D. K. (2006). *Personality differences and level of success in traders with and without competitive athletic background.* Ph.D, Capella University, Minnesota.

Jarvis, M. (2006). *Sport psychology: A student's handbook.* London: Routledge.

Judge, T. A., and Bono, J. E. (2001). Relationship of core self-evaluations traits—self-esteem, generalized self-efficacy, locus of control, and emotional stability—with job satisfaction and job performance: A meta-analysis. *Journal of Applied Psychology, 86*, 80-92. doi: 10.1037/0021-9010.86.1.80.

Kling, K. C., Hyde, J. S., Showers, C. J., and Buswell, B. N. (1999). Gender differences in self-esteem: A meta-analysis. *Psychological Bulletin, 125*, 470-500. doi: 10.1037/0033-2909.125.4.470.

Kose, S. (2003). Psychobiological model of temperament and character: TCI. *Yeni Symposium, 41*, 86-97.

Koss, M. P. (1990). The women's mental health research agenda: Violence against women. *American Psychologist, 45*, 374-380. doi: 10.1037/0003-066x.45.3.374.

Luby, J. L., Svrakic, D. M., McCallum, K., Przybeck, T. R., and Cloninger, C. R. (1999). The junior temperament and character inventory: preliminary validation of a child self-report measure. *Psychological Reports, 84*, 1127-1138. Retrieved from http://www.apa.org/pubs/journals/bul/index.aspx

Lyoo, I. K., Han, C. H., Lee, S. J., Yune, S. K., Ha, J. H., Chung, S. J., . . . Hong, K.-E. M. (2004). The reliability and validity of the junior temperament and character inventory. *Comprehensive Psychiatry, 45*, 121-128. doi: 10.1016/j.comppsych.2003.12.002

Maccoby, E. E. (1990). Gender and relationships: A developmental account. *American Psychologist, 45*, 513-520. doi: 10.1037/0003-066x.45.4.513

Mageau, G. A., Vallerand, R. J., Charest, J., Salvy, S.-J., Lacaille, N., Bouffard, T., and Koestner, R. (2009). On the development of harmonious and obsessive passion: The role of autonomy support, activity specialization, and identification with the activity. *Journal of Personality, 77*, 601-645. doi: 10.1111/j.1467-6494.2009.00559.x

Marsh, H. W., and Kleitman, S. (2003). School athletic participation: Mostly gain with little pain. *Journal of Sport and Exercise Psychology, 25*, 205-228. Retrieved from http://ovidsp.ovid.com/ovidweb.cgi?T=JSandCSC=YandNEWS=NandPAGE=fulltextandD=psyc4andAN=2003-05573-007

McDowell, I. (2010). Measures of self-perceived well-being. *Journal of Psychosomatic Research, 69*, 69-79. doi: 10.1016/j.jpsychores.2009.07.002

Morgan, W. P. (1980). The trait psychology controversy. *Research Quarterly for Exercise and Sport, 51*, 50-76. Retrieved from http://www.aahperd.org/rc/publications/rqes/

Morris, T. (2000). Psychological characteristics and talent identification in soccer. *Journal of Sports Sciences, 18*(9), 715-726. doi: 10.1080/02640410050120096

Norges, I. (2007). Idrettens barnerettigheter: Bestemmelser om barneidrett Retrieved April 18, 2012, from http://www.idrett.no/tema/barneidrett/bestemmelserogrettigheter/barnerettigheter/Sider/default.aspx

Pelissolo, A., Mallet, L., Baleyte, J. M., Michel, G., Cloninger, C. R., Allilaire, J. F., and Jouvent, R. (2005). The Temperament and Character Inventory-Revised (TCI-R): Psychometric characteristics of the French version. *Acta Psychiatrica Scandinavica, 112*, 126-133. doi: 10.1111/j.1600-0447.2005.00551.x

Piedmont, R. L., Hill, D. C., and Blanco, S. (1999). Predicting athletic performance using the five-factor model of personality. *Personality and Individual Differences, 27*, 769-777. doi: 10.1016/S0191-8869(98)00280-3.

Rip, B., Fortin, S., and Vallerand, R. J. (2006). The relationship between passion and injury in dance students. *Journal of Dance Medicine and Science, 10*, 14-20. Retrieved from http://www.iadms.org/displaycommon.cfm?an=1andsubarticlenbr=153.

Rosenberg, M. (1979). *Conceiving the self*. New York: Basic Books.

Rosenberg, M., Schooler, C., and Schoenbach, C. (1989). Self-esteem and adolescent problems: Modeling reciprocal effects. *American Sociological Review, 54*, 1004-1018. doi: 10.2307/2095720.

Ruble, T. L. (1983). Sex stereotypes: Issues of change in the 1970s. *Sex Roles, 9*, 397-402. doi: 10.1007/bf00289675

Sadker, M. (1994). *Failing at fairness: How our schools cheat girls*. New York: Simon and Schuster.

Saint-Phard, D., Van Dorsten, B., Marx, R. G., and York, K. A. (1999). Self-perception in elite collegiate female gymnasts, cross-country runners, and track-and-field athletes. *Mayo Clinic Proceedings, 74*(8), 770-774. doi: 10.4065/74.8.770.

Schmeck, K., Goth, K., Poustka, F., and Cloninger, R. C. (2001). Reliability and validity of the Junior Temperament and Character Inventory. *International Journal of Methods in Psychiatric Research, 10*, 172-182. doi: 10.1002/mpr.113

Schurr, K. T., Ashley, M. A., and Joy, K. L. (1977). A multivariate analysis of male athlete characteristics: Sport type and success. *Multivariate Experimental Clinical Research, 3*, 53-68.

Singer, R. N. (1988). Psychological testing: What value to coaches and athletes? *International Journal of Sport Psychology, 19*(2), 87-106.

Skaalvik, E. M., and Hagtvet, K. A. (1990). Academic achievement and self-concept: An analysis of causal predominance in a developmental perspective. *Journal of Personality and Social Psychology, 58*, 292-307. doi: 10.1037//0022-3514.58.2.292

Smith, D. J., Duffy, L., Stewart, M. E., Muir, W. J., and Blackwood, D. H. R. (2005). High harm avoidance and low self-directedness in euthymic young adults with recurrent, early-onset depression. *Journal of Affective Disorders, 87*, 83-89. doi: 10.1016/j.jad.2005.03.014

Snopek, M., Hublova, V., Porubanova, M., and Blatny, M. (2011). Psychometric properties of the Temperament and Character Inventory-Revised (TCI-R) in Czech adolescent sample. *Comprehensive Psychiatry, In Press, Corrected Proof*. doi: 10.1016/j.comppsych.2011.01.008.

Vallerand, R. J. (2008). On the psychology of passion: in search of what makes people's lives most worth living. *Canadian Psychology, 49*, 1-13. doi: 10.1037/0708-5591.49.1.1.

Vallerand, R. J., Blanchard, C., Mageau, G. A., Koestner, R., Ratelle, C., Léonard, M., and Gagné, M. (2003). Les passions de l'âme: On obsessive and harmonious passion. *Journal of Personality and Social Psychology, 85*, 756-767. doi: 10.1037/0022-3514.85.4.756

Vallerand, R. J., Mageau, G. A., Elliot, A. J., Dumais, A., Demers, M.-A., and Rousseau, F. (2008). Passion and performance attainment in sport. *Psychology of Sport and Exercise, 9*, 373-392. doi: 10.1016/j.psychsport.2007.05.003.

Vallerand, R. J., Salvy, S.-J., Mageau, G. A., Elliot, A. J., Denis, P. L., Grouzet, F. M. E., and Blanchard, C. (2007). On the role of passion in performance. *Journal of Personality, 75*, 505-534. doi: 10.1111/j.1467-6494.2007.00447.x

Vangberg, H. C. B., Eisemann, M., and Richter, J. (2011). *A validation of the Norwegian version of JTCI.* Tromsø.

Von Soest, T. (2005). Rosenbergs selvfølelsesskala: Validering av en norsk oversettelse. *Tidsskift for Norsk Psykologforening, 42*, 226-228.

Weinberg, R. S., and Gould, D. (2011). *Foundations of sport and exercise psychology* (5 ed.). Champaign, Ill.: Human Kinetics.

West, S. G., Finch, J. F., and Curran, P. J. (1995). Structural equation models with nonnormal variables: Problems and remedies. In R. H. Hoyle (Ed.), *Structural equation modeling: Concepts, issues, and application* (pp. 56-75). Thousand Oaks, CA: Sage Publication.

In: Innovative Writings in Sport and Exercise Psychology
Editor: Robert Schinke

ISBN: 978-1-62948-881-3
© 2014 Nova Science Publishers, Inc.

*Chapter 2*

# EXPLORING THE MOTIVATIONS UNDERPINNING TRACK AND FIELD OFFICIALS' DECISIONS TO VOLUNTEER

## *Casey E. Gray*[*1] *and Philip M. Wilson*[2]
[1]School of Kinesiology
University of Western Ontario
London, Ontario, Canada
[2]Department of Kinesiology
Brock University, St. Catharines, Ontario, Canada

### ABSTRACT

Little is known about the factors that promote behavioural persistence among volunteer track and field officials. This preliminary qualitative study examined the explanations a sample of Canadian officials offered for their initial and continued involvement in track and field over time. Certified track and field officials ($N = 79$) responded to 3 open-ended survey items exploring their reasons for initial, current, and future involvement in officiating. Content analysis indicated a varied and dynamic pattern of motivations that informed decisions to volunteer in the sport. Among them, intrapersonal factors were often cited as reasons for initial and current motivations for officiating, while a combination of intra- and interpersonal factors appeared salient reasons for anticipated future involvement. The current findings also support the important role played by satisfaction of the basic psychological needs outlined within Self-Determination Theory (Deci and Ryan, 2002) with respect to current involvement.

**Keywords:** Self-determination theory, motivation, volunteering, officiating

---

[*] The raw data used in the thematic content analysis outlined in this study can be obtained from the first author upon request.

# INTRODUCTION

The experiences and behaviours of sports officials have often drawn the attention of researchers (e.g., Rainey 1995; 1999). Interest in the topic is likely a response to the escalating attrition rates among certified officials that threaten the delivery of sport programs across North America (Deacon, 2001; VanYperen, 1998). Increased attrition of qualified officials has placed undue burden on the sport delivery system by creating staffing shortages and increasing the costs associated with the recruitment and training of new officials (Deacon, 2001; VanYperen, 1998). The net effect of this participation trend is that a high priority has been placed on identifying factors that can facilitate the retention of qualified officials (Weinberg and Richardson, 1995).

Theoretical frameworks can provide insight into the dynamics of intentional behaviour, and inform individual and group decisions about how to affect change. Initial studies conducted to examine attrition behaviour in sports officials were focused almost exclusively on frameworks centered on stress and/or coping-based models. Rainey and colleagues (Rainey, 1995; 1999; Rainey and Hardy, 1999), for example, conducted a series of studies with baseball/softball (Rainey, 1995), basketball (Rainey, 1999), and rugby union (Rainey and Hardy, 1999) officials, and suggested different causes of stress were evident across sports, which predicted burnout. Rainey et al. observed that when burnout was elevated, intentions to terminate officiating increased, leading them to implicate burnout as a central mechanism involved in termination-based decision making amongst officials. Anshel and colleagues (Kaissidis and Anshel, 1993; Anshel and Weinberg, 1999) suggested the stress-intention relationship may be more complicated, and appears to be impacted by a number of factors, such as age and coping resources. Kaissidis and Anshel (1993) found that younger officials often exhibited more stress compared to older officials, while Anshel and Weinberg (1999) discovered the development of coping mechanisms offset the debilitating effects attributed to acute or chronic stressors. Collectively, these studies are informative given that they provided conceptual accounts based largely on stress-based models for attrition intentions, and showed that coping mechanisms may impact the effects of stress-perceptions on intentions to terminate sport involvement in officials.

While the aforementioned investigations are insightful and grounded in relevant frameworks for understanding precursors to attrition, a number of issues warrant further consideration if sustained involvement amongst officiating groups is to be understood. First, previous researchers (Anshel and Wienberg, 1999; Kaissidis and Anshel, 1993; Rainey, 1995; 1999; Rainey and Hardy, 1999) examined termination intentions without considering intentions to continue and the potentially unique determinants. Second, the use of cross-sectional designs and reliance on stress-based frameworks may not be sufficient to interpret the dynamic processes motivating sustained involvement. Finally, researchers have relied extensively on modeling techniques to understand statistical relationships between antecedents such as burnout and coping mechanisms with attrition-laden intentions that may not fully capture the subtle processes involved in intention formation or subsequent behaviour.

Representing a possible alternative or adjunct to stress-based approaches, Self-Determination Theory (SDT; Deci and Ryan, 1985; 2002) is a framework for understanding human behaviour that offers practical strategies for intervention. Within SDT, Deci and Ryan

(2002) posit that, domain specific (or global) fulfillment of three innate psychological needs (i.e., autonomy, competence, and relatedness) will facilitate motivation and well-being and energize behavioural persistence. Competence refers to a sense of feeling mastery with regard to one's abilities to be effective in a particular context, relatedness refers to feeling meaningfully connected and/or involved with others, and autonomy refers to feeling self-governing such that behaviour is consistent with one's interests and integrated values (Ryan and Deci, 2002). Shedding light on the role of perceived relatedness in relation to continuance intentions of track and field officials, Gray and Wilson (2008) showed that perceiving a meaningful connection with fellow officials was an important predictor of intentions to continue officiating in the future. There are, however, many groups whom a person could interact with in the officiating role (i.e., novice and elite athletes, coaches, parents, and volunteers) that may exert varying levels of influence on intentions to continue officiating sport, and yet have not been fully examined. Furthermore, Gray and Wilson (2008) focused exclusively on the relative importance of the role played by feelings of perceived relatedness in relation to behavioural intentions. However, sport participation researchers have illustrated the importance of all three needs associated with SDT in forming intentions to drop out (e.g., Sarrazzin, Vallerand, Guillet, Pelletier, and Cury, 2002), and in athlete engagement (thought to be the conceptual opposite of burnout; Schaufeli, Salanova, Gonzalez-Roma, and Bakker, 2002) in a variety of sport cohorts including elite athletes (Hodge, Lonsdale, and Jackson, 2009). Clearly, these are complex relationships that are only beginning to be understood.

The extant research on the dynamic factors that could shape investment decisions in sport officials, although informative, is limited in scope. As such, it seems reasonable that qualitative approaches to the study of behavioural intentions may facilitate an understanding of the breadth of cognitive precursors to intentional behaviour. The purpose of this study, therefore, was to explore the motivational underpinnings associated with initial, present, and future involvement in the sport of track and field amongst officials certified with Athletics Canada. A secondary purpose was to consider the framework offered by Deci and Ryan (2002) within the context of the basic psychological needs housed within SDT as a model for interpreting officials' responses. An exploratory qualitative design was used to develop an initial, broad understanding of the motivations to volunteer as a track and field official as they have developed over time from the officials' perspectives. The theoretical framework provided by SDT was used in this preliminary study to interpret the data about current reasons for officiating.

# METHOD

## Participants and Recruitment

Purposive sampling criteria specified that each respondent (a) held current certification from Athletics Canada's National Officials Certification Program (NOCP) to officiate events, and (b) was actively involved in track and field officiating at the time of data collection. Following clearance from Brock University's Research Ethics Board, initial access to officials was gained by contacting executive board members of the National Officials Committee via email. The first author provided eligible participants with a flyer that advertised the study ($n = 200$). Contact was made in person during scheduled breaks over the duration of a track and field competition, or by email using publicly available contact information obtained from officiating websites in each Canadian province. Interested officials contacted in person at competition locations completed their questionnaires on site, or where time was an issue, returned them to the first author via mail at a subsequent time. Snowball sampling was employed to supplement the strategies designed to recruit study participants for this investigation. The first author contacted the head official of each province who distributed a flyer advertising this study to officials within each provincial organisation. Interested participants contacted the first author by email and were sent the questionnaire package by post. Finally, the flyer advertising this study was posted in the spring 2005 National Officials Committee newsletter that was posted on the Athletics Canada website. Participants recruited through this method were instructed to contact the researcher by email to have the questionnaire package sent to them by post. As recruitment and data collection for this qualitative study were conducted in conjunction with a larger quantitative investigation, rolling recruitment was employed in an attempt to maximize sample size and heterogeneity. This approach resulted in ongoing participant recruitment between January and August of 2005.

The questionnaire package included a letter of information, an informed consent form, a demographics questionnaire, and the survey used for the current study. An additional questionnaire used for a separate study published elsewhere was also distributed (Gray and Wilson, 2008). Participants provided written informed consent, completed the questionnaire package, and placed both study documents in a sealed envelope before returning them to the first author either in person or by post. The final sample represents 26.7 percent of the total number of eligible officials approached initially to participate.

All participants were certified by and were registered with their provincial officials committee for at least one full athletics season prior to data collection. Officials represented the full spectrum of certification levels available with Athletics Canada (Level 1 = 9.3 percent; Level 2 = 10.7 percent; Level 3 = 26.7 percent; Level 4 = 13.3 percent; Level 5 = 38.7 percent; 1.3 percent did not report their current level of certification) and had been engaged in officiating for varied lengths of time ($M$ = 18.60 years; $SD$ = 12.67 years; Range = 1 to 50 years).

## Instrumentation

*Demographics.* Seventy-nine officials representing 7 provincial track and field organisations volunteered for this study. Each official responded to at least 1 of 3 open-ended items posed within the study questionnaire. The following response patterns were noted across the 3 questions: (a) 77 participants responded to question 1; (b) 60 participants responded to question 2; and (c) 51 responded to question 3. Participants were aged between 22 and 83 years ($M_{age}$ = 58.83 years, $SD$ = 12.14), and were predominately male (67.1 percent) and well educated (41.3 percent had completed graduate school).

*Open-Ended Elicitation Questions.* A questionnaire containing 3 open-ended, elicitation questions was presented to each participant to provide insight into the dynamics influencing volunteer officials' participation in the sport of track and field.

These questions were: (a) How and why did you initially become involved in officiating track and field?; (b) Why are you currently volunteering to officiate track and field?; and (c)

What changes would encourage you to continue volunteering as a track and field official? The questions were designed specifically to encourage participants to reflect on initial factors that motivated them to become involved in the sport's officiating, describe who or what motivated their involvement at the time of data collection, and finally, provide an opportunity to describe what factors would influence their continued involvement in officiating track and field competitions in the future. However, the word 'motivation' was purposefully avoided in the questions presented to the sample in an attempt to alleviate social desirability response bias that can distort participant responses in research of this nature (Trochim, 2001).

## Data Analyses

Participants' responses varied greatly in length and structure, with several responses provided in point form. Written data were transcribed verbatim and yielded 15 pages of transcription. After reading all of the transcripts thoroughly, data were subjected to cross-case analysis (Miles and Huberman, 1994) by the first author using primarily inductive (i.e., data driven) approaches that have been successfully used in previous research concerning physical activity involvement (Weiss, Smith and Theeboom, 1996) and sport participation (Farrell, Crocker, McDonough, and Sedgwick, 2004). The first author read all of the transcripts carefully and thoroughly to get a sense of the data and then inspected the transcribed text using a line-by-line approach. Words, sentences, and paragraphs of raw data were coded into meaning units (Miles and Huberman, 1994), which served as the basis for subsequent analyses. Using open coding (Strauss and Corbin, 1990), meaning units were examined for commonalities and similar meaning units were grouped together to form categories. Axial coding (Strauss and Corbin, 1990) was conducted by grouping and regrouping categories to make new connections and look for meaning in the data, further reducing the data into overarching themes. Interpretations of meaning units associated with question 2 (i.e., Why are you currently volunteering to officiate track and field?) were simultaneously analysed deductively. Specifically, data were interpreted against SDT as a broader theory-based concept accounting for motivational processes (Deci and Ryan, 2002). Deductive comparisons with theoretical frameworks may illuminate central mechanisms influencing sport officials' intentions to continue. Selective coding, "the process of selecting the core category, systematically relating it to other categories, validating those relationships, and filling in categories that need further refinement and development" (Strauss and Corbin, 1990, p.116), was not conducted in this study.

The first author decided that the central focus of the topic within each question used to collect the data would serve as the linking story. The first author was responsible for the transcription of all participants' raw data, identification and extraction of meaning units for further analyses, and initial grouping of meaning units into categories and themes. When reviewing transcripts ceased to present new information the first author concluded that saturation had been achieved, yet all transcripts were analysed. The second author served as a critical friend (Sparkes and Partington, 2003) during the analysis and interpretation of the data derived from the transcriptions. Culver and associates note that the presentation of data in tabular format with frequencies and associated example quotations is the most common way of presenting qualitative data in the sport psychology literature (Culver, Gilbert, and Trudel, 2003).

To be consistent with Culver et al. (2003), an indication of the most frequently recurring patterns emerging (or derived) from the participant data were presented in this study in tabular form. The number of participants who endorsed each category presented by gender, and the total number of meaning units coded within each category, as well as the frequency with which meaning units appeared are presented in Tables 1, 2 and 3.

### Table 1. Number of Meaning Units (MU) and Frequency of Participants Identifying Specific

### Thematic Subcategories Pertaining to Initial Sport Involvement

| Categories/ Sub-categories | Male ($n = 50$) | Female ($n = 27$) | MU ($n = 152$) | Frequency MU /MU total |
|---|---|---|---|---|
| *Connection to the Sport* | | | | |
| Child/ other involved | 17 | 14 | 31 | 20.39 |
| Social | 2 | 2 | 4 | 2.63 |
| Training was available | 5 | 0 | 5 | 3.33 |
| *Helping Reasons* | | | | |
| Community service/volunteer | 9 | 6 | 15 | 9.87 |
| To give back/facilitate the sport | 13 | 7 | 20 | 13.16 |
| Was asked to help | 11 | 6 | 17 | 11.18 |
| *Extension of Role* | | | | |
| Coach | 12 | 5 | 17 | 11.18 |
| Physical Education Teacher | 3 | 1 | 4 | 2.63 |
| Athlete/former athlete | 11 | 10 | 21 | 13.82 |
| *Personal Reasons* | | | | |
| Interest | 6 | 2 | 8 | 5.26 |
| Enjoyment | 7 | 3 | 10 | 6.58 |

*Note.* MU = meaning unit. Frequency is the number of respondents citing the MU/all MU's provided by this sample of respondents. Question 1 stated: "Explain how and why you initially became involved in officiating track and field?"

## RESULTS

Results are reported in three sections, each providing a detailed experiential account of the factors underlying initial, current, and future involvement in the sport of track and field by this sample of Canadian officials. A summary of the major themes emerging from the analysis, as well as, the relative frequency with which similar meaning units occurred are presented in Tables 1, 2 and 3.

*Initial sport involvement.* Of the seventy-nine participants who provided a response to at least 1 of the 3 questions, seventy-seven participants responded to question 1. The analysis revealed 4 major themes led to officials' entry into officiating track and field (see Table 1).

**Table 2. Number of Meaning Units (MU) and Frequency
of Participants Identifying Specific**

**Thematic Subcategories Pertaining to Current Sport Involvement**

| *Categories/* Sub categories | Male ($n = 38$ ) | Female ($n = 22$ ) | Total MU (n =158) | Frequency MU/ MU total |
|---|---|---|---|---|
| *Sport Orientation* | | | | |
| Fan of track and field | 17 | 8 | 25 | 15.82 |
| Athlete development | 8 | 8 | 16 | 10.13 |
| Facilitate the sport | 5 | 0 | 5 | 3.16 |
| *Personal Reasons* | | | | |
| Perceived obligation | 10 | 5 | 15 | 9.49 |
| Emotional fulfillment | 3 | 4 | 7 | 4.43 |
| Enjoyment | 19 | 7 | 26 | 16.46 |
| Opportunities | 4 | 3 | 7 | 4.43 |
| *Basic Psychological Need Satisfaction* | | | | |
| Autonomy | 4 | 3 | 7 | 4.43 |
| Competence | 3 | 7 | 10 | 6.33 |
| Relatedness | 22 | 18 | 40 | 25.32 |

*Note.* MU = Meaning Unit. Frequency was calculated by dividing the number of respondents citing a particular meaning unit by the total number of MU's provided by the participants providing a response to question two. Question two stated: "Why are you currently volunteering to officiate track and field?"

Themes were labelled as connections to sport, helping, role extension, and personal reasons. Evident in the officials' data were a series of complex links to the sport of track and field through the involvement of another family member, typically a child, as a venue for spending time with friends while being involved in sport, or by the lure of mentorship opportunities within the track and field community. One respondent exemplified this last point by indicating his initial reasons for getting involved in officiating track and field as follows:

In our area (there) was a retired person who had great knowledge at the international level. He came out to help. He invited me to go with him to higher level meets. I did. He showed me what to do I just continued moving up the ranks of officiating. (M80)

Altruistic reasons were cited by officials who had wished to provide assistance either in terms of helping to run a track and field meet, or volunteering a service to the local community or a recognized athletic catchment area. Closer inspection of the raw data underpinning the helping theme showed a strong influence of life changes that alleviated participants' time constraints, thereby eliminating a barrier to track and field officiating. Most of these changes concerned restructuring of occupational tasks, for example: "I retired from an executive position and I finally had some flexibility with my time" (F79), and "I find that officiating is a good retirement pastime which allows me to interact with younger people and to give something back to the community" (M21). Similarly, barriers were removed by a shift in family structure as highlighted by one official who wrote: "Coaching was great until I had a family. Then I turned to administration and officiating" (F48). Also embedded within participant responses was the notion of reciprocating the benefits sport afforded to them by committing time to others. The following example written by participant M46 exemplifies this category:

Track and field was always my favourite and my best sport. I have always wanted to become an official, but didn't have a good opportunity, since I was moving so often and so busy with the Military. I wanted to keep in touch with track (and) field and give back what I enjoyed. I saw the application form on the OTFA (Ontario Track and Field Association) website about how to join as an official. Today everyone needs to be a volunteer at something either as a coach, official (or) for administration.

Complementing the themes labelled connections to sport and helping were the final two themes labelled role extensions and personal reasons, which collectively characterize early involvement as an official in track and field. Many participants viewed officiating as a natural extension of a related role they currently occupied such as coach, athlete, or teacher. For instance, one participant indicated "Being a (physical education) teacher wanted to learn more about the rules of each discipline" (F45). In addition to extending roles into track and field officiating, a number of participants noted the salience of personal reasons that reflected intrinsic processes as key factors shaping their initial participation. Such processes appeared to indicate officials initiated their involvement due to self-interest as one participant indicated: "I chose a sport I enjoyed in my youth" (F60), or enjoyment of either the sport or officiating as explained by others, for example: "I love the event. (I) knew that being an athlete could not last forever. (I) wanted to know the rules" (M05).

*Current sport involvement.* Content analyses of raw data provided by sixty of the total seventy-nine officials led to the creation of 3 themes describing the motives underlying current officiating involvement in Canadian track and field competitions (see Table 2). Themes were reflected by the labels sport orientation, personal reasons, and need satisfaction. A common thread through a majority of participant responses was a sense of orientation within or towards the sport of track and field. This theme was exemplified by participants indicating an appreciation of the sport from a spectator's perspective. One official captured the essence of being an athletics fan with the following comment: "…enjoy seeing the competitors always trying to improve themselves… enjoy seeing the success of competitors…" (M43). Taking this 'fan status' theme one step further, several officials expressed an interest in offering support for track and field athletics as a sport. A considerable number of responses from this sample of officials reflected internal motives to continue officiating as indicated by this study participant: "I would like to support track and field and encourage young athletes to participate in it" (M34).

Additional responses implied more external motives, rather than feeling motivated by their own interests, that underpinned current involvement as an official in track and field. As one official aptly noted, "I feel an obligation to help with the sport" (M55). Officials pointed to the athletes as a second intended target for their behaviour and expressed an interest in promoting their development: "I also enjoy helping athletes at lower or younger levels, who have no had proper coaching, to learn the proper techniques of their events as well as competition rules" (M35).

**Table 3. Number of Meaning Units (MU) and Frequency of Participants Identifying Specific Thematic Subcategories for Future Sport Involvement**

| Categories/ Sub-categories | Male (*n* = 31 ) | Female (*n* = 20 ) | MU (n =75 ) | Frequency MU/Total MUs |
|---|---|---|---|---|
| *Organisational / Structure* | | | | |
| Financial Support | 4 | 4 | 8 | 10.67 |
| Recruit new officials | 8 | 7 | 15 | 20 |
| Schedule | 3 | 3 | 6 | 8 |
| *Transparency* | | | | |
| Upgrade criteria | 3 | 5 | 8 | 10.67 |
| Standardize and enforce rules/ roles | 4 | 2 | 6 | 8 |
| Equality of meet assignments | 5 | 5 | 10 | 13.33 |
| *Personal* | | | | |
| Communication | 4 | 0 | 4 | 5.3 |
| Treatment | 7 | 4 | 11 | 14.67 |
| Recognition | 5 | 2 | 7 | 9.33 |

*Note*. MU = Meaning Unit. Frequency was calculated by dividing the number of respondents citing a particular MU by the total number of MU's provided by participants responding to question three. Question three stated: "What changes would encourage you to continue volunteering as a track and field official?"

Consistent with the insights pertaining to initial involvement in track and field, officiating incentives for current participation centred on a complex series of personal reasons. Enjoyment while officiating was the most prominent category within the personal reasons theme, as exemplified by the following quote: "I am currently volunteering to officiate track and field because I enjoy doing the tasks. Sometimes it is quite a challenge; other times it is truly relaxing" (F36).

Others acknowledged that emotional satisfaction stemming from officiating contributed to decisions to continue participation: "I have always enjoyed…the feeling of helping someone to achieve success" (F40).

Participants conveyed a need for effective officials in the sport and took it upon themselves to accept invitations to help by officiating competitions or educating novice officials, as one experienced official noted: "(I) realize there is still a need for competent officials and I don't see too many coming into the sport" (M37).

A number of officials felt a strong obligation to reciprocate opportunities or experiences afforded to them previously by sport in general, or by track and field in particular. One participant commented: "I am (an) exathlete and now is the time I give back what I learned in the past" (M33). A final thread within this theme concerned a minority of officials who indicated that they continued to officiate because of the opportunities afforded to them through their involvement. This predominately referred to opportunities to travel. As on official noted: "...officiate around the world" (M31).

At the core of the final theme were the three basic psychological needs forwarded within SDT by Deci and Ryan (1985; 2002). Relatedness, the psychological need most highly endorsed within this sample, was illustrated by a series of statements that detailed feelings of connection with individuals they regularly interacted with during track and field competitions. Exemplifying this, one official wrote: "I have always enjoyed the camaraderie that is prevalent among officials..." (F40).

Although less prominent than feelings of relatedness, participant responses aligned with the concept of perceived autonomy while officiating, and an identified belief in the personal importance of volunteering emerged as an important motive behind current involvement as explained by this official: "I consider it a meaningful and worthwhile contribution to the development of youth, as they need officials to be able to have competitions, and they need competitions to be able to develop further" (F79), and similarly, "...volunteering is part of my lifestyle...thing that I feel contributes to a better society" (M51).

Responses conveying an interest in being effective in the sporting milieu as an official emerged from the data provided by this sample. As one official noted, "We have given seminars around the world on track + field officiating + my husband + myself are the 2 experts in Canada when it comes to officiating disabled events – ex. Wheelchairs, amputee, C.P. + Blind" (F57). Such commentary implies that perceived competence may be an important factor behind the persistence behaviours of track and field officials.

*Future sport involvement.* Analysis of raw data provided by fifty-one of the total seventy-nine respondents produced three major themes in response to the item querying changes that would motivate continued involvement in officiating at track and field competitions (see Table 3). Organisational/structural, personal, and increased transparency were the central themes created to convey major issues expressed by this sample that pertain to future involvement in the sport of track and field as an official. Organisational/structural changes related to improving day-to-day operations were the most frequently endorsed theme emerging from the data, followed by transparency, and personal themes respectively. Recruitment and suitable treatment of new officials into the sport was the most dominant category emerging within the organisational/structural theme. One official described a need to treat new track and field officials as valued members of the community to increase retention by stating the following:

> Changes: positive recruitment of younger officials. An(sic) once recruited, no "screwing around" when it comes to asking them, instead of someone in their dotage, to officiate at major provincial national and international meets. This has happened in the

past. We need them. When we do not use them (and) treat them well---we lose them. (F61)

Additional issues in participant responses included, in order of endorsement, financial support and scheduling. There was a belief expressed among officials that the sport of track and field in Canada is underfunded to optimally run competitions when compared against other organisations. This was expressed by one track and field official in the following manner: "Through the 1980's until 1993 our Province received funding to send 1 official every year to Nationals. But, because of fiscal constraints, Newfoundland has not sent any official for over 10 years to Nationals!" (F60). Furthermore, a subset of officials voiced a collective belief that track and field meets regularly run too long, placing undue burden on those who volunteer. A desire to see increased transparency and changes to political parameters were apparent in participant responses. These focused on egalitarian treatment of officials within the sport, and the removal of political and administrative boundaries that were perceived to tarnish the experience of officiating in the sport of track and field. Abolishment of politics in terms of administrative governance within the sport, particularly with respect to equality of meet assignments was clear from participant responses. One official remarked:

> It bothers me that high level officials are not required to work community level meets. I discovered this last track season that I worked 15 meets culminating in international meets, whereas, higher level officials came out at the end of the season to work 2 or 3 national (and)/or international meets. Athletics Canada then does not credit me for the extra hours. (F35)

The final theme that emerged from participant responses to the question focused on future sport involvement concerned evidence that continued investment in track and field as an official would only be forthcoming if officials' own interests were better served. Increased opportunities and greater individual recognition were the dominant categories in the theme labelled 'personal'. One official noted: "Most of the time we, as officials are taken for granted, and that is unfortunate as without two groups of people, athletes and officials, there would be no track and field meets" (M47). A smaller contingent of officials felt their colleagues should become less self-indulgent and remember that they provide a service role in the operation of track and field competitions. As one track and field official stated:

> I would like to see more officials become less "officious" and remember that they are (there) to serve the athletes. I would like to see officials, especially the higher ranked ones, treat lower ranked officials and uncertified volunteers with more respect and consideration at track meets. (M34)

## DISCUSSION

The purpose of this investigation was to explore the motivational underpinnings associated with initial, present, and future involvement in the sport of track and field amongst officials certified with Athletics Canada. A secondary purpose was to consider the theoretical framework offered within SDT by the concept of basic psychological needs for interpreting officials' responses. Overall, the results suggest considerable variability around reasons motivating initial, current, and future involvement with volunteering in track and field. There was notable consistency in the dominance of intra-personal reasons motivating initial and current participation. It seems apparent that interpersonal reasons embedded within the broader context of sport dominated participant accounts of changes that would motivate continued involvement. Collectively, these results indicated the reasons underpinning volunteer behaviour in Canadian track and field officials are complex and likely vary as a function of prolonged involvement in the sport as an official.

Unlike previous studies examining the factors contributing to termination-based intentions in sport officials, content analysis of past, present, and anticipated future motivating factors provided by this sample of Canadian track and field officials gives a degree of support for the tenability of stress-based frameworks for understanding continuance intentions. It may be argued that the responses elicited from questions probing changes to encourage future sport involvement may be loosely conceived as sources of potential stress. On the contrary, the results of this study make it apparent that the framework for understanding behaviour provided by the concept of basic psychological needs may be a useful approach for understanding continuance based intentions in sports officials. Quantitative data collected by Gray and Wilson (2008) indicated that 60.0 percent of participants scored above the 75th percentile on intentions to continue officiating over the next 2 years, signifying the majority of officials had very strong intentions to continue with their role as a track and field official in the near future. In contrast, less than 26.7 percent of officials' intention scores fell below the 25th percentile for this variable. Thus, it is possible the officials in this study present a biased sample which may explain the lack of stress-laden language in the data.

Several links were evident in the results of this study to previous research focused on volunteer officials in other sports (e.g., basketball, baseball/softball; Rainey, 1995; 1999). First, it seems clear based on the results of this study that time-pressures can represent a salient source of stress for volunteer officials that is likely to dissuade continued involvement over time. As one track and field official commented: "…the meet schedules need to have a reasonable time frame. Some of us work full time and need to be ready to go back to work the next day" (F64). Rainey's (1995; 1999) investigations noted that time-based pressures function as a stressor leading to dropout intentions as officials experience heightened levels of burnout. Second, a number of track and field officials in this study reported feeling their efforts and involvement in the sport were not sufficiently recognized by other members of the track and field community. One track and field official commented: "Most of the time we, as officials are taken for granted, and that is unfortunate as without two groups of people, athletes and officials, there would be no track and field meets" (M47). This notion of being 'under-appreciated' was noted as a mild concern linked to the stress of volunteer officiating amongst basketball referees (Rainey, 1995), although not strongly linked with termination intentions. Overall, some consistencies (and differences) can be observed between intentions to terminate sports officiating provided by stress-based models and the current study that warrant further scrutiny.

*Theoretical frameworks.* The current data make it apparent that stress-based frameworks are informative, although possibly limited, as a framework for understanding initial, current, and future sport involvement as a volunteer official. The present study offers at least partial support for arguments presented by Deci and Ryan (2002) within SDT, highlighting basic psychological needs as important elements associated with optimal human functioning. One such psychological need concerns a felt sense of mastery and effectance in action referred to as perceived competence. The need for relatedness concerns the tendency to connect with, and be integral to, and accepted by others within and across one's social milieu. Finally, the need for autonomy concerns the feeling of being self-governing insofar as one's actions emanate from a true sense of self and integrated value system (Ryan and Deci, 2002).

Evidence in this study provided by personal insights of track and field officials working within the organisational structure of Athletics Canada highlighted the potential role of basic psychological need fulfillment at different stages of involvement as a volunteer sport official. Prominent examples that symbolise the importance of fulfilling each psychological need were most evident in the data reflecting officials' current involvement. However, it is reasonable to speculate that relatedness could be linked with categories labelled as 'Connections to the Sport' and 'Helping Reasons' listed as reasons for initiating participation as a track and field official. Moreover, the data comprising the 'Organisational/Structural' category implicated as an important factor linked with future officiating involvement aligns with the importance of providing opportunities for self-governance and agency rather than stifling personal autonomy. Given that opportunities to satisfy psychological needs promote self-motivation, which are in turn associated with positive behavioural outcomes (Baard, 2002) it is plausible that need fulfillment is important to behavioural persistence for track and field officials.

## Practical Recommendations

The participants in this study provided informative descriptions of circumstances and factors that shaped their initial, current, and, potential future involvement volunteering in the role of a track and field official. A number of practical recommendations can be extrapolated from these data that could be of use to the governing organisations (e.g., Athletics Canada, the National Officials Committee) in recruiting and retaining officials in track and field.

One strategy for attracting new officials is to improve 'how' governing organisations target potential officials who have an established connection with track and field. Attracting new officials was the most frequently expressed change noted by officials in this study that would promote continued involvement. Several participants indicated they began officiating track and field competitions because of an ongoing or previous involvement with the sport. Others noted they became involved as a function of a family member or friend's participation in the sport. Current officials indicated a mixture of initial trajectories leading to their involvement in the sport, including being provided a request to participate and taking initiative by volunteering. On the basis of these findings, it would seem prudent for governing organisations to target the search for new officials towards candidate groups with previous or ongoing sport involvement (e.g., former athletes, athletes' family members, etc.). Once potential new officials have been identified by governing organisations it may be beneficial to provide information about officiating and highlight the importance of new volunteers to the continued development of the sport. Making use of social connections between current and candidate officials seems to be one important communication strategy given that current officials noted that any direct invitations to volunteer came from a person with a pre-existing social connection. Enhancing global awareness of the need for volunteer officials appears to be a likely avenue to recruit new volunteer officials for track and field.

Issues concerning the retention of qualified and experienced officials also emerged as a priority in the personal accounts provided by this sample of volunteers. Retaining the involvement of volunteer officials is an important goal for many governing organisations delivering sport programs. The reasons for current and future investment noted in this study may warrant consideration in this regard. A synopsis of research using SDT as a guiding framework (Deci & Ryan, 2002) highlights the integral role of competence, autonomy, and relatedness needs satisfaction in promoting behavioural persistence in many areas of life including sport. A portion of the data in this study further supported the importance of fulfilling each psychological need central to SDT in a diverse sample of track and field officials volunteering in a Canadian sport delivery system. Extrapolating from the framework set forth within SDT, Baird (2002) notes that organisational leaders can communicate with members in such a way to support the key psychological needs endorsed by Deci and Ryan's (2002) theorizing. Specifically, Baird (2002) notes that interactions characterised as autonomy supportive, empathic with reference to the challenges of behavioural change and persistence (i.e., involvement; Deci and Ryan, 2002), and that offer clear and realistic expectations for success (i.e., structure; Deci and Ryan, 2002) can foster the satisfaction of competence, autonomy, and relatedness needs.

Combining the data presented here with the theoretical backdrop offered by SDT (Deci and Ryan, 2002) provides a number of opportunities for sport governing organisations (e.g., Athletics Canada) to develop strategies that ultimately are geared towards retention of qualified sport officials. The provision of support for autonomy is likely to facilitate feelings of self-governance and personal agency that characterise autonomous functioning (Baird, 2002; Deci and Ryan, 2002). Sport governing bodies could embrace the notion of autonomy support by finding avenues for officials to experience a sense of empowerment. The notion of feeling empowered was echoed in one participant's comments provided in this study that targeted future investment as a sports official: "Let event officials discuss with meet directors how their events are run on meet day" (M12). The importance of providing structure to volunteer sport officials was apparent in the current study, for example improved training and support, removing barriers that impede optimal performance including physical and procedural impediments, and improving mechanisms for progressive advancement of officials in track and field (e.g., "...upgrading based on experience and not who you know..." [M31]). Lastly, the data provided in this study indicated that officials felt connected to their fellow colleagues, although select data indicated a perceived disconnect between officials at the lower and higher echelons of certification, and between officials and meet organisers as well as Athletics Canada employees (e.g., "The politics at the provincial level, but more especially at the national level NEED to change. Athletics Canada does little, if anything for us [and the National Officials Committee] has become an old boys club [F48]). Increased quality of communication between organisational members, treating officials with respect, and acknowledging the contribution of volunteer officials to sport represent key ways that governing organisations can act with involvement towards members of officiating cohorts.

## Limitations and Future Research Directions

While the results of this study are novel and provide insight into the accounts of Canadian officials regarding their involvement in track and field, a number of limitations should be recognized and future directions outlined to advance our understanding of the motives underpinning involvement in sport by volunteer officials. First, the use of an open-ended survey presented a key challenge in the current study. Although valuable information was gained via written responses from a variety of individuals within the officiating population, some opted to avoid responding to certain questions without providing a reason for this omission. As such we do not know if those individuals had different ideas to their officiating colleagues, were not motivated to continue officiating, or simply had nothing to say on the focal topic in question. Nevertheless, the information gleaned from the current study was informative and could serve as a foundation for future research into this topic. Conducting individual interviews, with questions based on the current findings may overcome the non-response issue noted in this study and allow for follow-up probing questions to provide clarity around responses.

A second limitation of the present investigation is the cross-sectional administration of the survey. The collection of data on a single occasion is fraught with a number of difficulties when the central question of interest is concerned with changes in motivation over time. Cresswell and Eklund (2007) presented evidence arguing for the viability of longitudinal data collection techniques using qualitative methods in sport to illuminate mechanisms of change of interest to sport psychologists and coaches. Future studies would do well to consider adopting such longitudinal methods integrated with various approaches to qualitative research (e.g., participant observation, autoethnography, etc.) to capitalise on the richness and diversity of change mechanisms as they fluctuate across meaningful time periods. One potential concern with this approach based on the results of the present investigation stems from the length of time sport officials remain engaged in the sport of track and field, which on the basis of our data, can be exceptionally prolonged. Future studies will need to establish time periods over which to follow track and field officials if their interest is in motivating future sport involvement given that such changes could take extended periods of time to manifest or fully impact decision-making in volunteer officials.

Notwithstanding the limitations of this study, it is clear that the data provided by this sample of volunteer track and field officials offers a meaningful account of the experiences of volunteer sports officials working in conjunction with Athletics Canada. Future research could augment and extend the present study by directly testing the framework provided within SDT (Deci and Ryan, 2002) using representative samples of sports officials. Practical strategies to enhance persistence behaviour in other domains (e.g., education, sports) have been forthcoming and could be adapted to foster prolonged investment in sports officiating. Such practical strategies lend themselves well to further testing using experimental designs to ascertain their effectiveness before wholesale application on behalf of sport governing organisations.

## AUTHORS' NOTE

This study was conducted by the first author under the supervision of the second author in partial fulfillment of degree requirements for Master of Arts at Brock University. The second author was supported by a grant from the Social Sciences and Humanities Research Council of Canada (SSHRC Grant #410-2005-1485) during the preparation of this manuscript. Dr. Wilson is affiliated with the Behavioural Health Sciences Research Lab and the Center for Bone and Muscle Health (Brock University).

## REFERENCES

Anshel, M., and Weinberg, R. (1999). Re-examining coping among basketball referees following stressful events: Implications for coping interventions. *Journal of Sport Behavior, 22*, 141-161.

Baard, P. (2002). Intrinsic need satisfaction in organizations: A motivational basis of success in for-profit and not-for-profit settings. In E. Deci, and R. Ryan, *Handbook of self-determination research* (pp. 255-275). Rochester, NY: University of Rochester Press.

Cresswell, S. L., and Eklund, R. C. (2007). Athlete burnout: A longitudinal qualitative study. *The Sport Psychologist, 21*, 1–20.

Culver, D. M., Gilbert, W. D., and Trudel, P. (2003). A decade of qualitative research in sport psychology journals: 1990 – 1999. *The Sport Psychologist, 17*, 1-15.

Deacon, J. (2001, March 26). Rink rage. *Maclean's.* pp. 20-24.

Deci, E. L., and Ryan, R. M. (1985). *Intrinsic motivation and self-determination in human behavior*. New York, NY: Plenum.

Deci, E. L., and Ryan, R. M. (2002). *Handbook of self-determination research*. Rochester, NY: University of Rochester Press.

Farrell, R., Crocker, P., McDonough, M., and Sedgwick, W. (2004). The driving force: Motivation in Special Olympians. *Adapted Physical Activity Quarterly, 21*, 153-166.

Gray, C. E., and Wilson, P. M. (2008). The relationship between organizational commitment, perceived relatedness, and intentions to continue in Canadian track and field officials. *Journal of Sport Behavior, 31*, 44-63.

Hodge, K., Lonsdale, C., and Jackson, S. A. (2009). Athlete engagement in elite sport: An exploratory investigation of antecedents and consequences. *The Sport Psychologist, 23*, 186-202.

Kaissidis, A., and Anshel, M. (1993). Sources and intensity of acute stress in adolescent and adult Australian basketball referees: A preliminaryy study. *Australian Journal of Science and Medicine in Sport, 25*(3), 97-103.

Miles, M. B., and Huberman, M. A. (1994). *Qualitative data analysis: An expanded sourcebook* (2nd Ed.). Thousand Oaks, CA: Sage Publications.

Rainey, D. (1995). Stress, burnout, and intention to terminate among umpires. *Journal of Sport Behavior, 18*, 312-323.

Rainey, D. (1999). Sources of stress, burnout, and intention to terminate among basketball referees. *Journal of Sport Behaviour, 22*, 578-590.

Rainey, D., and Hardy, L. (1999). Sources of stress, burnout, and intention to terminate among rugby union referees. *Journal of Sport Sciences, 17*, 797-806.

Ryan, R. M., and Deci, E. L. (2002). Overview of self-determination theory: An organismic dialectical perspective. In E. L. Deci and R. M. Ryan (Eds.), *Handbook of self-determination research* (pp. 3-34) Rochester, NY: University of Rochester Press.

Ryan, R. M., and Deci, E. L. (2006). Self-regulation and the problem of human autonomy: Does psychology need choice, self-determination, and will? *Journal of Personality, 74,* 1557-1586.

Sarrazzin, P., Vallerand, R., Guillet, L., Pelletier, L., and Cury, F. (2002). Motivation and dropout in female handballers: A 21-month prospective study. *European Journal of Social Psychology, 32,* 395 - 418.

Schaufeli, W. B., Salanova, M., Gonzalez-Roma, V., and Bakker, A. B. (2002). The measurement of engagement and burnout: A two sample confirmatory factor analytic approach. *Journal of Happiness Studies, 3,* 71–92.

Sparkes, A. C., and Partington, S. (2003). The narrative practices and its potential contribution to sport psychology: The example of flow. *The Sport Psychologist, 17,* 292-317.

Strauss, A. and Corbin, J. (1990). *Basics of qualitative research: Grounded theory procedures and techniques.* Newbury Park, CA: Sage.

Trochim, W. M. K. (2001). *The research methods knowledge base* (2nd ed.). Cincinnati, OH: Atomic Dog.

VanYperen, N. (1998). Predicting stay/leave behavior among volleyball referees. *The Sport Psychologist, 12,* 427-439.

Weinberg, R. S., and Richardson, P. A. (1995). *Psychology of officiating.* Champaign, IL: Leisure Press.

Weiss, M. R., Smith, A. L., and Theeboom, M. (1996). "That's what friends are for": Children's and teenagers' perceptions of peer relationships in the sport domain. *Journal of Sport and Exercise Psychology, 18,* 347-379.

In: Innovative Writings in Sport and Exercise Psychology
Editor: Robert Schinke

ISBN: 978-1-62948-881-3
© 2014 Nova Science Publishers, Inc.

*Chapter 3*

# PSYCHOLOGICAL AND INSTRUCTIONAL ASPECTS OF SERVING IN TENNIS AND BADMINTON – A REVIEW AND IMPLICATIONS FOR COACHING

## *Ronnie Lidor*[*1] *and Gal Ziv*[1,2]
[1]The Zinman College of Physical Education and Sport Sciences,
Wingate Institute, Israel
[2]Faculty of Education,
University of Haifa, Israel

## ABSTRACT

The purpose of this article was to review a series of studies ($n = 16$) on psychological and instructional aspects of serving in two racquet sports – tennis and badminton. The main findings of this review were that (a) imagery and self-talk can help players improve their serves in tennis and badminton; (b) task-pertinent learning strategies which are introduced at the beginning of the learning process, or at some time after some knowledge of the serve was acquired, can enhance serving performances of beginning learners; (c) although there are not enough data to indicate what type of feedback benefits serving performances, instructional feedback based on the correct movement of the server should be useful in practicing the serve; (d) contextual variety appears to improve the learning of the badminton serve. Implications for coaching are discussed based on the reviewed studies, taking into account a number of research limitations associated with these studies.

**Keywords:** Serving, tennis, badminton, psychological preparation, instructional considerations

---

[*] Please send all correspondence to: Dr. Ronnie Lidor, Professor, The Zinman College of Physical Education and Sport Sciences, Wingate Institute, Netanya 42902, Israel, Fax: +972-9-8650960, E-mail: lidor@wincol.ac.il.

# INTRODUCTION

"There is a saying in tennis that you are only as good as your serve" (Yandell, 1999).

Serving is an important offensive fundamental of racquet sports (e.g., badminton, squash, and tennis) and can sometimes decide the outcome of a point or even a match. Statistical reports from the 2005 and 2006 French Open indicated that players won more points when serving (62.1%) than when receiving (37.9%), as well as when serving first serves (67.3%) compared to second serves (53.8%) (Gillet, Leroy, Thouvarecq, and Stein, 2009). These reports also indicated that players who used a flat serve won more points than top-spin serves (24.1%) or slice first serves (18.3%).

Serving in racquet sports is considered to be a self-paced task, namely the server is able to determine when to initiate the serving act (Lidor, 2007). Racquet players are provided with a number of seconds to prepare themselves for the serving act. Players who stand on the serving line and prepare themselves for the serve can hit the ball when they feel comfortable and ready to do so. They can decide not only what to do during this preparation interval, but also how to use the time officially allotted to them, taking into consideration their professional needs and preferences.

To enhance the ability of racquet players to serve effectively in practice sessions and matches, coaches should not only allocate the time to allow their players to repeatedly practice the serving skill, but also to plan the practice sessions so that the players will benefit from them. This is to say that in order to plan effective practice aimed at preparing players to enhance their serving performances, those professionals who work with racquet players, such as coaches, strength and conditioning coaches, and sport psychology consultants, should obtain relevant information on different aspects associated with the serving act, among them psychological and instructional aspects. Knowledge about these aspects of serving can be implemented by the coaches in their specific serving training programs, as well as integrated with the general training programs aimed at preparing the players for practices and games.

The purpose of this article was threefold: (a) to review a series of studies (n = 16) on psychological and instructional aspects associated with serving in two racquet games – tennis and badminton; (b) to discuss a number of research limitations and methodological concerns associated with the reviewed studies; (c) to propose several practical implications for coaches who work with tennis and badminton players on their serving ability.

The reviewed articles were selected from an extensive search of the English language literature, including major computerized databases (PubMed and SPORT Discus) and library holding searchers. The search included a combination of the following terms: badminton, tennis, serve, serving, and service. The inclusion criterion was that the studies included psychological and instructional aspects of serving in tennis and badminton. The search yielded 16 articles that were included in our review. These articles were grouped into two categories: psychological aspects of serving and instructional aspects of serving.

# PSYCHOLOGICAL ASPECTS OF SERVING

In this section we review studies on imagery and self-talk, learning strategies, and hypnosis.

## Imagery and Self-talk

In this section we discuss six studies: four studies examined the use of imagery in serving, one study focused on both imagery and self-talk, and one on self-talk. In one study (Coelho, de Campos, da Silva, Okazaki, and Keller, 2007), tennis players (mean age = 17.2 years) served more accurately at the end of a 2-month imagery program (12.3±2.1 successful out of 20 serves) than at the beginning of the program (10.8±2.2 out of 20). This difference represents a moderate effect size of .68. The 23 players in the imagery group underwent three weekly imagery sessions for the duration of the study. These sessions included watching a videotape of winning tennis athletes, relaxation, and imagery for building self-confidence. The control group (no-imagery) in this study ($n = 25$), were given technical instructions only during their sessions and showed no improvement in serving performances.

In another study (Noel, 1980), imagery and relaxation seemed to improve tennis serving performances in high ability players ($n = 6$; participated in intercollegiate competitions) but not low ability players ($n = 8$; did not participate in intercollegiate competitions). Serving performances were assessed in a pre-tournament match. Then, half of the players served as controls while the other half completed an intervention that was composed of three days of relaxation training (i.e., listening to a relaxation tape for 30 minutes per day) and four days of visualization training (i.e., listening to a visualization tape for 30 minutes per day). The posttest was an actual tennis tournament. While no differences were found between the pre-tournament match serving accuracy in the control group and in the low ability intervention group, participants in the high ability group who underwent the intervention improved their serving performance from 59.70% to 68.33%. The authors suggested that it is possible that lower ability players could benefit more from actual practice rather than imagery practice, or that the imagery program was more suitable for high ability players. Two limitations of this study are noteworthy. First, only six participants were in the high ability players group (three in the imagery program and three in the control condition). Second, the data from the pretest were obtained during a practice match while the data from the posttest were obtained during an actual tournament.

While the imagery interventions in the previous studies occurred before the day of testing, the acute effects of imagery and self-talk on tennis serving were examined in a study of 61 male and 54 female adult tennis players (mean age = 37.7±4.3 years) (Malouff, McGee, Halford, and Rooke, 2008). A serving accuracy competition was established in which each player performed 20 tennis serves while trying to hit a specific target area in the service zone. Zero points were given for missed serves, one point for hitting the service zone, and two points for hitting the specific target area within the service zone. The players were divided into three experimental groups: (a) control – serve as usual, (b) imagery – imagining the whole serve and seeing the ball hitting the target zone before each serve, and (c) self-talk – giving one-self silent instructions before each serve. The results showed better accuracy in both the imagery (19.05±4.35 points) and self-talk (18.71±5.16 points) groups compared to the control group (15.67±6.46 points), with effect sizes ranging from .51 to .6. In addition, the results of an instructional compliance questionnaire revealed that the participants mostly followed the given instructions. It appears that instructional self-talk and positive imagery that are performed right before the serve can improve performances.

Instructional self-talk was also found useful in the performance of badminton serves (Theodorakis, Weinberg, Natsis, Douma, and Kazakas, 2000). Twenty-eight male and 20 female physical education students performed badminton serves while trying to hit a specific location in the other side of the court. After a baseline performance of two blocks of 10 serves, the participants were divided into three groups: (a) control – do your best, (b) motivational self-talk – repeat the words "I can" before each serve, and (c) instructional self-talk – repeat the words "I see the net, I see the target" and performed another four blocks of 10 serves each. The instructional self-talk group performed better than both the motivational self-talk group and the control group, while no differences in performance were found between the two latter groups.

In contrast to a previous study (Malouff et al., 2008), mental imagery was found to be the least effective method of a warming-up method developed to reduce post-rest serving decrements (Anshel and Wrisberg, 1993). Running in place, striking the ball with the racquet and catching it, and performing practice swings were found to be more useful. In this study (Anshel and Wrisberg, 1993), 55 male and 15 female tennis players performed 20 tennis serves twice: (a) the serves were followed by a 5-min rest period, after which another four serves were performed, and (b) the serves were followed by a 15-min rest period, after which another four serves were performed. The last two minutes of the rest period were devoted to one of the strategies developed to reduce decrements in performance. The best strategy leading to the least reduction in performance was the practice swings and the worst strategy was the mental imagery. The results of this study are not necessarily surprising as practicing the task at hand is intuitively better than imagining it.

Lastly, the effects of kinesthetic and visual mental imagery on serving performances were examined in 50 male university students with no prior experience in tennis (Fery and Morizot, 2000). The participants' tennis serving performance was recorded in a pretest after which they were divided into four experimental groups: (a) kinesthetic modeling and kinesthetic mental practice, (b) visual modeling and visual mental practice, (c) kinesthetic modeling with no mental practice, and (d) visual modeling with no mental practice. Visual modeling was accomplished by directing the attention of the participants to a model's correct movements while completing the serve. Kinesthetic modeling was accomplished by blindfolding the participants and manually guiding them through the motions of the serve. During mental imagery, the participants in the imagery groups were asked to imagine performing the serve six times, while the participants in the no-imagery groups performed a distracting counting backwards task. The results showed that modeling (kinesthetic or visual) was useful only when mental imagery was allowed. More specifically, kinesthetic imagery led to better serve form scores and better serve velocity scores. When it came to serve accuracy, visual imagery and kinesthetic imagery led to similar improvements when compared to the no-imagery condition. Since serving success is a combination of both velocity and accuracy, this study suggests that kinesthetic modeling followed by kinesthetic mental imagery can lead to improved performance of a tennis serve.

Five of the six studies reviewed in this section suggest that mental imagery and/or instructional self-talk can be advantageous to the performance of tennis serves. However, only one of those studies (i.e., Fery and Morizot, 2000) took into account the velocity of the ball. Serving in tennis involves both accuracy and velocity. It is possible that the imagery groups in the reviewed studies reduced their velocity in order to improve the accuracy of the serve. In such a case, the serve overall quality may not be improved. Future studies should examine both accuracy and velocity in order to better understand whether mental imagery indeed benefits serving performances.

## Learning Strategies

A learning strategy refers to the behaviors and thoughts that a learner activates deliberately or subconsciously to improve a skill or to accomplish a goal (Lidor and Singer, 2005). We found two studies that examined the effects of the Five-Step Approach on the learning of the tennis serve (Bouchard and Singer, 1998; Tennant, Murray, and Tennant, 2004). The Five-Step Approach was established for learning a self-paced motor task (such as serving in tennis and badminton). This strategy is composed of five steps: (a) readying, (b) imaging, (c) focusing attention, (d) executing, and (e) evaluating (Singer, 1988).

In one of the two studies (Bouchard and Singer, 1998), 63 recreational tennis players were randomly assigned into three experimental groups: (a) the Five-Step Approach with video modeling, (b) the Five-Step Approach on audiotape, and (c) no strategy. The participants in the first group watched the performance of the five-step strategy on video and simultaneously performed the first three steps (readying, imaging, and focusing attention) after which they continued to watch the model perform the last two steps (executing and evaluating). The audiotape group heard (but did not watch) the same instructions delivered on the videotape and the no strategy group watched a general video clip on tennis. All participants performed two baseline blocks, three acquisition blocks, and two retention blocks of 10 serves each. The results showed that serving accuracy increased in all groups across blocks and performance was maintained during the retention blocks. However, no significant differences were found between groups. The authors of this study noted that the variance in skill level between participants (some were beginners and some were of intermediate and high levels) may have led to the lack of differences between groups.

The second study (Tennant et al., 2004), examined whether the point of introduction of the Five-Step Approach influenced the learning of the badminton serve in 50 novice badminton players. Participants were divided into five groups: (a) the Five-Step Approach was introduced for all trial blocks, (b) the strategy was introduced after the first block, (c) the strategy was introduced after three blocks, (d) the strategy was introduced after five blocks, and (e) no strategy. Participants performed six blocks in total and were given accuracy points based on target areas in the service court. Each participant received the same taped instructions regarding the Five-Step Approach except for the no-strategy group, which listened to a tape about various aspects of the sport of badminton. In the acquisition phase, participants who received the instructions after three blocks (50% of the blocks), or right at the beginning, performed better than those who received the instructions after the first block and after five blocks, and than those who did not receive instructions. No differences between groups were found in the retention phase. It appears that a learning strategy such as the Five-Step Approach should be introduced with the learning of a new skill or after individuals have some familiarity with the skill. Additional research is needed to increase our understanding of the optimal point of introduction of task-pertinent learning strategies.

## Hypnosis

We found one study on the effectiveness of hypnosis on the accuracy of the short serve in badminton in four female university players (Pates and Palmi, 2002). After testing baseline serving accuracy, each player underwent a two-stage hypnosis intervention in which the first stage included mental and muscular relaxation, and the second stage included regression to an experience of a previous excellent performance. When the memory of this performance was achieved, a trigger was introduced in order to create an association between the trigger and the visual, tactile, auditory, olfactory, and gustatory sensations during reliving the memory of the excellent performance. The trigger was holding the badminton racquet. The hypnosis session was taped and each player had played it once a day for seven days before a posttest of serving accuracy was completed. In the posttest, the players were asked to imagine the trigger every time they held the racquet before each serving attempt. All four players improved their serving accuracy: Player 1 improved from 18 (out of a maximum of 50) points to 28 points, Player 2 improved from 14 to 22, Player 3 from 9 to 25, and Player 4 from 15 to 27. In addition, three out of the four players improved their flow (i.e., feeling of being in the zone) scores. While this is only one study and additional research is needed, it appears that hypnosis can be a useful tool in improving accuracy while serving in badminton.

## INSTRUCTIONAL ASPECTS OF SERVING

In this section we review studies on feedback, contextual interference, and environmental factors associated with serving in tennis and badminton.

### Feedback

Feedback (sensory information that indicates something about the actual state of a person's movements; (Schmidt and Wrisberg, 2008) is used by coaches, instructors, and teachers to enhance performance of athletes. This section examines whether different types of feedback are beneficial when performing the tennis or the badminton serve. We found six studies examining the use of different types of feedback in serving: video modeling, video feedback, performance information feedback, environmental information feedback, correction cues, error cues, visuo-spatial feedback, proprioceptive feedback, and biofeedback.

In one study of 40 tennis novices (Emmen, Wesseling, Bootsma, Whiting, and Van Wieringen, 1985), video modeling, video feedback, or a combination of the two failed to produce improvements in serving performances when compared to regular tennis service training (a no-feedback condition). In fact, over five training sessions, 30 minutes of regular tennis service training produced similar results to those achieved during 45 minutes of regular training, or during sessions that incorporated 15 minutes of video-modeling, or video feedback, into the 45-minute sessions.

The findings of the previous study (Emmen et al., 1985) were supported in 72 intermediate tennis players who failed to show improved tennis service performances when using video feedback when compared to traditional training (no-feedback group) (Van Wieringen, Emmen, Bootsma, Hoogesteger, and Whiting, 1989). In this study, the participants were divided into three experimental groups (video feedback, traditional training, and control), and received two 40-minute training sessions per week for five weeks. During these sessions, the video-feedback group spent 10 minutes discussing video recording of their performance, and 30 minutes were spent on practical training. The traditional training group spent 30 minutes on practical training and watched videos of different types of tennis strokes for the remaining 10 minutes. Lastly, the control group did not receive any training. It was found in this study that the tennis service performances of the participants in the control group were poorer than those of the other two experimental groups.

Unlike the previous studies, video feedback seemed to improve tennis serving performances in 42 female high-school physical education students (Cooper and Rothstein, 1981). Students were divided into three experimental groups: (1) performance information feedback (PIF), (2) environmental information feedback (EIF), and (3) both. Specific verbal cues were given to each group when watching the replay of their serving performances on videotape. For example, the participants in the PIF group were asked whether they took the racquet arm back, did they follow through in the direction of the intended hit, and was the swing smooth. The participants in the EIF group were asked where was the ball toss in relation to the body, how high was the ball toss, and what was the flight path of the ball. The participants practiced 10 tennis sessions over five weeks. Five of these sessions were devoted to practicing the serve. Tennis serving performances were the highest in the group that used both EIF and PIF, while EIF was the least effective type of feedback. As the authors of this study suggested, it appears that, when learning the tennis serve, environmental information alone is not enough and a combination of both environmental and performance information should be emphasized during videotape feedback.

A different type of feedback was found to benefit badminton novices who were learning how to serve. This was shown in a group of 48 10-14-year old male participants who learned a badminton forehand long serve (more difficult) and a backhand short serve (less difficult) (Tzetzis and Votsis, 2006). The participants were divided into three feedback groups: (1) correction cues – positive feedback and instructions on how to correct the technique, (2) error cues – positive feedback and instructions on errors of execution, and 3) error and correction cues – positive feedback and instructions on errors and directions on how to make corrections. Practice was conducted twice a week for 12 weeks; each training session lasted 60 minutes. A pretest, a posttest, and a retention test (2 weeks after the end of the intervention) of serving performances were performed. All groups improved their serving accuracy from pretest to the retention test. However, at the retention test for the backhand short serve (less difficult task), the correction cues group performed better than the two other groups. Similarly, in the retention test for the forehand long serve (more difficult task), the correction cues group and the errors and correction cues group outperformed the errors cues group. These results suggest that providing beginning learners with positive feedback with the addition of instructional cues on correcting the technique can facilitate the learning of the badminton serve.

Another study (Graydon and Townsend, 1984) of young participants (12-13 year-old) examined the effectiveness of visuo-spatial feedback and proprioceptive feedback on tennis serving performance. The proprioceptive group was blindfolded and was given verbal feedback emphasizing the feel of the movements (e.g., hit the shuttle a little harder), and feedback on their score after every attempt. In addition, at the first trials, they were manually positioned by the researchers. The visuo-spatial group was not blindfolded and was shown visually what bodily positions to adopt. Verbal feedback on the distance and direction of the ball was also given to this group. The training lasted 10 weeks, with two weekly sessions. The results showed similar accuracy results in both groups. Subjective reports from the researchers suggest that the form of the proprioceptive group was superior to that of the visuo-spatial group. As the authors suggested, a better serving form may have proven useful if the training duration was longer.

One study examining the effectiveness of biofeedback training (regulating the athlete's relaxation and arousal state) on tennis service accuracy in six male national junior (13-14 year-old) elite athletes was found (Galloway, 2011). Five participants underwent a mental training intervention while the sixth participant served as control. The intervention was based on the Wingate Five-Step Approach for mental training incorporating biofeedback. Phase 1 included 12 office sessions in which the participants were familiarized with the biofeedback equipment and the psychological skills trained (i.e., excitation, relaxation, imagery, and centering). During Phase 2, the player's most efficient biofeedback response was identified, and the player learned what psychological and physiological indicators could help him develop his service accuracy. During Phase 3, each participant practiced mental training with biofeedback for 12 sessions. Phase 4 included shorter sessions of imagery, centering, and self-talk during training when play stopped, and Phase 5 was conducted in a competitive environment. Participants performed 20 serves during a baseline test, during each phase of the intervention, and during a posttest. Serving accuracy improved throughout the biofeedback intervention in all participants except for the control participant. The biggest gains in performance were observed between Phase 1 and Phase 2, while no differences were seen between baseline and Phase 1, and between Phase 4 and Phase 5.

The studies reviewed in this section lead to the following conclusions: in badminton, it seems that instructional feedback that emphasizes how to correct serving technique improves serving performance. In tennis, video feedback does not improve tennis performance in novice and intermediate level adults, but can have a positive effect on high-school physical education students. However, three factors could have affected the results of these studies: (a) the participants in the badminton study (Tzetzis and Votsis, 2006) were children (10-14 year-old) and it is not known whether adults would benefit similarly from the feedback introduced in this study; (b) the length of the training program of the badminton study (Tzetzis and Votsis, 2006) was 12 weeks compared to five weeks in the intermediate tennis players (Van Wieringen et al., 1989), and only five sessions in the novices (Emmen et al., 1985). Therefore, it is possible that either the age of the participants, the length of the training program, or both, influenced the results of these studies; (c) since only a small number of studies were performed on the use of feedback in learning a serve in tennis and badminton, there are not enough data to assess the effects of different types of feedback on tennis or badminton serving performance.

## Contextual Interference

Two studies on the contextual interference effect in learning to serve were found. Contextual interference has been defined as the interference in performance and learning that arises from performing one task in the context of other tasks (Schmidt and Lee, 2011). In one study (Goode and Magill, 1986), 30 females with no badminton experience tried to learn three types of badminton serves – short, long, and drive. The participants were divided into three experimental groups: (a) blocked – each type of serve was learned independently, (b) serial – all serves were practiced in each session in a predictable order, and (c) random – all serves were practiced in each session in random order. During acquisition, participants practiced three sessions per week for three weeks, and each session included three blocks of 12 serves. The blocked group performed the same serve 36 times during each session (and a different serve in the next session). The serial and random groups practiced all three serves in each session by performing a different serve each trial in a serial or a random order. The retention and transfer phases included 18 randomly set trials each. The transfer task involved serving to the left instead of to the right side of the court. During the acquisition phase, all groups improved their accuracy in all three serves over time, with no differences between groups. During retention and transfer, serving accuracy of the random group for the short serve was better than the accuracy of the serial and blocked groups. As the authors of this study suggested, the contextual variety allowed the participants to be context independent, and therefore able to make the transition from one serving task to a new serving task more successfully.

Similar results were found in a study of 32 male and 20 female university students enrolled in an elementary badminton class (Wrisberg and Liu, 1991). The participants were divided into two experimental groups: blocked and alternating. In each practice session, the blocked group performed nine trials of the short serve and nine trials of the blocked serve in a counterbalanced manner. The alternating group performed a different type of serve each trial (e.g., short, long, short long…) in a counterbalanced manner. After five practice sessions, a retention and transfer tests (12 long and 12 short serves in an alternating manner) were performed. Accuracy of the short serve was higher for the blocked group on practice days 4 and 5. During the retention phase, the accuracy of the alternating group was significantly higher than that of the blocked group for the short serve. During the transfer phase, the accuracy of both serves was higher in the alternating group. These results suggest that contextual variety can facilitate learning in real-life situations (e.g., physical education classes) and not only in laboratory settings.

In both of these studies, the retention and transfer phases were performed in the same manner as the random or alternating acquisition groups. Therefore, it is possible that the better performance of the random group in one study (Goode and Magill, 1986) and the alternating group in the other study (Wrisberg and Liu, 1991) during the retention and transfer phases was due the contextual similarity to the one presented in the acquisition phase. However, evidence from at least one study (Wrisberg, 1991) shows that it is more likely that the superior performance of the random or alternating groups was indeed due to the difference in contextual variety. In this study (Wrisberg, 1991), the retention and transfer phases were performed in a blocked manner, and still the participants who practiced in alternating manner showed higher badminton serving accuracy when compared to participants who practiced in a blocked manner.

## Environmental Effects

Two studies, one in tennis (Atkinson and Speirs, 1998) and one in badminton (Edwards, Lindsay, and Waterhouse, 2005) which examined the effects of time of day on serving performances were found. In the tennis study (Atkinson and Speirs, 1998), three male and three female competitive tennis players performed a first serve followed by a second serve fifteen times, on three occasions during one day – at 09:00, 14:00, and 18:00. Dependent variables included body temperature, grip strength, subjective alertness, racquet head velocity, ball velocity, and serve accuracy. Body temperature and grip strength were higher at 14:00 and 18:00. First serves were faster than second serves, but accuracy was similar between the first and second serves. For first serves, ball velocity was highest at 18:00, lower at 14:00 and lowest at 09:00. In contrast, accuracy was higher at 09:00 and 14:00 compared to 18:00. A closer examination of the data reveals that the differences in velocity were small: 23.3 m·s$^{-1}$ at 09:00, 23.8 m·s$^{-1}$ at 14:00, and 24.2 m·s$^{-1}$ at 18:00, representing an effect size of no more than .25. Differences in accuracy were larger: 32.3 points at 09:00, 26.6 points at 14:00, and 20.3 points at 18:00, representing an effect size of 1.5. No differences were found in velocity and accuracy in second serves.

Similar results were found in the badminton study (Edwards et al., 2005). Eight male recreational badminton players performed 10 long and 10 short serves at 08:00, 14:00, and 20:00, and tried to hit the shuttle into the center of a grid on the service court. Accuracy for both the long serve and the short serve was higher at 14:00 than 08:00 and 20:00.

While both studies suggest that serving accuracy is better during the day when compared to the evening, a number of variables that were not controlled may have affected these results. For example, fatigue could have played a role in the reduced accuracy during the evening since all of the participants began the experiment in the morning and completed it in the evening. A counterbalanced design in which players begin at different hours is needed in order to control for possible fatigue. Such a counterbalanced design would also prevent a testing effect. In addition, both studies included small sample sizes. Lastly, participants were of intermediate level at best, and it is not clear whether similar diurnal variations would occur in high level athletes.

## IMPLICATIONS FOR COACHING

Before implementing those psychological and instructional interventions found to assist coaches to improve the serving ability of their players, we outline a number of research limitations associated with the reviewed studies. Then, we provide coaches with practical advice on how to use these interventions in actual serving practices.

### Research Limitations

Based on the studies reviewed in this article, the following four research limitations are discussed:

*The lack of data on elite racquet players.* Most of the participants who participated in the reviewed studies were beginning players. Not much empirical data have been collected on the serving ability of elite tennis or badminton players. The use of findings that emerged from studies on beginning racquet players in training programs developed for elite players is questionable. Additional data should be collected on how elite racquet players practice the serving skill, and what psychological techniques they use to prepare themselves for the serving act.

*The lack of data on psychological interventions.* We found data on only a small number of sport psychology interventions used in serving in tennis and badminton: imagery, self-talk, learning strategies, and hypnosis. Additional studies on sport psychology techniques that can be used in serving should be conducted. Among the techniques that can help the server achieve better, but up to now have not been examined, are focusing attention, goal setting, and task orientation.

*The lack of qualitative studies.* Not many qualitative studies on psychological and instructional aspects of serving in racquet sports were found. Descriptive and experimental studies are essential for examining the effectiveness of psychological (e.g., imagery and self-talk) and instructional (e.g., feedback and contextual interference) interventions on performance enhancement in serving. However, in qualitative studies data can be gathered on psychological and instructional aspects related to the serving act, such as the feelings, perceptions, and thoughts of the players from the moment they know that they are going to serve until the moment they actually perform the serve. These qualitative data can help coaches to better understand the psychological needs of the server, and subsequently to plan effective psychological and instructional interventions that reflect these needs.

*The lack of studies on on-court serving performances.* We did not find empirical data on what tennis and badminton players do before, during, and after the serving act. A systematic analysis of the main actions demonstrated by servers during actual practices and matches while preparing themselves for the serving act should be carefully performed. The analysis of real-game actions demonstrated by servers can help coaches in understanding what servers actually do when readying themselves for the serving act. Based on these analyses, appropriate psychological and instructional interventions can be selected for the server.

## Practical Advice for Coaches

Based on the data discussed in our review, five practical implications are suggested for coaches who aim at preparing tennis and racquetball players for the serving act:

*Imagery should be used in training programs aimed at improving serving performances.* Imagery was found to be a contributing technique in improving serving performances. Imagery should be used when working with beginning and advanced servers. Servers can perform imagery during practice sessions and actual matches. It is recommended for coaches and sport psychology consultants to teach their players to imagine the following aspects of the serve: (a) the ready position, (b) the racket drop, (c) the contact point, and (d) the finish position (Yandell, 1999).

*Self-talk routines should be introduced to the server.* Self-talk was also found to be a contributing technique to enhance serving performances. Servers can establish a self-talk routine prior to each time they are going to perform the serving act (e.g., using the same words / short sentences). Self-talk can help servers to stay focus before they serve the ball, as well as assist them in feeling control over what they are doing in the serve.

*Task-pertinent learning strategies should be taught to beginning learners.* Learning strategies, such as the Five-Step Approach (Singer, 1988), can help beginning learners effectively organize effectively their thoughts before they perform the serve. In addition, these strategies enable servers to imagine themselves and be focused when they readying themselves for the serving act. However, not only beginning learners can benefit from the use of learning strategies, but also skilled servers who can adopt them as pre-performance routines (see, for example, Lidor and Singer, 2003).

*Feedback should be provided throughout all stages of learning/performance.* Although there are not enough data to indicate what type of feedback benefits serving performances, coaches should provide servers with feedback. Correction of performance errors is one of the most essential instructional techniques in the learning and performance of motor skills (Halden-Brown, 2003; Schmidt and Wrisberg, 2008). Servers are not able to observe all the segments of their serving motion, and therefore they should rely on feedback provided to them by their coaches. The use of video showing the servers' serving performances as part of the provision of feedback can also help them in understanding what they have to do in order to improve their serves.

*Learning conditions of contextual interference can be adopted by coaches when working with beginning servers.* When working with beginning servers, coaches are recommended to alter the learning conditions by presenting one type of serve (e.g., a short serve in badminton) in the context of other types of serves (e.g., a long serve or a drive serve in badminton). Learning conditions of contextual interference help the beginning server strengthen the foundations of the serving act, and better understand the specific requirements of each of the different learned types of serves. In addition, alternating the serving conditions allows the beginning learner to be context independent, and therefore able to make an efficient transition from one type of serve to a new type of serve.

## REFERENCES

Anshel, M. H., and Wrisberg, C. A. (1993). Reducing warm-up decrement in the performance of the tennis serve. *Journal of Sport and Exercise Psychology, 15*, 290-303.

Atkinson, G., and Speirs, L. (1998). Diurnal variation in tennis service. *Perceptual and Motor Skills, 86*, 1335-1338.

Bouchard, L. J., and Singer, R. N. (1998). Effects of the five-step strategy with videotape modeling on performance of the tennis serve. *Perceptual and Motor Skills, 86*, 739-746.

Coelho, R. W., de Campos, W., da Silva, S. G., Okazaki, F. H. A., and Keller, B. (2007). Imagery intervention in open and closed tennis motor skill performance. *Perceptual and Motor Skills, 105*, 458-468.

Cooper, L. K., and Rothstein, A. L. (1981). Videotape replay and the learning of skills in open and closed environments. *Research Quarterly for Exercise and Sport, 52*, 191-199.

Edwards, B., Lindsay, K., and Waterhouse, J. (2005). Effect of time of day on the accuracy and consistency of the badminton serve. *Ergonomics, 48*, 1488-1498.

Emmen, H. H., Wesseling, L. G., Bootsma, R. J., Whiting, H. T., and Van Wieringen, P. C. (1985). The effect of video-modelling and video-feedback on the learning of the tennis service by novices. *Journal of Sports Sciences, 3*, 127-138.

Fery, Y. A., and Morizot, P. (2000). Kinesthetic and visual image in modeling closed motor skills: the example of the tennis serve. *Perceptual and Motor Skills, 90*, 707-722.

Galloway, S. M. (2011). The effect of biofeedback on tennis service accuracy. *International Journal of Sport and Exercise Psychology, 9*, 251-266.

Gillet, E., Leroy, D., Thouvarecq, R., and Stein, J. F. (2009). A notational analysis of elite tennis serve and serve-return strategies on slow surface. *Journal of Strength and Conditioning Research, 23*, 532-539.

Goode, S., and Magill, R. A. (1986). Contextual interference effects in learning three badminton serves. *Research Quarterly for Exercise and Sport, 57*, 308-314.

Graydon, J. K., and Townsend, J. (1984). Proprioceptive and visual feedback in the learning of two gross motor skills. *International Journal of Sport Psychology, 15*, 227-235.

Halden-Brown, S. (2003). *Mistakes worth making – How to turn sports errors into athletic excellence*. Champaign, IL: Human Kinetics.

Lidor, R. (2007). Preparatory routines in self-paced events: Do they benefit the skilled athletes? Can they help the beginners? In G. Tenenbaum and R. C. Eklund (Eds.), *Handbook of sport psychology* (3rd ed., pp. 445-465). New York, NY: Wiley.

Lidor, R., and Singer, R. N. (2003). Pre-performance routines in self-paced tasks: Educational, developmental, and psychological considerations. In R. Lidor and K. Henschen (Eds.), *The psychology of team sports* (pp. 69-88). Morgantown, WV: Fitness Information Technology.

Malouff, J. M., McGee, J. A., Halford, H. T., and Rooke, S. E. (2008). Effects of pre-competition positive imagery and self-instructions on accuracy of serving in tennis. *Journal of Sport Behavior, 31*, 264-275.

Noel, R. C. (1980). The effect of visuo-motor behavior rehearsal on tennis performance. *Journal of Sport Psychology, 2*, 221-226.

Pates, J., and Palmi, J. (2002). The effects of hypnosis on flow states and performance. *Journal of Excellence, 6*, 48-62.

Schmidt, R. A., and Lee, T. D. (2011). *Motor control and learning – A behavioral emphasis* (5th ed.). Champaign, IL: Human Kinetics.

Schmidt, R. A., and Wrisberg, C. A. (2008). *Motor learning and performance – A situation-based learning approach* (4th ed.). Champaign, IL: Human Kinetics.

Singer, R. N. (1988). Strategies and metastrategies in learning and performing self-paced athletic skills. *The Sport Psychologist, 2*, 49-68.

Tennant, K., Murray, N. P., and Tennant, L. M. (2004). Effects of strategy use on acquisition of a motor task during various stages of learning. *Perceptual and Motor Skills, 98*, 1337-1344.

Theodorakis, Y., Weinberg, R., Natsis, P., Douma, I., and Kazakas, P. (2000). The effects of motivational versus instructional self-talk on improving motor performance. *The Sport Psychologist, 14*, 253-271.

Tzetzis, G., and Votsis, E. (2006). Three feedback methods in acquisition and retention of badminton skills. *Perceptual and Motor Skills, 102*, 275-284.

Van Wieringen, P. C. W., Emmen, H. H., Bootsma, R. J., Hoogesteger, M., and Whiting, H. T. A. (1989). The effect of video-feedback on the learning of the tennis service by intermediate players. *Journal of Sports Sciences, 7*, 153-162.

Wrisberg, C. A. (1991). A field test of the effect of contextual variety during skill acquisition. *Journal of Teaching in Physical Education, 11*, 21-30.

Wrisberg, C. A., and Liu, Z. (1991). The effect of contextual variety on the practice, retention, and transfer of an applied motor skill. *Research Quarterly for Exercise and Sport, 62*, 406-412.

Yandell, J. (1999). *Visual tennis – Using mental imagery to perfect your stoke technique* (2nd ed.). Champaign, IL: Human Kinetics.

In: Innovative Writings in Sport and Exercise Psychology
Editor: Robert Schinke

ISBN: 978-1-62948-881-3
© 2014 Nova Science Publishers, Inc.

*Chapter 4*

# A Phenomenological Examination of Depression in Female Collegiate Athletes

## *Alyson L. Jones, Ted M. Butryn\*, David M. Furst and Tamar Z. Semerjian*
San José State University, San José, CA US

## Abstract

Despite the well-known mental health benefits of exercise, collegiate athletes may be at an increased risk of depression due to the number of stressors they face (Gill, 2008; Yang et al., 2007), and this risk may be even greater for female athletes (Donohue et al., 2004; Storch, Storch, Killikany, and Roberti, 2005). It has been suggested that a greater understanding of personal experiences would be helpful in increasing awareness and improving treatment. Therefore, the purpose of the current study was to explore the lived experience of depression in female collegiate athletes. In-depth, unstructured interviews were conducted with 10 current and former female collegiate athletes. The interviews were recorded, transcribed, and analyzed using phenomenological research methods (Dale, 1996, 2000). Thematic analysis revealed one ground (the role of sport) and four general categories (weariness, self-doubt, out of control, and nowhere to go). Practical implications and recommendations are made for athletes and coaches.

## Introduction

Research investigating the relationship between sport participation and mental health has led to conflicting results (Proctor and Boan-Lenzo, 2010; Storch et al., 2005; Wyshak, 2001). A number of studies have suggested that participation in sport is associated with psychological benefits and that it acts as a buffer against various sources of stress (Proctor

---

\* Correspondence: Ted M. Butryn, San Jose State University, One Washington Square, San Jose, CA 95192-0054. Theodore.butryn@sjsu.edu. (408) 924-3068 (phone). (408) 924-3053 (fax).

and Boan-Lenzo, 2010). The Profile of Mood States (POMS), developed for use in counseling and psychotherapy as a means of measuring the current mood of patients, has often been employed in studies measuring athletes' emotional states (Snow and LeUnes, 1994). Through this research, the "iceberg" profile was identified, in which athletes displayed high levels of vigor alongside low levels of anger, depression, tension, fatigue, and confusion (Morgan, 1980; Morgan and Pollock, 1977; Puffer and McShane, 1992; Terry, 1995). Overall, research utilizing the POMS in sport appears to point to positive mental health among athletes, including decreased levels of depression, compared to other populations (Terry, 1995).

Contrary to these findings, a significant body of research has pointed to mental health detriments associated with sport participation, particularly in the collegiate athletic population (Gill, 2008; Storch et al., 2005). Theories posited to explain these research findings hinge on the assertion that the collegiate athlete is exposed to an increased number of stressors, including time demands, decreased autonomy, pressures of meeting expectations and pleasing those around them, negotiating relationships, increased competition, retirement from sport after graduation, and performance anxiety (Proctor and Boan-Lenzo, 2010; Storch et al., 2005; Yang et al., 2007). In addition, student-athletes are expected to meet the demands of being a student as well (Storch et al., 2005; Yang et al., 2007). Balancing different identity roles can be a significant challenge for the collegiate athlete, and role conflict or interference has been found to negatively affect mental health (Killeya-Jones, 2005; Settles, Sellers, and Damas, 2002). Finally, college is a time often characterized by transition, which can add additional stress to the lives of student-athletes (Storch et al., 2005; Yang et al., 2007).

A wide range of potential psychiatric disorders may present within the collegiate athletic population as a result of these varied and significant stressors, including depression, anxiety, bipolar disorder, attention-deficit/hyperactivity disorder, disordered eating, and substance abuse (Broshek and Freeman, 2005; Puffer and McShane, 1992). In the general population, depression is the most common mental health issue. Nicknamed the "common cold" of psychiatric disorders, nearly one in six people will experience depression in their lifetime (Cogan, 2000; Mentink, 2001). The college-aged population may experience depression at even higher levels than the general population. According to recent research, 18.9% of college students reported feeling depressed within the past 12 months (American College Health Association [ACHA], 2008). These numbers appear to be on the rise during recent years, with colleges and universities reporting growing numbers of reports of depression and suicidal ideations and intentions at their mental health facilities (Sisk, 2006). In fact, suicide ranks as the second-leading cause of death among college students with 12.5 deaths per 100,000 young people between the ages of 20 and 24 (National Institute of Mental Health [NIMH], 2009a; Sisk, 2006).

A significant gender difference exists in the prevalence of depression, with women outnumbering men by nearly a 2:1 ratio (NIMH, 2009b). Previous studies have reported a greater incidence of depression among female collegiate athletes compared to males (Donohue et al., 2004; Storch et al., 2005; Yang et al., 2007).

Various theories have been proposed to explain the reported gender difference in the prevalence of depression. Typically these theories have pointed to potential hormonal or cognitive differences (LaFrance and Stoppard, 2006). Gender role socialization, or an increased willingness to report symptoms and seek help, have also been suggested as possible reasons for gender differences (Yang et al., 2007). Additional theories specific to the collegiate athletic population include exposure to more stressors than male athletes, greater internalization of stress and negative feedback, or less involvement in non-sport social activities (Storch et al., 2005). It is clear that female collegiate athletes are at significant risk of experiencing depression, and this can lead to potentially harmful outcomes.

The experience of depressive symptoms in the collegiate athletic population should be of great concern for a number of reasons. First, the typical age of onset for depression is the mid-twenties, making depression a significant risk for this group (Broshek and Freeman, 2005). Second, collegiate athletes face a unique set of challenges that place them at an increased risk for mental health disorders such as depression and maladaptive coping behaviors like alcohol abuse (Ford, 2007; Gill, 2008; Miller, Miller, Verhegge, Linville, and Pumariega, 2002). Third, an individual suffering from depression is unlikely to be functioning at optimal levels, and for an athlete that could mean impaired sport performance (Cogan, 2000). Finally, the health, safety, and happiness of individuals suffering from depression rely on recognition and proper care.

Depression is a significant risk factor for suicidal ideations and attempts, highlighting the critical importance of appropriate attention and intervention (ACHA, 2008; NIMH, 2009b, Sisk, 2006). This need may be especially pressing in collegiate sport because college students, and athletes in particular, underutilize mental health support resources available to them, leaving them susceptible to potentially harmful outcomes (Andersen, Denson, Brewer, and Van Raalte, 1994; Cogan, 2000; Glick and Horsfall, 2005; Mentink, 2001; Sisk, 2006; Watson, 2005; Yang et al., 2007). Understanding the symptoms, prevalence, and associated risk factors of mental illness is vital in ensuring proper attention and care (Andersen et al., 1994; Glick and Horsfall, 2005). Obtaining an in-depth understanding of the experience of depression from the point of view of the athlete can also provide valuable assistance in treating this at-risk population.

As previously discussed, the majority of research investigating the relationship between mental health and sport participation has relied heavily on quantitative measurements. Qualitative research, however, could provide another valuable means of understanding the relationship between depression and sport participation. Indeed, existential phenomenology has been suggested as a potent means of exploration due to its ability to investigate complex experiences from a first-person perspective and subjectively define what is meaningful within those experiences (Allen-Collinson, 2009; Bain, 1995; Dale, 1996; Fahlberg, Fahlberg, and Gates, 1992; Kerry and Armour, 2000; Pollio, Henley, and Thompson, 1997; Ryba, 2007; Solomon, 1972; Sorenson, Czech, Gonzalez, Klein, and Lachowetz, 2009; Spillman, 2006; Valle, King, and Halling, 1989). The melding of the philosophical underpinnings of existentialism and phenomenology–namely, the interest in human experience as it exists in the world–with qualitative research methods allows for a richness of results and a depth of understanding greater than what could be obtained through other modes of inquiry (Allen-Collinson, 2009; Dale, 1996; Giorgi, 2002; Heidegger, 1962; Kerry and Armour, 2000).

In recent years, there has been an increased use of existential phenomenology within sport psychology research, exploring a wide variety of topics. Also, existential phenomenological research studies in psychology have investigated the experiences of depression among various demographic groups. Farmer (2002) explored adolescents' experiences of depression with five depressed adolescents aged 13 to 17, and concluded that the essential structures of their experiences were anger and fatigue. Spillman (2006) explored men's experiences of depression with 10 participants, ranging in age from 30 to 61, who had been diagnosed with depression and were currently receiving psychotherapy. Central to their experiences was feeling out of control, which represented the participants' feelings of unpredictability and powerlessness with regard to their depression. The lack of qualitative research exploring the depression experiences of women, however, leaves researchers and practitioners "wandering in the dark" (Schreiber, 2001, p. 86), demonstrating a need for more research in this area.

In order to explore the experience of depression in sport, Mentink (2001) utilized a case study approach with three collegiate athletes (two male, one female). Mentink was particularly interested in how the athletes used the resources available to them to cope with depression. Semi-structured interviews were conducted in addition to two surveys to assess depressive symptoms. Additionally, a parent or coach of each athlete was interviewed. Results revealed a disconnect between the participants' experiences of depression and what their coach or parent perceived. In addition, the participants were reluctant to come forward with their mental health struggles, demonstrating a clear need for a better understanding of the symptoms of depression in this population.

Leno (2007) conducted an existential phenomenological investigation of African American male athletes' experiences of depression. Ten collegiate and professional basketball and football players were interviewed using open-ended questions. Similar to Mentink's (2001) findings, Leno suggested that the experiences of an athlete may differ significantly from the perceptions held by others and may be characterized by a balancing of the positive aspects of an athletic career with pressure and struggles with performance. Leno suggested that more qualitative research is necessary in order to increase knowledge and debunk misconceptions and stereotypes regarding depression. Therefore, the purpose of the current study was to explore the lived experiences of depression in female collegiate athletes from an existential phenomenological perspective.

## METHOD

### Participants

The purpose of phenomenological research is to describe the fundamental structure of an experience, not the statistical characteristics of the individuals in the group under study. Therefore, participants are not chosen randomly in order to achieve statistical generalization, but are instead purposefully selected due to their experience with a given phenomenon (Czech et al., 2004; Dale, 1996, 2000). Ideally, these participants are able to richly describe their experiences, providing varying accounts of a particular phenomenon that when taken as a whole will create an understanding of the lived experience under investigation (Polkinghorne, 1989; Ryba, 2007). Participants were recruited through local Division I collegiate athletic programs. Criteria for inclusion in the current study were: (a) being a current or former female collegiate athlete, and (b) self-identifying as having experienced depression (Leno, 2007; Mentink, 2001). Ten current and former female collegiate athletes participated in the study. Participants ranged in age from 18 to 27 years. Participants included athletes from five sports: water polo (4), swimming (3), basketball (1), lacrosse (1), and gymnastics (1). See Table 1 for profiles of the participants.

## Table 1. Participant Profiles

| Name | Sport | Year | Precipitating Events |
|---|---|---|---|
| Alisha | Basketball | 5 | Major injuries; difficulties with coach; eligibility issues |
| Dee | Swimming | 3 | Performance problems |
| Emily | Lacrosse | Former | Difficulties with coach; role confusion; homesickness |
| Erin | Gymnastics | 1 | Personal relationship issues |
| Heather | Water polo | Former | Major injuries; teammate relationship issues |
| Heidi | Swimming | 4 | Major injury; teammate/coach relationship issues |
| Jodi | Water polo | 4 | Concern about upcoming retirement from sport |
| Katy | Water polo | 2 | Performance problems |
| Maddy | Swimming | 1 | Homesickness; struggle with time demands |
| Renee | Water polo | 2 | Personal relationship issues |

## Interview Strategy

Phenomenological interviews are open-ended, unstructured, and designed to create a conversation or discourse investigating the experience of interest (Czech et al., 2004; Johnson, 1998; Leno, 2007; Polkinghorne, 1989; Ryba, 2007; Sorenson et al., 2009). The role of the researcher is to encourage self-reflection by the participant and to seek clarification when necessary (Czech et al., 2004; Johnson, 1998; Polkinghorne, 1989).

Prior to conducting participant interviews, the researcher took part in a bracketing interview in order to better understand her preconceived notions regarding the current topic of study (Dale, 1996; Garland, 2005). While it is impossible to completely discard researcher assumptions, the awareness of those assumptions gained through the bracketing interview allowed for the minimization of bias (Allen-Collinson, 2009; Dale, 1996; Krane, Andersen, and Strean, 1997). Next, a pilot interview was conducted with an athlete who met the criteria necessary for the current study. The interview was an opportunity for the researcher to practice appropriate phenomenological interview techniques (Dale, 1996). The pilot interview also raised additional dimensions of interest that were not identified during the self-reflective bracketing interview (Polkinghorne, 1989), and the interviewee gave feedback regarding the interview.

After receiving university IRB approval, interviews were arranged at times convenient for the participants. Nine interviews were conducted in person, and one interview was conducted via web-cam using the online phone service Skype. Each participant was fully informed about the focus of the study and signed an Informed Consent Form at the time of the interview.

The interviews began with an open-ended prompt designed to guide the direction of the interview: "Tell me about your experience of depression during your time as an athlete." If the participant found it difficult to know where to begin, they were asked to first describe their sport background. This approach often helped the participants feel comfortable before delving into subjects that were quite personal and perhaps more difficult to articulate. Follow-up questions were asked based on how the participant responded and sought to clarify the participant's responses, such as "Could you tell me more about that?" or "What was that like for you?" The format of the interview was circular instead of linear, resembling a natural conversation, and the dialogue was set primarily by the participant (Dale, 1996; Polkinghorne, 1989). The interviews lasted as long as the participants needed in order to cover the topics they felt were relevant, and ranged from 35 minutes to just over 90 minutes. Each interview was transcribed verbatim and all names and other identifying information were changed or removed in order to protect the participants' privacy. Transcripts were returned to the participants in order to be checked for errors, omissions, or corrections.

## Thematic Analysis

Data analysis involved the creation of multiple levels of data themes. First, meaning units were identified in the transcripts by locating key words or phrases (Garland, 2005; Gratton and Jones, 2004; Sorenson et al., 2009). Next, the meaning units were grouped based on similarities into themes (Côté, Salmela, Baria, and Russell, 1993; Czech et al., 2004; Dale, 1996; Gratton and Jones, 2004). The themes were then merged again into general categories. This final level of analysis represents the fundamental structure of the data (Dale, 1996; Gratton and Jones, 2004). The hermeneutic circle was employed during the process of thematic analysis. This procedure involves the continuous interpretation of one piece of data, or interview transcript, in relation to the whole of the data (Dale, 1996; Pollio et al., 1997). By continually going back over earlier interviews in relation to later ones, and vice versa, the researcher is able to recognize how each one resembles others, and eventually arrive at themes and general categories that are representative of the data (Dale, 1996; Pollio et al., 1997).

## Establishing Academic Rigor

A number of steps were taken in the interest of establishing academic rigor: the aforementioned bracketing and pilot interviews; a reflexive journal detailing decisions made in relation to methods used and the reasons for those decisions (Côté et al., 1993; Dale, 1996); peer review, in which another researcher not involved with the study read and raised questions about the interview transcripts and analysis; first-person, thick description through the use of direct quotes when reporting the participants' experiences (Allen-Collinson, 2009; Dale, 1996; Krane et al., 1997; Sparkes, 1998; Strean, 1998); and member checking, in which the interview transcripts were returned to the respective participants in an effort to allow the participants to check for accuracy (Appleby and Fisher, 2009; Dale, 1996; Polkinghorne, 1989).

## RESULTS

Analysis of the 10 interview transcripts revealed one ground, the role of sport, and four general categories that embodied the participants' experiences of depression: weariness, self-doubt, out of control, and nowhere to go (see Table 2). The following section describes the ground and the four general categories.

# A Phenomenological Examination of Depression in Female Collegiate Athletes

## Table 2. Thematic Categories

| Ground | Theme | |
|---|---|---|
| The role of sport | "I enjoy sport" | |
| | "It takes up so much time" | |
| | "It's part of my identity" | |
| | "It's an out for me" | |
| Weariness | "I was sad all the time" | Feeling sad (5) |
| | | Crying (7) |
| | | Bed/ sleep (3) |
| | | Breaking down (2) |
| | "I had nobody" | Feeling lonely (2) |
| | | Feeling homesick (4) |
| | | Excluded by teammates (3) |
| | "I was overwhelmed" | Dealing with a lot (2) |
| | | Feeling overwhelmed (1) |
| | | Feeling drained (1) |
| | | Feeling mentally weak (1) |
| Self-Doubt | "What's wrong with me?" | Self-Doubt (4) |
| | | What's wrong with me? (2) |
| | | Question yourself (2) |
| | | Can I do this? (2) |
| | | Why am I not improving? (2) |
| | | Second guessing (1) |
| | | In a rut (1) |
| | | In a funk (1) |
| | | Plateau (1) |
| | | Not in the groove (1) |
| | "I was hard on myself" | Hard on myself (2) |
| | | Get down on yourself (2) |
| | | Self-Criticism (1) |
| | | Feeling worthless (1) |
| | | Feeling disappointed (1) |
| | | High expectations not met (1) |
| | | Feel like a failure (1) |
| Out of control | "Sport was taken from me" | Someone else says "no" (3) |
| | | Injury (3) |
| | | Physical pain (3) |
| | | Rehab (2) |
| | "It made me angry" | Feeling angry (2) |
| | | Feeling insulted (2) |
| | | Feeling betrayed (1) |
| | | Not fair (1) |
| | "I've tried and tried..." | I don't know what to do (3) |
| | | Why is this happening? (2) |
| | | Out of my hands/ control (1) |
| | | I don't understand (1) |
| | | Come to terms (1) |
| Nowhere to go | "Why am I doing this?" | Why am I doing this? (6) |
| | | I don't want to do this (6) |

**Table 2. (Continued)**

| Ground | Theme | |
|---|---|---|
| | "I tried to get away" | Wanted to quit (5) |
| | | Feeling trapped (1) |
| | | Feeling torn (1) |
| | | Distance/ seclusion (5) |
| | | Get away from it (3) |
| | | Don't think about it (2) |
| | | Bottle it up (2) |
| | | Keep to myself (2) |
| | | Making excuses (2) |
| | | Not trying (1) |
| | | Drugs (1) |
| | | Embarrassment/ hiding (1) |
| | "I couldn't give up" | I couldn't give up (6) |
| | | I get through things (6) |
| | | Push through (2) |
| | "This is all I have" | Scared to end sport (5) |
| | | What to do without sport (4) |

*Note.* Numbers in parentheses represent the number of participants coded as referring to each meaning unit.

## The Role of Sport

No one aspect of human experience exists without connection to the experience as a whole. When discussing a specific aspect of first-person experience (figure), it must be considered as it relates to the whole of the experience (ground). This relationship is referred to as the "figure/ground structure of experience," in which the ground serves as a backdrop for understanding figural themes, providing them with necessary context (Pollio et al., 1997, p. 13). The role of sport is the ground in the current study and represents the psychological, emotional, temporal, and physical commitment the athletes have made to sport as a major part of their lives.

The participants discussed different aspects of the role of sport in their lives, the most prominent of which was an enjoyment of sport. As Dee explained, "I enjoy swimming. I enjoy racing. I enjoy being with my teammates, and that's really what keeps me together."

Not surprisingly, being an athlete had become a major part of the participants' identity. As Jodi stated, "Maybe it's just that it's always been my thing. I've always been an athlete, and I've always felt really great about working really hard." Heidi also discussed her relationship to sport:

> I guess [sport] being part of my identity has overall been a good thing. I mean, obviously I love the sport. I've taken it all the way through college; it's taken *me* all the way through college [laughs]. And it is my life; swimming is my life.

Participants discussed the significant time commitment required to be a collegiate athlete. For Katy, the time commitment to sport left her wondering what to do when she had time to herself:

When you play a sport at such a high level, it's like all you do. So all I basically do is I go to school, I sleep, I eat, and I play water polo.... Since you do it so much in the year, without it is like an emptiness... you don't know what to do with all that time.

Sport was seen as an escape from negative events in the participants' lives. They explained that sport helped them to feel relaxed and happy when they were otherwise stressed or upset, often referring to sport as an "outlet." In the following passage, Alisha explained how basketball helped her feel better when she was angry or upset:

When I was younger, if my brothers and sisters were arguing, or my mom was arguing with my dad, or I got in trouble... I'd just grab the basketball and go outside and start shooting. And it was like I could just forget about it in that moment. It was like my coping mechanism. And I know maybe it sounds stupid, but some people eat when they're depressed; I play basketball.

In short, sport contributed greatly to the participants' views of themselves, their social relationships, their college lives, and their futures. However, sport often took on a new and complex role as the source of, or reprieve from, depression. Sometimes, it was perceived as both. The following sections detail the difficult experience of depression for these participants. Each aspect of their experience was influenced heavily by the ground of the role of sport in their lives.

## Weariness

Feelings of sadness, loneliness, and mental and emotional exhaustion permeated many areas of the participants' lives and all related to the general category of weariness. Five of the participants discussed feeling sad, upset, or unhappy during their experience of depression. As Erin described, she remembered the sadness as being pervasive:

I was sad all the time. And I don't know; it was just kind of routine. I'd get up and go to school, but I wouldn't really talk much. And when I got home, I'd just listen to sad music.

Three participants remembered their desire to do not much more than stay in bed and sleep when they were depressed, and seven participants discussed crying as part of their experience. Being upset to the point of "breaking down" was an experience described by two of the participants in this study. As Emily recalled, "I was like water works for 3 hours, I couldn't even get a word out. It was just a complete breakdown; crying, lots of tears." Pervasive and sometimes overwhelming feelings of sadness were ongoing during participants' experiences of depression.

Six participants recalled struggling with feelings of loneliness and homesickness. For some of them, it was due to being away from family and friends for the first time. Due to the obligations of being a collegiate athlete, participants often found that they were unable to travel home at times when their non-athlete friends could. These restrictions exacerbated their feelings of loneliness. Emily described her experience:

I don't think I ever knew it would be so hard to be so far from my friends and family. Not even that they were far, but that they were so far that I couldn't even drive six hours or so to see them, which I would have done. But I couldn't. I had nobody. It was a really isolating feeling.

Three participants explained feeling lonely because an event had caused their teammates to exclude them. For Heidi, a conflict with teammates led to feelings of ostracism and loneliness when they excluded her from their social circle:

They were like, "You messed up; we don't want you here." And it was really hard, because this was like my family; these were like my older sisters. So that was very, very depressing.

Sport placed many demands on their time, as discussed in the ground, which led four participants to feel overwhelmed and exhausted. Juggling many obligations or worries while also struggling with depression can lead to a feeling of being unable to deal with it all. Heather recalled how she felt overwhelmed and less capable during her experience of depression:

When I feel overwhelmed, it's like emotionally overwhelmed. If something's bad, I think it's 10 times worse than it is, and then I just get really sad about it. Normally I'd be like, "Oh, that sucks." But [instead] it was like, "Oh my god, the world's going to end. I can't deal with this."

Heather's depression led her to overestimate the size of the problems she faced while also underestimating her ability to meet them. She discussed how being overwhelmed led her to feel depleted and mentally drained:

It was so hard. It took all my mental energy to be positive through my injury. Pull myself through, start playing, be cool with my teammates, and then [getting injured] again, and rehabbing through that. My brain was just tired.... I just felt like I had tapped out my mental bank.

## Self-Doubt

This general category is comprised of participants' experiences of questioning and criticizing themselves and their athletic abilities during their struggles with depression and other challenges. Six participants discussed doubting themselves when faced with poor performance or a lack of expected improvement. Dee struggled with self-doubt during a plateau in her performance when she was training but not improving. She remembered asking herself, "If my competitors are doing better than me and they've been swimming just as long as me, then what is wrong with me?" Self-doubt about her athletic abilities caused Dee to question other aspects of her life as well: "I think the hardest part about when I was plateauing, the most confusing part was, 'Ok, if I'm not good at this, then what am I good at?'" Sport had long seemed like solid ground for the participants. Consequently, being faced with new questions about their performance or their place within sport caused significant distress.

Four participants described feelings of perfectionism and heightened self-criticism when they believed they fell short of their goals. Katy described having extremely high expectations for her performance, and Dee described feelings of worthlessness: "I didn't really feel like I was worth anything anymore. I didn't feel like my hard work did anything for me." Emily admitted: "You almost feel like a part of you is a failure, a little bit."

Sport had always been a source of confidence and enjoyment, but when faced with unexpected plateaus or periods of poor performance, the participants suddenly felt self-doubt creeping in. Questions regarding their athletic abilities were exacerbated by perfectionism and harsh criticism of their performance, spiraling until their sport foundation had been truly shaken.

## Out of Control

Feeling out of control was a common experience for eight of the participants. It took many forms and appeared in narratives about being unwillingly restricted from sport participation, reacting in anger towards themselves and others, and feeling helpless to regain control of their athletic fate.

Sport participation was restricted for six participants because of injury, rehabilitation, physical pain, or discipline for academic or extracurricular issues. This left participants feeling as if they had lost an important aspect of their lives and they lacked the control to get it back. They felt as if external and uncontrollable sources had taken sport away from them, and they had no say in the decision.

A salient aspect of this category was the experience of somebody else telling them they could not participate. "When they said I couldn't even go [play], I was like, 'Oh my goodness, this is my life, and they're taking it away,'" Heidi explained. Alisha echoed feelings of her life being controlled by external sources when she struggled with school officials over her athletic eligibility: "I mean, this is my life. I even told them that; I was like, 'This is my *life*.'"

Injuries, especially career-ending injuries, have been found to lead to feelings of identity loss and depression for athletes, as discussed by Leno (2007) and others. In the current study, injuries that restricted sport participation contributed to feeling out of control. When Heather could not play water polo due to an injury, she felt as though she was blocked from the one thing that would ease her depression:

> I just needed to get back to water polo for my sanity. That's what I felt would solve everything.... I felt like I could go back to water polo and it would all be erased and I would be happy and cool again.

Four participants described feeling angry as a major part of their experiences. Often their anger was directed at something over which they had no control. Other times their anger was a response to a lack of control over their situation; an experience described by many participants. If attempts to reclaim control were unsuccessful, they felt powerless and helpless as a result. An example of this experience was provided by Alisha, who had struggled with an accumulation of negative and unpredictable setbacks—multiple injuries, conflict with coaches, and disagreement over her eligibility–that left her feeling out of control of her situation. In the following passage she discussed feeling powerless to clear up the eligibility disagreement:

> I don't know what to do anymore. It's out of my hands really, as far as I see it. [Researcher: What's that like, to feel like it's out of your hands?] Yeah, it's out of my control, and it is very frustrating. I mean, I've done everything I can do about it, and I've tried and tried and tried.... I'm like getting emotional talking about it, it's just so wrong. It is *wrong*.... I just don't understand.

The experience of being out of control represented participants' struggles with being restricted from playing sport and feelings of anger, powerlessness, and helplessness when their attempts at control were unsuccessful. Another way participants attempted to regain control in the face of depression and other sport-related challenges was to re-evaluate their commitment to sport entirely.

## Nowhere to Go

Depression and frustration with sport led participants to consider leaving sport in order to alleviate their pain. Yet, they expressed being unwilling to give up sport because it was such a big part of their lives and identity, and had served as an emotional outlet during times of stress. For some, sport was seen as all they had going for them and struggled to imagine what they would do instead of sport. Thus, they had nowhere to go. Even though sport created problems, they could not imagine their lives without it. This general category discusses how participants balanced these conflicting thoughts and desires regarding their athletic future.

Five participants recounted times in which they nearly quit sport as a way out of their struggle with depression. While vacillating over the idea of quitting sport, participants often asked themselves, somewhat rhetorically, what their reasons were for continuing to play. They wondered what the point of getting up early for practice was when they were not seeing any improvement in their performance, or if their injury rehabilitation was worth the pain and effort it required. Most importantly, they wondered why they were continuing to play when they were no longer enjoying it, as Katy described in the following passage:

> I'd be like, "I'm quitting; I'm not doing this anymore".... But of course the next year I'd go back. It happened every year; every week I was like, "I'm *not* doing this." It was like, "Why am I doing this? I'm not having any fun, I'm not getting any better, and I'm not even that good, where am I going to go?"

No longer finding enjoyment in previously enjoyed activities, or meaning in previously valued activities, are hallmark signs of depression. Heather felt a waning enjoyment of sport as she neared the end of college, yet was unable to move on to the next phase of her life:

> At that point, I felt trapped with water polo. [Researcher: So what was that feeling like, being trapped?] I just realized that, you know, I did what I wanted to do with water polo; I was done. Yeah, I liked playing, I liked to train, but I just didn't want to do it anymore. And I wasn't sad about it, I was just sad that I would go to practice and I would have feelings that I didn't want to be there, and I'd never really experienced that before. I didn't want to be at practice at six in the morning... it was like, "I have a big paper to

write; I just want to sleep; I don't want to do this; I want to go out to the bars with my friends," you know, but I couldn't. All my other friends who were done playing had lives, and I still couldn't. I felt like I didn't have a life.

Because quitting sport completely was not seen as a viable option, eight participants described efforts to try to separate themselves from the issue they saw as the source of their depression. Physical distance was placed between them and their team. Mental distance was created by bottling up their emotions, ignoring the problem, or taking drugs. They felt they could avoid pain and frustration by using these strategies to sidestep the problems they faced. Temporary and noncommittal forms of distance from sport were desirable because they could experience independence without having to give up sport completely, something they felt they could never do. In fact, despite struggling with depression and other significant issues that were affecting their enjoyment of sport, participants described feeling as though they could not give up on their commitment to sport.

For example, one reason that participants gave for being unwilling to quit was how much they had already committed to their athletics. Dee discussed why she rejected the thought of giving up on swimming after a long period of frustration over her performance:

Swimming was such a big part of me; I couldn't just let it go.... I did not want to lose what I already had. Because it was such a big part of my life, I didn't want to lose all of it.

A conviction that they "finish things" or "get through things" was mentioned by a number of participants as a reason they would not give up on sport despite struggles they were facing. Compounding that commitment for some was the belief that sport was the best thing they had going. Struggling with sport, as many of the participants were, left them in an uncomfortable predicament. Katy explained this difficult situation:

If you hate water polo, then you're like, "Well, my life's over. What am I going to do? This is all I have. If I quit water polo, I don't have my scholarship. If I quit water polo, what else am I going to do?".... It's just all you have.

Katy's quote articulated the worries a number of participants had when considering the ramifications of no longer having sport in their lives. They had difficulty imagining what they would do, who they would be, and what their lives would be like without sport. Therefore, no matter the struggles they faced, giving up sport was not an option. Of course, as collegiate athletes, they will soon reach the end of their collegiate athletic career, whether they are ready for it or not. In Jodi's interview, she discussed the dread she felt about her upcoming retirement from sport:

I went through a pretty severe depression, just thinking about... life after sports, you know. And it took a while for me to realize that it's not like my life is going to be over, but it still really makes me scared.

The experience of having nowhere to go represents the way participants were trapped between the positive and negative aspects of sport. Though they struggled with depression due to plateaus in sport performance, significant injuries, declining enjoyment in sport, tense

# DISCUSSIONS

This study revealed that the sources of the participants' depression were varied; yet their experiences were characterized by key similarities. These similarities were the focus of the results, but it is important to note that each participant's experience consisted of a unique configuration of the general categories. For each individual, certain general categories were more or less salient than others, reflecting their own personal experience. Nevertheless, the results identified represent essential themes in the experiences described by the participants.

The results from this study are in many ways congruent with the findings from previous studies on the experience of depression. For example, the experience of weariness described in this study echoed the results of Farmer (2002) and Spillman (2006), who reported participant descriptions of feeling physically drained and weak from their experiences of depression. Leno (2007) described how participants placed a great deal of pressure on themselves while they were struggling with depression and felt as though there was no room for mistake or injury, similar to how participants of this study described experiencing self-doubt and being overly critical of their performance and abilities.

Also, Spillman (2006) identified the feeling of being out of control, a general category in the current study, as the ground in men's experiences of depression. The participants in that study described depression as unpredictable, and they felt powerless to control it. In their research on the experience of falling apart, Pollio et al. (1997) also described a theme of being out of control. Participants in that study described feeling a lack of control over their lives, behavior, and emotions. The participants in the study by Pollio et al. also described feeling vulnerable or helpless, feelings echoed by participants in the current study as well.

Finally, Farmer (2002) and Spillman (2006) both found that anger was a significant aspect of the participants' experiences of depression, as it was in the current study as well. In Farmer's study, adolescents with depression described feelings of anger the most frequently and used the anger as a barometer for how they were handling their depression. According to Jackson and Finney (2002), young adults often respond to stressful life events with anger.

Other aspects of the results are also worthy of note, including the language used by participants to describe their experiences of depression. Language is important in phenomenological research because it enables the expression of experience, yet it may also serve as a limitation (Allen-Collinson, 2009; Willig, 2008). Participants may rely on certain words or phrases that they feel comfortable with while shying away from other descriptions, or have a difficult time locating the words to describe their experiences, as Spillman (2006) noted. In the present study, participants struggled at times with the same problem. Perhaps due to the negatively loaded term *depression* (Mentink, 2001) participants often found more casual descriptors. For example, they often said they had felt *down*, or used the terms *hard*, *tough*, or *shitty* to describe their experiences.

Interestingly, gender did not seem to play a large role in the current study, as participants rarely mentioned it as an important aspect of their experience. Further, the results that emerged were similar to previous phenomenological studies of depression conducted with male participants (Leno, 2007; Spillman, 2006) or both male and female participants (Farmer, 2002; Mentink, 2001). The reason for these similarities cannot be determined without further research, but may be more reflective of participants' age or athletic status than gender. However, it is certainly possible that the role of gender did play a role in the sources participants cited as contributing to their depression: interpersonal relationships, perfectionism and self-criticism, or the lack of viable post-collegiate sport options, for example. These precipitating events, and the degree to which they may or may not have been gendered, were unexplored by the participants and by the researcher, as the focus of the current study was on the experience of depression itself, not its causes. Future research should certainly address these issues.

## CONCLUSION AND RECOMMENDATIONS

Participants described a variety of ways depression had affected their lives. Spillman (2006) discussed how depression can be pervasive, affecting multiple areas of life in significant ways. Participants in this study described a similar experience, highlighting weight gain or loss, changes in eating habits, changes in sleeping patterns, and mood swings, all of which are commonly reported symptoms of depression.

The experience of depression is difficult and unpleasant, and the participants seemed to reflect deeply in an effort to find reasons for the struggles they had faced. Many participants described finding positive lessons to learn and use to move forward in life, and discussed feeling as though they had grown as a result of their experiences. They also felt that they had gained resiliency and explained that their experiences had helped them to feel as if they were ready to move on from sport when the time came. Leno (2007) also found that the experiences of depression had helped participants gain resiliency, and to recognize that there is life after being an athlete.

On the other hand, a depressive episode should never be taken lightly, and receiving care and support early is of vital importance. However, it can be difficult for others to determine if and when to intervene and suggest help for a struggling athlete.

Participants expressed often receiving either too little support or ineffective support from others. Support was ineffective if the athlete was not yet ready to accept help, or if the support was perceived to be shallow or unrealistic. It was vital to the participants that they felt those providing them support truly cared and understood what they were going through. According to the participants in this study, effective and empathetic support from others who are experiencing the same struggles, or had in the past, would have been invaluable.

The present study also demonstrated that the coach's role in providing support to athletes struggling with depression can be difficult to navigate. Coaches were sources of support for five participants, but the others reported not turning to their coach or feeling unsupported by them. Mentink (2001) found that athletes often did not want to approach their coach about their struggles with depression out of fear of rejection or retribution (i.e., removal from team, reduced playing time, etc.).

It is also extremely important for coaches to be familiar with the symptoms of depression and the ways in which athletes may express how they are feeling. This study provided some real-life examples, however, it is important to note that each instance will be different. It is challenging to approach athletes about personal issues such as depression, but it can be extremely important for their health and their future (Andersen et al., 1994; Cogan, 2000; Gill, 2008; Glick and Horsfall, 2005).

Finally, guiding athletes through injury or rehabilitation, and negotiating the transition out of sport upon graduation is an important role for the coach. Participants in the current study felt that their coaches did not do much, if anything, to support them through these times. There should be ongoing support for injured athletes so that they do not feel abandoned, and discussions of life after college sport to aid in the transition of graduating athletes. College athletic departments could organize support groups for injured or retiring athletes with the guidance of qualified sport psychologists.

Finally, with respect to future research, while the current study was delimited only to self-reported depression, future studies may be interested in adding a diagnostic delimitation prior to participant selection. It is not possible to predict how results would differ, but investigating the depression experiences of a clinical population could provide an interesting comparison to the results of the current study.

It may also be potentially beneficial to utilize quantitative measures used in previous studies of depression in collegiate athletes (Armstrong and Oomen-Early, 2009; Donohue et al., 2004; Proctor and Boan-Lenzo, 2010; Storch et al., 2005; Wyshak, 2001; Yang et al., 2007). Though it would not conform to strict existential-phenomenological research methods, using a mixed-methods design with quantitative methods could provide additional depth to the results. Relying solely on interview-based research methods may be a potential limitation, as participants may feel uncomfortable discussing all aspects of their experiences.

Finally, future studies may wish to conduct multiple interviews over a longer period of time, or include interviews with family members or coaches that are familiar with the athlete participating in the study, as with Mentink (2001). These approaches may allow for a greater depth of understanding of the experience of depression.

## REFERENCES

Allen-Collinson, J. (2009). Sporting embodiment: Sports studies and the (continuing) promise of phenomenology. *Qualitative Research in Sport and Exercise, 1*, 279-296.

American College Health Association. (2008). *American College Health Association-National College Health Assessment: Reference Group Executive Summary Fall 2007.* Baltimore, MD: Author.

Andersen, M. B., Denson, E. L., Brewer, B. W., and Van Raalte, J. L. (1994). Disorders of personality and mood in athletes: Recognition and referral. *Journal of Applied Sport Psychology, 6,* 168-184.

Appleby, K. M., and Fisher, L. A. (2009). Running in and out of motherhood: Elite distance runners' experiences of returning to competition after pregnancy. *Women in Sport and Physical Activity Journal, 18*, 3-17.

Armstrong, S. A., and Oomen-Early, J. (2009). Social connectedness, self-esteem, and depression symptomatology among collegiate athletes versus nonathletes. *Journal of American College Health, 57*, 521-526.

Bain, L. L. (1995). Mindfulness and subjective knowledge. *Quest, 47,* 238-253.

Broshek, D. K., and Freeman, J. R. (2005). Psychiatric and neuropsychological issues in sport medicine. *Clinics in Sport Medicine, 24*, 663-679.

Cogan, K. D. (2000). The sadness in sport: Working with a depressed and suicidal athlete. In M. B. Anderson (Ed.), *Doing sport psychology* (pp. 107-119). Champaign, IL: Human Kinetics.

Côté, J., Salmela, J. H., Baria, A., and Russell, S. J. (1993). Organizing and interpreting unstructured qualitative data. *The Sport Psychologist, 7,* 127-137.

Czech, D. R., Wrisberg, C. A., Fisher, L. A., Thompson, C. L., and Hayes, G. (2004). The experience of Christian prayer in sport: An existential phenomenological investigation. *Journal of Psychology and Christianity, 23*(1), 3-11.

Dale, G. A. (1996). Existential phenomenology: Emphasizing the experience of the athlete in sport psychology research. *The Sport Psychologist, 10,* 307-321.

Dale, G. A. (2000). Distractions and coping techniques of elite decathletes during their most memorable performances. *The Sport Psychologist, 14,* 17-41.

Donohue, B., Covassin, D., Lancer, K., Dickens, Y., Miller, A., Hash, A., and Genet, J. (2004). Examination of psychiatric symptoms in student athletes. *The Journal of General Psychology, 131*, 29-35.

Fahlberg, L. L., Fahlberg, L. A., and Gates, W. K. (1992). Exercise and existence: Exercise behavior from as existential-phenomenological perspective. *The Sport Psychologist, 6,* 172-191.

Farmer, T. J. (2002). The experience of major depression: Adolescents' perspectives. *Issues in Mental Health Nursing, 23,* 567-585.

Ford, J. A. (2007). Alcohol use among college students: A comparison of athletes and nonathletes. *Substance Use and Misuse, 42,* 1367-1377.

Garland, K. M. (2005). *An existential phenomenological investigation of resiliency in triathletes* (Unpublished doctoral dissertation). St Mary's University, TX.

Gill, E. L. (2008). Mental health in college athletics: It's time for social work to get in the game. *Social Work, 53*, 85-88.

Giorgi, A. (2002). The question of validity in qualitative research. *Journal of Phenomenological Psychology, 33*, 1-18.

Glick, I. D., and Horsfall, J. L. (2005). Diagnosis and psychiatric treatment of athletes. *Clinics in Sport Medicine, 24*, 771-781.

Gratton, C., and Jones, I. (2004). Analyzing data II: Qualitative data analysis. In C. Gratton and I. Jones (Eds.), *Research methods for sport studies* (pp. 217-227). New York: Routledge.

Heidegger, M. (1962). *Being and time.* New York: Harper and Row.

Jackson, P. B., and Finney, M. (2002). Negative life events and psychological distress among young adults. *Social Psychology Quarterly, 65*, 186-201.

Johnson, M. S. (1998). *The athlete's experience of being coached: An existential phenomenological investigation* (Unpublished doctoral dissertation). University of Tennessee, Knoxville.

Kerry, D. S., and Armour, K. M. (2000). Sport sciences and the promise of phenomenology: Philosophy, method, and insight. *Quest, 52,* 1-17.

Killeya-Jones, L. A. (2005). Identity structure, role discrepancy and psychological adjustment in male college student-athletes. *Journal of Sport Behavior, 28*, 167-185.

Krane, V., Andersen, M. B., and Strean, W. B. (1997). Issues of qualitative research methods and presentation. *Journal of Sport and Exercise Psychology, 19,* 213-218.

LaFrance, M. N., and Stoppard, J. M. (2006). Constructing a non-depressed self: Women's accounts of recovery from depression. *Feminism and Psychology, 16,* 307-325.

Leno, M. (2007). *The experience of depression in African American male athletes* (Doctoral dissertation). Available from ProQuest Dissertations and Theses database. (UMI No. 3288616)

Mentink, J. W. (2001). *Major depression in collegiate student-athletes: Case study research* (Unpublished doctoral dissertation). Washington State University, Pullman.

Miller, B. E., Miller, M. N., Verhegge, R., Linville, H. H., and Pumariega, A. J. (2002). Alcohol misuse among college athletes: Self-medication for psychiatric symptoms? *Journal of Drug Education, 32,* 41-52.

Morgan, W. P. (1980). Test of champions. *Psychology Today, 14,* 92-108.

Morgan, W. P., and Pollock, M. L. (1977). Psychologic characterization of the elite runner. *Annals of the New York Academy of Sciences, 301,* 382-403.

National Institute of Mental Health. (2009a). *Suicide in the U.S.: Statistics and prevention.* Retrieved from http://www.nimh.nih.gov/health/ publications/suicide-in-the-us-statistics-and-prevention/index.shtml

National Institute of Mental Health. (2009b). *Women and depression: Discovering hope.* Retrieved from http://www.nimh.nih.gov/health/publications/ women-and-depression-discovering-hope/complete-index.shtml

Polkinghorne, D. E. (1989). Phenomenological research methods. In R. S. Valle and S. Halling (Eds.), *Existential-phenomenological perspectives in psychology* (pp. 41-60). New York: Plenum.

Pollio, H. R., Henley, T., and Thompson, C. B. (1997). *The phenomenology of everyday life.* New York: Cambridge.

Proctor, S. L., and Boan-Lenzo, C. (2010). Prevalence of depressive symptoms in male intercollegiate student-athletes and nonathletes. *Journal of Clinical Sport Psychology, 4,* 204-220.

Puffer, J. C., and McShane, J. M. (1992). Depression and chronic fatigue in athletes. *Clinics in Sport Medicine, 11,* 327-338.

Ryba, T. V. (2007). Cartwheels on ice: A phenomenological exploration of children's enjoyment in competitive figure skating. *Athletic Insight, 9*(2), 58-73.

Schreiber, R. (2001). Wandering in the dark: Women's experiences with depression. *Health Care for Women International, 22,* 85-98.

Settles, I. H., Sellers, R. M., and Damas, A. (2002). One role or two? The function of psychological separation in role conflict. *Journal of Applied Psychology, 87,* 574-582.

Sisk, J. (2006). Depression on college campuses: The downside of higher education. *Social Work Today, 6*(5), 17-21.

Snow, A., and LeUnes, A. (1994). Characteristics of sports research using the Profile of Mood States. *Journal of Sport Behavior, 17,* 207-211.

Solomon, R. C. (1972). Existential phenomenology: Introduction. In R. C. Solomon (Ed.), *Existentialism and phenomenology* (pp. 289-290). Lanham, MD: Rowman and Littlefield.

Sorenson, L., Czech, D. R., Gonzalez, S., Klein, J., and Lachowetz, T. (2009). Listen up! The experience of music in sport: A phenomenological investigation. *Athletic Insight, 10*(2). Retrieved from http://www.athleticinsight.com/Vol10Iss2/ Music.htm

Sparkes, A. C. (1998). Validity in qualitative inquiry and the problem of criteria: Implications for sport psychology. *The Sport Psychologist, 12,* 363-386.

Spillman, B. D. (2006). *Men's experiences of depression: A phenomenological investigation* (Doctoral dissertation). Available from ProQuest Dissertations and Theses database. (UMI No. 3235516)

Storch, E. A., Storch, J. B., Killikany, E. M., and Roberti, J. W. (2005). Self-reported psychopathology in athletes: A comparison of intercollegiate student-athletes and non-athletes. *Journal of Sport Behavior, 28,* 86-97.

Strean, W. B. (1998). Possibilities for qualitative research in sport psychology. *The Sport Psychologist, 12,* 333-345.

Terry, P. (1995). The efficacy of mood state profiling with elite performers: A review and synthesis. *The Sport Psychologist, 9,* 309-324.

Valle, R. S., King, M., and Halling, S. (1989). An introduction to existential-phenomenological thought in psychology. In R. S. Valle and S. Halling (Eds.), *Existential-phenomenological perspectives in psychology* (pp. 3-16). New York: Plenum.

Watson, J. C. (2005). College student-athletes' attitudes toward help-seeking behavior and expectations of counseling services. *Journal of College Student Development, 46,* 442-449.

Willig, C. (2008). A phenomenological investigation of the experience of taking part in extreme sports. *Journal of Health Psychology, 13,* 690-702.

Wyshak, G. (2001). Women's college physical activity and self-reports of physician-diagnosed depression and of current symptoms of psychiatric distress. *Journal of Women's Health and Gender-Based Medicine, 10,* 363-370.

Yang, J., Peek-Asa, C., Corlette, J. D., Cheng, G., Foster, D. T., and Albright, J. (2007). Prevalence of and risk factors associated with symptoms of depression in competitive collegiate student athletes. *Clinical Journal of Sport Medicine, 17,* 481-487.

In: Innovative Writings in Sport and Exercise Psychology
Editor: Robert Schinke

ISBN: 978-1-62948-881-3
© 2014 Nova Science Publishers, Inc.

*Chapter 5*

# SUBJECTIVE BELIEFS AMONG SPORT COACHES ABOUT COMMUNICATION DURING COACH-ATHLETE CONVERSATIONS

## *Frode Moen[*] and Ragnvald Kvalsund*
Norwegian University of Science and Technology, Trondheim, Norway

### ABSTRACT

The purpose of this study was to explore subjective beliefs among coaches in elite sports about what they think are effective communication during performance appraisals with their athletes. A Q-sample of 36 different opinions about different underlying aims for communication, and how this affects athletes' abilities to understand better (knowing), to perform better (doing), and/ or improve their focus, were presented to sport coaches from different top level sports. A sample of statements drawn from the actual concourse of communication was presented to 19 elite coaches who were asked to consider and rank-order the statements regarding performance appraisals through Q-sorting procedure.

The authors will discuss their analysis using Q methodology, where a three factors solution was chosen from the factor analysis. In general, the coaches share some common viewpoints across the three factors (consensus), and believe that the communication process should be aimed at stimulating both coaches' and their athletes' understanding about their performances. Attending behaviour such as the ability to ask their athletes open questions and listen to what they are saying seems to be a necessity for coaches during performance appraisals. Interestingly, the importance of instructive behaviour is also emphasized among two of the three factors.

**Keywords:** Communication, coaching, sport, performance appraisals

---

[*] Correspondence concerning this article should be addressed to Frode Moen, Department of Education, Norwegian University of Science and Technology, Loholt Allé 87, Pav. C Dragvoll, 7491 Trondheim. E-mail: frmoe@online.no.

# INTRODUCTION

Research states that the coach plays an important role in the development of a successful athlete within sport (Baker, Yardley and Côté, 2003; Blom, Watson II, and Spadaro, 2010; Jowett and Cockerill, 2003; Moen and Verburg, 2012). Previous studies have found that communication skills are fundamental in creating an optimal helping relationship in general (e.g., as in counselling and business), and particularly between a coach and his or her athletes in sport (Baker, Côté, and Hawes, 2000; Bloom, Schinke and Salmela, 1997; Ivey and Ivey, 2006; Jones and Wallace, 2006; Lafrenière, Jowett, Vallerand, Gonahue and Lorimer, 2008; Schein, 2009). However, sport coaches in elite sport are engaged with multiple tasks related to different situations, and it will be a challenge to meet these different situations with suitable and proper communication (Gould, Greenleaf, Chung and Guinan 2002; Jones, 2006; Mallett and Côté, 2006). As an example, research shows that instructions seem to characterize a coach's behaviour during practice and that training and instructions are found to be the preferred coaching leadership style among athletes (Lacy and Darst, 1989; Nazarudin, Fauzee, Jamalis, Geok and Din, 2009; Pilus and Saadan, 2009; Potrac, Jones and Cushio, 2007). However, optimal coach-athlete relationships are defined by mutuality between coaches' and athletes' feelings, thoughts and behaviours (Jowett, 2007; Jowett and Meek, 2000). To establish and develop such relationships, coaches also need to communicate with their athletes in other manners than instructive manners: coaches need to communicate with intentions to establish mutual understanding and sharing power with their athletes (Jones and Standage, 2006; Jowett, 2007). Importantly, communication is central in the coaching process, and the coach's communication skills will determine how successful the coach-athlete relationship will be (Bloom, 1996; Spink, 1991). To achieve a successful coach-athlete relationship, a coach and an athlete need to spend time together and communicate effectively both in- and outside the practice arena (Jones, 2006; Jowett, 2005a). Since situations in the practice arena are distinguished by instructive communication by coaches, coach-athlete conversations outside the practice arena are important in order to establish coach-athlete relationships that are built on mutuality (Jones and Standage, 2006; Jowett, 2007; Pilus and Saadan, 2009; Potrac, et al., 2007). This study will explore coaches` viewpoints about their communication during coach- athlete conversations outside the practice arena, where conversations related to their athletes' learning and development are in focus. The question to be addressed is therefore: *What are sport coaches` subjective beliefs about their communication during performance appraisals?*

# THEORETICAL BACKGROUND

The field of psychological counselling has traditionally been occupied with questions about the counselling process, where the communication process between a therapist and a client is found to be one key factor (Hargie, 2006; Heppner, Leong and Chiao, 2008; Ivey and Ivey, 2006). A formal coach-athlete conversation that focuses on the athlete's learning and development in sport, share much of the same elements regarding the communication process (Jowett and Meek, 2000). Literature from both counselling and sports are therefore used in this study.

Communication is defined as the scientific study of the production, processing and effects of signal and symbol systems used by humans to send and receive messages (Hargie, Dickson and Tourish, 2004; Ivey and Ivey, 2006). Communication is therefore the exchange and flow of information from one person to another; it involves a sender transmitting information, and a receiver who receives the information and decodes it (Hargie, 2006). The receiver decodes the message based on both verbal and non-verbal information, interprets the message's content, and makes a judgement about how he or she feels about it (Bloom, et al., 1997). Successful communication is achieved when there is concordance between the intended message being sent by a sender and its perception by the receiver (Ivey and Ivey, 2006; Martens, 2012).

## THE COMMUNICATION PROCESS

The core elements in the communication process therefore consists of at least four possible perspectives: It starts with an intention within a sender to communicate a message. The self-perspective is the sender's own world, as he or she experiences it based on his or her own experiences, personality, attitudes and knowledge (Martens, 2012). The message is then being encoded by the sender and sent to a receiver. The receiver starts his or her communication process by decoding (interpretation) the message being sent. The decoding process might result in an intention to reply to the message being sent, and the intention is then encoded and sent back to the sender as shown in figure 1 below (Fouss and Troppmann, 1981; Weinberg and Gould, 2007). This is the receiver's perspective reflecting the receiver's internal world. Both the sender and the receiver communicate based upon their subjective perception of reality. Importantly, this is not reality as such, it is the individual's model of reality based on the individual's experiences and knowledge (Hargie, et al., 2004). Each individual's own model of reality might be different, because each perspective is based on each individual's experiences and knowledge. This makes communication both important and challenging since successful communication aim to achieve accordance between the message that is communicated and the perception of it by a receiver. This is especially important between coaches and athletes within sport (Jones, 2006; Jowett, 2007).

The communication process is aimed at achieving an intersubjectively experienced fellowship, which implies a mutual understanding of one another's different worlds (Kvalsund and Allgood, 2008; Shotter, 1995). Hargie, Dickson and Tourish (2004) point to different phases in the communication process, from just being aware of each other in the beginning phase, to an intermediary phase developing a surface contact potentially leading to a process-phase of giving and receiving self-disclosure, and thereby understand each other on a deeper mutual level. Thus, effective communication seems to emerge when the receiver gains a mutual understanding with the sender about the message being sent, and vice versa (Jowett, 2007). The last perspective is the interaction perspective, which is about understanding the interaction process and the relationship between the communicators as such (Martens, 2012). The interaction perspective is the communicators' awareness about the communication process, how they influence one another in the process through their relational responsive and their emphatic understanding (Shotter, 1995).

As figure 1 shows, the communication process is characterized by an underlying intention, or an interest, to achieve something. Communication could be characterized by three universal intentions: control, common understanding and emancipator reflections (Bloom, et al., 1997; Chelladurai and Saleh, 1980; Jowett and Cockerill, 2003; Jowett and Ntoumanis, 2004; Williams, et al., 2003). As an example, training and instruction, and democratic behaviour, are two important factors in the leadership scale for sports (LSS), which share important similarities with the intentions to respectively control and achieve common understanding in communication (Chelladurai and Saleh, 1980). Also, the coach behaviour questionnaire (CBQ) emphasizes these two dimensions (Williams, et al., 2003), whereas the 3Cs model emphasizes the importance of common understanding (Jowett and Cockerill, 2002; Jowett and Ntoumanis, 2004). Both common understanding and emancipator reflections are emphasized as important intentions for coaches (Jones, 2006).

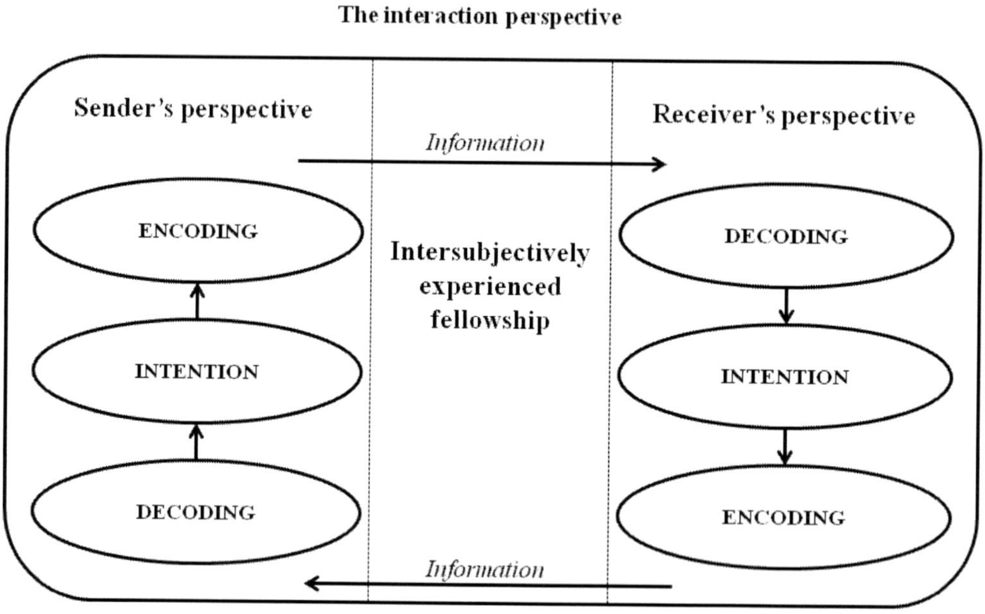

**The interaction perspective**

Figure 1. The Communication Process.

*Control.* Control is when a coach's intention is to control an athlete and influence him or her in a certain directio n (Jowett and Lavallee, 2007). Instructions are used to influence others in specific directions. Research shows that instructions seem to characterize a coach's behaviour during practice (Lacy and Darst, 1989; Potrac, et al., 2007). Interestingly, training and instructions are also found to be the preferred coaching leadership style among athletes (Nazarudin, et al., 2009; Pilus and Saadan, 2009). An instruction can include telling an athlete a specific behaviour that should be performed, the level of proficiency that should be achieved, or the level of proficiency that a performer should achieve in a desired skill or activity (Weinberg and Gould, 2007).

*Common understanding.* Common understanding, as a wish, represents a coach's intention to understand an athlete and develop a common understanding about a given situation. Jowett claims that effective coach-athlete relationships are defined by mutuality between coaches' and athletes' feelings, thoughts and behaviours (Jowett, 2005a; Jowett and Meek, 2000). The importance of common understanding in sport is emphasized through studies of the 3+1 C's constructs: Closeness, Commitment, Complementary, and Co-orientation (Jowett, 2007). Closeness is to which degree the coach and the athlete are connected or the depth of their emotional attachment (Jowett and Cockerill, 2002). Commitment reflects coaches' and athletes' intention or desire to maintain their athletic partnership over time. Complementary defines if the interaction between the coach and the athlete is perceived as cooperative and effective, and co-orientation defines the degree of similarity and emphatic understanding (Jowett, 2007).

Communication techniques such as open-ended questions and active listening are used to ensure common understanding between individuals (Ivey and Ivey, 2006). Interrogative questions give the receiver the power to generate rich descriptions and detailed answers with regards to his or her own experiences, feelings and interpretations (Hargie, 2006). In this way, the sender is given the opportunity to achieve a deeper- and common understanding of the receiver's perspective. Active listening is the most important attending skill because the receiver needs to know that the sender has heard and understood what he or she has been saying, seen his or her point of view, and has an understanding of the receiver's perspective as he or she experiences it (Heron, 2001).

*Emancipator reflections.* Emancipator reflections represent a coach's intention to stimulate the athlete to discover something new through becoming fully aware, so that he or she can be liberated from unfortunate and unconscious behaviour. Powerful questioning and confrontations are used to stimulate reflections (Hargie, 2006; Ivey and Ivey, 2006). Powerful questioning invites the receiver into a mental exercise, establishing awareness, reflecting and making decisions that relate to the information that is being discussed (Jones, 2006). Confrontation is defined as a statement or question calculated to motivate the receiver to make a decision or face the reality of a situation (Heron, 2001). Thus, confrontations can often involve conflict and differences of opinion, and has the potential to achieve raised awareness (Moen and Kvalsund, 2008). However, to achieve a positive outcome, it is necessary to confront with care, respect and empathy (Jowett, 2005a). Thus, awareness about the underlying intentions in communication is important, because inter-human dialogue is characterized by the intentions that people have towards one another in the meetings (Stein, Bloom and Sabiston, 2012).

The coach has an essential influence on an athlete's performance, motivation and well being within sport (Cockerill, 2002; Côté, et al., 1999; Lyle, 1999; Mageau, 2003). Thus, it is the coach-athlete relationship that contributes to the most growth and development of an athlete. Importantly, coaching in sport can be considered to entail the teaching and instruction of technical skills and tactics (Nazarudin, et al., 2009; Pilus and Saadan, 2009; Potrac, et al., 2007). However, coaching must also entail elements of reciprocity, trust, and a genuine and helping nature (Bloom, Durand-Bush, Schinke and Salmela, 1998; Jowett and Cockerhill, 2003; Poczwardowski, Barott and Henschen, 2002). Research shows that instructions seem to characterize a coach's behaviour during practice (Jones, 2006; Lacy and Darst, 1989; Potrac, et al., 2007), and that teaching and instructions seem to be the preferred coaching leadership style among athletes (Nazarudin, et al., 2009; Pilus and Saadan, 2009). At the same time, coach-athlete relationships must be based on a mutuality of dependence, which involves a power balance between the coach and an athlete as in "give and take" (Jowett and Lavallee, 2007, p.21). Since instructions seem to be the dominant coaching style during practice, which involves that coaches communicate to control their athletes towards specific standards, coach-athlete conversations outside practices must be build on other intentions in order to achieve a relationship built on mutuality. In order for both a coach and an athlete to achieve a shared level of reciprocity and trust for helping one another, there must be effective communication that is aimed at achieving common understanding and emancipator reflections (Jowett, 2005b). Importantly, the communication process requires a vast repertoire of skills, such as intrapersonal and interpersonal processing, listening, observing, speaking, questioning and reflecting, explaining, analysing, evaluating and self-disclosing (Hargie, et al., 2004; Jowett and Lavallee, 2007).

Thus, communication is an important element of both the coach-athlete relationship and the act of coaching in general (Chelladurai and Saleh, 1980; Jowett and Cockerill, 2002; Jowett and Ntoumanis, 2004). As a result of the many and varied roles and situations that a coach is responsible for undertaking, it is essential that the coach have a clear understanding of his or her intention in the given situation, and how to communicate effectively in order to successfully accomplish what he or she intend to achieve (Mallett, and Côté, 2006). Interestingly, it seems to be a need for studies that investigates coach-athlete conversations within sport, where the athlete's learning and development is in focus, but still seen from the subjective perspective of the coaches (Jowett and Cockerill, 2002; Jowett and Ntoumanis, 2004; Williams, et al., 2003). The performance appraisal in this connection entails the conversational subjective communication going on between the coach and the athlete evaluating the course of athlete performances so far, in its recent past, in the here and now - and opening up for the potential improvements in the nearby emergent future. Thus, the research question to be addressed in this study is: *"What are sport coaches` subjective beliefs about their communication during performance appraisals?"*

# METHODOLOGY

The research question in this study invites to an exploration of the subjectivity among sport coaches regarding the research question. Q methodology provides a basis for a systematic study of subjectivity (Watts and Stenner, 2012). Thus, Q methodology is rooted in the qualitative research tradition and subjectivity is revealed by a systematic categorizing of people's thoughts, feelings, values and experiences related to the current research issue from their own first person perspective (Brown, 1996; Watts and Stenner, 2012). The process is completed through a series of five steps: 1) Definition of the concourse, 2) Development of Q sample, 3) The selection of P sample, 4) Q sorting, and 5) Analysis and interpretations.

## 1. Definition of the Concourse

The first step in Q methodology is to establish a "concourse," originally called a "trait universe" (Stephenson, 1950), which is a collection of thoughts, feelings, values and experiences related to a specific topic (Stephenson, 1986). The concourse in this study was established through an analysis of relevant literature within the field.

We compiled a list of about 80 statements, which covered different possible viewpoints about the research issue. Then the statements from this process were systematically organized, analysed and presented as the concourse, i.e., within the segment of the actual communication universe. In principle, the concourse contains many diverse ways of communicating about the actual topic within a specific culture (Brown 1996; Kvalsund,

1998). We then sat about to reduce the concourse into a meaningful Q sample in order to create a balanced sample for stimulating the Q-sorters to use the subjective statements (sample) to rank-order them *self-referentially* and draw a picture of their own self-conceived view on the topic (McKeown and Thomas, 1988).

## 2. Development of Q Sample

The Q sample is a comprehensive selection of the views within the concourse (Kvalsund, 1998). The size of a Q sample is dependent upon how many statements it takes to represent the concourse.

It is important to grasp as much breadth as possible so that the viewpoints from the concourse are represented. During this phase it is important to organize all the sub themes emerging from the concourse. In the present study, two main themes (what Stephenson, 1950, calls effects) emerged in the concourse; intention and benefit. Within the theme "intention" four sub-themes (what Stephenson calls levels (1950)) seemed to be relevant; goal oriented control, mutual understanding and agreement, emancipatory reflections, and the need for information.

Within the theme "benefit" three other subthemes or effects seemed to be relevant; learning in form of understanding, learning in form of performing, and focus. In this study, it is important to differentiate whether coaches in sport believe that their intention in communication is based on goal oriented control, mutual understanding and agreement, emancipatory reflections, or the need for information, or a combination of some of the four. It is further interesting to investigate what they believe is the benefit from their communication. As a result, the design for the statements was created as shown in Table 1.

### Table 1. The Design of the Statements Based on Cultural Effects

| Effects | Levels | | | |
|---|---|---|---|---|
| Intention | a. Goal oriented control. | b. Mutual understanding and agreement. | c. Emancipatory reflections. | d. The need for information. |
| Benefit | e. Learning in form of understanding (knowing). | f. Learning in form of performing (doing). (operational competence) | g. Focus | |

Each combination of independent effects and levels becomes a categorical cell. Based on this, we must look to the levels to see all possible combinations of cells, since they are the multiplication of levels by all four effects. Using the design in Table 1, twelve combinations of statements are obtained, as shown in Table 2. In principle, there are 4x3 cells. Each cell consists of statements that are interrelated but are somewhat different. After studying the statements in the concourse and the different levels that emerged, the authors decided to use three statements from the concourse to represent each of the 12 cells. The statements that most clearly represented the viewpoint in the different cells were picked for the Q sample. The Q sample resulted in 36 statements. To make it impossible for the sorter to see the structure in the sample, statements were randomly allocated a number from 1 to 36.

| most strongly disagree | very strongly disagree | strongly disagree | disagree | disagree | Neutral | agree | agree | strongly agree | very strongly agree | most strongly agree |
|---|---|---|---|---|---|---|---|---|---|---|
| -5 | -4 | -3 | -2 | -1 | 0 | +1 | +2 | +3 | +4 | +5 |
| | | | | | | | | | | |
| | | | | | | | | | | |
| | | | | | | | | | | |
| | | | | | | | | | | |
| | | | | | | | | | | |
| | | | | | | | | | | |

Figure 2. The Scoreboard for the Q Sorting.

# Subjective Beliefs among Sport Coaches ...

## Table 2. The Combination of Levels in the Design

| Effects | Combination of levels | | | | | | | | | | | |
|---|---|---|---|---|---|---|---|---|---|---|---|---|
| Intention. | a | a | a | b | b | b | c | c | c | d | d | d |
| Benefit. | e | f | g | e | f | g | e | f | g | e | f | g |
| | | | | | | | | | | | | |
| Statement No | 12 | 2 | 3 | 4 | 5 | 6 | 7 | 8 | 9 | 10 | 11 | 1 |
| | 13 | 14 | 15 | 16 | 17 | 18 | 19 | 20 | 21 | 22 | 23 | 24 |
| | 25 | 26 | 27 | 28 | 29 | 30 | 31 | 32 | 33 | 34 | 35 | 36 |

## 3. The Selection of P Sample

The data was collected from sports coaches attending a course organized by the Norwegian Olympic Committee and the Norwegian University of Science and Technology (NTNU) in Trondheim. Nineteen elite coaches participated at the sorting. The course was aimed at elite coaches[1] who are working with national elite teams in Norway. The coaches who participated in the course were from different sports such as cross country skiing, biathlon, ski jumping, Nordic combined, ice hockey, alpine skiing, swimming, rowing, athletics, bicycling, wrestling, dancing, figure skating, orienteering and handball. Their average age was 35 ½ years (youngest 23 and oldest 53), and their formal educational background varied from master degree to no formal education after high-school. Their experience as coaches at elite level varied from 1 year to 25 years.

Whereas quantitative methods normally require larger samples, Q methodology uses much smaller samples (Brown, 1996). In Q methodology the aim is to discover and find general views (factors) of subjectivity that exist in the communication culture one set out to study. The operant factors quantified must be interpreted qualitatively and be discovered for their meanings and reasons (abduction). Explanations such as age, relational dynamics, gender, etc. might be influencing and represent reasonable causes, however they can hardly be predicted but only disclosed through a process of interpretative comprehension. Q-factor interpretations are, therefore, about discovering general subjective meanings from within an abductive logic, systematized for understanding holistic subjective viewpoints and their impact on communication (Kvalsund 1998).

## 4. The Q Sorting

The coaches were asked to read through each statement in the Q sample and to consider what they thought was effective communication during a typical performance appraisal with their athletes. Specifically, they were asked to select the statements that described the most optimal type of communication that should be utilized, and to consider what type of communication had the most effect on learning in the form of understanding, performing, and/or the athletes' ability to focus. Thus, it was emphasized that they should rank the statements with regards to their ideal beliefs. Each statement had to be evaluated from the extreme positive to the extreme negative end of a continuum. Zero indicates a neutral viewpoint or no meaning. This is an operation referred to as "Q sorting" (McKeown and

---

[1] Coaches who are coaching athletes who are on National A-teams in Norway.

Thomas, 1988). The scores range from a score of +5 for "most strongly agree" to -5 for "most strongly disagree" under the so-called forced quasi-normal distribution of the statements, as shown in Figure 2 (Brown, 1996).

The coach is free to place an item anywhere within the distribution, but forced to keep to the distribution form in order to make all the necessary nuanced evaluations of the statements (Kvalsund 1998). However, the scoreboard has less cells at both ends (+5, +4, +3, -5, -4, -3) than in the middle. This is done to provoke psychological significance among the coaches by forcing them to rank the statements by considering stringent options. While performing the Q sort, the coaches draw distinctions on the basis of psychological significance. The statements placed in the middle area (-1, 0, +1) evoke little or no emotional feelings for the coaches. This low emotional state represents low psychological meaning as well, that is, that all meaning spreads out from zero, taking on more and more psychological meaning as they extend. The statements in the zero column are more or less psychologically insignificant. At each end of the scale, are statements that the coaches relate most strongly to, both positively (+5) and negatively (-5). These are the statements that are most psychologically significant (Brown, 1996). The coaches continued their Q sorting until all the statements were distributed into the scoreboard. It took approximately one hour for the coaches to distribute the 36 statements. Each scoreboard was signed by the coaches, so that the researchers had the opportunity to make interviews with them during interpretations of their Q sortings.

## 5. Analysis and Interpretations

The different Q sorts arranged by the coaches were then entered into the computer program PQMethod (Schmolck, 2002), which is a statistical program tailored for Q studies (Rhoads, 2000). For any $n$ Q sorts, the correlations produce a matrix of size $n \times n$, or in this case 19 x 19 cells in the overall matrix. If the correlation coefficient is high this indicates that two coaches sorted the Q sample statements in a similar manner. The 19 x 19 correlation matrix was then subjected to a Centroid factor analysis, initially with the default value of seven factors extracted. The Centroid factor analysis showed that one of the factors had an Eigen value of 11, counting for 57 % of the variance, whereas three other factors had Eigen values exceeding 1. All of this indicates the possibility for at least three factors since the rule of thumb is that unrotated factors with an eigenvalue above 1 can be estimated as factors. It is important to decide how high a factor loading should be if a particular sort is to be regarded as an important contributor to a factor (Pett, Lackey, and Sullivan, 2003, p. 208). In Q methodology an estimate is used to decide if a sort is contributing to a factor or not (Kvalsund, 1998; Pett et al., 2003). The minimum factor loading that is used for defining Q sorts (Q sorts marked by an X in the factor matrix) is the standard deviation of the forced distribution (2.58) multiplied with the result of 1 divided on the square root of the number of statements in the q-sample (36). In this study .43 was estimated to be the minimum contributor to a factor. Those Q sorts that define the factor have influence on the content of the factor that emerges. After experimenting with various alternatives by manual rotation, the authors decided to consider a varimax rotation with a three-factor solution. The coaches who sorted the statements approximately similar, produced this factor solution (McKeown and Thomas, 1988). Thus, the factor represents natural categories of subjectivity that can be discovered by the researchers (Brown, 1996). Stephenson points out that Q data and Q methodology is abductive in its approach, and its interest is in understanding reasons, causes and laws, and not on a search for facts by testing hypotheses (Stephenson, 1950). This implies that the researcher must work to understand the Q sorters mind through gaining insight regarding the subjectivity that is disclosed (Stephenson, 1986, p. 53). After the first analysis and interpretations of the factors each Q sorter was interviewed by the researchers in order to check whether or not the factors did represent the common conversational modes for the individuals on the factors. Q analysis has therefore their centre point in each case, the view from the individual's perspective, whereas quantitative methods tend to view the same events from an external perspective. Thus, our analysis is mapping the coaches subjective beliefs based on the concourse that represents possible beliefs regarding this research issue. Q-methodology therefore refers to factors as operant factors or operant subjectivity, and uses different criteria's in their analysis compared to what is seen in traditional quantitative methods (Brown, 1996).

# RESULTS

The computer programme PQMethod[2], a statistical program tailored to Q studies, was used to statistically analyse the data for this project. It computes intercorrelations among Q sorts, which are then factor analysed using either the Centroid or Principal Component method.

The 19 x 19 correlation matrix was subjected to a Centroid factor analysis, initially with the default value of seven factors extracted. After experimenting with various alternatives, the authors decided to consider a three-factor solution.

As shown in the factor matrix in table 3, factor A has 9 sorts that load on the factor, which were marked "x" after each factor loading; factor B, 9; and factor C, 10. There were 18 mixed cases (rather 9 persons having mixed loadings) where sorts loaded on more than one factor, as shown in loadings in boldface in table 3.

The remainder of this paper focused on analysis of these three types reflected in their sorting. The statements on the extreme side in Figure 1, with rank scores of +5, +4, +3, -3, -4, and −5, reflect the intense feelings and attitudes of each respondent and characterize the factor, so analysis was mainly focused on the interpretation of those statements (Brown, 1996).

*Factor A: Reflections and Clear Instructions*
The most extreme statements loading on factor A (+ 5 and +4) emphasize the importance of stimulating reflections in order to achieve understanding (statement number 7). The statements also emphasizes that communication must be clear and direct in order to keep focus on what is appropriate (statement number 1 and 3). The most extreme statements on the negative side (-5 and -4) also emphasize the importance of stimulating reflections in order to achieve understanding about performance (statement number 32 and 31). The importance of understanding and common understanding is also emphasized to keep focus (statement number 30).

---

[2] PQMethod- 2.11 by Peter.Schmolck@unibw-muenchen.de, http://www.rz.unibw-muenchen.de/-p41bsmk/qmethod/

## Table 3. The Matrix of Rotated Factors and their Loadings

| QSORT | Factors | | |
| --- | --- | --- | --- |
| | A | B | C |
| 1 | 0.74x | 0.32 | 0.03 |
| 2 | *0.55x* | *0.61x* | 0.17 |
| 3 | 0.40 | -0.01 | 0.74x |
| 4 | 0.68x | 0.30 | 0.37 |
| 5 | 0.25 | *0.75x* | *0.45x* |
| 6 | *0.52x* | 0.15 | *0.71x* |
| 7 | 0.33 | 0.34 | 0.68x |
| 8 | -0.23 | 0.42 | 0.71x |
| 9 | 0.16 | *0.55x* | *0.67x* |
| 10 | 0.37 | *0.63x* | *0.45x* |
| 11 | 0.18 | 0.84x | 0.23 |
| 12 | *0.59x* | *0.49x* | 0.33 |
| 13 | 0.78x | 0.03 | 0.12 |
| 14 | 0.34 | 0.84x | 0.05 |
| 15 | 0.14 | 0.87x | 0.27 |
| 16 | *0.54x* | 0.41 | *0.54x* |
| 17 | 0.64x | 0.33 | 0.44 |
| 18 | 0.40 | *0.49x* | *0.56x* |
| 19 | *0.66x* | 0.33 | *0.47x* |
| | | | |
| % expl. Var. | 24 | 27 | 23 |

*Note.* Factor loadings with bold faces are pure cases loading on a factor, and loadings with italic faces are mixed cases loading on more than one factor.

## Table 4. Distinguished Statements Loading on Factor A

| Number | Statement | Strength |
| --- | --- | --- |
| 7 | When I am asked open-ended questions that stimulate deep, personal reflections, my understanding about the level of my performance develops. | +5 |
| 1 | It is easier for me to focus on what is appropriate when I receive both clear and direct information in small amounts. | +4 |
| 3 | To stay focused on what is appropriate, it is important that the communication is clear and precise. | +4 |
| | | |
| *32* | *When I'm asked questions that stimulate new perspectives and thoughts, it makes it difficult for me to know which idea will allow me to have the strongest performance.* | -4 |
| *31* | *The understanding about my performance is reduced when I'm asked open questions that stimulate me to discover new perspectives.* | -4 |
| *30* | *It is more difficult to keep focused when I am understood and understand what is communicated.* | -5 |

Note: Included mixed cases, 9 cases loaded on factor A.

## Subjective Beliefs among Sport Coaches ...

*Factor B: Active Involvement and Common Understanding*

The most extreme statements loading on factor B (+ 5 and +4) emphasize the importance of stimulating mutual and clear understanding in order to perform better and keep focused (statement number 5 and 6). Open ended questions that stimulate reflections are also emphasized in order to achieve a deep understanding (statement number 7). The most extreme statements on the negative side (-5 and -4) all emphasize the importance of common understanding in order to perform and develop a clear understanding (statement number16, 17 and 28). The statements loading on factor B state the importance of stimulating mutual understanding through active involvement in order to develop understanding and perform.

**Table 5. Distinguished Statements Loading on Factor B**

| Number | Statement | Strength |
|---|---|---|
| 5 | I perform better when I have a clear understanding of what I am told and when other's listen to my needs. When I'm understood by others and understand what I am told, my tasks are performed better. | +5 |
| 7 | When I am asked open-ended questions that stimulate deep, personal reflections, my understanding about the level of my performance develops. | +4 |
| 6 | In order to keep my focus on what is important, it is essential that I have a clear understanding of the task and that I am included in the decision-making process. | +4 |
| 17 | *I feel no need for common understanding to improve the execution of my tasks.* | -4 |
| 16 | *I understand how to develop and improve my performance, regardless if I feel understood or not by others.* | -4 |
| 28 | *When I am able to voice my opinions and I am included in the decision-making process, it is difficult for me to develop a clear understanding about my performances.* | -5 |

*Note.* Included mixed cases, 9 cases loaded on factor B.

*Factor C: Attending Behaviour and Clear Mutual Understanding*

The most distinguished statements loading on factor C (+ 5 and +4) emphasize the importance of stimulating understanding through attending behaviour (statement number 5 and 4). Clear and direct information is also emphasized in order to keep focus (statement number 1). The most extreme statements on the negative side (-5 and -4) all emphasize the importance of receiving clear instructions in order to develop understanding and performance (statement number 25, 26 and 13).

## DISCUSSION AND CONCLUSION

This study investigates 19 elite coaches' perceptions about what they believe is effective communication during performance appraisals, where their athletes' learning and development is focused. The results demonstrate that the coaches share some common views about what they believe is effective communication. Their views cluster around three significant factors that 9, 9 and 10 coaches respectively load on, when mixed sorts are included (Table 3, Factor A, B and C): (A) Reflections and clear instructions, (B) Active involvement and common understanding, (C) Attending behaviour and clear mutual understanding. Interestingly, there seem to be individual mixed views among 9 of the coaches about what they believe is effective communication (Table 3). Thus, coaches that load on factor A, also load on factor B and C. Thus, even if the factors are significant, they also seem to share something that they have in common, or make them interconnect.

**Table 6. Distinguished Statements Loading on Factor C**

| Number | Statement | Strength |
|---|---|---|
| 1 | It is easier for me to focus on what is appropriate when I receive both clear and direct information in small amounts. | +5 |
| 5 | I perform better when I have a clear understanding of what I am told and when other's listen to my needs. When I'm understood by others and understand what I am told, my tasks are performed better. | +4 |
| 4 | The understanding concerning my performance develops when I am listened to and acknowledged. | +4 |
| 25 | *It is difficult for me to develop an understanding of my performance when explanations are both clear and evident.* | *-4* |
| 26 | *If I'm not told exactly what to do, it is difficult for me to perform.* | *-4* |
| 13 | *I feel no need to understand the focused case or being told how things are connected.* | *-5* |

*Note.* Included mixed cases, 10 cases loaded on factor C.

## Reflections and Clear Instructions

The most psychologically significant statements loading on factor A support that the coaches loading on factor A believe that effective communication during performance appraisals should both stimulate athletes' reflections and be based on clear and direct information (No. 1, 3, 7, 31, 32). This is an interesting finding. Both counselling-, and sport psychology claim that questioning is stimulating the receiver to reflect, which indicate that the coach's questioning skills are important during performance appraisals (Hargie, 2006; Ivey and Ivey, 2006; Jowett and Lavallee, 2007). Further, research shows that the amount of deliberate practice is an important factor in the development of an expert athlete (Farrow, Baker and MacMahon, 2008). Thus, instructions that are explaining the performance that is most predictive of the attainment of an expert athlete also seem to be an important skill for coaches in these settings (Abernethy, 2008). This result could indicate that coaches loading on factor A think that effective communication during performance appraisals must be driven by two underlying intentions: 1) To ask questions that stimulate the athletes to discover something new through emancipator reflections, and 2) To take control when it is necessary and influence the athletes in the direction of improving the performance that is most predictive to achieve goal attainment. If this is the case, the communication process seems to be a balancing act between being mutual interdependent and sharing power on the one side, and act in an instructive manner and take control on the other (Jones and Standage, 2006; Jowett and Lavallee, 2007; Potrac, et al., 2007). Coaches need to involve their athletes with open - ended questions and when it is necessary they need to be clear and direct in their instructions. One interpretation could be that the coaches think that when they stimulate their athletes toward reflections and new discoveries, they also have to help them in their considerations based on their new discoveries, to conclude by being clear and direct in their communication. Thus, coaches both involve their athletes in the process and instruct them to do the right thing when it is necessary (Horton and Deakin, 2008; Jowett, 2007). The statements loading on factor A show that reflections and clear and direct instructions are supposed to affect the athletes' understanding about their performances and their focus in the process (No. 1, 3, 7, 30, 31, 32). Thus, the coaches loading on factor A in this study, believe that performance appraisals are supposed to develop their athletes' understanding about their sport and affect their focus to be more appropriate (Cushion, Armour and Jones, 2003). Further research should investigate if coaches believe that there is a relationship between understanding and focus. Thus, if an athlete's understanding of sport specific tasks and behaviours is influencing his or her ability to stay focused during action.

## Active Involvement and Common Understanding

The most psychologically significant statements loading on factor B support that the coaches loading on factor B believe that effective communication during performance appraisals should be aimed at achieving common understanding with their athletes, by actively involving them in the communication process (No. 5, 6, 7, 16, 17, 28). This result indicates that the communication process must be based on mutuality. Interestingly, mutuality is described as the optimal relationship between a coach and an athlete (Jowett, 2007). The 3+1Cs model captures the specific interdependence structures in which coaches and athletes cause one another to experience good versus poor outcomes (Jowett, 2007). The statements loading on factor B might indicate that the coaches believe that if they attempt to cooperate with their athletes by actively involving them, showing them respect and act in a trustful manner, this will ensure a positive outcome of the communication process, as in accordance with the 3+1 Cs model (Jowett, 2007). Therefore, coaches loading on factor B seem to think that effective communication during performance appraisals must be driven by the underlying intention to achieve a common and mutual understanding with their athletes about important factors that are relevant for their performances. The coaches are especially emphasizing that this will affect the athletes' understanding about their own performances (No. 5, 6, 7, 16, 28). As a consequence, attending skills such as listening skills and the ability to ask questions that stimulate understanding seems to be important during performance appraisals according to the coaches loading on factor B (Hargie, et al., 2004).

## Attending Behaviour and Instructions

The most psychologically significant statements loading on factor C give reason to believe that the coaches loading on factor C believe that attending behaviour is important during performance appraisals, and that attending behaviour will affect the athletes' understanding of their own performances (No. 5, 4). Thus, factor C shares similarities with factor B, but states the importance of attending behaviour even more clearly. As with factor

B, this result supports research that claims that communication must be built on trust and respect-, commitment-, and a cooperative attitude for one another, (i. e., high levels of closeness, commitment, complementarity and co-orientation) (Jowett, 2007; Lafrenière , et al., 2008; Lorimer and Jowett, 2009; Olympiou, Jowett and Duda, 2008). Attending behaviour is also found to be important in order to motivate athletes to promote a long-term commitment to become expert athletes (Young and Medic, 2008). Interestingly, as in similarity with factor A, also this factor emphasizes the importance of communicating clear instructions in small amounts, and that clear instructions in small amounts will affect the athletes' ability to focus, their understanding of their own performances, and their actual achievements (No. 1, 13, 25, 26). Research from expert coaches during practice supports this notion; good coaches spend the majority of their time instructing their athletes (Horton and Deakin, 2008). However, this was a formal coach-athlete conversation, which could indicate that the coaches find it necessary to behave in an instructive manner when it is necessary also during performance appraisals (as with factor A).

As a conclusion, coaches loading on factor C seem to think that effective communication during performance appraisals must be driven by two underlying intentions: 1) To achieve a common and mutual understanding with their athletes, and 2) To take control and influence the athlete when it is necessary. An interpretation could be that the coaches loading on factor C believe that they have to balance their communication during performance appraisals, from attending behaviour such as open questions that stimulates deep reflections, listening skills in order to understand their athletes' perspectives on the one side, and clear instructions to conclude with what is right and wrong regarding the focused case on the other side. Thus, an interpretation might be that empathizing with the athlete seems to be a prerequisite to hit the right or helpful target instructional point. The coaches loading on factor C especially highlight that this will affect the athletes understanding about their performances, but also their focus and performances.

## General Findings between the Factors

Research shows that coach-athlete interactions during practises mainly are based on instructive manners (Farrow, et al., 2008). However, research states that the coach-athlete relationship, especially on the elite level, must be based on a mutuality of dependence, which involves a power balance between them as in "give and take" and sharing power (Jowett and Lavallee, 2007, p.21).

To achieve this, coach-athlete interactions outside practises, such as during formal coach-athlete conversations, seem to be very important. To achieve a sense of mutuality for both parts in the relationship when practises mainly are based on instructive manners, formal coach-athlete conversation must be completed in a more balanced manner where the athlete experiences that powered is shared. It is therefore interesting that all factors emphasize the importance of attending behaviour during performance appraisals, especially factor B and C. In conclusion, the coaches in this study seem to agree that one fundamental intention in their communication during performance appraisals is to communicate to stimulate common understanding by actively involve their athletes in the communication process.

On the other hand, both factors A and C emphasize the importance of an instructive manner during performance appraisals. Research indicates that instructions that are explaining the performance that is most predictive of goal attainment are important in order to complete the amount of deliberate practice that is necessary to become an expert athlete (Abernethy, 2008; Farrow, et al., 2008). Thus, it seems that coaches believe that they need to take control when it is necessary, i. e., when their athletes are struggling with their understanding, and explain to them what they need to think or do. Further research should investigate if coaches believe that their athletes are more open for instructions during performance appraisals when they are heard and understood initially, and that it is a necessity to stimulate common understanding and active involvement initially in such conversations in order to influence the athletes directly through instructions (as in accordance with counselling psychology Ivey and Ivey, 2006).

Even if factor A is focusing on the importance of stimulating reflections during performance appraisals, it is surprising that this is not preferred even more among the coaches. To achieve a relationship that is built on mutuality, both parts in the relationship should cooperate to stimulate the other to achieve new discoveries and raised awareness through reflections, especially high performance coaches and athletes (Jowett, 2007; Moen, 2010; Young and Medic, 2008). A possible interpretation could be that the coaches in reality have a pre-set agenda, but need to give their athletes an illusion of mutuality through the use of attending behaviour (Jones and Standage, 2006). This should be investigated further in future research.

Whereas the general view among all the factors is that the intention in communication should be to achieve a common understanding, and that communication should affect the athletes understanding about their own performance, there are nuanced and significant differences between the factors. Factor A emphasizes the importance of stimulating reflections in combination with instructions, whereas factor B emphasizes the importance of active involvement in combination with common understanding, and factor C emphasizes the importance of attending behaviour in combination with instructions.

This result confirms that the interpersonal process of communication is complex, ever-changing, and directly affected by a large number of interrelated factors, and that the communication process is a dynamic process (Jones, 2006; Williams, et al., 2003).

The data from this study cannot draw conclusions regarding causal predominance between communication and effects. However, these issues should be investigated and explored in future research. Also, the problem addressed in this study should be investigated further among athletes in sport and in different situations in sport, such as during practises, planning and preparations, and evaluations.

## REFERENCES

Abernethy, B. (2008). Developing expertise in sport- how research can inform practice. In D. Farrow, J. Baker, and C. MacMahon (Eds.), *Developing sport expertise: Researchers and coaches put theory into practice* (pp. 1-15). NY: Routledge, Taylor and Francis Group.

Baker, J., Côté, J., and Hawes, R. (2000). The relationship between coaching behaviours and sport anxiety in athletes. *Journal of Science and Medicine in Sport, 3*, 110-119.

Baker, J., Yardley, J., and Côté, J. (2003). Coach behaviours and athlete satisfaction in team and individual sports. *International Journal of Sport Psychology, 34*, 226-239.

Bloom, G. A. (1996). Competition: Preparing for and operating in competition. In J. H. Salmela (Ed.), *Great job coach! Getting the edge from proven winners* (pp. 138-179). Ottawa, Canada: Potentium.

Bloom, G. A., Durand-Bush, N., Schinke, R. J., and Salmela, J. H. (1998). The importance of mentoring in the development of coaches and athletes. *International Journal of Sport Psychology, 29,* 267-281.

Bloom, G. A., Schinke, R. J., and Salmela, J.H. (1997). The development of communication skills by elite basketball coaches. *Coaching and Sport Science Journal, 2,* 3-10.

Blom, L. C., Watson II, J. C., and Spadaro, N. (2010). The impact of a coaching intervention on the coach-athlete dyad and athlete sport experience. *Athletic Insight. The Online Journal of Sport Psychology,* 12. Retrieved from http://www.athleticinsight.com/Vol12Iss3/Feature.htm.

Brown, S. R. (1996). Q methodology and qualitative research. *Qualitative Health Research, 6,* 561-567.

Chelladurai, P., and Saleh, S. D. (1980). Preferred leadership in sports. *Journal of Sport Psychology, 2,* 34-45.

Côté, J., Yardley, J., Hay, J., Sedgwick, W., and Baker, J. (1999). An exploratory examination of the coaching behaviour scale of sport. *Avante, 5,* 82-92.

Cushion, C., Armour, K. and Jones, R. (2003). Coach education and continuing professional development: Experience and learning to coach. *Quest 55,* 215-230.

Farrow, D., Baker, J., and MacMahon, C. (2008). *Developing sport expertise: Researchers and coaches put theory into practice.* NY: Routledge, Taylor and Francis Group.

Fouss, D. E., and Troppmann, R. J. (1981). *Effective coaching: A psychological approach.* NY: Wiley.

Gould, D., Greenleaf, C., Chung, Y., and Guinan, D. (2002). A survey of U.S. Atlanta and Nagano Olympians: variables perceived to influence performance. *Research Quarterly Exercise and Sport, 73,* 175-86.

Hargie, O. D. (2006). *The handbook of communication skills.* NY: Routledge.

Hargie, O. D., and Dickson, D. (2004). *Skilled interpersonal communication: Research, theory and practice.* Hove, England: Routledge.

Hargie, O. D., Dickson, D., and Tourish, D. (2004). *Communication skills for effective management.* NY: Palgrave Macmillan.

Heppner, P., Leong, F. T. L., Chiao, H. (2008). A growing internationalization of counselling psychology. In S. D. Brown, and R. W. Lent (Eds.), *Handbook of counselling psychology* (4th ed., pp.68-85). Hoboken, NJ: John Wiley and Sons.

Heron, J. (2001). *Helping the client.* 5th ed. London: Sage.

Horton, S., and Deakin, J. M. (2008). Expert coaches in action. In D. Farrow, J. Baker, and C. MacMahon (Eds.), *Developing sport expertise: Researchers and coaches put theory into practice* (pp. 75-88). NY: Routledge, Taylor and Francis Group.

Ivey, A. E., and Ivey, M. B. (2006). *Intentional interviewing and counselling. Facilitating client development in a multicultural society,* 6th ed. Emeryville, CA: Wadsworth.

Jones, R. L. (2006). *The sports coach as educator: re-conceptualising sports coaching.* NY: Routledge, Taylor and Francis Group.

Jones, R. L., and Standage, M. (2006). First among equals. Shared leadership in coaching context. In R. L. Jones (Ed.), *The sports coach as educator: re-conceptualising sports coaching* (pp. 65-76). NY: Routledge, Taylor and Francis Group.

Jones, R. L., and Wallace, M. (2006). The coach as "orchestrator". More realistically managing the complex coaching context. In R. L. Jones (Ed.), *The sports coach as educator: re-conceptualising sports coaching* (pp. 51-64). NY: Routledge, Taylor and Francis Group.

Jowett, S. (2005a). The coach-athlete partnership. *The Psychologist, 18*, 412-415.

Jowett, S. (2005b). On repairing and enhancing the coach–athlete relationship. In S. Jowett, and M. Jones (Eds.), *The psychology of coaching. Sport and exercise psychology division* (pp. 14–26). Leicester: The British Psychological Society.

Jowett, S. (2007). Interdependence analysis and 3+1 Cs in the coach-athlete relationship. In S. Jowett, and D. Lavallee (Eds.), *Social psychology in sport* (pp.15-28). Champaign, IL: Human Kinetics.

Jowett, S., and Cockerill, I. M. (2002). Incompatibility in the coach–athlete relationship. In I. M. Cockerill (Ed.) *Solutions in sport psychology* (pp. 16–31). London: Thomson Learning.

Jowett, S., and Cockerill, I. M. (2003). Olympic medalists' perspective of the athlete-coach relationship. *Psychology of Sport and Exercise, 4*, 313-331.

Jowett, S., and Lavallee, D. (2007). *Social psychology in sport.* Champaign, IL: Human Kinetics.

Jowett, S., and Meek, G. A. (2000). The coach–athlete relationship in married couples: An exploratory content analysis. *The Sport Psychologist, 14*, 157–175.

Jowett, S., and Ntoumanis, N. (2004). The coach–athlete relationship questionnaire (CART-Q): Development and initial validation. *Scandinavian Journal of Medicine and Science in Sports, 14*, 245–257.

Kvalsund, R. (1998). *A theory of the person.* Department of Education Faculty of Social Science and Technology Management. The Norwegian University of Science and Technology Trondheim.

Kvalsund, R., and Allgood, E. (2008). Person-in-relation. Dialogue as transformative learning in counselling. In G. Grazina (Ed.), *Santykis ir Pokytis. Tarpasmeniniu rysiu gelmines prielaidosir pscihoterapija* (pp. 84–106). Vilnius: Universiteto Leidykla.

Lacy, A. C., and Darst, P. W. (1989). The Arizona State University observation instrument (ASUOI). In P. W. Darst, D. B. Zakrajsek, and V. H. Mancini (Eds.), *Analyzing physical education and sport instruction* (2nd ed., pp. 369- 378). Champaign, IL: Human Kinetics.

Lafrenière, M. A., Jowett, S., Vallerand, R. J., Gonahue, E. G., and Lorimer, R. (2008). Passion in sport: On the quality of the coach-athlete relationship. *Journal of Sport and Exercise Psychology, 30*, 541-60.

Lorimer, R., and Jowett, S. (2009). Empathic accuracy in coach-athlete dyads who participate in team and individual sports. *Psychology of Sport and Exercise, 10*, 152-158.

Lyle, J. (1999). Coaching philosophy and coaching behaviour. In N. Cross, and J. Lyle (Eds.), *The coaching process: Principles and practice for sport* (pp. 25–46). Oxford: Butterworth-Heineman.

Mageau, G. A. (2003). Coach-athlete relationship: A motivational model. *Journal of Sport Sciences, 21*, 883-904.

Mallett, C., and Côté, J. (2006). Beyond winning and losing: Guidelines for evaluating high performance coaches. *The Sport Psychologist, 20*, 213-221.

Martens, R. (2012). *Successful Coaching,* 4th ed., Champaign, IL: Human Kinetics.

McKeown, B., and Thomas, D. (1988). *Q Methodology.* London: Sage.

Moen, F., and Kvalsund, R. (2008). What communications or relational factors characterize the method, skills and techniques of executive coaching? *Journal of Coaching in Organizations*, 102-123.

Moen, F., and Verburg, E. (2012). Subjective beliefs among athletes about how relational factors affect intrinsic motivation, responsibility and development in sport. *The International Journal of Coaching and Science. 6*, 81-100.

Nazarudin, B. H. N. M., Fauzee, O. S. M., Jamalis, M., Geok, K. S., and Din, A. (2009). Coaching leadership styles and athlete satisfaction among Malaysian University Basketball team. *Research Journal of International Studies, 9*, 4-11.

Olympiou, A., Jowett, S., and Duda, J. L. (2008). The psychological interface between the coach-created motivational climate and the coach-athlete relationship in team sports. *The Sport Psychologist, 22*, 423-438.

Pett, M. A., Lackey, N. R. and Sullivan, J. J. (2003). *Making sense of factor analysis: The use of factor analysis for instrument development in health care research.* Thousand Oaks, CA: Sage.

Pilus, A. H., and Saadan, R. (2009). Coaching leadership styles and athlete satisfaction among hockey team. *Journal of Human Capital Development, 2*, 77- 87.

Poczwardowski, A., Barott, J. E., and Henschen, K. P. (2002). The athlete and coach: Their relationship and its meaning. Results of an interpretive study. *International Journal of Sport Psychology, 33*, 116–140.

Potrac, P., Jones, R. L. and Cushion, C. J. (2007). Understanding power and the coach's role in professional English soccer: A preliminary investigation of coach behaviour. *Soccer and Society, 8*, 33-49.

Rhoads, J. C. (2007). Q methodology. In N. J. Salkind, and K. Rasmussen (Eds.), *Encyclopedia of measurement and statistics* (pp. 799- 802). Thousand Oaks, CA, London, and New Delhi: Sage.

Schein, E. (2009). *Helping: How to offer, give, and receive help.* San Francisco, California: Berrett-Koehler Publishers.

Schmolck, P. (2002). PQMethod Download Mirror Retrieved from http://www.qmethod.org/ Tutorials/pqmethod.htm

Shotter, J. (1995). In conversation: Joint action, shared intentionality, and ethics. *Theory and Psychology, 5*, 49-73.

Spink, K. (1991). The psychology of coaching. *New Studies in Athletics, 6*, 37-41.

Stein, J., Bloom, G. A., and Sabiston, C. M. (2012). Influence of perceived and preferred coach feedback on youth athletes' perceptions of team motivational climate. *Psychology of Sport and Exercise, 13*, 484-490.

Stephenson, W. (1950). A statistical approach to typology: The study of trait universes. *Journal of Clinical psychology. 6*, 26-38.

Stephenson, W. (1986). Protoconcurcus: The concourse theory of communication. *Operant Subjectivity, 9*, 37-58, 73-96.

Watts, S., and Stenner, P. (2012). *Doing Q methodological research.* CA: Sage.

Weinberg, R. S., and Gould, D. (2007). *Foundations of sport and exercise psychology,* 4th ed. Champaign, IL: Human Kinetics.

Williams, J. M., Jerome, J. G., Kenow, L. J., Rogers, T., Sartain, T. A., and Darland, G. (2003). Factor structure of the coaching behaviour questionnaire and its relationship to athlete variables. *The Sport Psychologist, 17*, 16-34.

Young, B. W., and Medic, N. (2008). The motivation to become an expert athlete. How coaches can promote long-term commitment. In D. Farrow, J. Baker, and C. MacMahon (Eds.), *Developing sport expertise: Researchers and coaches put theory into practice* (pp. 43-59). NY: Routledge, Taylor and Francis Group.

In: Innovative Writings in Sport and Exercise Psychology
Editor: Robert Schinke

ISBN: 978-1-62948-881-3
© 2014 Nova Science Publishers, Inc.

*Chapter 6*

# THE RELATIONSHIP BETWEEN ATHLETIC IDENTITY AND PHYSICAL ACTIVITY AMONG FORMER COLLEGE ATHLETES

## *Erin J. Reifsteck\*, Diane L. Gill, and DeAnne L. Brooks*

[1,2]The University of North Carolina at Greensboro, Greensboro, NC, US
[3]Greensboro College, NC, US

### ABSTRACT

The purpose of this study was to examine the relationship between athletic identity and physical activity among former college athletes. The relationship was first examined with former Division I athletes ($N$=56) and then in a second sample of former Division III athletes (N=18) and non-athletes (N=31) from a small college. All participants (N=105) completed the Athletic Identity Measurement Scale (AIMS), the Godin Leisure Time Exercise Questionnaire, and the Stage of Exercise Behavior Change measure. The AIMS was a positive predictor of physical activity, and this relationship was stronger for alumni who had participated in college athletics. While former college athletes had higher AIMS scores, they were not more active than alumni who did not participate in college athletics. Former athletes were also more likely than non-athletes to report a decrease in physical activity after college. Substantial decreases in physical activity after the conclusion of a collegiate athletic career have important health implications for former college athletes, which warrant the development of transitional programs that promote lifelong physical activity participation among NCAA student-athletes.

### INTRODUCTION

There are currently more than 400,000 student-athletes competing in intercollegiate sports sponsored by the National Collegiate Athletic Association (NCAA, 2010), and the number of former student-athletes is exponentially more than that. Although the NCAA

---

\* Email: ejreifst@uncg.edu, Phone: (336) 334-4683, Fax: (336) 334-3070.

recognizes that retirement from sports after college is inevitable for most of its members, there are few programs designed to prepare student-athletes for the transition out of collegiate sports. Much of the existing research and programming related to the transition revolve around the construct of athletic identity and its relationship to career planning and the retirement process (Grove, Lavallee, and Gordon, 1997; Lally, 2007; Lally and Kerr, 2005; Lavallee, Gordon, and Grove, 1997; Taylor and Ogilvie, 1994). Research and programs like the NCAA-sponsored Student-Athlete Affairs Program have not typically emphasized physical activity and health behaviors for student-athletes after they retire from their collegiate careers.

The position statement on recommended physical activity for healthy adults released by the American College of Sports Medicine (ACSM) contends that physical activity is extremely important and provides many health-related and psychological benefits (Haskell, et al., 2007). For instance, regular physical activity participation can reduce the risk for cardiovascular disease, osteoporosis, type 2 diabetes, anxiety, and depression (ACSM, 2010). A major concern for public health officials is that many Americans are not meeting physical activity guidelines and are insufficiently active (*Healthy People 2020*). Given that athletes are often characterized as being physically active, the athlete population is usually not a focus of exercise adherence or physical activity promotion studies or interventions. This gap in research and programming is significant because studies show that, contrary to popular understandings, athletic participation may not necessarily predict post-competitive physical activity across the lifespan (Dishman, Sallis, and Orienstein, 1985; Koukouris, 1991; Stephan and Bilard, 2003). Further, the athlete population may have unique health concerns, which would make maintaining lifelong physical activity levels after retirement from competitive sports of particular importance for this subgroup. For instance, research suggests that former elite athletes may be more susceptible to inactivity-related increases in risks for certain types of chronic diseases such as diabetes and cardiovascular disease (Witkowski and Spangenburg, 2008). Witkowski and Spangenburg (2008) contend that cessation of regular exercise among athletes who retire from their athletic careers can lead to issues with insulin sensitivity, plasma lipids, and body composition. Thus, it is particularly important for athletes to continue to be active even after retirement from competitive sports. The authors warn that athletes who stop physical activity upon retiring from sports will have the same or greater risk for chronic diseases compared to non-athletes who have been sedentary all of their lives. Given these health concerns, the inclusion of the retired athlete population in studies that track and promote physical activity is imperative.

In order to gain a better understanding of physical activity among retired athletes, it is important to acknowledge that athletic retirement is "a coping process with potentially positive or negative outcomes" (Stambulova, Alfermann, Statler, and Cote, 2009, p. 396). According to Taylor and Ogilvie (1994), retirement from an athletic career is a transitional process. Maintaining physical activity after retirement is a possible adjustment difficulty an athlete might experience through the transition (Stephan and Bilard, 2003). Self-identity is perhaps the most important factor that can impact transition into retirement (Taylor and Ogilvie, 1994). Because athletic identity is a major source of self-identity for athletes, it is appropriate to focus on the role of athletic identity in the transition process, and specifically in maintaining physical activity.

According to identity theory, identity can be defined as "meanings one attributes to oneself in a role" (Burke and Reitzes, 1981), and it is formed and maintained through social processes. Through interaction with others who confirm and validate one's self-concept, individuals are able to establish identities. Beyond serving as a means for defining oneself, identity also impacts the performance of behaviors consistent with a given identity. According to identity theory (Burke and Reitzes, 1981), an individual monitors his or her behavior based on whether or not the meaning of that behavior is in line with the meaning of his or her respective identity role. Greater identification with an identity role is predictive of greater frequency of engagement in behaviors consistent with that role (Callero, 1985).

Athletic identity is a specific type of identity defined as the extent to which one identifies with the athletic role (Brewer, Van Raalte, and Linder, 1993). In applying identity theory, in order to *identify* as an athlete one must *behave* as an athlete. Because physical activity is a behavior that is consistent with the role of athlete, having a strong athletic identity logically is related to physical activity behavior. Indeed, having a more salient athletic identity has been shown to be related to greater engagement in physical activity (Anderson, 2004; Brewer, Van Raalte, and Linder, 1993). It is important to note that physical activity is not the only behavior associated with athletic identity. Furthermore, the type of physical activity associated with athletic identity may be specific to the athletic setting. Athletic identity is complex and not the same as exerciser identity. Those who identify as exercisers are more likely to participate in greater physical activity (Anderson and Cychosz, 1995), but that exercise activity may or may not be related to athletics or athletic identity. Athletic identity is rooted more specifically in competitive sport. As such, athletic identity may be related to participation in certain modes or intensities of physical activity that are consistent with competitive sport training.

With their Athletic Identity Measurement Scale (AIMS), Brewer, Van Raalte, and Linder (1993) introduced athletic identity as an identity rooted in participation in competitive sports. The AIMS has been the most widely used measurement of athletic identity. Research has shown that greater involvement in athletics is indeed associated with a stronger athletic identity, and men tend to score higher on the AIMS than women (Brewer, Van Raalte, and Linder, 1993). This may reflect the extensive body of research which suggests that athletics is stereotypically viewed as a more masculine space (Gill, 2007; Gill and Kamphoff, 2010; Messner, 1992). Brewer and colleagues (1993) found a positive relationship between the AIMS and amount of physical activity among college students. Research has not examined this relationship among former college athletes specifically, although a similar relationship would seem plausible. Public health reports and large sample research with the general population indicate that women are less active than men across all age groups and other categories (Caspersen, Pereira, and Curran, 2000; CDC, 2011). Whether these gender patterns are similar among former college athletes as well has yet to be determined.

Athletic identity has also been linked to problematic issues in retirement, such as emotional difficulties and poor career transition (Lally, 2007; Lally and Kerr, 2005; Lavallee, Gordon, and Grove, 1997), particularly when an athlete's identity is rooted in a performance narrative in which his/her single-minded dedication to sport comes at the expense of developing other identities (Douglas and Carless, 2009). Because of these issues, some have suggested (Lally, 2007; Lally and Kerr, 2005; Lavallee, Gordon, and Grove, 1997) that athletes will transition better if they take proactive steps to disengage from their athletic identity and focus on fostering other identities during retirement in order to avoid maladjustment. Indeed, research shows that the saliency of athletic identity does drop off after retirement from sport (Houle, Brewer, and Kluck, 2010). If athletic identity is facilitative of engagement in physical activity (Brewer et al., 1993), this decrease in saliency of athletic identity could be one important factor related to a decline in physical activity after the conclusion of collegiate sport participation.

While research has not documented the physical activity patterns of former college athletes specifically, Calfas, Sallis, Lovato, and Campbell (1994) found that one third of recent college graduates they surveyed were presently inactive, and almost half of the alumni reported being less active now compared to when they were in college. Sparling and Snow (2002) reported similar findings when they surveyed college alumni who had graduated within the past ten years and found that 44% of the participants reported being less active now than they were in college. Persistence of physical activity behaviors after college was related to how physically active individuals were while in college: 84.7% of those who reported being regular exercisers in college were as active or more active now while 81.3% of those who did not participate in exercise during college reported being about the same or even less active now.

These findings indicate that some people, especially those who had developed regular physical activity patterns in college, continued to maintain some level of physical activity after graduation, while many other individuals had a clear drop in the amount of time spent engaged in physical activity. Based on these findings, it is plausible that alumni who were athletes during college might continue to be physically active; however, it is difficult to make such comparisons because current research on this topic has not specifically looked at former college athletes.

The general college population is not as active as collegiate athletes and the type and structure of that exercise is different as well. There is a need for studies geared specifically toward athletes to determine their physical activity patterns after retirement from collegiate sports. Additionally, an even greater drop in physical activity after college may occur for former student-athletes who would have difficulty maintaining the high amount of physical activity they engaged in during their college sports career (Galloway, 2007; Zielinski, Krol-Zielinska, and Kusy, 2006). Such a decline in physical activity has been shown to have negative health implications for former athletes (Witkowski and Spangenburg, 2008).

## Purpose and Hypothesis

The purpose of this study was to examine the relationship between athletic identity and physical activity among former college athletes. The main research question was, How is athletic identity related to physical activity levels of former college athletes? A positive relationship was hypothesized in that college alumni who scored higher in athletic identity, as measured by the AIMS, would report higher levels of physical activity compared to alumni with lower athletic identity scores.

In addition to former Division I athletes, both athlete and non-athlete alumni from a small Division III college were included for comparison. It was expected that alumni who were former college athletes would report higher athletic identity scores than non-athletes. Although it was expected that the former athletes would report experiencing a greater drop in physical activity after college, it was expected that they would still be more physically active than non-athlete alumni.

Given that research has suggested men tend to score higher on athletic identity than women (Brewer, Van Raalte, and Linder, 1993), it was expected that male participants would have higher athletic identity scores. Finally, because population-wide surveillance data suggest that American men are more active than American women (CDC, 2011), it was expected that men in this study would report being more physically active than women.

## METHOD

Survey methods were used with college alumni in two phases to address the research question. Participants completed the Athletic Identity Measurement Scale, the Godin Leisure Time Exercise Questionnaire, a stage of exercise measure, and one item comparing current physical activity with the previous physical activity during college.

## Participants

Participants were college alumni who graduated within the past five years (2005-2010). In the first phase, former Division I student-athletes (*N*=56) were surveyed from one southeastern university with permission and cooperation of the university athletic department. In the second phase, former Division III student-athletes (*N*=18) and non-athlete alumni (*N*=31) from a smaller southeastern college were surveyed with the permission and cooperation of the college's alumni office. Data from 105 male (*n*=37) and female (*n*=68) alumni were included in this study. Recruitment was limited to recent graduates to focus on the more immediate transition from college to life after college.

The total sample was comprised of Caucasian (*n*=82), African American (*n*=15), Asian/Pacific Islander (*n*=5), and Other (*n*=2) individuals with an average age of 28.3 (*SD*=8.01) years old. Of the 105 graduates, 2% had earned an associates' degree, 78% of the participants had obtained a bachelor's degree, and 20% had earned a master's degree. Former athletes in soccer, basketball, baseball, football, volleyball, lacrosse, golf, tennis, wrestling, cross country/track, swimming, softball, cheerleading, and dance were represented in the sample.

## Measures

Athletic identity and physical activity levels were the main variables measured in this study. Athletic identity was measured using the AIMS (Brewer, Van Raalte, and Linder, 1993). Physical activity levels were measured using the Godin Leisure-Time Exercise Questionnaire (Godin and Shepard, 1985) and the Stage of Exercise Behavior Change measure (Marcus et al., 1992).

*AIMS.* The AIMS consists of 10 items rated on a 7-point Likert scale (1= strongly disagree, 7= strongly agree), and a higher total score is interpreted as a more salient athletic identity. The AIMS has been previously (Brewer, Van Raalte, and Linder, 1993; Martin, Mushett, and Eklund, 1994) shown to be a valid, reliable, and consistent measure of athletic identity: $\alpha$= .93 for internal consistency and $r$=.89 for test-retest reliability. Validity has been demonstrated by correlating the AIMS to Fox's (1990) Perceived Importance Profile, $r$=.83 (Brewer, Van Raalte, and Linder, 1993). Reliability of the measure was confirmed in the current study, $\alpha$= .895, with all positive item-total correlations, indicating that all items contribute to the total reliability.

*Godin.* The Godin Leisure-Time Exercise Questionnaire (Godin and Shepard, 1985) measures physical activity levels based on self-reported weekly frequencies of strenuous, moderate, and light activities. The Godin asks respondents to report the number of times they engage in strenuous, moderate, and light physical activity in at least fifteen minute bouts during the week.

The Godin provides an approximate MET value for weekly physical activity using the equation: (frequency of strenuous activity/wk X 9) + (frequency of moderate activity/wk X 5) + (frequency of light activity/wk X 3).

A higher score indicates greater MET expenditure and thus higher physical activity levels. Validity for this measure was assessed by positive correlations with $VO_2$ max performance, and the Godin was found to have a test-retest reliability of $r$=.74 (Godin and Shepherd, 1985). Jacobs et al.'s (1993) review of physical activity measures supports the use of this questionnaire.

*Stage of Exercise.* In addition to the Godin, a stage of exercise behavior change measure developed by Marcus and colleagues (1992) was used to assess former athletes' current physical activity.

The measure, which is based on intention to exercise and exercise behavior, is widely used in research and programs (e.g., Marcus and Forsyth, 2009) to assess stage of exercise (precontemplation, contemplation, preparation, action, and maintenance) and provides an added, broader measure of physical activity levels. Stages range from being sedentary with no intention to begin regular exercise (precontemplation) to being regularly active for more than 6 months (maintenance). With this stage measure, a higher stage number (Stage 5 = maintenance) represents more regular engagement in physical activity.

*One-Item Physical Activity Comparison.* Participants were also asked to indicate whether they were less active now than they were in college, more active now, or about the same.

*Demographics.* The participants were asked to provide background information including gender, age, race, occupation, sport(s) played in college, current sport participation, and amount of time that has passed since their last collegiate competition. These demographics were used to provide relevant information about the sample participating in this study.

## Procedures

Prior to the main study, the electronic survey was pilot-tested with former Division I field hockey players ($N$=13) from a different institution.

No issues were raised with the measures or methods and the same measures and electronic survey format were used in the main study. Following approval from the university Institutional Review Board and from the university athletic department, an email containing a hyperlink for the informed consent and survey was sent out through the larger university's athletic department's alumni/booster club.

The same procedures were followed in the second phase with messages sent through the smaller college's alumni office. Using the provided link, the AIMS, the Godin, demographics, and the added questions were administered electronically through the *Qualtrics* online survey software.

The Relationship between Athletic Identity and Physical Activity ...

Voluntary consent and directions were provided, and participants submitted their answers electronically on the website.

Of 127 surveys that were returned, 22 were excluded from data analysis due to not fully completing the questionnaires for a final total of 105 participants.

# RESULTS

Descriptive statistics were calculated for the athletic identity and physical activity measures as well as for demographic information. Tables 1 and 2 provide descriptive information for the AIMS and Godin measures.

**Table 1. Descriptive Statistics for AIMS and Godin – Division I Athletes**

|  | Division I | | | |
|  | Male *(n=22)* | | Female *(n=34)* | |
|  | M | SD | M | SD |
| AIMS Total | 44.23 | 10.70 | 42.94 | 9.60 |
| Godin Total | 48.86 | 25.38 | 44.79 | 25.71 |

**Table 2. Descriptive Statistics for AIMS and Godin – Division III Athletes and Non-Athletes**

|  | Division III | | | | Non-Athletes | | | |
|  | Male *(n=7)* | | Female *(n=11)* | | Male *(n=8)* | | Female *(n=23)* | |
|  | M | SD | M | SD | M | SD | M | SD |
| AIMS Total | 46.57 | 10.10 | 40.55 | 12.36 | 37.13 | 12.70 | 24.91 | 11.88 |
| Godin Total | 75.14 | 33.54 | 38.50 | 20.43 | 53.50 | 18.94 | 42.28 | 24.24 |

The results are presented in three phases: 1) results of the first group surveyed including Division I athletes, 2) results of the second group of athletes and non athletes surveyed from a small Division III college, and 3) combined group comparisons.

## Division I Athletes

*Athletic Identity and Physical Activity Relationships.* Pearson's correlation and regression analysis were used to determine the relationship between athletic identity and physical activity. Specifically, the AIMS total was used as a predictor of the Godin total to address the main research question. The AIMS total score was positively related to the Godin total ($r=.360, p<.01$).

The results of the regression analysis showed that the AIMS explained 12.9% of the variance in physical activity scores, $F(1, 54)= 8.030, p<.01$.

*Gender Differences.* A one-way ANOVA was used to compare the effect of gender on physical activity scores. Results revealed no significant differences in physical activity levels among male and female Division I athletes, $F(1,54)= .338, p=.563$. A second ANOVA was also used to compare the effect of gender on athletic identity scores. Again, there were no significant gender differences in athletic identity, $F(1,54)= .219, p= .642$.

## Division III Athletes and Non-Athletes

*Athletic Identity and Physical Activity Relationships.* Pearson's correlations and regression analysis were repeated with the second group of Division III athlete and non-athlete alumni to investigate the primary research question regarding the relationship between athletic identity and physical activity. Pearson's correlation indicated that the AIMS was positively related to physical activity for the alumni of the small college ($r=.371, p<.01$). Results of the regression analysis showed that the AIMS significantly explained 13.7% of the variance in physical activity among the small college alumni, $F(1, 47)= 7.481, p<.01$.

*Gender and Group Differences.* A two-way ANOVA was used to compare the effects of athlete status and gender on physical activity levels. In contrast to the findings with the Division I former athlete sample, the male alumni from the small college reported significantly higher physical activity than the female alumni, $F(1,45)= 9.72, p<.01$; however, there was no significant difference in physical activity participation between the former athletes and non-athletes, $F(1,45)=1.354, p= .251$. There was no significant interaction, $F(1,45)= 2.743, p=.105$.

A second two-way ANOVA was used to compare the effects of athlete status and gender on athletic identity scores. Again contrasting the findings with the Division I former athlete sample, male alumni had significantly higher athletic identity scores than female alumni, $F(1,45)= 5.839, p=.02$. The former Division III athletes also reported higher athletic identity than the non-athletes, $F(1,45)= 11.040, p<.01$. There was no significant interaction, $F(1,45)= .672, p=.417$.

## Combined Groups

*Athletic Identity and Physical Activity Relationships.* To reflect the primary research question comparing athletic identity and physical activity relationships, Pearson's correlations and regression analyses were used with the three groups combined. The overall correlation between the AIMS and Godin total was positive and significant, $r=.322, p=.001$. The regression analysis indicated that the AIMS explained 10.4% of the variance in physical activity scores, $F(1, 103)= 11.956, p=.001$. However, when non-athletes were removed from the analysis, athletic identity had a higher correlation with physical activity ($r=.428, p<.001$) and significantly explained 18.3% of the variance, $F(1,72)=16.14, p<.001$. Thus, the relationship between athletic identity and physical activity appears to be particularly strong for former athletes compared to the non-athletes ($r=.196, p=.291$).

*Physical Activity and Athletic Identity Group Differences.* A 2x3 factorial ANOVA was used to compare the effects of gender and athlete status (former Division I athlete, former Division III athlete, non-athlete) on physical activity levels. Results of the ANOVA indicated male alumni were significantly more active than female alumni, $F(1,99)= 9.068$, $p= .003$. There were no group differences in physical activity levels based on athlete status, indicating that amount of reported weekly physical activity did not differ among Division I former athletes, Division III former athletes, or non-athlete alumni, $F(2,99)=1.065$, $p=.349$. The interaction effect did not reach significance, $F(2, 99)= 2.760$, $p= .068$.

A second 2x3 factorial ANOVA was used to compare the effect of gender and athlete status on AIMS scores. Results of the ANOVA revealed that male alumni had significantly higher AIMS scores than female alumni, $F(1, 99)= 6.691$, $p =.011$. There was also a main effect for athlete status, $F(2,99)= 11.732$, $p<.001$. Tukey's post hoc analyses clarified that both Division I and Division III former athletes had higher athletic identity scores than non athlete alumni ($p<.001$). Athletic identity scores of former Division I and Division III athletes were not significantly different ($p=.981$). There was no significant interaction effect for gender and athlete status, $F(2,99)= 2.082$, $p= .130$.

**Table 3. Stage of Exercise for Former Athletes and Non-Athletes**

|  | Stage 1 | Stage 2 | Stage 3 | Stage 4 | Stage 5 |
|---|---|---|---|---|---|
| Former Athletes |  |  |  |  |  |
| Div I | 1 | 5 | 7 | 6 | 37 |
| Div III | 0 | 1 | 2 | 2 | 13 |
| Total (M/F) | 1 (0/1) | 6 (1/5) | 9 (3/6) | 8 (2/6) | 50 (23/27) |
| Non-Athletes (M/F) | 1 (0/1) | 4 (2/2) | 5 (1/4) | 10 (4/6) | 11 (1/10) |

**Table 4. Changes in Physical Activity Since College**

|  | Less Active | Same | More Active |
|---|---|---|---|
| Former Athletes |  |  |  |
| Div I | 47 | 6 | 3 |
| Div III | 11 | 4 | 3 |
| Total (M/F) | 58 (21/37) | 10 (5/5) | 6 (3/3) |
| Non-Athletes (M/F) | 8 (4/4) | 12 (3/9) | 11 (1/10) |

*Physical Activity Levels and Changes Across Groups.* In addition to the main measures of athletic identity and physical activity, participants were asked to complete the stage of exercise change measure. Participants were asked to indicate how regularly active they were based on the following five stages: 1) currently inactive with no intention of exercising regularly within the next 6 months, 2) currently inactive with the intention to start exercising regularly within the next 6 months, 3) currently inactive but intend to start exercising regularly in the next 30 days, 4) currently active but exercising regularly for less than 6 months, and 5) currently active and exercising regularly for more than 6 months. Table 3 provides frequency counts for former athletes (Division I and III) and non-athletes who fell into each of the five stages. Results of a chi-square analysis indicated that a higher proportion of former athletes reported being in the maintenance stage (exercising regularly for more than 6 months), $\chi^2(4)=10.922$, $p=.027$. Similar proportions of athletes and non-athletes reported being in the inactive stages. A similar chi-square analysis revealed no gender differences across the stages, $\chi^2(4)=1.960$, $p=.743$.

In addition to the stage measure, participants responded to a one-item question regarding how their physical activity had changed since college: less active now, about the same, or more active now. Table 4 shows change in physical activity frequencies for the former athletes (Division I and III) and non-athletes. A chi-square analysis comparing changes in physical activity levels after college revealed that there was a clear difference between the former athlete groups and the non-athlete group, $\chi^2(4)= 29.404$, $p<.001$. In general, the former athletes tended to report a drop in their physical activity after college whereas non-athletes were just as likely to stay the same or even increase their physical activity after college. No gender differences were observed, $\chi^2(2)= 1.235$, $p=.539$.

## DISCUSSION

The main purpose of this study was to investigate the relationship between athletic identity and physical activity levels among male and female former college athletes. Consistent with our hypothesis, higher athletic identity scores were related to higher physical activity levels. The Athletic Identity Measurement Scale (AIMS) showed a moderate, positive relationship with physical activity engagement among alumni who were college athletes. The relationship was stronger for former athletes than non athletes. These results support identity theory framework and suggest that physical activity behavior is consistent with and predicted by athletic identity.

As we had expected, male college alumni reported a higher athletic identity than female alumni overall, though there were no gender differences among the Division I former athletes. Further, differences in athletic identity between athletes and non-athletes were stronger than were gender differences. Both Division I and Division III former collegiate athletes identified more as athletes than the non athlete alumni did, and did not differ from each other. Male college alumni were also on average more active than their female counterparts, which is consistent with patterns in the general population (Caspersen, Pereira, and Curran, 2000; CDC, 2011), although again, there were no gender differences among the Division I former athletes. The gender patterns for athletic identity and physical activity among the Division I athletes contradict findings with the general population (Brewer, Van Raalte, and Linder, 1993; CDC, 2011). Perhaps athletes who have competed at more elite levels, such as the Division I sample, maintain athletic identities that preclude clear gender differences in athletic identity and physical activity. This is consistent with Gill, Kang and colleagues' (Gill, 1999; Kang, Gill, Acevedo and Deeter, 1990) findings that gender differences in sport competitiveness do not hold at more elite levels of sport.

While the former athletes reported higher athletic identity, the former athlete alumni were not significantly more active presently than alumni who were not collegiate athletes, and this effect was consistent across gender. This finding contradicted our hypothesis that former athletes would report higher physical activity levels than non-athletes. Although former athletes reported higher athletic identity scores, this apparently did not translate into significantly more physical activity engagement among former athletes. Self-concept is multidimensional (Marsh, 1990), and individuals may have several salient, and possibly confounding, identities that may influence their behaviors. Given that a lot of variance in physical activity was still unexplained by athletic identity, future studies might consider other identity roles and factors that may contribute to or interfere with physical activity engagement among college graduates.

It appears that although college athletes are very active while in college, they are no more active than non-athletes after college. While a greater proportion of former athletes reported being in the maintenance stage of exercise, their overall physical activity levels were not different from non-athletes, and a similar proportion of former athletes and non-athletes reported being inactive. This contradicts Sparling and Snow's (2002) findings that amount of physical activity participation after college was related to how active individuals were while in college. Clearly, athletes engage in very active lifestyles while participating in college; however, once they conclude their college athletic careers they may be no more likely to participate in physical activity than non-athletes.

Overall, an evident decline in physical activity after college was found for this sample - even greater than numbers reported by Calfas and colleagues (1994) or Sparling and Snow (2002). This is clearly due to the specific inclusion of former athletes in the present sample. As we had anticipated, the former athletes were more likely to report a drop in physical activity compared to alumni who were not college athletes. The large majority (78.4%) of former athletes reported being less active now than they were in college compared to 25.8% of non-athlete alumni. In fact, non-athlete alumni were likely to report maintaining their physical activity and even becoming more physically active after college. Close to a third of the former athletes, who once participated in the rigorous physical activity demands of collegiate athletics, reported that they were currently inactive or had been so at one point in the past six months.

Because the primary goal of collegiate athletes' training and physical activity is skill improvement and preparation for success during competition (Adler and Adler, 1991), the decline in participation seen in members of this study may reflect a loss of these motivational factors. Further, Theberge (2007) has suggested that competitive athletes do not engage in physical activity for the purpose of maintaining or improving health. Because maintenance of mental and physical health is a great benefit and motivator of lifelong physical acitivty for many post-collegiate adults, former athletes who lack this value for activity may not continue to engage in physical activity post-competitively. Many highly competitive athletes may value physical activity because it serves as a means for improving their ability to play their chosen sport. Once they retire from that sport, athletes may find it difficult to engage in those same types of physical activity because it no longer serves its original purpose. This may be a particular challenge for those athletes whose identities revolve around a performance narrative focused solely on competitive sport (Douglas and Carless, 2009). Future interventions that promote physical activity engagement among former athletes might help athletes focus on other positive benefits of physical activity besides enhancing sport performance.

If, as Witkowski and Spangenburg (2008) suggest, cessation of regular exercise among former athletes leads to metabolic issues, changes in body composition, and increased susceptibility to certain types of chronic diseases such as diabetes and cardiovascular disease, then a substantial portion of the current sample may be at risk for these health concerns. Additionally, research suggests that physical activity can play a protective role against depression among former elite athletes as they age (Backmand, Kaprio, Kujala, and Sarna, 2003). Thus, interventions that track and promote lifestyle physical activity among graduating student-athletes are warranted. These interventions should focus on educating retiring and retired student-athletes about health-related physical activity options and, specifically, how they differ from the physical activity involved in collegiate sports participation. Specific information regarding goal setting, exercise programming, and skill development in areas outside of the athletes' sport should be addressed.

## Limitations and Future Directions

The current study is limited in several ways, including the descriptive survey methodology and sample from only two institutions located in the same city. It is impossible to draw conclusions about any causal relationship, and the factors underlying the positive relationship between athletic identity and physical activity are not fully explained. Future research might further explore this complex relationship with larger samples and varied methodologies. A longitudinal study with interview, focus group, and survey data collected before, during, and after retirement from college sports might better demonstrate how physical activity and athletic identity actually change through the retirement process and in relation to each other.

While there are limitations, this study is one of the first to examine athletic identity and physical activity levels of former college athletes. This information is essential if we are to design effective programs to foster lifelong physical activity participation among transitioning student-athletes. Given the high visibility of college sports and the large number of college athletes, understanding the issues related to retirement from sport, including continued engagement in healthy physical activity, is important. Researchers and practitioners are charged with the task of discovering ways to encourage healthy lifestyles and participation in lifelong physical activity among the 400,000 NCAA student-athletes who participate in college sports each year, all of whom will eventually retire from college sports and face their own set of post-college challenges.

## REFERENCES

Adler, P., and Adler, P. (1991). *Backboards and blackboards: College athletes and role engulfment.* New York: Columbia University Press.

American College of Sports Medicine. (2009). *ACSM's guidelines for exercise testing and prescription* (8th ed.). Philadelphia, PA: Lippincott Williams and Wilkins)

Anderson, C.B. (2004). Athletic identity and its relation to exercise behavior: Scale development and initial validation. *Journal of Sport and Exercise Psychology, 26*, 39-56.

Anderson, D.F. and Cychosz, C.M. (1995). Exploration of the relationship between exercise behavior and exercise identity. *Journal of Sport Behavior, 18*(3), 159.

Backmand, H., Kaprio, J., Kujala, U., and Sarna, S. (2003). Influence of physical activity on depression and anxiety of former elite athletes. *International Journal of Sports Medicine, 24*(8), 609-619.

Brewer, B.W., Van Raalte, J.L., and Linder, D.E. (1993). Athletic identity: Hercules' muscles or Achilles heel? *International Journal of Sport Psychology, 24*(2), 237-254.

Burke, P.T., and Reitzes, D. (1981). The link between identity and role performance. *Social Psychology Quarterly, 44*(2), 83-92.

Calfas, K.J., Sallis, J.F., Lovato, C.Y., and Campbell, J. (1994). Physical activity and its determinants before and after college graduation. *Medicine, Exercise, Nutrition and Health, 3*(6), 323-334.

Callero, P.L. (1985). Role-identity salience. *Social Psychology Quarterly, 48*(3), 203-215.

Caspersen, C.J., Pereira, M.A. and Curran, K.M. (2000). Changes in physical activity patterns in the United States by sex and cross-sectional age. *Medicine and Science of Sport and Exercise, 32*(9), 1601-1609.

CDC (2011). Behavioral risk factor surveillance system: prevalence and trends data. Center for Disease Control. Retrieved November 22, 2012 from: http://apps.nccd.cdc.gov/ brfss/sex.asp?cat=PAandyr=2011andqkey=8291andstate=UB.

Dishman, R. K., Sallis, J., and Orenstein, D. (1985). The determinants of physical activity and exercise. *Public Health Reports , 100* (2), 158-171.

Douglas, K., and Carless, D. (2009). Abandoning the performance narrative: Two women's stories of transition from professional sport. *Journal of Applied Sport Psychology, 21,* 213-230.

Fox, K.R. (1990). *The Physical Self-Perception Profile manual.* DeKalb, IL: Office for Health Promotion, Northern Illinois University.

Galloway, S. (2007). Consulting with Olympic track and field hopefuls: It can't be this easy...or could it? *Athletic Insight, 9*(4), 29-36.

Gill, D. L. (1999). Gender and competitive motivation: From the recreation center to the Olympic arena. In D.J. Bernstein (Ed.), Vol. 45 of the *Nebraska Symposium on Motivation: Gender and Motivation* (pp. 173-207). Lincoln, NE: University of Nebraska Press.

Gill, D.L. (2007). Gender and cultural diversity. In G. Tenenbaum and R.C. Eklund (Eds.), *Handbook of Sport Psychology* (3rd ed.) (pp. 823-844). Hoboken, NJ: Wiley.

Gill, D.L. and Kamphoff, C.S. (2010). Gender and cultural diversity. In J.M. Williams (Eds.), *Applied sport psychology*, (6th ed.) (pp. 417-439). New York, NY: McGraw Hill.

Godin, G., and Shepherd, R.J. (1985). A simple method to assess exercise behavior in the community. *Canadian Journal of Applied Sport Sciences, 10,* 141-146.

Grove, J.R., Lavallee, D., and Gordon, S. (1997). Coping with retirement from sport: The influence of athletic identity. *Journal of Applied Sport Psychology, 9*(2), 191-203.

Haskell, W.L., Lee, I-M., Russell R., Pate, R.R., Powell, K.E., Blair, S.N., Franklin, B.A., Macera, C.A., Heath, G.W., Thompson, P.D., and Bauman, A. (2007). Physical activity and public health: updated recommendation for adults from the American College of Sports Medicine and the American Heart Association. *Medicine and Science in Sport and Exercise,39*(8), 1423-1434.

Healthy People 2020. (2010, Dec. 2). 2020 Healthy People Objectives: Physical Activity. Retrieved from http://healthypeople.gov/2020.

Houle, J.L.W., Brewer, B.W., and Kluck, A.S. (2010). Developmental trends in athletic identity: A two-part retrospective study. *Journal of Sport Behavior, 33*(2), 146-159.

Jacobs, D.R., Jr., Ainsworth, B.E., Hartman, T.J., and Leon, A.S. (1993). A simultaneous evaluation of 10 commonly used physical activity questionnaires. *Medicine and Science in Sport and Exercise, 25,* 81-91.

Kang, L., Gill, D.L., Acevedo, E.O. and Deeter, T.E. (1990). Competitive orientations among athletes and nonathletes in Taiwan. *International Journal of Sport Psychology, 21,* 146-157.

Koukouris, K. (1991). Quantitative aspects of the disengagement process of advanced and elite Greek male athletes from organized competitive sport. *Journal of Sport Behavior, 14*(4), 227-247.

Lally, P. (2007). Identity and athletic retirement: A prospective study. *Psychology of Sport and Exercise, 8,* 85-99.

Lally, P.S., and Kerr, G.A. (2005). The career planning, athletic identity, and student role identity of intercollegiate student-athletes. *Research Quarterly for Exercise and Sport, 76*(3), 275-285.

Lavallee, D., Gordon, S., and Grove, J.R. (1997). Retirement from sport and the loss of athletic identity. *Journal of Loss and Trauma, 2,* 129-147.

Marcus, B.M. and Forsyth, L.H. (2009). *Motivating people to be physically active.* (2nd ed). Champaign, IL: Human Kinetics.

Marcus, B.H., Selby, V.C., Niaura, R.S., and Rossi, J.S. (1992). Self-efficacy and the stages of exercise behavior change. *Research Quarterly for Exercise and Sport, 63*(1), 60-66.

Martin, J.J., Mushett, C., and Eklund, R. (1994).Factor structure of the Athletic Identity Measurement Scale with adolescent swimmers with disabilities. *Brazilian Journal of Adapted Physical Education Research, 1(1)*, 87-100.

Marsh, H.W. (1990). A multidimensional, hierarchical model of self-concept: Theoretical and empirical justification. *Educational Psychology Review, 2*(2), 77-172.

Messner, M.A. (1992). *Power at play: Sports and the problem of masculinity.* Boston: Beacon Press.

National Collegiate Athletic Association. (2010). *Guide for the college-bound student-athlete: Where academic and athletic success is your goal.* Retrieved from NCAA website: http://www.ncaastudent.org/NCAA_Guide.pdf

Sparling, P.B., and Snow, T.K. (2002). Physical activity patterns in recent college alumni. *Research Quarterly for Exercise and Sport, 73*(2), 200-205.

Stambulova, N., Alfermann, D., Statler, T., and Cote, J. (2009). ISSP position stand: Career development and transitions of athletes. *International Journal of Sport and Exercise Psychology, 7,* 395-412.

Stephan, Y., and Bilard, J. (2003). Repercussions of transition out of elite sport on body image. *Perceptual and Motor Skills , 96,* 95-104.

Taylor, J., and Ogilvie, B.C. (1994). A conceptual model of adaptation to retirement process among athletes. *Journal of Applied Sport Psychology, 6,* 1-20.

Theberge, N. (2007). It's not about health, it's about performance. In J. Hargreaves, and P. Vertinsky (Eds.), *Physical culture, power, and the body* (pp. 176-194). New York: Routledge.

Witkowski, S., and Spangenburg, E.E. (2008). Reduced physical activity and the retired athlete: a dangerous combination? *British Journal of Sports Medicine, 42*(12), 952-953.

Zielinski, J., Krol-Zielinska, M., and Kusy, K. (2006). Changes in physical activity of elite track and field athletes in selected age categories. *Studies in Physical Culture and Tourism, 13* (Supplement), 185-187.

Revision Submission Date: 11/30/2012

In: Innovative Writings in Sport and Exercise Psychology
Editor: Robert Schinke

ISBN: 978-1-62948-881-3
© 2014 Nova Science Publishers, Inc.

*Chapter 7*

# NETWORKING AS AN AMERICAN SPORT PSYCHOLOGY DOCTORAL STUDENT: CREATING AND MARKETING YOUR PERSONAL BRAND

## *Scott Barnicle[*] and Damon Burton*
Department of Movement Sciences
University of Idaho, ID, US

### ABSTRACT

The field of applied sport and performance psychology is booming. More graduate education programs are emerging, attracting increasing numbers of qualified students, and growing the exposure and knowledge base of the field (Quinn, 2011). Coupled with a strong theoretical and research foundation, applied sport psychology consulting experiences are vital to developing well-rounded professionals in the field (Balague, 2011). Guided by the three fundamentals of positive relationships, exchange relationships, and positive self-efficacy, Network Theory (Turnbull, Ford, and Cunningham, 1996) can provide graduate students with the opportunities and experiences in which to practice their applied sport psychology skills. Future applied sport psychology consultants will need to mesh their academic foundation with solid business, marketing, advertising, and branding skills and techniques to grow their personal consulting brand as well as the field of sport psychology. This article provides theory-driven practical applications of Network Theory for sport psychology students whose goal is to enhance their depth of knowledge through applied sport psychology consulting experiences.

---

[*] E-mail: sbarnicle@uidaho.edu.

# Introduction

The idea of starting a doctoral program can be daunting for even the most gifted and confident student. With a change in environment, culture, curriculum, and classes, it can be difficult to reach beyond the confines of the academic department and make new professional contacts. Part of learning to become an effective applied sport psychology consultant involves meeting as many people as possible, and broadening personal horizons to embrace every consulting development experience (Tod, 2007) while pursuing doctoral coursework and conducting research in sport and exercise psychology. Networking is often discussed as a concept and/or skill that consultants should develop (Prajapati & Biswas, 2011), but what are the real-world skills that doctoral students can utilize to gain greater access to applied consulting experiences with athletes and coaches while enhancing their marketability around campus and beyond? *Network theory* has been developed and promoted in the field of business (Turnbull et al., 1996) and marketing (Lusch and Brown, 1996), yet the field of sport psychology has yet to develop research-proven strategies to integrate Network Theory into training programs, which could potentially enhance consulting opportunities, particularly for graduate students. The skills and techniques detailed in this article are framed by Network Theory, promoting strategies to expand consulting opportunities in applied sport psychology settings.

# Network Theory Basics

Developed in the business world, Network Theory basics provide a framework for personal and professional interaction within business relationships (Turnbull et al., 1996). This idea has grown in use and is currently applied across fields outside of business (Lusch and Brown, 1996), including the growing trend of social networks, which may lack face-to-face interactions, yet contain their own set of social norms (Konetes and McKeague, 2011). Network Theory places emphasis on fundamentals of psychology such as personal constructs, self-efficacy, and positive self-image (Turnbull et al., 1996), with a key goal being personal and professional image consistency. Above all, Network Theory is about developing personal and professional relationships, with these relationships producing more business opportunities and subsequently more business capital. This mindset of relationships producing capital has been a mainstay of the business world, and conceptually could be adopted by plied sport psychology professionals who run their own knowledge-based business on a daily basis. With business at the core of creating an applied sport psychology consulting career, it seems natural to adopt ideas from the business world, with Network Theory being a readily available and easily transferable framework.

Network Theory shares constructs with classical social interaction theories, such as actor-Network Theory which examines social relationships from a scientific role perspective (Law, 1992) and social theory which examines interpersonal relationships from a sociological and philosophical viewpoint (Harrington, 2005). Network Theory uses similar ideas to explain social interaction in a modern business environment, consisting of three fundamental social-interaction attributes: positive relationships and interactions, exchange relationships, and self-efficacy in professional image and skills (Turnbull et al., 1996).

## POSITIVE RELATIONSHIPS AND INTERACTIONS

The importance of positive relationships and interactions is constant across settings, as shown in an organizational or corporate environment (Turnbull, 1996), and is a pillar of networking in all business environments. Interpersonal communication traits such as humility, professionalism, empathy, kindness and respect are important aspect of developing and maintaining positive relationships and interactions (Law, 1992). Networking skills can be optimized in proper settings, which need a basis of positivism and solidarity between the parties, developed in part from positive relationships and interactions with peers, client, or anyone who consultants may provide services to in the future.

### Exchange Relationships

Exchange relationships are at the heart of any business interaction (Homans, 1958) and are vital to Network Theory. Exchange relations are built on mutual cooperation, with the idea that give-and-take is the key to promoting effective mutually beneficial relationships (Homans, 1958). Applied sport psychology professionals provide a service which the client needs in exchange for compensation (typically), which is a basic example of an exchange relationship at its' core. However, other subtle client benefits include personal enjoyment and satisfaction with the relationship, word of mouth advertising to friends and colleagues and reputation enhancement. Given both parties share similar understanding of how the relationship operates within their defined roles, the desired outcome should be successful. The importance of understanding how business-networking relationships are structured and maintained is a vital component of Network Theory in applied settings. In an academic setting, a graduate student and faculty advisor may share an exchange relationship as the student may often contribute to the research project of the advisor, and in turn the advisor provides mentorship, advanced education, and professional role modeling. Exchange relationships are a part of daily life (Law, 1992), and although normal life interactions may not be defined as exchange relationships, the idea of give-and-take is common and easily understood.

### Consulting Self- Efficacy

Acting in a confident and professional manner has been shown to increase business success, marketability, professional reputation and self-efficacy (Lee and Wong, 2005), and ultimately networking and communication skills (Prajapati & Biswas, 2011). Professionals' belief in their abilities as well as their external impression to others is a key component of networking and gaining entry to mutually beneficial consulting relationships. Consultants' confidence to make contacts, develop networks, promote cooperative relationships, maintain partnerships and build a business with a solid foundation of positive exchange relationships is necessary to impart applied skills successfully (Tod, 2007, Tod, Marchant, and Anderson, 2007).

Outside of the American university setting, students have opportunities to establish a private consulting business that also generates numerous personal clients while gaining invaluable experiences and insight into what it takes to be a private consultant. By using the skills and strategies detailed in this article, graduate students can enhance the depth and breadth of their applied knowledge beyond the research and theory of the classroom, while getting their career as an applied sport psychology consultant off on the right foot. Although established sport psychology professionals have shared consulting experiences (Halliwell, 1989; Poczwardowski, Sherman, and Ravizza, 2004) and sport psychology students have shared their "novice" experiences (Andersen, Van Raalte, and Brewer, 2000; Stambulova and Johnson, 2010), this manuscript fosuces on personal insights into experiences and opportunities available beyond the classroom during a doctoral program.

## Branding: Developing Your Personal Brand

As students embark on new graduate program adventures and gain exposure to conceptual and empirical knowledge, it is beneficial to look for opportunities to apply this knowledge, identify how it could improve consulting opportunities and develop themselves as a "brand name" (Adams, 2011) for consulting excellence. Network Theory places emphasis on relationships and positive interactions (Turnbull et al., 1996) which can be implemented in many ways such as taking time to interact with a wide range of groups including: fans, athletic donors, and alumni. Listening to others rather than dominating the conversation, and being courteous and respectful are traits that are valued and allow one to thrive in a small college town (Mitchell, 2009). Consistent with the self-efficacy component of networking theory, outward displays of professionalism and respect are important, the old cliché is "look good, feel good", with first-impressions being vital. Emerging applied consultants may find it necessary to always be aware of their surroundings, the people and the places, adjusting their consulting approach to fit the person and situation while earning the most coveted of distinctions in consulting: a sterling reputation (Tod, Andersen, and Marchant, 2009).

### Marketing Your Personal Brand on Campus – A Personal Case Example

My decision to attend the University of Idaho was influenced by many factors, yet I was careful to explore the consulting opportunities I had available before I committed to any doctoral program. Ultimately, this research about applied consulting opportunities at Idaho set me apart from some of my peers looking at similar doctoral programs, and it allowed me to hit the ground running. Once I arrived on campus, I was excited to meet as many people as possible, prompting me to email coaches and local sports organizations informing them that I was looking for applied experience through mutually beneficial relationships.

Quintessential small college towns often pose an intimate atmosphere where it seems like everyone knows what's going on in the community (Mitchell, 2009), making it easy to market yourself quickly. For students who are charismatic and personable, this is a perfect built-in marketing environment. Network Theory defines this idea as interdependency and contracting (Lucas and Brown, 1996), yet it is a crucial element of learning about one's environment and gathering as much environmental information as possible. My advisor is well known in town, as well as around the country, and thus being his student was a way to get a foot in the door. However, it was my enthusiasm to gain as many applied consulting experiences as possible and build my personal brand that created opportunities for me.

## Your Brand May Be Stronger Off-Campus

With the goal of producing more applied consulting experiences and skills, every situation should be viewed as an opportunity. Network Theory emphasizes positive relationships and maintaining a professional image (Lee and Wong, 2005). When one identifies themselves as a sport psychology doctoral student, eyes widen and ears open. I once sat next to the editor of a golf publication on an airplane. By take-off, we were engaged in an intense conversation about the profession, and he soon became interested in publishing my research on stress and expectations in golf. Although during the conversation I was not thinking about the tenants of Network Theory, my knowledge of self-efficacy (Prajapati and Biswas, 2011) and projecting a positive self-image (Lee and Wong, 2005) was displayed naturally, eventually producing a new business relationship.

Networking requires being open to any opportunity (Adams, 2010). While playing a recreational round of golf with my father on vacation, I met a man who became a client. Events like these convinced me to take further steps to grow my personal brand in a more professional manner, including developing a well crafted and illustrative "elevator pitch" (Adams, 2010). This speech is vital when meeting potential clients, because it represents how you would sell yourself to someone in ten seconds in order to interest them in what you do. Emerging consultants must serve multiple roles, including publicist, marketer and brand manager (Tod et al., 2007). If a potential client or fellow professional is interested in learning about your applied consulting skills, being able to quickly and effectively describe yourself and your abilities is a must (Tod, 2007). It is through practice, as well as trial-and-error, that these elevator speeches become clear and concise.

One planning strategy students may find useful is the idea of devoting time to specific areas of specialty and interest. As an avid golfer and having worked in numerous roles in the golf industry, it was an easy choice. However, I had two backup sport foci: soccer and basketball, both sports in which I have extensive competitive experience. Although an established sport psychologist should be able to apply mental skills training to any sport or profession (Tod, 2007), I found it useful to specialize in sports for which I had extensive knowledge and high level playing experience. This focus allowed me to spend as much time with those three sports as possible, thus getting to know the coaches and their philosophy, the intricacies of Division 1 athletics, and most importantly, the individual needs of the athletes.

## Networking Strategies for Doctoral Students

One drawback of the business perspective of Network Theory is the constant professionalism required in the business world (Turnbull et al., 1996). Many students who pursue sport psychology consulting seem to enjoy sports and personal interaction, as well as informal and collegial settings. This strays from strict Network Theory, yet I have found professionals in the world of sport enjoy seeing personality and a sense of humor, thus

Network Theory's ideas of constant professionalism and maintaining a professional self-image can be adjusted for the setting.

## Take Risks

Sometimes risk-taking is an important part of the consulting success. I received a piece of great advice from my mother who told me, "What's the worst thing that can happen? If they say no, then you are right where you started. Nothing lost!" This mentality is perfect for a student looking for applied sport psychology experience. Coaches are always looking for volunteer assistants, and the only way to learn about these opportunities is to ask! Email, call, drop by their office. Whatever the means of communication, ask questions and be persistent. If someone says no, do not fret. Either offer your services whenever they need it, or explore a different path. Too often students may feel trapped by the classroom and a research-driven curriculum, when in reality coaches and administrators jump at the opportunity when a qualified and competent doctoral consultant comes knocking seeking to volunteer time to gain experience. Lastly, when entering new applied consulting venues, one must be confident and competent in their ability to help their client, as the only thing worse than not helping, is hurting.

## "Hanging Out" Approach to Networking

Athletes become comfortable with those in their team's inner circle (Drummond, Hostetter, Laguna, Gillentine, and Del Rossi, 2007), which is why it is vital for would-be consultants to simply be exposed to the sport with whom you would like to consult. Let's take the example of golf. During the first few weeks of school, a student could spend some time at the university's golf course, hitting balls on the range, trying to make connections with the athletes and coaches, volunteering my time when needed. This approach allows coaches and players to recognize a name, face, and become familiar with my personality. Most coaches embrace volunteer help, especially regarding sport psychology, and adopting a plan to work without pay for a couple months may allow a student to become entrenched in the athletic department. Not only will you gain a better understanding about the coaches and athletes, but the exposure and publicity will promote your abilities in a way classrooms alone cannot. If opportunities occur, maintaining the proper role of "consultant" is vital, as dual-relationships may develop which can be harmful to both parties.

## Embrace New Opportunities

Aside from being afraid to ask, the thought of exploring a new situation or sport may seem daunting to the inexperienced student consultant (Tod et al., 2009). The cliché of "diving in head first" may not apply to all situations, but it does when one wants to gain consulting experience. Being open to new situations and challenges is an extremely attractive trait to coaches and administrators. During the Fall semester of my second year, I was contacted by the head swimming and diving coach. He extended a potential opportunity to work with his athletes. Even though I had no experience or extensive knowledge of the sport, which I readily divulged upfront, I approached my initial meeting with this sport focusing on a saying I borrowed from my advisor: "I trust you will teach me all you can about the sport of swimming, and I hope you can trust me to teach you everything I know about sport psychology".

## Utilize Technology

As a product of "Generation Y," I cannot remember a time without the internet or cell phones. Like many of my generation, my skills with such technology were developed at a young age and seem second nature (Dobson, 2010). Unfortunately, many older professionals are not as adept with such technology, thus do not know how to use it advantageously in consulting. Many of my golf clients text me before and after every tournament, seeking a pre-round refresher or a debriefing on the completed round. Another amazing tool that is growing as a consulting medium is Skype, which has been shown to be an effective substitute for live sessions (Wright and Griffiths, 2010). My counseling psychology background taught me the adage that only 20 percent of communication is what is said and 80 percent is how it is said. Technology such as web cameras may not be a perfect substitute for live sessions, but programs such as Skype are tremendous tools for long-distance consulting. As a consultant, I have a Facebook page, a Twitter account, and a website, which act as marketing tools that allow prospective clients to learn more about my services, experience, and resume, as well as read testimonials from previous clients. These technological tools have been shown to improve social capital and exposure (Konetes and McKeague, 2011) as well as further connectivity and grow community consulting partnerships (Dawson, 2010). Without question, the publicity and exposure provided by these tools are vital for the growth of a student consultant. Technology is not without its concerns though, as confidentiality when using emerging technologies must be kept in mind. Maintaining appropriate consultant-client confidentialities must be at the forefront of any use of new technology, which may be a growing issue in the future.

## Highlight Strengths and Develop Collaborative Partnerships

One of my clients on the women's golf team is a senior advertising major who consistently reinforces the idea of "highlighting one's strengths." In the world of applied sport psychology, this basic advertising slogan holds true (Poczwardowski et al., 2004). From a purely superficial standpoint, it is always vital to look professional, prepared, and well-groomed, with shirt tucked in, pants ironed, and appropriate shoes. Professional dress depends on the setting (Adams, 2010). It may not be appropriate to wear a coat and tie when meeting a golfer on the driving range, just as jeans and a T-shirt may be inappropriate for an initial meeting with a coach. As a 20-something year old doctoral student, it is important to portray a sense of professionalism and knowledge, while at the same time being approachable for the collegiate and youth athlete. These mixed demands may be more difficult for a more experienced and older consultant, but it is certainly a trait I portray and highlight when meeting a new client.

## Utilize Existing Networks

Another old adage that I have found important in consulting is "It is not what you know but who you know." The importance of personal and professional relationships has been shown as a pillar of Network Theory (Harrington, 2005), with equal importance on developing and maintaining relationships. I was fortunate enough to attend Clemson University for my undergraduate degree and Boston College for my masters degree in counseling psychology, both well known national institutions with strong alumni networks. I have found these networks extremely helpful, even though many graduate students simply ignore them, or think they are designed for older alumni. Join the alumni network of your past institutions! These provide venues to meet potential employers, and offer a good learning experience for developing virtual networking skills such as email etiquette, developing professional email writing skills, facilitating opportunities online, and generally conducting oneself in a professional manner in the virtual environment. When a coach, administrator, or employer is provided with your resume or you are introducing yourself via email, it is important to highlight qualities which set you apart. If you attended a well respected university or well known program, don't be bashful, and make sure you highlight your quality education. It is your degree; you earned it the old fashioned way, so use it to your advantage.

## CONCLUSION

Utilizing Network Theory as a graduate-level sport psychology student can bring about opportunities outside of the traditional classroom walls. Supported by the evidence-based research literature, the personal examples detailed in this article are designed to shed light on opportunities which may not be commonly conceptualized by a graduate student, and also aid in highlighting other aspects of the graduate sport psychology experience for both student and faculty. The basis of most graduate students' network is the network of their advisor and program, and it is the aim of this article to give both student and faculty information to take into consideration.

## Student-Mentor Cohesiveness

Through an understanding an appreciation for the content of this article, faculty members may gain insight into the often unsaid wants and desires of an aspiring applied sport psychology student. Some graduate programs focus on research, while other may focus more heavily on teaching or applied consulting, yet one of the most important aspects of the program-search process should be the fit of student and mentor (or program). The personal example detailed in this article illustrates the potential long-term benefits and importance of a positive student-mentor fit, both personally, theoretically, and professionally. If the goal of a graduate program is to provide applied opportunities outside of the traditional classroom setting or curriculum, a faculty's appreciation of Network Theory and the importance of positive interpersonal exchange relationships could go a long way to ensuring a successful graduate experience for students and mentors.

## Supervision

One of the most important factors in choosing a graduate program should be the relationship between the student and their supervisor (Andersen et al., 2000). A supervisor will not only train and mentor an emerging consultant, but ensure the educational and consulting experiences are ethical and professional in nature. AASP and APA both maintain strict ethical guidelines, of which students may be naïve of in their early consulting experience, and it is the role of the supervisor to ensure proper support and growth in the consulting experiences of their students. Supervision is a great opportunity to reflect on consulting experiences, both positive and negative. Choosing the right fit may take time and effort, but will lead to a long-lasting and fulfilling relationship.

## Formula for Student Consulting Success

Self-awareness and confidence can be two of the most important skills a graduate student must have in order to grow their consulting experience (Tod, 2007). The quiet confidence portrayed when meeting a new coach or client is the product of all the skills I detailed above: highlighting playing and consulting experience, being proud of your educational background, awareness of your outward appearance, and acting in accordance with developing a strong personal brand – polite, professional, and personable. Sport and exercise psychology students can transform their consulting future by using these networking skills to grow their marketability, expose, and experience.

## REFERENCES

Adams, S. (2010). *How to craft a job search elevator pitch*. Retrieved from Forbes: http://www.forbes.com/2010/03/30/elevator-pitch-interview-leadership-careers-hiring.html

Andersen, M. B., Van Raalte, J. L., and Brewer, B. W. (2000). When sport psychology consultants and graduate students are impaired: Ethical and legal issues in training and supervision. *Journal of Applied Sport Psychology, 12,* 134–150.

Balague, G. (2011). *Exercise and Sport Psychology*. Retrieved from American Psychological Association: http://www.apadivisions.org/division-47/index.aspx

Dawson, S. (2010). 'Seeing' the learning community: An exploration of the development of a resource for monitoring online student networking. *British Journal of Educational Technology, 41,* 736-752.

Dobson, L. (2010). The net generation. *Therapy Today, 21,* 28-31.

Drummond, J.L., Hostetter, K., Laguna, P.L., Gillentine, A., and Del Rossi, G. (2007) Self-reported comfort of collegiate athletes with injury and condition care by same-sex and opposite-sex athletic trainers. *Journal of Athletic Training, 42,* 106-112.

Halliwell, W. (1989). Delivering sport psychology services to the Canadian sailing team at the 1988 Summer Olympic Games. *The Sport Psychologist, 3,* 313-319.

Harrington, A. (2005). *Modern social theory: An introduction.* Oxford, UK: Oxford University Press.

Homans, G. C. (1958). Social behavior as exchange. *American Journal of Sociology, 63* , 597-606.

Konetes, G., and McKeague, M. (2011). The effects of social networking sites on the acquisition of social capital among college students: A pilot study. *Global Media Journal: American Edition, 11*, 1-10.

Law, J. (1992). *Notes on the Theory of the Actor Network: Ordering, Strategy and Heterogeneity.* Retrieved 1 7, 2012, from Centre for Science Studies Lancaster University: http://www.lancs.ac.uk/fass/sociology/papers/law-notes-on-ant.pdf

Lee, L., and Wong, P.K. (2005) The role of self-efficacy, opportunity perception, social network, and fear of failure on nascent entrepreneurial propensities. Available at SSRN: http://ssrn.com/abstract=856225.

Lusch, R., and Brown, J. (1996) Interdependency, contracting and relational behavior in marketing channels, *Journal of Marketing, 60*, 19-38.

Mitchell, K. (2009) More than a college town. *BusinessWest*, 26, 10-49.

Stambulova, N., and Johnson, U. (2010). Novice consultants' experiences: Lessons learned by applied sport psychology students. *Psychology of Sport and Exercise, 11*, 295-303.

Prajapati, K., and Biswas, S. (2011). Effect of entrepreneur network and entrepreneur self-efficacy on subjective performance. *Journal of Entrepreneurship, 20*, 227-247

Poczwardowski, A., Sherman, C. P., and Ravizza, K. (2004). Professional philosophy in the sport psychology service delivery: Building on theory and practice. *The Sport Psychologist,18* , 443-463.

Quinn, E. (2011, 7 21). *Sports psychology degree programs - how to become a sports psychologist.* Retrieved 1 29, 2012, from sportsmedicine.com: http://sportsmedicine. about.com/od/sportspsychology/a/sportpsychedu.htm

Tod, D. (2007). The long and winding road: Professional development in sport psychology. *The Sport Psychologist, 21*, 94–108.

Tod, D., Andersen, M. B., and Marchant, D. (2009). A longitudinal examination of neophyte applied sport psychologists' development. *Journal of Applied Sport Psychology, 21*, S1-S16.

Tod, D., Marchant, D. B., and Andersen, M. B. (2007). Professional development in student sport psychologists. *Journal of Sports Sciences, 25*, 327–328.

Turnbull, P., Ford, D., and Cunningham, M. (1996), "Interaction, relationships and networks in business markets: An evolving perspective," *Journal of Business and Industrial Marketing, 11* (3/4), 44-62.

Wright, J., and Griffiths, F. (2010). Reflective practice at a distance: Using technology in counseling supervision. *Reflective Practice, 11*, 693-703.

In: Innovative Writings in Sport and Exercise Psychology
Editor: Robert Schinke

ISBN: 978-1-62948-881-3
© 2014 Nova Science Publishers, Inc.

*Chapter 8*

# COMMON FEATURES IN OVERTRAINED ATHLETES AND INDIVIDUALS WITH PROFESSIONAL BURNOUT: IMPLICATIONS FOR SPORTS MEDICAL PRACTICE

### *Harri Selänne[*1], Tatiana V. Ryba[2] and Juhani Leppäluoto[3]*

[1]LIKES Research Center, Jyväskylä, Finland
[2]Department of Public Health, Aarhus University, Denmark
[3]Department of Physiology, University of Oulu, Finland

### ABSTRACT

In this paper, the authors discuss the symptoms of overtraining and burnout— two syndromes in which the etiology, after the decades of research, is still poorly understood. Overtraining is caused by an imbalance between exercise and rest, and often triggered by increased neuromuscular loading. There are no reliable diagnostic tests for overtraining. The neurological mechanisms underpinning burnout are similarly not known; however, it is generally accepted that the main cause is mental overloading. Both conditions are stress-related developmental processes suggesting malfunction of adrenal cortex and hypothalamus, mainly the pituitary. The two syndromes are also related to a variety of individual, environmental, and organizational factors. Based on the first author's extensive practical experience of working with overtrained athletes and individuals with occupational burnout, the authors draw on both literatures to offer invaluable insights into a medical assessment and treatment of athletes suffering from overtraining.

**Keywords:** Overtraining, burnout, POMS, sports medicine

---

[*] Corresponding author: Harri Selänne, LIKES Research Center, Viitaniementie 15 a, Jyväskylä, 40720 Finland, Email: harri.selanne@likes.fi.

# INTRODUCTION

Overtraining is defined as an imbalance between exercise and rest, occurring when athletes are subjected to an intensive training load without adequate rest and recovery. In addition to the physical effects, the overtraining syndrome manifests in simultaneous negative changes in the athlete's psychosocial environment. According to Budgett (1998), the overtraining syndrome is "a condition of fatigue and underperformance, often associated with frequent infections and depression which occurs following hard training and competition" (p. 107). Hence repeated physical exercises stimulate the metabolism and improve physical performance; yet long-lasting exercises may result in overtraining, with decreased performance and disturbances in organ functions. Athletes suffering from overtraining typically display irritation, carelessness, sleep disturbance, and frequent infections.

Biochemical indices of overtraining include high plasma cortisol and low testosterone, low responses of ACTH, cortisol and growth hormone to the insulin stimulation test, low salivary immunoglobulin and also decreased heart rate variation. Overtraining has been observed to lead to increased secretion of inflammatory cytokines, which offer an explanation for the syndrome's symptoms: tiredness, vulnerability to infection, and changes in hormonal secretions and the autonomic nervous system.

Work-related burnout shares many common features with overtraining. The concept of professional burnout was introduced by Freudenberger (1974) to describe exhaustion experienced by workers, suggesting that the predominant cause of burnout was mental stress. The most often cited definition of the burnout syndrome states that it is a psychological syndrome developed "in response to chronic interpersonal stressors on the job. The three key dimensions of this response are an overwhelming exhaustion, feelings of cynicism and detachment from the job, and a sense of ineffectiveness and lack of accomplishment" (Maslach, Schaufeli, and Leiter, 2001, p. 399). While most authors agree that stress is the key factor in the development of burnout, a comprehensive theoretical framework is still lacking (Schaufeli and Buunk, 2003) and the etiology of burnout is poorly understood.

Athletes affected by burnout likewise experience tiredness, poor concentration, decreased confidence and self-esteem, and sleep disturbance. Questionnaires, such as rating of perceived exertion (RPE; Borg, 1975), the recovery-stress questionnaire for athletes (RESTQ-Sport; Kellmann and Kallus, 2001) and the profile of mood states (POMS) questionnaire (McNair, Lorr, and Droppelman, 1971/1992) have been used in the analyses of overtraining and burnout. Yet there is very little available information about the roles of hormones, cytokines, and the autonomic nervous system in the development of burnout.

# SYMPTOMS OF OVERTRAINING AND BURNOUT

Natural selection has led to strength and endurance as positive attributes in the evolution of *Homo sapiens*. However, in modern societies, these attributes relate primarily to sport and are no longer required in working life. Physical activity training improves an athlete's performance only to a certain extent. When the frequency and intensity of training exercises surpass this limit, the *condition of overtraining* will develop with long-lasting symptoms. Overtraining is preceded by an *overreaching condition*, which is a normal response to progressive overload. Overreaching is necessary for improved performance and the symptoms should cease within a few weeks of adequate rest. The development of both overtraining and burnout takes a long time, and recovery is likewise a lengthy process, often lasting several months. Diseases, such as infection and malnutrition, frequently hasten breaking out of the overtraining cycle. In addition to the impairment of an athlete's physical performance, other symptoms, such as carelessness, loss of appetite, and mood changes, are likely to occur. Though symptoms vary among individuals, sleep disturbances appear to be the most common (Kalimo and Toppinen, 1997; Winsley and Matos, 2011). Common symptoms of overtraining and burnout are summarized in Table 1.

**Table 1. Common Symptoms of Overtraining and Burnout**

| Overtraining | Burnout |
| --- | --- |
| Physical performance impairs | Working capacity impairs |
| Tiredness | Tiredness |
| Irritability | Irritability |
| Sleep disturbances | Sleep disturbances |
| Sensitivity to infections | Sick absences |
| Cardiovascular changes | Cardiovascular changes |
| Hormonal changes | Inconclusive |
| Activation of inflammations | Inconclusive |

Several studies have been done to reveal the etiology of overtraining, as well as to determine diagnostic methods (e.g., Green, Batada, Cole, Burnett, Kollias, McKay, et al., 2012; Xiao, Chen, and Dong, 2012). According to this research, the overtraining condition will develop fastest with an increase in volume of exercise (running distance or repetition of strength exercises), whereas an increase in intensity (running speed or load of strength exercises) has a noticeably smaller effect. For example, during a two-week training camp, featuring daily stepwise-increasing cycling tests, running of 40 minutes, and additional cycling of 60 minutes, an altered cardiovascular activity towards parasympathetic inhibition and sympathetic activation were observed (Baumert, 2006). In the absence of recovery, physical performance, oxygen uptake, and muscular strength will worsen. Exhaustion will follow from disturbances in muscle energy production and hormonal secretions. The final etiology of overtraining is not known, but physical exercise uncompensated for by adequate recovery markedly disturbs the hypothalamic neuroendocrine functions and the autonomic nervous system.

Work-related stress with symptoms of burnout is one of the most common occupational health problems. A European survey found that more than 60% of workers experience stress in their jobs for over 50% of the time (European Foundation for the Improvement of Living and Working Conditions, 1995/6). In Finland, approximately 7% of working population suffers from *severe* burnout (Kalimo and Toppinen, 1997), with main symptoms reported as tiredness, underestimation of working capacity, and weak self-confidence. Disruption of sleep is also common. Burnout is diagnosed largely through interviews and questionnaires. There is scant knowledge about the changes in organ function in individuals suffering from burnout. It is possible that work-related stress causes similar changes in the hypothalamic neuroendocrine system and autonomic nerves as does overtraining.

Athletic overtraining and professional burnout share several similar mental symptoms. In both situations, psychometric tests as diagnostic instruments are utilized. Heavy, excessive physical training is the major cause for overtraining, but has a minor role in the development of burnout. Whereas the continuation of heavy training is deleterious for overtraining athletes, light training may, on the contrary, prove beneficial for burnout individuals. At brain level, insensitivity of hypothalamic neuroendocrine neurons leading to suppression of stress hormones appears to be one diagnostic feature for overtraining symptoms, yet presently there exists no information about the role of hypothalamus in causing burnout. From a clinical point of view, comparisons between different psychometric tests used in the diagnosis of overtraining and burnout would be beneficial. In addition, measurements of blood concentrations of stress hormones would prove novel diagnostic tools in burnout subjects.

## OVERTRAINING AND HORMONAL CHANGES

A single bout of heavy physical exercise immediately stimulates large parts of the endocrine system. Hormonal secretions from the pituitary and adrenal gland cortex will increase during the exercise and last for several hours. Increased cortisol levels mobilize glucose and fatty acids to muscle as a source of energy. On the other hand, the secretion of testosterone, an anabolic hormone responsible for increasing muscle protein synthesis and innervation, decreases after physical exercise (Adlercreuz, Härkönen, and Kuoppasalmi, 1986). For these reasons, anabolic compounds were previously used to improve recovery and to prevent the overtraining condition. The ratio of testosterone to cortisol concentration has been used as a marker, with a decrease of this ratio by 30% (or to smaller than $35 \times 10^{-5}$) suggesting overtraining. Some studies have, however, shown that the testosterone/cortisol ratio does not always provide an accurate prediction (Fry, Kraemer, and van Borselen, 1994; MacKinnon, Hooper, Jones, Gordon, and Bachmann, 1997). For instance, a squatting press-up exercise completed regularly for two weeks decreased maximal muscle strength by 11%, indicating an overtraining condition, yet testosterone, cortisol, and growth hormone levels did not change (Fry, et al., 1994). The authors therefore argued that reliance on the testosterone/cortisol ration as a sign of overtraining is not recommended.

Few studies on severe overtraining exist. In a South African study, overtraining was diagnosed in four male runners training for a marathon (Barron, Noakes, and Levy, 1985). They were tired, careless, did not sleep well, and their training volumes were lowering. Basal hormone levels were unchanged, with the exception of high cortisol levels. The functions of their neuroendocrine systems were studied by an insulin stimulation test. Responses of growth hormone, prolactin, ACTH, and cortisol to insulin were clearly decreased (Barron, et al., 1985). Recovery for the athletes lasted several months. The authors of this study recommend rest and light exercise for the prevention of overtraining symptoms if an increase of cortisol in the insulin test to below 180 nmol/l is observed.

In another study, three months of heavy endurance exercises resulted in the overtraining syndrome, with high cortisol, low testosterone, and low semen count (Roberts, McClure, and Weiner, 1993). Intensified endurance concentration in female athletes was found to decrease maximal oxygen uptake by 6% and lead to low adrenaline, noradrenaline, and cortisol responses to exercise – all signs of overtraining (Uusitalo, Uusitalo, and Rusko, 1998). Several recent studies have also focused on the effects of long-term exercise periods on the pituitary-adrenal and pituitary-gonad axes. An Iranian study showed that high intensity treadmill running for 24 weeks led to decreases in basal and stimulated testosterone, FSH and LH levels, but increased levels of sex hormone binding globulin, SHBG (Safarinejad, Azma, and Kolahi, 2009). LHR (GnRH) was used for the stimulation of LH and FSH for testosterone. Semen quality also worsened, and the authors concluded that overtraining has a deleterious effect on reproduction. The suppressed reproductive hormones returned following 12 weeks of detraining, suggesting that the overtraining was not grave.

Overtraining is preceded by overreaching conditions, and it is difficult to make a differential diagnosis between these syndromes. Usually, overtraining is distinguished by its duration, lasting, for instance, 6-12 months. For the purpose of analyzing these differences, ten underperforming athletes were studied using a two-bout exercise protocol, and ACTH, growth hormone, prolactin, testosterone, and lactic acid were measured after both sessions (Meeusen, Nederhof, Buyse, Roelands, de Schutter, and Piacentini, 2010). The first maximal test was performed at 9:00-10:00, followed by another at 14:00-15:00 on the same day. The authors were able to show that athletes with overtraining syndrome had suppressed ACTH and prolactin responses to the *second* exercise bout, but those with overreaching condition maintained normal responses. It would appear that in the overtraining condition, hypothalamic CRH-neurons become insensitive to glucocorticoids and are no longer capable of stimulating ACTH.

In an interesting study conducted with young men entering compulsory military service in Finland, cortisol, testosterone, SHBG, and lactic acid were monitored during an eight-week basic military training period (Tanskanen, Kyröläinen, Uusitalo, Huovinen, Nissilä, Kinnunen, et al., 2011). After the training period, one-third of conscripts had the overreaching condition, implied by high basal cortisol and SHBG, an unchanged testosterone/cortisol ratio, and low lactic acid response. The authors conclude that the basic training period is physically too demanding and recovery-type training should be implemented to avoid the development of overtraining. They further present cortisol, testosterone, and lactic acid response measurements as potentially useful tools to monitor training.

Heavy physical exercises have been observed to result in transient or long-lasting amenorrhea (Warren, 1992). The phenomenon is common in high-level endurance sportswomen, with 10-40% of female athletes as sufferers. It thus appears that hypogonadotrophic hypogonadism follows heavy exercises, perhaps due to the insensitivity of hypothalamic neurons to LRH. Female swimmers and cyclists appear to have less amenorrhea than endurance athletes (Sanborn, Albrecht, and Wagner, 1987). Amenorrhea is not specific to physical exercise, as moving to a new school in another country or repeated intensive heat exposures can also be causes, especially in young women (Leppäluoto, Huttunen, and Hirvonen, 1986). Physical exercise amenorrhea is treated with estrogen, which additionally protects from osteoporosis and stress fractures.

## EXERCISE-INDUCED CARDIOVASCULAR RESPONSES

Heart rate has long been a measure for physical activity. New monitors can register the RR intervals and calculate heart rate variability from the intervals registered for several minutes (HRV). This is a noninvasive and effective method for studying the balance between sympathetic and parasympathetic tone. HRV changes have been traced both during and after physical exercises, and then related to the changes in physical performance or to the development of overtraining. Orthostatic heart rate responses have likewise been used for estimating the effects of training. Heart rate and HRV are measured in supine and standing positions – blood pressure can also be measured at this time. Findings which relate to overtraining are increased heart rate, slow recovery during standing, and smaller HRV. More specifically, an increase of 6% or higher in heart rate and a 25% decrease in HRV suggests overtraining (Uusitalo, Uusitalo, and Rusko, 2000). HRV responses should be tracked when athletes are relocating to distant training camps or going to competitions. Full-scale training can begin after HRV responses have returned to normal levels.

Endurance training increases high-frequency power domain in HRV recordings, which is known to reflect parasympathetic activity. Increases in that domain correlates positively to maximal oxygen uptake (Uusitalo, et al., 1998, 2000). Overtraining athletes had decreased HRV, meaning a shift from parasympathetic to sympathetic activity. In another study, in which HRV was studied in severely overtraining athletes during night sleep and after awakening, similar findings were obtained (Hynynen, Uusitalo, Konttinen, and Rusko, 2006). No changes in heart rate and HRV were found during sleep, but after waking, overtraining athletes exhibited variation in heart rate and the low-frequency domain in HRV was lower than in their healthy peers, indicating an increase of sympathetic tone and a parasympathetic withdrawal. However, HRV recordings show great inter-individual differences, problematizing their use in overtraining diagnoses. It is not known whether HRV recordings can be applied to evaluate work-related burnout conditions.

## PHYSICAL EXERCISE AND IMMUNE SYSTEM

Moderate levels of physical activity have been observed to decrease the occurrence of upper airway infections, but intensive activity appears to have the opposite effect, sensitizing top-level athletes in particular to infection (Nieman, Nehlen-Cannarella, and Henson, 1998; Nieman and Pedersen, 1999). Long-lasting heavy physical exercise impairs the response of the immune system (see Table 2): activity of white blood cells and lymphocytes is suppressed and cytokines may activate or inhibit inflammatory reactions. Furthermore, physical exercise induces the secretion on tumor necrosis factor alpha (TNF-α), interleukines 1b, 6, 10, and IL-1 receptor antagonist (Nieman, et al., 1998; Stensberg, van Hall, and Osada, 2000).

**Table 2. Heavy Physical Exercise-induced Immune System Response**

| Immune Reactions |
| --- |
| Increased neutrophil count, lymphopenia (cortisol effect) |
| Increased phagocytosis |
| Decreased oxidative activity in granulocytes |
| Decreased activity of natural killer cells and T-cells |
| Delayed skin hypersensitivity |
| Increased release of proinflammatory cytokines (TNF-α, IL-1, IL-6) |
| Increased release of anti-inflammatory cytokines (IL-1 receptor antagonist, soluble TNF receptors, IL-4) |
| Decrease of salivary immunoglobulin A |

Cytokines prove interesting in the development of overtraining. Interleukine 6 (IL-6) presents a dramatic, over-100-fold increase after marathon running (Ostrowski, Rohde, and Asp, 1999), yet moderate exercises (e.g., cycling for 60 minutes at 60% level of the maximal oxygen uptake) do not have any effect on plasma IL-6 levels (Smith, 2000). Heavy exercises do not always lead to inflammations, as the release of anti-inflammatory cytokines increases accordingly.

Cytokines are released through blood cells, but muscle and fat cells also produce them. Muscle cells contain IL-6 messenger RNA, which increases in response to training (Ostrowski, Rohde, and Zacho, 1998). IL-6 has pleiotropic effects, inducing the secretion of IGF-1, C-reactive protein, and glucose from the liver (Tsigos, Papanicolaou, Kyrou, Defensor, Mitsiadis, and Chrousos, 1997).

During heavy exercise, muscle glycogen stores diminish and increased IL-6 levels have compensatory effects, increasing glucose release from the liver. Cytokines also affect the central nervous system, potentially resulting in the tiredness, feeling sick, and negative mood states observed as symptoms of the overtraining condition.

Recently, studies have shown that physical exercise causes inflammatory damages in muscle cells and increases the release of pro-inflammatory cytokines from muscle and blood cells (Xiao, et al., 2012). At the same time, anti-inflammatory cytokines are released to limit the inflammation. Cytokines further affect the hypothalamus by stimulating the secretion of ACTH (Paulsen, Mikkelsen, Raastad, and Peake, 2012), which may relate to the activation of the general stress reaction in response to heavy physical exercise.

Besides inflammation and cytokine release, heavy exercises can cause muscle damage (myofibre ruptures). During a recovery phase, some muscle precursor cells called satellite cells accumulate in the damaged area and produce new fibers. Overtraining causes large muscle damages and the recovery may last for weeks. Anti-inflammatory steroids delay this exercise induced muscle recovery (Paulsen, et al., 2012).

## PREVENTION OF OVERTRAINING AND BURNOUT

Athletic overtraining denotes an imbalance between training and recovery, and it is evident that the best training responses are achieved at high intensity levels, bordering on those which lead to overtraining. Athletes' responses to training load, competition and life stressors are idiosyncratic and vary through the season; therefore, training must be individualized taking multiple factors into account. While individuals participating in physical exercise for recreation or for health purposes would benefit keeping track of workouts, training results, and diseases in a training diary, it is an absolute must for competing athletes. The diaries will monitor the training progress and alert to the possible development of overtraining.

There are several questionnaires which monitor an athlete's training level and can be used in the prevention of overtraining. The most familiar are rating of perceived exertion (RPE; Borg, 1975), profiling mood states (POMS; McNair, et al., 1971/1992), and the recovery-stress questionnaire for athletes (RESTQ-Sport; Kellmann and Kallus, 2001). The results of the questionnaires can be accompanied by body measures (e.g., weight), and heart rate monitoring is very useful when endurance level information is important. Training can be followed and adjusted according to the results of the monitoring. For detecting sleep disorders, a wrist activity monitor can be used. Since the occurrence of infections, anemia, and thyroid diseases are often associated with overtraining, medical check-ups are necessary. There is no simple test or method by which overtraining and its development can be diagnosed, but the combination of biochemical and physiological measurements to the results of questionnaires should provide sufficient information about the condition.

In Finland, a large-scale study of professional burnout was conducted by Kalimo and Toppinen (1997) revealing that work-related burnout was associated with long working hours, the uncertainty of employment, underestimation of own labor input and ageing. The authors developed a 16-item questionnaire to investigate an employee's experience, tiredness, and interest and motivation to work. The answers are then quantified and form an index, increases of which imply burnout. In this method, the questionnaire provides insight into an individual's mental state, and can be utilized for the prevention of the burnout condition.

## APPLYING RESEARCH IN PRACTICE: A CASE OF OVERTRAINING

As already discussed, it is very difficult to distinguish between overreaching and the overtraining syndrome. The first author of this paper has been working with several Finnish teams in their preparation for the Olympic Games. The POMS questionnaire proved to be useful in identifying athletes at a state of overreaching or overtraining, allowing for an intervention to prevent athletes' overreaching turning into the overtraining.

The standard POMS scale consists of 65 questions, which form scores for five negative and one positive item: tension-anxiety, depression-rejection, anger-hostility, fatigue-inertia, confusion-bewilderment, and vigor-activity. Successful performance in sport is usually associated with an "iceberg profile" (Figure 1), described by Morgan, Brown, Raglin, O'Connor, and Ellickson (1987) in their study of mood states observed in swimmers. In the "iceberg" profile assessed by POMS, vigor index is high while tension, depression, anger, fatigue, and confusion indices are low. Athletes suffering from overreaching or overtraining syndrome form an opposite POMS image.

The summary of the five negative POMS items minus vigor can be composed as TMS (total mood score), and the ratio of POMS vigor to POMS fatigue can be used as an energy index (Kenttä, 2006). POMS has been routinely used in our medical clinic to screen for burnout or overtraining syndrome, as well as during the follow-up on the healing process of these conditions. It can likewise be used in order to determine the state of health when performing health examinations for athletes or working people, and when observing the influence of a training program.

The POMS scale is well documented and easy to fill out, and the results can be attained instantly. It is useful both in observation of a single individual or of a group of people. Therefore, it can be applied to analyze the condition of an athlete or an employee, a team, working department, or even a whole company.

When the Finnish Olympic swimming team had a strenuous training weekend, we used POMS to observe the training effect and recovery. The scale was filled three times (i.e., three days before, during, and three days after the camp). The changes in the energy index of the team showed that both the training effect and the recovery were good, and hence further trainings could be planned according to this information (see Figure 2).

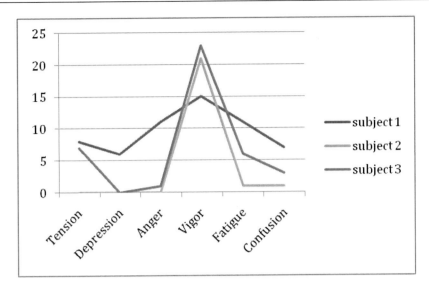

Figure 1. The "Iceberg Profile" of POMS Results in Three Healthy Athletes.

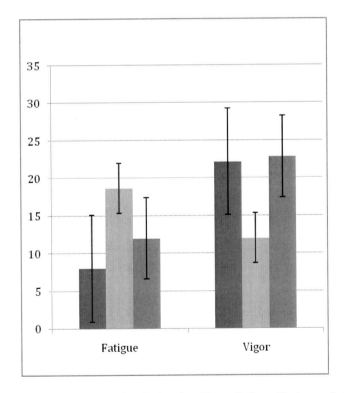

Figure 2. The Energy Index Changes of a Swimming Team Before, During and After a Strenuous Training Camp.

In another example, the Finnish Olympic judo team was abroad for a training camp when we received a phone call from the very concerned head coach and an e-mail from one of the athletes claiming "It's not working now". A preliminary review of the athlete revealed many symptoms associated with overtraining, such as exhaustion, muscle fatigue, and insomnia. No signs of infections were found.

Overtraining or overreaching was the possible diagnosis. To investigate further, a POMS questionnaire was sent by and replied to via e-mail. Total mood score and energy index were alarmingly abnormal. The athlete was advised to halt all training and competitions until further notice to allow full recovery. The questionnaire was filled in the beginning of the resting period and repeated monthly for follow-up. After four months of complete break, the total mood score (TMS) reflected the recovery (Figure 3). The athlete gradually returned to training and began to enter competitions, eventually qualifying for the London Olympics.

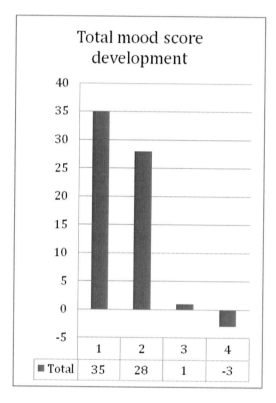

Figure 3. Total Mood Score Development of an Overtrained Athlete During Recovery. (Numbers 1-4 indicate months).

## CONCLUSION

Overtraining and burnout share many common symptoms, such as decreased performance, tiredness, sleep disturbance, carelessness, and sensitivity to infection. There is no single test for diagnosing professional burnout or overtraining syndrome. Burnout is assessed primarily through the use of questionnaires, but biochemical analyses might give important information about occupational stress and burnout mechanisms. In athletic overtraining, hypothalamic neuroendocrine functions are disturbed, sympathetic tonus is increased, and inflammatory factors possibly activated. It is not yet known how various factors (e.g., psychological, physiological, immunological) play a role in preventing athletes' recovery from training and competition. Considering the amount of factors shared between the two conditions, it is possible that even moderate exercise may worsen severe burnout.

In our experience, POMS is a practical tool when monitoring health condition, recovery, or the effects of training. The results are most valuable when observing the development of physical conditions of one person or a group of athletes over a period of time (having repeated measures of the POMS questionnaire) rather than drawing conclusions after a single visit. Clinical diagnoses of underperforming athletes remain to be based mainly on the athletes' medical history. In order to make the overtraining syndrome diagnosis, the physician needs to be able to rule out other underlying medical causes and to gather suitable results from questionnaires and physical tests.

## REFERENCES

Adlercreutz H., Härkönen M., and Kuoppasalmi K. (1986). Effect of training on plasma anabolic and catabolic steroid hormones and their response during physical exercise. *International Journal of Sports Medicine, 7*, Suppl 1, 27-8.

Barron, J. L., Noakes, T. D., and Levy, W. (1985) Hypothalamic dysfunction in overtrained athletes. *Journal of Clinical Endocrinology Metabolism, 60*, 803-806.

Baumert, M., Brechtel, L., Lock, J., Hermsdorf, M., Wolff, R., Baier, V., and Voss, A. (2006). Heart rate variability, blood pressure variability, and baroreflex sensitivity in overtrained athletes. *Clinical Journal of Sport Medicine, 16*, 412-417.

Borg G. (1975). Perceived exertion as an indicator of somatic stress. *Scandinavian Journal of Rehabilitative Medicine, 2*, 92-98.

Budgett, R. (1998). Fatigue and underperformance in athletes: the overtraining syndrome. *British Journal of Sports Medicine, 32*, 107-110.

European Foundation for the Improvement of Living and Working Conditions (1995/6). *Second European Survey on Working Conditions – Working Conditions in the European Union.* Luxemburg: Office for Official Publications of the European Communities.

Freudenberger, H. J. (1974). Staff burnout. *Journal of Social Sciences, 30*, 159-165.

Fry, A. C., Kraemer, W. J., and van Borselen. (1994). Performance decrements with high-intensity resistance overtraining. *Medicine and Science in Sports and Exercise, 26*, 1165-1173.

Green, H. J., Batada, A., Cole, B., Burnett, M. E., Kollias, H., McKay, S, et al. (2012). Muscle cellular properties in the ice hockey player: a model for investigating overtraining? *Canadian Journal of Physiology and Pharmacology, 90*, 567-578.

Hooper S. L., MacKinnon, L. T., Gordon, R. D., and Bachmann, A. W. (1993). Hormonal responses of elite swimmers to overtraining. *Medicine in Science of Sports and Exercise, 6*, 741-747.

Hynynen, E., Uusitalo, A., Konttinen, N., and Rusko, H. (2006). Heart rate variability during night sleep and after awakening in overtrained athletes. *Medicine and Science in Sports and Exercise, 38*, 313-317.

Kalimo, R., and Toppinen, S. (1997). Työuupumus Suomen työikäisellä väestöllä. Kirjassa: Työuupumus Suomen työikäisellä väestöllä. Työterveyslaitos, Helsinki, s. 1-63.

Kellman, M., and Kallus, K. W. (2001). *The recovery –stress questionnaire for athletes; user manual.* Champaign, IL, USA: Human Kinetics.

Kenttä, G., Hassmén, P., and Raglin, J. S. (2006). Mood state monitoring of training and recovery in elite kayakers. *European Journal of Sport Science, 6,* 245-253.

Kreher, J. B, and Schwartz, J. B. (2012). Overtraining syndrome: a practical guide. *Sports Health, 4,*128-138.

Leppäluoto, J., Huttunen, P., and Hirvonen, J. (1986). Endocrine effects of repeated sauna bathing. *Acta Physiologica Scandinavica, 128,* 467-470.

MacKinnon, L. T., Hooper, S. L., Jones, S., Gordon, R. D., and Bachmann, A. W. (1997). Hormonal, immunological and haematological responses to intensified training in elite swimmers. *Medicine and Science in Sports and Exercise, 29,* 1637-1645.

Maslach, C., Schaufeli, W. B., and Leiter, M. P. (2001). Job burnout. *Annual Review of Psychology, 52,* 397–422.

McNair, D., Lorr, M., and Droppelman, L. F. (1971/1992). *Profile of mood states manual.* San Diego: Educational and Industrial Testing Service.

Meeusen, R., Nederhof, E., Buyse, L., Roelands, B., de Schutter, G., and Piacentini, M. F. (2010). Diagnosing overtraining in athletes using the two-bout exercise protocol. *British Journal of Sports Medicine, 44,* 642-648.

Morgan, W. P., Brown, D. R., Raglin, J. S., O'Connor, P. J., and Ellickson, K. A. (1987). Psychological monitoring of overtraining and staleness. *British Journal of Sports Medicine, 21,* 107-114.

Nieman, D. C., and Pedersen, B. K. (1999). Exercise and immune function. Recent developments. *Sports Medicine, 27*(2), 73-80.

Nieman, D. C., Nehlen-Cannarella, S. L., and Henson, D. A. (1998). Immune response to exercise training and/or energy restriction in obese women. *Medicine and Science in Sports and Exercise, 30,* 679-686.

Ostrowski, K., Rohde, T., and Asp, S. (1999). Pro- and anti-inflammatory cytokine balance in strenuous exercise in humans. *Journal of Physiology, 515,* 287-291.

Ostrowski K., Rohde, T., and Zacho, M. (1998). Evidence that interleukin-6 is produced in human skeletal muscle during prolonged running. *Journal of Physiology, 508,* 949-953.

Paulsen, G., Mikkelsen, U.R., Raastad, T., and Peake, J.M. (2012). Leucocytes, cytokines and satellite cells: what role do they play in muscle damage and regeneration following eccentric exercise? *Exercise Immunology Review, 18,* 42-97.

Roberts, A. C., McClure, R. D., and Weiner, R. I. (1993). Overtraining affects male reproductive status. *Fertility and Sterility, 60,* 686-692.

Safarinejad M. R., Azma K., and Kolahi A. A. (2009). The effects of intensive, long-term treadmill running on reproductive hormones, hypothalamus-pituitary-testis axis, and semen quality: a randomized controlled study. *Journal of Endocrinology, 200,* 259-271.

Sanborn C. F., Albrecht, B. H., and Wagner, W. W. (1987). Athletic amenorrhea: lack of association with body fat. *Medicine and Science in Sports and Exercise, 19,* 207-211.

Schaufeli, W. B. and Buunk, B. P. (2003). Burnout: an overview of 25 years of research and theorizing. In M. J. Schabracq, Winnubst, J. A., and Cooper, C. L. (Eds.). *Handbook of work and health psychology* (pp. 383 – 425). Chichester: Wiley.

Smith, L. L. (2000). Cytokine hypothesis of overtraining: a physiological adaptation to excessive stress? *Medicine and Science in Sports and Exercise, 32,* 317-331.

Stensberg, A., van Hall, G., and Osada T. (2000). Production of interleukin-6 in contracting human skeletal muscles can account for the exercise-induced increase in plasma interleukin-6. *Journal of Physiology, 529,* 237-242.

Tanskanen, M. M., Kyröläinen, H., Uusitalo, A. L., Huovinen, J., Nissilä, J., Kinnunen, H,. et al. (2011). Serun sex hormone-binding globulin and cortisol concentrations are associated with overreaching during strenuous military training. *Journal of Strength and Conditioning Research, 25*, 787-797.

Tsigos C., Papanicolaou, D. A., Kyrou, I., Defensor, R., Mitsiadis, C. S., Chrousos, G. P. (1997). Dose-dependent effects of recombinant human interleukin-6 on glucose regulation. *Journal of Clinical Endocrinology and Metabolism, 82*, 4167-4170.

Uusitalo A. L., Uusitalo A. J., and Rusko, H. K. (1998). Exhaustive endurance training for 6-9 weeks did not induce changes in intrinsic heart rate and cardiac autonomic modulation in female athletes. *International Journal of Sports Medicine, 19*, 532-540.

Uusitalo A. L., Uusitalo A. J., and Rusko, H. K. (2000). Heart rate and blood pressure variability during heavy training and overtraining in the female athlete. *International Journal of Sports Medicine, 21*, 45-53.

Warren M. P. (1992). Clinical review 40. Amenorrhea in endurance runners. *Journal of Clinical Endocrinology and Metabolism, 75*, 1393-1397.

Winsley R., and Matos N. (2011). Overtraining and elite young athletes. *Medicine in Sport Science, 56*, 97-105.

Xiao W., Chen P., and Dong J. (2012). Effects of overtraining on skeletal muscle growth and gene expression. *International Journal of Sports Medicine, 33*, 846-853.

In: Innovative Writings in Sport and Exercise Psychology
Editor: Robert Schinke

ISBN: 978-1-62948-881-3
© 2014 Nova Science Publishers, Inc.

*Chapter 9*

# FANS' IDENTIFICATION AND COMMITMENT TO A SPORT TEAM: THE IMPACT OF SELF-SELECTION VERSUS SOCIALIZATION PROCESSES

## *Katrina Koch[*] and Daniel L. Wann*
Murray State University, Murray, KY, US

### ABSTRACT

Team fandom origin, self-selected or socialized, should play an important role in one's level of team identification with and commitment to a favorite team. It was hypothesized that fans who self-selected their favorite team would report higher levels of team identification on three dimensions of team commitment: personal identity, affective commitment, and calculative commitment. Fans who were socialized to prefer a team were expected to report higher levels of two dimensions of team commitment: social obligation and regional tribalism. Participants completed the Sport Spectator Identification Scale, the Scale of Commitment to Sport Teams, and assessments of team fandom origin. It was found that socialized fans reported higher levels of social obligation and regional tribalism to their teams than self-selected fans. Additional findings include: Male fans reported higher levels of team identification, personal identity, affective commitment, calculative commitment, and social obligation than female fans; older fans reported more self-selection than younger fans; and female fans reported more socialization than male fans.

### INTRODUCTION

Spectator sports are important recreational, entertainment, and social outlets for people, and specific teams can become important elements of a person's self-concept (Wann, Royalty, and Roberts, 2000). Considering the basic sports of football, men's and women's

---

[*] Portions of this research were presented at the Annual Sport Psychology Forum, Bowling Green, KY (February, 2011). Address correspondence to Daniel L. Wann, Department of Psychology, Murray State University, Murray, KY 42071 (270-809-2860) or to dwann@murraystate.edu via Internet.

basketball, baseball, soccer, and hockey, there are approximately 150 professional sport teams in the United States. College sports offer even more options, with well over 200 football teams and more than 300 men's and women's basketball teams at the Division I level alone. Although there seems to be no end to the possibilities, sport fans are able to discern favorites from among the various teams. They may make their own choice of which team to support, or they may be socialized to support the favorite team of family members or peers. Once fans have determined which teams they will support, they identify at various levels with the teams, sometimes mildly and sometimes intensely (Wann and Branscombe, 1993). Research has yet to investigate fans who choose their favorite team or the impact of that choice on team identification and team commitment. This research is important to investigating the underlying differences between choice and socialization on how fans identify with and commit to their teams. Knowing how people become fans and how fan origin influences their fandom has many implications for sport marketing, including recruiting new fans and team memorabilia consumption. This study examined the impact of choice on level of team identification and team commitment. Specifically, the focus was on variations in levels of sport team identification and sport team commitment between people who self-selected their favorite team versus those who were socialized to prefer a particular team.

## Sport Team Identification

Sport team identification is defined as "the extent to which a fan feels a psychological connection to a team and the team's performances are viewed as self-relevant" (Wann, 2006, pp. 3-4). Team identification influences many different responses. The categorization of the self into a group makes the group affiliation a central component of the individual, therefore, the reactions of highly identified fans to team-relevant events can be more intense than those who are not as highly identified (Wann, 2006; Wann et al., 2000). For example, affective responses are different for highly identified fans than for individuals with low levels of team identity. While fans typically experience happiness for a supported team's win and unhappiness at a loss, these emotions are much more intense for highly identified fans, who are happiest when a favorite team trounces a despised rival (Mahony and Moorman, 2000; Wann, Dolan, McGeorge, and Allison, 1994). Behavioral responses, such as consumption and aggression, also differ according to an individual's level of identification with a team. Consumption can be separated into game consumption, team-related consumption, and sponsorship. The most powerful influence on game consumption is identification level, as highly identified fans are more likely to attend games and follow them indirectly (Fisher, 1998; Wann, 2006). Similarly, the highest levels of fan aggression are typically exhibited by persons with high levels of team identification (Wann, 2006).

## Measuring Team Identification and Team Commitment

The ability to precisely measure team identification is paramount to its investigation. To aid in the assessment of this construct, Wann and Branscombe (1993) created the Sport Spectator Identification Scale (SSIS). The seven-item scale, which has been translated into many languages, has strong reliability and validity (Wann, 2006; Wann and Pierce, 2003; Wann, Melnick, Russell, and Pease, 2001).

Researchers have argued that commitment and identification are made up of several components (Allen and Meyer, 1990; Becker, Billings, Eveleth, and Gilbert, 1996; Mathieu and Zajac, 1990; O'Reilly and Chatman, 1986). Tajfel (1982) claimed that both cognitive and evaluative dimensions are necessary to social identity. Others claim an emotional dimension is also needed to fully explore social identity (Ellemers, Kortekaas, and Ouwerkerk, 1999; Stets and Burke, 2000). Not surprisingly, research on commitment has made similar arguments for numerous components. Allen and Meyer (1990) created a measure exploring affective, continuance, and normative components of organizational commitment. They described the affective component as "the emotional attachment to, identification with, and involvement in, the organization" (p. 1). They described the continuance component as the "commitment based on the costs . . . [associated] with leaving the organization," while the normative component was defined as "feelings of obligation to remain with the organization" (p. 1). They found that the affective and normative components of commitment seem to be related but are still empirically discernible, while affective and continuance components are discernible from one another (Allen and Meyer, 1990). O'Reilly and Chatman (1986) found support for internalization and identification as components of psychological commitment, and the authors suspect that compliance may also be important.

Based on the aforementioned literature on the multidimensional nature of identification and commitment, Matsuoka (2001; Matsuoka and Chelladurai, 2005) developed the multidimensional Scale of Commitment to Sport Teams (SCST). The SCST assesses five different components of team commitment: personal identity, affective commitment, calculative commitment, social obligation, and regional tribalism. Personal identity is described as the way that "fans . . . are psychologically committed to a sport team that helps them to express, maintain, and support their self-concepts and sense of personal identity" (p. 10). For example, the White Sox are known as Chicago's blue-collar team, and a fan might feel more committed to the team if she saw herself as blue-collar as well. The identity of the team lines up with the personal identity of the fan, and helps to maintain the sense of self. Laverie and Arnett (2000) found that as a team became a part of a fan's self-concept, the attachment to the team also increased. Affective commitment is defined as the "emotional attachment based on the fan's liking for the team and the desire to associate with the team" (p. 16). For example, fans who like the team will be more affectively committed to the team.

The third dimension is calculative commitment and depends on the cost, which can be monetary, temporal, energetic, and/or psychological, of leaving the team (Matsuoka, 2001; Matsuoka and Chelladurai, 2005). This is similar to the continuance commitment described by Allen and Meyer (1990) which is based on "magnitude and/or number of investments" as well as the "perceived lack of alternatives" (p. 4). For example, an Oakland Raiders fan with a closet full of team jerseys, a full stock of black and silver body paint, and thousands of dollars spent on travel and game tickets has a large investment in his/her fandom of the team. A change to support the San Francisco 49ers would mean taking quite a financial loss.

Social obligation is the fourth dimension assessed by the SCST. Like normative commitment described by Allen and Meyer (1990), this dimension refers to commitment to a team based on the social pressure felt by fans, that is, the extent to which fans feel that they ought to remain affiliated. Research suggests that social obligation can be influenced by friends and family through the inherent persuasive power of socialization (Allen and Meyer,

1990; James, 2001; Matsuoka, 2001; Wann, Tucker, and Schrader, 1996). For example, a fan whose commitment is influenced by pressure from friends, family, and peers feels social obligation to maintain the fandom to his favorite team.

Regional tribalism is a final dimension of commitment. Proximity can increase identification in a sport fan through media coverage and socialization with nearby fellow fans (Wann, 2006). Matsuoka's (2001; Matsuoka and Chelladurai, 2005) regional tribalism is thought to be a dimension of commitment due to pride and feeling a connection to a particular place. Fans who live in Boston might find they are committed to the Red Sox because they are attached to Boston itself, and the team has such a connection to the city.

## Self-Selection of Groups

Ellemers and colleagues (1999) looked at three components of social identity: a cognitive component, an evaluative component, and an emotional component. The purpose of their investigation was to empirically study the relationships among the components of social identity and different characteristics of groups, including group formation. With respect to the group formation variable, participants were either told they were in one particular group (assigned group formation) due to their problem-solving style, or allowed to choose the group (self-selected group formation) that they thought best fit their problem-solving style. The results found one significant interaction for group self-esteem, the evaluative component of social identity. Members who self-selected their memberships to low-status majority groups had lower self-esteem. Affective commitment, the emotional component of social identity, was lowest for individuals who were assigned to majority groups, while membership in high-status groups led to higher levels of affective commitment. Most importantly to this investigation, self-selection of group membership led to higher levels of affective commitment than did assigned group membership (Ellemers et al., 1999). Self-selecting group members also were found to have higher levels of affective commitment by showing ingroup favoritism for the group they chose.

## Hypotheses

The current study investigated possible differences between levels of team identification and team commitment between fans who self-selected a favorite team and fans who were socialized to follow a team. Self-selection of team fandom was operationally defined as fans who reported that they actively chose to follow their favorite team, or that they were not actively encouraged by others to follow their favorite team. Socialization was operationally defined as fans who reported that they were actively encouraged by others to follow their favorite team.

The current investigation tested one research question and six hypotheses. The research question examined the topic of age and gender as they relate to team fandom origin. The fandom literature indicates that both of these variables may be related to fan behaviors (Wann et al., 2001). For instance, males often report higher levels of fandom than females (Bahk, 2000; Wann, 2002) and male and female fans often report different patterns of behaviors and reasons for becoming a fan (Dietz-Uhler, Harrick, End, and Jacquemotte, 2000). Age also can play a role in fandom with age showing a positive correlation with fandom (Lee and Zeiss, 1980; Murrell and Dietz, 1992). However, the interrelation among age, gender, and fandom origin had not been examined. Thus, specific hypotheses were not warranted. Therefore, we investigated these relationships within the framework of a research question asking, "In what way do age and gender impact with origin of fandom?"

The first hypothesis dealt with the Sport Spectator Identification Scale (SSIS) (Wann and Branscombe, 1993). It was predicted that team identification would be higher in fans who self-selected their favorite team than in people who were socialized to follow their favorite team. Actively choosing the team to support (rather than being encouraged by others to follow a team) would likely result in the role of team follower becoming a more central component of the individual's identity. This hypothesis was derived from the findings that affective commitment is higher in group members who self-select their groups than in members who are assigned to a group (Ellemers et al., 1999). Although socialization is not assignment, it seemed likely that there will be similar outcomes when opposing self-selection of group membership.

Hypotheses 2 through 6 dealt with the five dimensions of commitment (personal identity, affective commitment, calculative commitment, social obligation, and regional tribalism) included in the Scale of Commitment to Sport Teams (SCST) (Matsuoka, 2001; Matsuoka and Chelladurai, 2005). The second hypothesis stated that personal identity would be higher in fans who self-selected their favorite team. It was reasonable to expect that individuals would make choices that were more relevant and important to them than would socializing agents. They were essentially choosing their own identities, rather than being molded into a persona.

The third and fourth hypotheses stated that affective commitment and calculative commitment, respectively, would be higher in fans who had self-selected their favorite team. Fans should be more attached to and involved in their chosen groups than socialized fans (Ellemers et al., 1999; Wann and Branscombe, 1993). Also, fans who chose their favorite team should be willing to spend more time, money, and energy on endeavors that they have chosen (Wann and Branscombe, 1993). Likewise, according to Matsuoka (2001) these fans should be less willing to pay the costs of deserting their team fandom.

Hypothesis 5 stated that the social obligation dimension of team commitment would be higher in fans who were socialized to prefer their favorite team. Social obligation and socialization both require influence from others, and should therefore go hand in hand. Normative commitment occurs when individuals remain a part of an organization because they feel as if they ought to (Allen and Meyer, 1990). Normative commitment could begin with one's socializing agents (Matsuoka, 2001). James (2001) asserts that the influence of socializing agents continues throughout life. The socializing agents that influenced individuals to become a fan of a team, as well as the members of an ingroup, were also likely to influence them to remain a fan. Meanwhile, those who self-selected their favorite team would not feel the same social pressures to maintain their fandom.

Sixth, it was expected that higher levels of the regional tribalism dimension of team commitment would be found in the socialized fans. Matsuoka (2001) mentions that people take pride in and feel loyalty for the places they grow up and live. These places are filled with the socializing agents of the individual's life (e.g., their family, friends, and others in the community). Proximity to the socializing influence was expected to increase the connection to and pride that an individual feels for the geographical area.

# METHOD

## Participants

The original sample contained 500 persons. These participants were either university students (who received extra credit for participation) or attendees at a university basketball game. Twenty questionnaire packets were discarded for being incomplete, leaving 480 participants. Because this investigation was focused on fans of a sport team, those persons who did not report a favorite team ($n = 126$) were dropped from the sample. This resulted in a final sample of $n = 356$. Of these participants, 140 were male and 216 were female. Their ages ranged from 18 years old to 86 years old, with a mean age of 24.92 ($SD = 11.05$). The favorite teams named by participants covered a variety of sports at all levels from scholastic to professional. A full list can be obtained from the corresponding author.

## Materials and Procedure

Participants were given a cover letter instructing them that their participation was voluntary and they could terminate their participation at any time without penalty. Participants then received a five-page questionnaire packet containing four questionnaires. The first questionnaire consisted of two demographic items (age and gender), and one contingency question that assessed whether the participants had a favorite team. A positive response to the third item necessitated the completion of the packet. A negative response to the third question terminated the session for those participants, and a written statement informed them that they were finished and free to leave.

The second questionnaire included an item designed to ascertain the fan's favorite team, and the Sport Spectator Identification Scale (SSIS), which targeted the favorite team. The SSIS is made up of seven Likert-scale items with response options varying from 1 to 8; a lower score indicates low identification and a higher score indicates high identification. The scale is both reliable and valid and has strong internal consistency, with a Cronbach's alpha of .91 (Wann and Branscombe, 1993).

The third questionnaire was the Scale of Commitment to Sport Teams (SCST), also targeting the fan's favorite team. The SCST is composed of 15 Likert-scale items with response options ranging from 1 (*Strongly Disagree*) to 7 (*Strongly Agree*), with 3 items for each of the 5 subscales. A higher score on each dimension indicated a higher level of that dimension of team commitment. The subscales of SCST are each reliable, with Cronbach's alphas of .79 for Personal Identity, .85 for Affective Commitment, .86 for Calculative Commitment, .74 for Social Obligation, and .95 for Regional Tribalism (Matsuoka, 2001). The questionnaires were counterbalanced for the SSIS and the SCST. The counterbalanced questionnaires were randomly assigned to the participants.

The fifth, and final, page of the questionnaire contained two questions that assessed team fandom origin (i.e., socialized or self-selected). The first question was dichotomous and asked the participants to circle the statement that best described their team fandom origin. The question read, "Some fans of sport teams began to follow the team because they were encouraged to do so by other people, such as their parents, siblings, and/or friends. Other fans followed a team because of their own choice, generally without the encouragement from others. Which of these possibilities best describes you?" Circling the response "I began to follow the team listed previously predominately because I was actively encouraged to do so by others (such as my parents, siblings, and/or friends)" placed the participants in the socialized group. Circling the other response, "I began to follow the team listed previously predominately because I chose to, without the encouragement of others (such as my parents, siblings, and/or friends)" placed them in the self-selection group. The second question asked, "What percentage of your fandom for the team listed above is due to the fact that your parents, siblings, and/or friends actively encouraged you to follow the team?" Participants were asked to indicate a response ranging from 0% to 100%.

After completing the questionnaire packet, the participants received a debriefing statement, which explained the purpose of the study. This form also provided contact information should the participant wish to obtain a copy of the results. The entire session lasted approximately 15 minutes.

## RESULTS

Items contained in each scale and subscale were summed to establish scale scores for each measure. Means, standard deviations, and Cronbach's reliability alphas for each scale and subscale are listed in Table 1. The means found in the current research were, for the most part, remarkably similar to those reported by Matsuoka and Chelladurai (2005). In fact, the mean scores found in the current data set were within one point of the means reported by Matsuoka and Chelladurai, with the lone exception being scores on the regional tribalism subscale in which the previously reported mean (15.06) was somewhat higher than the current mean of 11.10. Means on the SSIS are also consistent with past work (e.g., Grieve et al., 2009; Wann and Martin, 2008). The scores reported here are generally consistent with moderate to high levels of commitment and team identification (Matsuoka and Chelladurai, 2005; Wann et al., 2001).

**Table 1. Means, Standard Deviations, and Cronbach's Reliability Alphas for the Sport Spectator Identification Scale and the Five Subscales of the Scale of Commitment to Sport Teams**

|  | M | SD | alpha |
|---|---|---|---|
| SSIS | 39.60 | 10.97 | .92 |
| SCST-Personal Identity (PI) | 10.36 | 4.78 | .87 |
| SCST-Affective Comm. (AC) | 14.82 | 4.78 | .90 |
| SCST-Calculative Comm. (CC) | 9.40 | 5.06 | .88 |
| SCST-Social Obligation (SO) | 9.37 | 4.92 | .78 |
| SCST-Regional Tribalism (RT) | 11.10 | 6.81 | .93 |

*Note.* The response range for the SSIS is from 7 to 56. The response range for each subscale of the SCST is from 3 to 21.

Correlations among the scales and subscales are shown in Table 2. The counterbalancing of the SSIS and SCST was examined via a multivariate analysis of variance (MANOVA) with order as the independent variable and identification and commitment scale scores (i.e.,

SSIS and total SCST) as the dependent variables. A significant order effect was found, $F(2, 353) = 20.44$, $p = .001$. Respondents reported higher levels of identification/commitment for the first scale in the packet. However, because there were no significant interaction effects involving order of the questionnaires, subsequent analyses were collapsed across this variable.

**Table 2. Correlations Among the Sport Spectator Identification Scale and the Five Subscales of the Scale of Commitment to Sport Teams**

|           | 1       | 2       | 3       | 4       | 5       | 6     |
|-----------|---------|---------|---------|---------|---------|-------|
| SSIS (1)  | -----   |         |         |         |         |       |
| SCST-PI (2) | .641** | -----   |         |         |         |       |
| SCST-AC (3) | .785** | .660** | -----   |         |         |       |
| SCST-CC (4) | .547** | .658** | .544** | -----   |         |       |
| SCST-SO (5) | .461** | .641** | .478** | .731** | -----   |       |
| SCST-RT (6) | .195** | .264** | .217** | .206** | .232** | ----- |

*Note.* ** $p < .01$

On the dichotomous item, socialized fans were coded as a 1 while self-selected fans were coded as a 2. A point-biserial correlation was used to examine the relationship between the dichotomous and percentage fandom origin assessments before the tripartite split of the percentage assessment. They were significantly and negatively correlated, $r(354) = -.73$, $p = .001$. Thus, most fans who reported being self-selected on one assessment also indicated being self-selected on the other assessment; while most fans who indicated being socialized on one assessment also indicated being socialized on the other assessment.

A tripartite split was used on the percentage assessment of team fandom origin to categorize participants into the self-selected and socialized groups. One-third of participants reported that socializing agents influenced 0% to 20% of their team fandom, and thus were included in the self-selected group ($n = 120$, $M = 6.02$, $SD = 7.60$). One-third of participants reported that socializing agents influenced 70% to 100% of their team fandom, and thus were included in the socialized group ($n = 128$, $M = 85.47$, $SD = 10.36$). The remaining participants were dropped from the analyses ($n = 108$).

On the percentage item, self-selected fans were coded as a 1, while socialized fans were coded as a 2. Thus, a higher score on the first assessment (the dichotomous item), and a lower score on the second assessment (the percentage item) indicated self-selection of favorite team. Meanwhile, a lower score on the first assessment, and a higher score on the second assessment, indicated that the fan was socialized into the fandom of their favorite team.

Although the fandom origin assessments were correlated (see above), some participants did not answer consistently. An examination of the data revealed that eleven participants indicated they chose their favorite team on the dichotomous item but indicated they were socialized on the percentage item. Ten participants indicated that they were socialized on the dichotomous assessment and yet indicated they chose their favorite team on the percentage item. Consequently, these 21 inconsistent participants were dropped from the analyses.

A 2 (Gender: male or female) x 2 (Team Fandom Origin: self-selected or socialized) MANOVA with 6 dependent variables (SSIS, SCST-personal identity, SCST-affective commitment, SCST-calculative commitment, SCST-social obligation, and SCST-regional tribalism) was used to test the hypothesized pattern of effects. Follow up tests were conducted using a 2 x 2 ANOVA on each dependent variable. A gender multivariate main effect was found, $F(6, 218) = 4.98$, $p < .001$. Follow up univariate analyses found that male fans had significantly higher levels of team identification, personal identity, affective commitment, calculative commitment, and social obligation than did female fans (see Table 3).

**Table 3. Means, Standard Deviations, and F Scores of the Univariate Analysis of Gender for the Supplemental Analyses**

|  | Males | | Females | | | |
|  | *M* | *SD* | *M* | *SD* | *F* | *p* |
|---|---|---|---|---|---|---|
| SSIS | 42.69 | 10.51 | 37.23 | 10.91 | 13.27 | .001 |
| SCST-PI | 10.77 | 4.85 | 9.49 | 4.47 | 4.72 | .031 |
| SCST-AC | 16.11 | 4.71 | 13.65 | 4.96 | 13.22 | .001 |
| SCST-CC | 10.14 | 5.39 | 8.40 | 4.82 | 7.63 | .006 |
| SCST-SO | 10.47 | 5.26 | 7.92 | 4.49 | 20.25 | .001 |
| SCST-RT | 11.18 | 7.08 | 10.95 | 7.01 | 0.45 | .502 |

*Note.* The response range for the SSIS is from 7 to 56. The response range for each subscale of the SCST is from 3 to 21.

A team fandom origin multivariate main effect was also found, $F(6, 218) = 3.98$, $p < .001$. Follow up univariate analyses found that socialized fans had significantly higher levels of social obligation and regional tribalism than did fans who self-selected their favorite team (see Table 4). There was not a significant multivariate interaction between gender and team fandom origin, $F(6, 218) = 1.33$, $p = .246$. Correlations were used to assess the relationships between age and team fandom origin, and gender and team fandom origin. A point-biserial correlation computed on age and team fandom origin found a significant and positive correlation, $r(225) = .268$, $p = .001$. Thus, older participants tended to actively choose their favorite team, while younger participants reported more socialization. A Pearson chi-square analyzed gender and team fandom origin. Female fans were found to have reported significantly more socialization than male fans, $\chi 2(1, N = 227) = 6.50$, $p = .011$.

**Table 4. Means, Standard Deviations, and F Scores of the Univariate Analysis of Team Fandom Origin for the Supplemental Analyses**

|  | Self-selected | | Socialized | | | |
|  | *M* | *SD* | *M* | *SD* | *F* | *p* |
|---|---|---|---|---|---|---|
| SSIS | 40.77 | 11.17 | 38.47 | 10.88 | 0.47 | .492 |
| SCST-PI | 9.88 | 4.84 | 10.19 | 4.53 | 0.84 | .360 |
| SCST-AC | 15.18 | 4.96 | 14.27 | 5.00 | 0.31 | .581 |
| SCST-CC | 8.84 | 4.98 | 9.45 | 5.27 | 2.02 | .157 |
| SCST-SO | 8.24 | 4.70 | 9.76 | 5.15 | 10.59 | .001 |
| SCST-RT | 9.93 | 7.08 | 12.11 | 6.84 | 6.57 | .011 |

*Note.* The response range for the SSIS is from 7 to 56. The response range for each subscale of the SCST is from 3 to 21.

# DISCUSSION

The current investigation examined differences in team identification and team commitment between self-selected fans and socialized fans. Self-selected fans were fans who reported that they actively chose to follow their favorite team (i.e., they were generally not actively encouraged to follow their favorite team by others). Conversely, socialized fans were fans who reported they were actively encouraged to follow their favorite team by others.

Hypothesis 1 predicted that team identification (i.e., SSIS scores) would be higher in fans who self-selected their favorite teams than in fans who were socialized into their team fandom. The current investigation found that this hypothesis was not supported. Fans reached the same levels of team identification whether they were socialized into their team fandom or chose their favorite team.

Personal identity, a component of team commitment, is "a sense of oneness with or belonging to a team that defines self-identity" (Matsuoka, 2001, p. 11). Hypothesis 2 stated that personal identity would be higher in fans who self-selected their favorite team than in fans who were socialized into their team fandom. The current investigation found that this hypothesis was not supported. Apparently, a team becomes a part of the fans' personal identities whether they self-selected their team or were socialized into their team fandom by others. Perhaps fans fit their identification to the group they become members of, instead of seeking a group that fits their self-concept.

Affective commitment is the fan's emotional attachment to the team. Hypothesis 3 predicted that affective commitment would be higher in fans who self-selected their favorite team than in fans who were socialized into their team fandom. The current investigation found that this hypothesis was not supported. Interestingly, team identification and the affective commitment component of team commitment had the strongest correlation among the scale and subscales. Items measuring team identification and items measuring affective commitment were similar (i.e., "During the season, how closely to you follow the team listed above via any of the following: a) in person or on television, b) the radio, c) television news or a newspaper, and/or d) the Internet?" and "I am a devoted fan of the team."; Matsuoka, 2001; Wann and Branscombe, 1993). However, there is a slight difference between team identification and affective commitment to a team. Where team identification is measuring the connection to and relevancy of the team to the fan, affective commitment measures the liking of and attachment to the team. Perhaps this small distinction is enough to allow for the lack of support found for affective commitment.

Calculative commitment involves a fan's unwillingness to incur the costs to no longer support the team. Hypothesis 4 stated that calculative commitment would be higher in fans who self-selected their favorite team than in fans who were socialized into their team fandom. The current investigation found that this hypothesis was not supported. Cognitive dissonance is a state of discomfort created when a person's behavior does not match his/her thoughts (Festinger, 1957). When a person has sufficient justification for his/her behavior, the state of discomfort is avoided (Festinger and Carlsmith, 1959). When discontinuing their fandom of a team, self-selected fans may experience cognitive dissonance because their behavior (i.e., time, energy, and money spent on their fandom) does not match their thoughts (i.e., their decision to leave the team fandom). Meanwhile, socialized fans may experience less cognitive dissonance when discontinuing their fandom of a team, because the social influence of others may act as sufficient justification for their behavior (i.e., they spent time, energy, and money to interact with their family and friends).

On the other hand, socialized fans may experience more social pressure on their sport consumption costs than self-selected fans, resulting in higher amounts of time, energy, and money spent. Choice decreases as calculative commitment and normative commitment (i.e., social obligation) increase (Bloemer and Oderkerken-Schröder, 2007). Game attendance for highly identified fans is a social activity that benefits psychological well-being (Wann, Martin, Grieve, and Gardner, 2008). Shopping is also a social activity, often done with friends and family (Bellenger and Korgaonkar, 1980; Evans, Christiansen, and Gill, 1996). It seems logical that sport team related purchases would be made in the company of socializing agents, or at least for social reasons such as fitting in with fellow sport fans. Perhaps no differences in calculative commitment were found because both self-selected and socialized fans have strong factors that influence their calculative commitment to their team fandom.

Social obligation occurs when fans feel "a sense of obligation fostered by social norms and pressures" (Matsuoka, 2001, p. 10). Regional tribalism occurs from "perception of connection between the team and the place to which the fan is attached" (Matsuoka, 2001, p. 11). Hypotheses 5 and 6 predicted that social obligation and regional tribalism would be higher in fans that were socialized into their team fandom than in self-selected fans. Indeed, as expected, this investigation found that social obligation and regional tribalism were both higher in fans that were socialized into the fandom of their favorite team. Socializing agents generally live in close proximity to the fan. Not only will the fan feel social pressure to maintain his fandom of the team, it is reasonable to conclude that the fan and his socializing agents will attend local games to socialize. Perhaps teams should have more promotions focused on bringing family and friends to games, as well as deals for locals, as a way to recruit more fans.

This investigation also found that older participants tended to actively choose their favorite team while younger participants reported more socialization. Consumer research has found that older individuals' brand loyalty increases with age (Evanschitzky and Woisetschläger, 2008). The same study suggests trying to "'win' older consumers by providing brand experience" (Evanschitzky and Woisetschäger, 2008, p. 632). This would be beneficial to the sport industry because populations are aging, creating legions of potentially loyal fans. It is unknown why the age differences occur. Perhaps older participants were contemporaries with the inceptions or expansions of teams. Related to this, since the vast number of options in teams is relatively new, older fans may not have had as many team fandom socializing agents.

Another possibility is that older participants had fewer opportunities to interact with others during sporting events in the past (i.e., fewer ESPN channels and less free time to attend games), or acknowledgement of socializing agents' influence diminishes over time. Future research should ask how long the participants have been fans of their favorite teams.

The investigation also found that there are gender differences in team fandom origin. Female fans reported significantly more socialization than male fans. Past research has found that women value groups for the relational attachments, whereas men value groups for the relational attachments and the collective identity of the group (Seeley, Gardner, Pennington, and Gabriel, 2003). Therefore, it seems that women may often become fans as a way to bond with their socializing agents; men may become fans both to bond with their socializing agents and to be a member of the group of fans.

Although this investigation assessed the differences in fandom between fans who reported choosing their favorite team and fans who reported being socialized into their team preference, it did not try to discern why self-selected fans were less likely to report being socialized. Perhaps some fans initially gain awareness of the team from a socializing agent, but later actively choose to pursue the fandom of that team. For example, imagine a college student who becomes aware of her parent's favorite team. When deciding where to attend college, the parent's favorite team is among the choices, and is eventually selected by the student. Although she was initially socialized, ultimately her team fandom was cemented by her choice and she may consider herself a self-selected fan. When choice is threatened or taken away, individuals seek to reestablish their freedom to choose (Brehm, 1989). They often do this by rejecting the recommended option and instead choosing the threatened option (Biner, 1988; Brehm, 1989). Choice is valuable to individuals; once reactance is activated, people tend to choose the option that leads to more choices (Liebhart, 1973).

Using the previous example, imagine that the college student's parent instructs the student she must attend her parent's favorite college. The student may rebel because her choice of which college to attend is being taken away. Once reactance is initiated, the student would choose the option with the most freedom (perhaps a distant college or the parent's most despised rival team). However, emphasizing that the student has a choice (such as which college to attend) leaves both options on the table. This could explain how some socialized fans might report they self-selected their favorite team. Future research may discern where socialization ends and choice begins. Another investigation might ask whether the fan's favorite team is the same as his/her socializing agents, and if not, if his/her favorite team is a despised rival of the favorite team of his/her socializing agents.

The current study found yet more support for gender differences in team identification and team commitment. Male fans were significantly higher on four types of team identification and team commitment than were female fans. This is consistent with previous research that men are more likely to derive social identities from their sport fandom than are women (James and Ridinger, 2002; Wann et al., 2001). One study found that group members who were told they were attitudinally similar to other group members had higher identification to that group (Reynolds et al., 2007). Perhaps because sport fandom is a traditional male activity, more attitudinal comparisons are drawn between men and sport fans. This may lead to higher levels of team identification regardless of whether the fan self-selected his team or is socialized into his team fandom.

## CONCLUSION

This study found that socialized fans report higher levels of both social obligation and regional tribalism than do self-selected fans. Male fans have higher levels of team identification, personal identity, affective commitment, calculative commitment, and social obligation than female fans. Older fans report more self-selection of their favorite team than younger fans. Finally, female fans report more socialization than male fans. This investigation into the origin of sport team fandom was the first to examine choice as a starting point for fandom and how age and gender played a role in the team fandom origin.

This study was also the first to examine the differences between self-selection of, and socialization to, a favorite team on team identification and team commitment. The findings of this study provide information on how membership within a group of fans was influenced by the origin of the fandom, information sport marketers would likely find valuable.

# REFERENCES

Allen, N. J., and Meyer, J. P. (1990). The measurement and antecedents of affective, continuance and normative commitment to the organization. *Journal of Occupational Psychology, 63,* 1-18

Bahk, C. M. (2000). Sex differences in sport spectator involvement. *Perceptual and Motor Skills, 91,* 79-83.

Becker, T. E., Billings, R. S., Eveleth, D. M., and Gilbert, N. L. (1996). Foci and bases of employee commitment: Implications for job performance. *Academy of Management Journal, 39,* 464-482.

Bellenger, D. N., and Korgaonkar, P. K. (1980). Profiling the recreational shopper. *Journal of Retailing, 56,* 77-92.

Biner, P. M. (1988). Effects of cover letter appeal and monetary incentives on survey response: A reactance theory application. *Basic and Applied Social Psychology, 9,* 99-106.

Bloemer, J., and Odekerken-Schröder, G. (2007). The psychological antecedents of enduring customer relationships: An empirical study in a bank setting. *Journal of Relationship Marketing, 6,* 21-43.

Brehm, J. W. (1989). Psychological reactance: Theory and applications. *Advances in Consumer Research, 16,* 72-75.

Dietz-Uhler, B., Harrick, E. A., End, C., and Jacquemotte, L. (2000). Sex differences in sport fan behavior and reasons for being a sport fan. *Journal of Sport Behavior, 23,* 219-231.

Ellemers, N., Kortekaas, P., and Ouwerkerk, J. W. (1999). Self-categorisation, commitment to the group and group self-esteem as related but distinct aspects of social identity. *European Journal of Social Psychology, 29,* 371-389.

Evans, K. R., Christiansen, T., and Gill, J. D. (1996). The impact of social influence and role expectations on shopping center patronage intentions. *Journal of the Academy of Marketing Science, 24,* 208-218.

Evanschitzky, H., and Woisetschläger, D. M. (2008). Too old to choose? The effects of age and age related constructs on consumer decision making. *Advances in Consumer Research, 35,* 630-636.

Festinger, L. (1957). *A theory of cognitive dissonance.* Oxford, England: Row, Peterson, and Company.

Festinger, L., and Carlsmith, J. M. (1959). Cognitive consequences of forced compliance. *Journal of Abnormal and Social Psychology, 58,* 203-210.

Fisher, R. J. (1998). Group-derived consumption: The role of similarity and attractiveness in identification with a favorite sports team. *Advances in Consumer Research, 25,* 283-288.

Grieve, F. G., Zapalac, R. K., Visek, A. J., Wann, D. L., Parker, P. M., Partridge, J., and Lanter, J. R. (2009). Identification with multiple sporting teams: How many teams do sport fans follow? *Journal of Contemporary Athletics, 3,* 283-294.

James, J. D. (2001). The role of cognitive development and socialization in the initial development of team loyalty. *Leisure Sciences, 23,* 233-261.

James, J. D., and Ridinger, L. L. (2002). Female and male sport fans: A comparison of sport consumption motives. *Journal of Sport Behavior, 25*, 260-278.

Laverie, D. A., and Arnett, D. B. (2000). Factors affecting fan attendance: The influence of identity salience and satisfaction. *Journal of Leisure Research, 32*, 225-246.

Lee, B. A., and Zeiss, C. A. (1980). Behavioral commitment to the role of sport consumer: An exploratory analysis. *Sociology and Social Research, 64*, 405-419.

Liebhart, E. H. (1973). Choice as a value. *European Journal of Social Psychology, 3*, 485-489.

Mahony, D. F., and Moorman, A. M. (2000). The relationship between the attitudes of professional sport fans and their intentions to watch televised games. *Sport Marketing Quarterly, 9*, 131-139.

Mathieu, J. E., and Zajac, D. M. (1990). A review and meta-analysis of the antecedents, correlates, and consequences of organizational commitment. *Psychological Bulletin, 108*, 171-194.

Matsuoka, H. (2001). *Multidimensionality of fans' psychological commitment to sport teams: Development of a scale* (Unpublished doctoral dissertation). The Ohio State University.

Matsuoka, H., and Chelladurai, P. (2005). *Multidimensionality of fans' psychological commitment to sport teams*. Manuscript submitted for publication.

Murrell, A. J., and Dietz, B. (1992). Fan support of sports teams: The effect of a common group identity. *Journal of Sport and Exercise Psychology, 14*, 28-39.

O'Reilly, C. A., and Chatman, J. A. (1986). Organizational commitment and psychological attachment: The effects of compliance, identification, and internalization on prosocial behavior. *Journal of Applied Psychology, 71*, 492-499.

Reynolds, K. J., Turner, J. C., Haslam, S. A., Ryan, M. K., Bizumic, B., and Subasic, E. (2007). Does personality explain in-group identification and discrimination? Evidence from the minimal group paradigm. *British Journal of Social Psychology, 46*, 517-539.

Seeley, E. A., Gardner, W. L., Pennington, G., and Gabriel, S. (2003). Circle of friends or members of a group? Sex differences in relational and collective attachment to groups. *Group Processes and Intergroup Relations, 6*, 251-263.

Stets, J. E., and Burke, P. J. (2000). Identity theory and social identity theory. *Social Psychology Quarterly, 63*, 224-237.

Tajfel, H. (1982). Social psychology of intergroup relations. *Annual Review of Psychology, 33*, 1-39.

Wann, D. L. (2002). Preliminary validation of a measure for assessing identification as a sport fan: The Sport Fandom Questionnaire. *International Journal of Sport Management, 3*, 103-115.

Wann, D. L. (2006). The causes and consequences of sport team identification. In A. A. Raney and J. Bryant (Eds.), *Handbook of Sports and Media* (pp. 331-352). Erlbaum.

Wann, D. L., and Branscombe, N. R. (1993). Sport fans: Measuring the degree of identification with their team. *International Journal of Sport Psychology, 24*, 1-17.

Wann, D. L., Dolan, T. J., McGeorge, K. K., and Allison, J. A. (1994). Relationships between spectator identification and specators' perceptions of influence, spectators' emotions, and competition outcome. *Journal of Sport and Exercise Psychology, 16*, 347-364.

Wann, D. L., and Martin, J. (2008). The positive relationship between sport team identification and social psychological well-being: Identification with favorite teams versus local teams. *Journal of Contemporary Athletics, 3*, 81-91.

Wann, D. L., Martin, J., Grieve, F. G., and Gardner, L. (2008). Social connections at sporting events: Attendance and its positive relationship with state social psychological well-being. *North American Journal of Psychology, 10*, 229-239.

Wann, D. L., Melnick, M. J., Russell, G. W., and Pease, D. G. (2001). *Sport fans: The psychology and social impact of spectators.* New York, NY: Routledge.

Wann, D. L., and Pierce, S. (2003). Measuring sport team identification and commitment: An empirical comparison of the sport spectator identification scale and the psychological commitment to team scale. *North American Journal of Psychology, 5*, 365-372.

Wann, D. L., Royalty, J., and Roberts, A. (2000). The self-presentation of sport fans: Investigating the importance of team identification and self-esteem. *Journal of Sport Behavior, 23*, 198-206.

Wann, D. L., Tucker, K. B., and Schrader, M. P. (1996). An exploratory examination of the factors influencing the origination, continuation, and cessation of identification with sports teams. *Perceptual and Motor Skills, 82*, 995-1001.

In: Innovative Writings in Sport and Exercise Psychology
Editor: Robert Schinke

ISBN: 978-1-62948-881-3
© 2014 Nova Science Publishers, Inc.

*Chapter 10*

# COACHES' PERCEPTIONS OF THE USE OF CHRONOLOGICAL AND BIOLOGICAL AGE IN THE IDENTIFICATION AND DEVELOPMENT OF TALENTED ATHLETES

## *Matthew F. Fiander, Martin I. Jones* and John K. Parker*

Faculty of Applied Sciences, University of Gloucestershire, Gloucestershire, UK

### ABSTRACT

Coaches and practitioners recognize that talent identification and development have a crucial role in the pursuit of excellence. National governing bodies routinely allocate youth participants, irrespective of biological age, to chronological age categories in an effort to ensure developmentally fair competition and opportunity. However, differences in the timing and tempo of maturation provide evidence to exclude chronological age and can lead to the misclassification of children in relation to their biological maturity. The purpose of this study was to explore coaches' perceptions of how they use chronological age and biological age in coaching practice, and the importance they place on the measurement and utilization of biological age to develop young athletes. We conducted semi-structured interviews with six coaches and analyzed data using a qualitative description methodology. The results revealed three main themes relating to the delivery of the long-term athlete development model, the limited or lack of knowledge of all aspects of the long-term athlete development model, and a desire for a different model. Results provide scholars and practitioners with a greater understanding of coaches' perspectives of the use of chronological and biological age in the identification and development of talented athletes.

---

* Correspondence: Martin I. Jones, Faculty of Applied Science, Oxstalls campus, Oxstalls lane, Gloucester, GLOS, GL2 9HW, United Kingdom, EMAIL: mjones2@glos.ac.uk.

## INTRODUCTION

Researchers recognize the crucial role talent identification and talent development play in the pursuit of excellence (Vaeyens, Lenoir, Williams, and Philippaerts, 2008). The focus from many sporting organizations, and top-level teams, has been on talent identification (i.e., the process of recognizing current participants with the potential to excel in a particular sport: Williams and Reilly, 2000). However, due to the lack of scientific grounding for most talent identification programs, scholars suggest that research efforts should be transferred from talent identification and detection to talent development (i.e., providing the most appropriate learning environment to realize this potential: Durand-Bush and Salmela, 2002; Williams and Reilly). Despite the change in research focus (Régneir, Salmela, and Russell, 1993), many national federations and club teams, particularly in professional sports, continue to invest considerable resources in an effort to identify exceptionally gifted youngsters at an early age in an attempt to accelerate the developmental process (Morris, 2000).

An issue within some current talent development programs is the use of physiological, physical, anthropometric, and technical measurements to assess the current levels of a child's performance in an attempt to predict future sporting success (Vaeyens et al., 2008). This creates concerns surrounding a child's maturation rate because of its significant impact upon performance characteristics (Malina, Bouchard, and Bar-Or, 2004). Since chronological age and biological maturity rarely progress at the same rate (Katzmarzyk, Malina, and Beunen, 1997), children may be at a disadvantage on performance tests due to their maturity status, especially when practitioners compare results to chronological age-specific norms (Armstrong, Welsman, and Kirby, 1998).

Within talent development programs, sporting governing bodies routinely allocate youth participants, irrespective of biological age, to chronological age categories in an effort to ensure developmentally fair competition and opportunity. However, differences in the timing and tempo of maturation provide evidence to exclude chronological age as an accurate index of physical potential (Maffulli, 1996) and can lead to the misclassification of children in relation to their biological maturity (Baxter-Jones, 1995).

Although there is no uniformly accepted theoretical framework to guide current practice within talent development programs (Vaeyens et al., 2008), authors have put forth conceptual frameworks in an attempt to clarify this lack of consensus. The contemporary view of sporting talent as being multidimensional and dynamic in nature (Abbott and Collins, 2004) is reflected within these talent development models. For example, dissatisfied with the often mistakenly interchanged terms talent, gifted and aptitude, Gagné (1993) introduced the Differentiated Model of Giftedness and Talent. The six components of the model sought to bring together in a dynamic way all the recognized determinants of talent and describe how it emerges from natural gifts through a complex choreography between various casual influences (van Rossum and Gagné, 2005). However, despite the contribution of this work from the educational field, it is unappreciated within the sporting domain (Tranckle and Cushion, 2006) which is demonstrated by a distinct lack in key reviews of the talent literature pertaining to sport (e.g., Durand-Bush and Salmela, 2002; Régnier, Salmela, and Russell, 1993; Williams and Reilly, 2000).

Currently, however, the most relevant and well-known talent development model to include such pediatric developmental considerations is the Long Term Athlete Development

(Balyi and Hamilton, 2004) model which, although not novel (Bompa, 1995), combines successful training methods with a greater scientific basis for children and adolescents (Balyi and Hamilton). The long-term athlete development model distinguishes six stages of training development that account for enhancing general athletic capabilities and sport specialization after pubertal changes (Balyi and Hamilton). Through objective physiological assessment tools (e.g., peak height velocity, peak weight velocity), coaches can account for individual maturation rates for each athlete so that they can apply the relevant training protocols depicted in each phase of the model. Also, by using appropriate training stimuli linked to natural growth and maturation processes, coaches can utilize "windows of opportunity" to accelerate and enhance physical development (Ford et al., 2011). What is more, a failure to maximize these windows will limit potential. Yet, the lack of supporting evidence has led some coaches and scholars to question if "windows of opportunity" exist and whether adhering to this philosophy would actually improve future performance or just allow a child to reach their genetic potential at a faster rate. In spite of claims of "windows of opportunity", a large body of empirical evidence available suggests that all aspects of physical fitness are trainable at all stages of development. Moreover, scholars and practitioners debate whether the misuse of "windows of opportunity," factual or fictitious, can lead to an increased likelihood of detrimental effects on adult participation (Bailey et al., 2010).

Another key issue of the long-term athlete development model is the exposure of elite child athletes to unnecessary and excessively high physical training loads. For example, the age range of approximately 11-16 years is the 'training-to-train' stage. This stage represents the adolescent years and the optimal time to develop physical fitness traits such as speed, endurance, and strength. Therefore, it is likely that coaches implementing the long-term athlete development model will expose adolescent athletes to training primarily designed to develop these fitness components. However, sport specific physical conditioning reflects a form of early specialization that may hinder physical, social, and psychological development (Baker, Cobley, and Fraser-Thomas, 2009).

Despite the aforementioned limitations, several national governing bodies (in the UK and across the world) and coaching organizations have adopted the long-term athlete development model. For example, the long-term athlete development model appears in the UK Government's 'Game Plan' strategy (Strategy Unit of Cabinet Office, 2002) and British national governing bodies need to have a sport-specific long-term athlete development plan if they wish to receive state funding (Day, 2011). Despite government and national governing body endorsement, the problem exists that the authors of long-term athlete development resources write for an audience of coaches who have a strong working knowledge of periodization and annual programs (Balyi and Way, 2009). This could create problems because a high proportion of coaches have limited formal coaching education and develop coaching guidelines based on experiences of trial and error or through modeling professional coaches who work with vastly different populations (Wiersma and Sherman, 2005).

The limited formal education of coaches presents problems with the utilization of "windows of opportunity," because understanding of maturation, its consequences, and the technique of measuring growth are important for coaches to be able to optimize training for young athletes (Balyi and Way, 2009). Young athletes consider coaches to be "experts" (Conroy and Coatsworth, 2006) and therefore coaches need to understand chronological and biological age, maturation, and measuring growth in relation to talent development if they are to provide young athletes with appropriate advice. To date, it is unclear whether coaches have this "expert" knowledge. To this end, the aim of this investigation was to describe coaches' perceptions of how they use chronological age and biological age in their coaching practice, and the importance they place on the measurement and utilization of biological age to develop young athletes. As the most prominent talent development model in youth sport, we adopted the long-term athlete development model as a point of reference for coaches to discuss their perceptions of talent identification and talent development.

# METHOD

The purpose of this study was not to explore differences between sub groups of participants (e.g., rugby union vs. rugby league). The purpose of this investigation was to describe coaches' perceptions of how they use chronological age and biological age in their coaching practice, and the importance they place on the measurement and utilization of biological age to develop young athletes. Triangulation, defined as "a validity procedure where researchers search for convergence among multiple and different sources of information to form themes or categories in a study" (Creswell and Miller, 2000, p. 126) was appropriate to describe coaches' perceptions of the use of chronological and biological age in the identification and development of talented athletes because triangulation allowed us to re-present a comprehensive summary of coaches perceptions.

We adopted a qualitative description methodology (Sandelowski, 2000; 2010) because qualitative descriptive studies generate a comprehensive summary of events in the everyday terms of those events (Sandelowski, 2000); therefore, a qualitative description was appropriate for our research question. Qualitative descriptive designs are an eclectic but reasonable combination of sampling, and data collection, analysis, and re-presentation techniques. Sandelowski stated that qualitative researchers often defend their efforts as something more than "mere" description. That is, researchers have sought epistemological credibility by labeling their work as phenomenology, grounded theory, ethnography, or narrative study. Sandelowski stated that it is often the case that authors claim to be conducting a phenomenology but re-presentation of results provides nothing more than the "subjective" experience of the participants. In this case, Sandelowski suggests that authors describe these types of studies as qualitative descriptions, albeit with phenomenological overtones (e.g., a study that has used a technique that might be associated with a phenomenology). Researchers conducting qualitative descriptive studies seek descriptive validity or an accurate accounting of events that most people (including the reader of research) observing the same event would agree is accurate.

In terms of the epistemological, ontological, and axiological foundations of qualitative descriptive studies, Sandelowski (2000) stated that qualitative descriptive studies are less "theoretical" than the spectrum of available qualitative methodologies. This does not mean that qualitative descriptive are conceptually naked. Rather, qualitative descriptions, as with all research, are grounded in researchers' pre-conceptions. The difference could be that researchers adopting one of the "more" theoretical methodologies (i.e., grounded theory, phenomenology, ethnography, or narrative enquiry) are required to establish epistemological credibility because editors and reviewers expect it. However, when using philosophical jargon, there is a danger of creating unnecessary obstacles to knowledge translation; particularly if researchers wish to achieve impact beyond the academic fraternity (e.g., knowledge translation to coaches, athletes, and policy makers). Qualitative descriptions are not atheorteical (Sandelowski, 2010), nor should they be used a default or salvage method for the epistemologically uninitiated. Sandelowski (2000) stated that qualitative descriptions tend to draw on tenets of naturalistic inquiry, a term / approach that seems to have fallen out of favor in the sport psychology literature. Sandelowski (2000) stated that naturalistic inquiry implies a commitment to studying something in its natural state, or as it is, to the extent that this is possible in a research enterprise (Lincoln and Guba, 1985). In any naturalistic study like a qualitative description, there is no pre-selection of variables to study, no manipulation of variables, and no a priori commitment to any one theoretical view of a target phenomenon (i.e., symbolic interactionism or social constructivism).

## PARTICIPANTS

Following ethical approval from a University ethics panel, the first author recruited participants to take part in the study. We did not specify the number of participants needed. Rather, we kept recruiting until we reached data saturation. We decided to stop recruiting after the sixth interview. We used a purposive sampling strategy to select information-rich participants who had experiences of the phenomena in question (i.e., coaching adolescent athletes). By employing a purposive sampling strategy we delimited the study to UK rugby coaches.

We recruited participants on the following criteria: (a) they had experience of coaching youth athletes between the ages of 10 and 25 years, (b) they had received a formal coaching qualification; and (c) had at least six months of coaching experience. We chose six months coaching experience because researchers (e.g., Cushion, Armour, and Jones, 2003; Lyle, 2002; Trudel and Gilbert, 2006) have shown that coach education/accreditation is less valued by coaches than experiential learning and other less formal opportunities. Therefore, six months gave the participants the opportunity to gain experience in less formal opportunities. We selected rugby union and rugby league coaches because of the first author's experience in both rugby codes.

Rugby league and rugby union are similar but distinct types of rugby with slightly different rules (e.g., rugby league teams comprise 13 rather than 15 players). The differentiation between rugby union and rugby league is similar to differentiation between American Football and Canadian football. As such, this criterion was for convenience, rather than for a specific purpose.

Participants ranged in age from 22 to 56 years, were male, were Caucasian, and classed themselves as middle class ($n=5$) and working class ($n=1$). All six participants were qualified in rugby league or rugby union or both, through the Rugby Football Union (RFU), Rugby Football League (RFL) or Sports Coach UK. We display the amount of practical experience, including the age ranges and codes of rugby in Table 1. The names in Table 1 are pseudonyms. The study complied with the UK Data Protection Act (The National Archives, 2011).

## Table 1. Research participant details

|         | Experience   | Ages of athletes coached | Sport(s)                    |
|---------|--------------|--------------------------|-----------------------------|
| Keith   | 5 years      | 11-21                    | Rugby League/ Rugby Union   |
| James   | 1 years      | 12-17                    | Rugby Union                 |
| Malcolm | 10 years     | 11-18                    | Rugby League                |
| Simon   | 8 – 9 years  | 5-16, 18-22              | Rugby League                |
| Damian  | 12 years     | 8-30/40+                 | Rugby League/Rugby Union    |
| Tim     | 12 years     | 5-50+                    | Rugby League/Rugby Union    |

## PROCEDURE

Semi-structured interviews were the most appropriate data collection technique because of the capacity of interviewing to provide in depth, individual data related to the phenomenon in question. The first author developed an interview guide around three types of questions: (a) opening questions to break the ice and encourage open and relaxed discussion, (b) main questions, to begin discussions on the appropriate information; and (c) probes to expand responses (Zeisel, 1984). The first author used relevant literature on coaches' perspectives on long-term athlete development, the long-term athlete development model, and the issues surrounding both of these topics to create a list of interview questions. Examples of main questions included "With regards to your own club, how do you adapt long-term athlete development for your players?", "How do you feel about children being separated by biological age as well as chronological age?", and "What methods do you use to separate your athletes?" Readers can request a copy of the interview guide from the corresponding author.

The first author conducted the interviews at a variety of locations that suited the convenience and comfort of the participants (for example, university campus, rugby club rooms), and the duration of interviews ranged from 30 to 90 minutes. The first author had received interview training during several undergraduate and postgraduate research methods courses. Furthermore, the second and third authors provided personal one to one tutoring and feedback to improve the first author's interview style. On arrival at the place of interview, the first author informed the participants of the interview procedure, its relevance to the research study, ethical procedures (e.g., confidentiality and anonymity), procedures of providing informed consent, and procedures regarding withdrawal from the research. The interviews were audio recorded and transcribed verbatim.

## DATA ANALYSIS

The first author conducted, digitally recorded, and transcribed each interview verbatim. The first author started data analysis immediately after transcription and before the subsequent interview. The cyclical process of data collection and analysis helped strengthen the data by developing new questions for the next interview (see Corbin and Strauss, 2008 and Morse, Barrett, Mayan, Olson, and Spiers, 2002) and by breaking down the analysis into manageable sections, rather than one pile of transcripts at the end of the study. When no new results emerged from the analysis, we made the decision that we had achieved data saturation and stopped collecting data. We stopped interviewing after six interviews; however, we reserved the option of collecting more data if we later decided that we had made the decision to stop interviewing prematurely.

The data analysis followed a set of steps recommended by Colaizzi (1978). The first author read the participants' descriptions and extracted significant statements, phrases and sentences that directly pertain to the investigated phenomenon. The first author made notes and memos regarding the meaning of each of these statements, phrases and sentences and began to cluster statements. Colaizzi stated that in this difficult step, the meanings arrived at must not sever the connection with the original description. Therefore, wherever possible the first author used in vivo codes that used the participants' words and the first author discussed coding with the second and third author to facilitate the description. Finally, we organized clusters of themes from the aggregate formulated meanings. This allowed for the emergence of themes common to all of the subjects' descriptions. We referred the clusters of themes back to the original descriptions in order to validate and/or re-examine them and to see if there was anything in the original that was not accounted for in the cluster of themes, and where the cluster proposed anything which was not in the original (i.e., constant comparison).

## Methodological Rigor

In line with the suggestions of Morse et al. (2002), we employed constructive and evaluative methods of ensuring rigor.

We selected a methodology and employed data collection techniques, analysis procedures, and re-presentation strategies in line with our research question (i.e., to describe coaches' perceptions of how they use chronological age and biological age in their coaching practice, and the importance they place on the measurement and utilization of biological age to develop young athletes).

By collecting and analyzing data, simultaneously, we could identify and rectify potential threats to the rigor of the research before conducting the next interview (Morse et al.). The second and third authors provided feedback to the first author during the process of data collection and analysis, once we decided to stop collecting data; both second and third authors checked the results framework to ensure transparency of the analysis process.

## RESULTS

The data analysis procedure resulted in three main themes related to coaches' perceptions of the use of chronological and biological age in the identification and development of talented athletes (See Figure 1).

These themes are (1) the delivery of the long-term athlete development model, (2) the limited or lack of knowledge of all the aspects of the long-term athlete development model, and (3) a desire for a different model. We presented the main themes with associated sub-themes in the following sections.

# DELIVERY OF THE LONG-TERM ATHLETE DEVELOPMENT MODEL

Coaches are not using the information supplied to them by their national governing bodies. Three of the participants stated that they found it difficult to implement the long-term athlete development model supplied to them by their national governing bodies in their coaching practices. For example, Simon stated:

> It's pretty difficult because...everybody's got mixed abilities, you're coming from people who've been playing the game since they were 10, you've got guys who have never played the game before...so you've got to try and fit something in that suits everybody in at once.

James supported Simon's sentiments; James claimed his national governing body was not trying to implement long-term athlete development with any great degree.

> They do push long-term athlete development but not as serious as I would have thought...they try to make it more fun to keep the player in the game rather than to see if he can become an elite athlete.

Concerning the information supplied about biological age, Simon said he did not feel comfortable implementing anything due to a lack of detail.

> From what I remember...it was a couple years ago now...from what I remember I think there was some talk about mental age and...Because that has to come into it... You can't just say this guy's born on the 30th of August and this guy's born on the 1st of September so they're a complete year apart...there's only one day different and everybody matures at a different rate. So, yeah there was stuff but...not in great detail for me to stick it in there and use it.

Malcolm suggested that he did not use the long-term athlete development that his national governing body provided him because he was getting advice regarding talent identification from a different source, namely the head coach of a professional rugby league club.

> Then [coach] has come along who is head coach at [club name], so he in a way...is in a nice way dictating on what he wants. The level that he is keen on now is under 14's. That is the age where you want to snatch the kids...you know they have rugby experience albeit union...umm and then we can have a few years developing them in the...in the grass roots club and then they feed into our academy.

**Coaches are creating a non-sport specific environment.** Four participants expressed their aspiration to create a non-sport specific environment for children to develop into a sport that suits them and not necessarily the coaches' sport.

Malcolm discussed this point in the following quote, "part of what our philosophy is...is if we keep them in an athletic environment...if they go off and play football then we have still done our job because we have encouraged sport." Simon said:

You cannot just start at the bottom and say "right you are four years old but I know you are going to be like this when you are older so you are going to play rugby." You have to have the basics first and then you can build from then and then let them find their own way. You cannot just say "I am going to direct you to do this because I think you will be good at this." So you let them find their own way . . . [if] you give them enough options...they will eventually fall into one that suits them.

**Most of the coaches had no experience of a long-term athlete development model as a player.** For four of the coaches, the lack of experience of a long-term athlete development model as a player is another avenue for them to gather information about long-term athlete development that they might well have missed.

James talked about his own development as a player. Malcolm talked about how he was coached as a junior rugby player, "In those days you were passed from pillar to post...that there wasn't any coaching structures really like we know it." Keith had similar memories:

So back then, 15 years ago, there was not a great deal of structure in sport in the sense of the long-term development of the athletes...they were all sort of individual governing bodies ways of doing things so there was not any clear directive until about 10 years ago when that started coming into play.

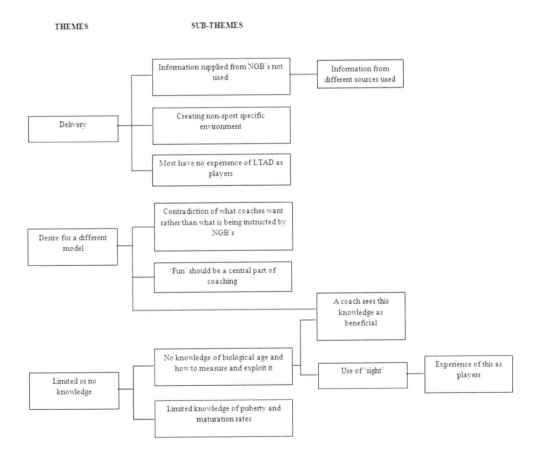

Figure 1. The Themes and Sub-Themes Arising from Data Analysis.

## A Desire for a Different Model

**When asked what their perfect talent development model would look like, coaches did not describe the current long-term athlete development model.** All of the coaches described something that was different to what their national governing bodies currently prescribed to them.

Keith discussed what he would like to see, "I think there needs to be more emphasis based on gymnastic ability and things like that and then from 14 onwards those national governing bodies coming in and starting to pick talented individuals to go into specific sports they're showing interest in."

While describing his ideal talent development model, James explicitly disregarded the use of biological age to separate children in conjunction with chronological age, "I'd probably keep it as age groups...I think that systems working at the moment. When you get to over 18 years, anyway it does not matter how old you are." However, four coaches expressed that they would find this knowledge useful in their model.

Discussing his model, Tim stated "definitely 100% think that should be in it." When describing their ideal talent development model, three coaches, described a model that had no specific sport at the center. Simon said:

> You can give them a wide range of sports...so you can do...all involving your motor skills, hand eye co-ordination, etc. You can give them netball, cricket, rugby, basketball, anything you know. Then just say well they are not your only options we also have football, we also have this; just leave the possibilities wide open for them. If you introduce them too sport specific stuff to early... then they could be missing so much more.

Simon added that talent development models for younger children should also eschew competition:

> Kids can't be put into a sport specific situation...I heard a theory and I actually agree with it that maybe you shouldn't introduce kids to competitive sport or maybe even sports specific until maybe 14 onwards...it would make it a more...not competitive as such but a more fairer kind of playing field.

Malcolm expressed his opinion that the children he was coaching should actually have an input into their long-term development plan, rather than following the current prescribed long-term athlete development model.

> I think basically what it would look like, as a system that would actually map out what you actually wanted from the kids, and what you thought their development should look like, but also I think there has to be an input in from the kids themselves. I think that is really...I think that sometimes we patronize kids, even 10 year olds.

**Coaches wanted fun to be at the heart of their coaching and their talent development model.** Three of the coaches believed that within the coaching they do and the long-term athlete development model, there should be an element of fun as the common denominator. For example, Tim said, "My perfect long-term athlete development model would have a massive focus on fun." James said, "It is just the element of keeping it fun rather than getting hurt or not enjoying it as a child and staying in the game." Malcolm also said:

> I think you get the kids at the earliest possible age, so you're talking about 5 or 6, you teach them a form of rugby so that they can run around, they can enjoy themselves, you do nice drills and basically make it as fun as possible.

## THE LIMITED OR LACK OF KNOWLEDGE OF ALL THE ASPECTS OF THE LONG-TERM ATHLETE DEVELOPMENT MODEL

None of the coaches displayed any knowledge of how to measure and exploit biological age. Simon said, "I am assuming there are specific methods of measuring biological age, etc.?" Tim asked, "How do you measure maturation? Umm...you would have people of similar size [pause] umm [pause] and [pause] uhh [pause] level of maturation so I would have to [pause]. In a perfect world, I would find a tool to measure maturation." The coaches described their own methods of measuring biological age and their own methods of separating their child athletes. The following quotes show that these methods are not evidence based. For example, Malcolm used his instinct to select players for open age (adult competition), "Instinct...you just know don't you? Yeah you know, I coach under 15's during the summer, and some of them, you know they would be quite happy playing with the open age no problem." Perhaps, the coaches' methods of measuring biological age and maturation had come from personal experience rather than from formal education or long-term athlete development resources. Keith talked about his experiences:

> For example, myself, I was one of the biggest people in our [school] year and I played rugby for the [school year] above, football two [school years] above because I was physically able to do that within that school environment. It may not have been right but in the sense of the physical aspects to it, I was able to do that.

However, four coaches explicitly expressed that this knowledge of biological age would be beneficial to them and their young athletes. Malcolm said, "Any help a coach can have of developing their kids in the right way has to be a good thing." A reason why coaches did not understand biological age and maturation may be the academic terminology used in the long-term athlete development model, which does not translate to every day coaching practice. Damien highlighted this point in the following quote, "I think the thing is though, that's all great from an academic who's doing it. However, there is no way of doing that [using peak height velocity] within, you know, within a session." Coaches have a limited knowledge about the development of a child during puberty and maturation rates. The coaches talked about puberty, maturation, and the development of talent. However, they were not able to explain these concepts in detail or provide a coherent rationale for the inclusion of maturation and puberty in the long-term athlete development model. For example, Simon said:

> From there [14 years old], you tend to find that people go and grow spurts and so on. Their hand eye co-ordination is disparate quite a lot because the depth and the vision and

things. Someone, all of a sudden, during the puberty stage, is quite short now, then they are quite tall...they are knocking on the ball a lot, and things like that.

Malcolm did not segregate his athletes based on maturation or gender:

The coaching I do is mixed. I do not say the girls over there and the boys over there. I have just told the girls, some of them and obviously, girls develop sooner than the boys and you can see that.

## DISCUSSION

The purpose of this study was to explore coaches' perceptions of how they use chronological age and biological age in their coaching practice, and the importance they place on the measurement and utilization of biological age to develop their young athletes. Three main themes emerged from the data analysis. These findings contribute to the literature by highlighting issues regarding the long-term athlete development model and the people that deliver it to young sporting talent. The first theme that emerged related to issues with the delivery of the long-term athlete development model. Coaches were receiving some level of information from their national governing bodies regarding the long-term athlete development model but it was either insufficient or not in enough detail for the coaches to use it. In addition, coaches suggested that the information supplied did not contain the necessary information. This issue could be caused by the limited amount of formal coaching education that most non-school youth coaches have (Wiersma and Sherman, 2005) and can create differences in sport systems across different clubs (Martindale, Collins, and Daubney, 2005). In addition, one of the coaches began to ignore the long-term athlete development model that his national governing body endorsed, and was implementing an athlete development model from a different source. This echoes trends from other sports where coaches have not embraced the coaching system adopted at higher levels (Black and Holt, 2009).

Deci and Ryan (1985) suggested that providing participants with perceptions of choice and control could increase their intrinsic motivation to act in particular ways. Therefore, when the current findings are interpreted in light of previous research in this area, the delivery of long-term athlete development could have been impeded by the lack of coach involvement in the creation of the program. This could be an important future research consideration (Black and Holt, 2009). Most of the coaches expressed that they did not experience the long-term athlete development model or other specific player development models when they were players. Therefore, this issue regarding the delivery of the current long-term athlete development model might be a result of an observation and imitation of their coaches' behavior (Bandura and Walters, 1963).

The second theme that emerged related to the limited or lack of knowledge of the key aspects of the long-term athlete development model. Coaches had a limited knowledge about the development of a child during puberty and maturation rates, and they did not understand biological age and how to measure and train athletes in a developmentally appropriate manner. With the maximization of a child's "window of opportunity" at the heart of the long-term athlete development model (Balyi and Hamilton, 2004); a lack of knowledge about the maturation rates and measurement of maturation could detrimentally affect the development of young athletes. Wiersma and Sherman (2005) suggested that coaches need further training in growth and developmental phases of young athletes. The current research support Wiersma and Sherman's statement. Unfortunately, despite the availability of coaching education programs, the current participants did not receive the necessary training to enable them to understand, measure, and exploit biological age (and therefore "windows of opportunity").

McCallister, Blinde, and Kolenbrander, (2000) suggested that the role of youth sport coaches carries a general perception that anyone can coach and that the criteria for selecting coaches was often based on either having a child in the team or a willingness to assume the role of coach if no one else was available. Coaches without formal education in biological development and the scientific underpinnings of the strategies that national governing bodies tell them to use, face aspects of youth sports that they are largely unprepared for (e.g., implementing developmentally appropriate coaching). If these coaches are to be prepared, national governing bodies need to provide the right coaching education (Libman, 1998).

With regards to the current results, all four coaches were using 'instinct' and 'sight' of a child's physical attributes to gauge biological status for the purpose of moving them up or down age groups, rather than to develop the child in their "windows of opportunity." Two of the coaches said they experienced this while they were younger, therefore personal experiences may have been instrumental in shaping future coaching practices (Rodgers, Reade, and Hall, 2007). Even though the validity of the detection and utilization of these "windows of opportunities" is a highly debated concept (Bailey et al., 2010), it remains an important part of the long-term athlete development model so knowledge of biological age is important for coaches. The current participants clearly did not grasp this concept; however, they all recognized that knowledge of biological development would be beneficial in assisting them to develop their child athletes in the most appropriate ways.

The final theme to emerge was the desire for a different athlete development model. This theme surfaced because of a conflict between what national governing bodies were asking coaches to deliver and what coaches actually wanted to deliver. As highlighted previously, research has shown the need for coaches to be involved in the creation and ongoing development of their sports specific athlete development programs so coaches have an opportunity to embrace the model and deliver it effectively (Black and Holt, 2009). However, Cassidy (2010) highlights the issue that although coaches may want change within current coaching practices, without any emotional commitment by a governing body to support change, coaches tend to lose hope, as well as faith, in the change process. Therefore drawing attention to role that governing bodies must play in listening to coaches desires and committing to change.

When asked to describe their 'perfect' athlete development model, all of the coaches described something that was different to the current long-term athlete development model. For example, two coaches described how they wanted children to avoid participating in specific sports until the age of 14 years. The current long-term athlete development model suggests competition could begin at eight or nine years of age. Although a difference of five years might seem small when compared to an athlete's career, evidence suggests that children's early learning experiences of sport is crucial to the development of high levels of expertise (Kirk, 2005).

All of the coaches expressed a desire to develop their athletes physically, yet there was no mention of any other aspects of development (e.g., psychosocial, cognitive, technical). Oliver (2010) suggested that there was a disproportionate focus on an unduly large amount of physical conditioning for elite child athletes, which can occur at the expense of other important developmental considerations, areas such as technical, tactical, social and psychological development.

Although the long-term athlete development model has provided some structure for national governing bodies and coaches, this issue can impede the holistic development of child athletes (Oliver). Two of the coaches expressed their desire for 'fun' to be at the heart of all coaching and the long-term athlete development model. In its current form, fun is not the primary concern of coaches adopting the long-term athlete development model (despite stage names like the FUNdamentals). Central to the long-term athlete development model is the notion that to become an expert performer it takes at least 10 years, or 10,000 hours, of highly structured activity (Ericsson, Krampe, and Tesch-Römer, 1993; Wall and Côté, 2007). Current results support the need for more emphasis on fun and enjoyment.

## CONCLUSION

The purpose of this study was to describe coaches' perceptions of how they use chronological age and biological age in their coaching practice, and the importance they place on the measurement and utilization of biological age to develop their young athletes. The findings of this study highlighted that coaches were not delivering the long-term athlete development model as prescribed to them by their national governing bodies. In addition, results suggest that coaches had limited knowledge of the biological and maturation aspects of the long-term athlete development model (specifically a lack of knowledge how to measure and exploit biological age). Lastly, results suggested that the current coaches wanted to deliver a different model to develop their young athletes.

The current study contributed to the literature by highlighting issues with coaches' perspectives of the long-term athlete development. Further research is required to substantiate whether these results are typical across coaching systems. As the issues from this study focused on the information supplied from national governing bodies and the knowledge of coaches, future research should further investigate the quantity and quality of the information being supplied to coaches by their national governing bodies, especially with reference to biological age, particularly when it has been demonstrated how influential national governing bodies can be to the change process in coaching practices.

## REFERENCES

Abbott, A., and Collins, D. (2004). Eliminating the dichotomy between theory and practice in talent identification and development: Considering the role of psychology. *Journal of Sport Sciences, 22,* 395-408.

Armstrong, N., Welsman, J., and Kirby, B. (1998). Peak oxygen intake and maturation in 12-Year olds. *Medicine and Science in Sport and Exercise, 30,* 165-169.

Bailey, R., Collins, D., Ford, P., MacNamara, A., Toms, M., and Pearce, G. (2010). *Participant development in sport: An academic review.* Leeds, UK: Sports Coach UK.

Baker, J., Cobley, S., and Fraser-Thomas, J. (2009). What do we know about early sports specialization? Not much! *High Ability Studies, 20,* 77-89.

Balyi, I., and Hamilton, A. (2004). *Long-term athlete development: Trainability in childhood and adolescence. Windows of opportunity. Optimal trainability.* Victoria, BC: National Coaching Institute British Columbia and Advanced Training and Performance Ltd.

Balyi, I., and Way, R. (2009). *The role of monitoring growth in long-term athlete development.* Retrieved from: Cross Country Canada Web site: http://www.cccski.com/main.asp?cmd=docandID=3967andlan=0.

Bandura, A., and Walters, R. (1963). *Social learning and personality development.* Lansing, MI: Holt, Rinehart, and Winston.

Baxter-Jones, A. (1995). Growth and development of young athletes: Should competition levels be age related? *Sports Medicine, 20,* 59-64.

Black, D., and Holt, N. (2009). Athlete development in ski racing: Perceptions of coaches and parents. *International Journal of Sport Science and Coaching, 4,* 242-260.

Bompa, T. (1995). *From childhood to champion athlete.* West Sedona, AZ: Veritas Publishing.

Cassidy, T. (2010). Understanding the change process: Valuing what it is that coaches do. *International Journal of Sports Science and Coaching, 5,* 143-147.

Colaizzi, P. (1978). Psychological research as the phenomenologist views it. In R. Vaile and M. King (Eds.), *Existential phenomenological alternatives for psychology.* New York, NY: Oxford University Press.

Conroy, D., and Coatsworth, J. (2006). Coach training as a strategy for promoting youth social development. *The Sport Psychologist, 20,* 128-144.

Creswell, J. W. and Miller, D. L. (2000). Determining validity in qualitative inquiry. *Theory into Practice, 39,* 124-131.

Day, D. (2011). Craft coaching and the 'discerning eye' of the coach. *International Journal of Sports Science and Coaching, 6,* 179-195.

Deci, E., and Ryan, R. (1985). *Intrinsic motivation and self-determination in human behavior.* New York, NY: Plenum.

Durand-Bush, N., and Salmela, J. (2002). The development of talent in sport. In R. N. Singer., H. A. Hausenblas., and C. M. Janelle (Eds.), *Handbook of sport psychology* (pp. 269-289). New York, NY: Wiley.

Ericsson, K., Krampe, R., and Tesch-Römer, C. (1993). The role of deliberate practice in the acquisition of expert performance. *Psychological Review, 100,* 363-406.

Ford, P., De Ste Croix, M., Lloyd, R., Meyers, R., Moosavi, M., Oliver, J., Till, K., and Williams, C. (2011). The long-term athlete development model: Physiological evidence and application. *Journal of Sport Sciences, 29,* 389-402.

Gagné, F. (1993). Constructs and models pertaining to exceptional human abilities. In K. A. Heller., F. J. Mönks., and A. H. Passow (Eds.), *International handbook of research and development of giftedness and talent* (pp. 63-85). Oxford, UK: Pergamon Press.

Golafshani, N. (2003). Understanding reliability and validity in qualitative research. *The Qualitative Report, 8,* 597-607.

Jones, M. I., and Lavallee, D. (2009). Exploring the life skills needs of adolescent athletes. *Psychology of Sport and Exercise, 10,* 159-167.

Katzmarzyk, P., Malina, R., and Beunen, G. (1997). The contribution of biological maturation to the strength and motor fitness of children. *Annals of Human Biology, 24,* 493-505.

Kirk, D. (2005). Physical education, youth sport and lifelong participation: The importance of early learning experiences. *European Physical Education Review, 11,* 239-255.

Libman, S. (1998). Adult participation in youth sports: A developmental perspective. *Child and Adolescent Psychiatric Clinics of North America, 4,* 725-744.

Maffulli, N. (1996). Children in sport. Towards the year 2000. *Sports Exercise Injury, 2,* 109-110.

Malina, R., Bouchard, C., and Bar-Or, O. (2004). *Growth, maturation and physical activity* (2nd Ed.). Champaign, IL: Human Kinetics.

Martindale, R., Collins, D., and Daubney, J. (2005). Talent development: A guide for practice and research within sport. *Quest, 57,* 353-375.

McCallister, S., Blinde, E., and Kolenbrander, B. (2000). Problematic aspects of the role of youth sport coach. *International Sports Journal, 4,* 9-26.

Morris, T. (2000). Psychological characteristics and talent identification in soccer. *Journal of Sport Science, 18,* 715-726.

Morse, J. M., Barrett, M., Mayan, M., Olson, K., and Spiers, J. (2002). Verification strategies for establishing reliability and validity in qualitative research. *International Journal of Qualitative Methods, 1,* Article 2. Retrieved from http://ejournals.library.ualberta.ca/index.php/IJQM/index

Oliver, J. (2010). Developing physical fitness and talent in elite child athletes. In C. Brackenridge and D. Rhind (Eds.), *Elite child athlete welfare: International perspectives* (pp. 34-40). Middlesex, UK: Brunel University.

Régneir, G., Salmela, J., and Russell, S. (1993). Talent detection and development in sport. In R. Singer., M. Murphy., and L. Tennant (Eds.), *Handbook of research on sport psychology* (pp. 290-313). New York, NY: Macmillan.

Rodgers, W., Reade, I., and Hall, C. (2007). Factors that influence coaches' use of sound coaching practices. *International Journal of Sport Science and Coaching, 2,* 155-170.

Sandelowski, M. (2000). Whatever happened to qualitative description? Research in Nursing and Health, 23, 334-340.

Sandelowski, M. (2010). What's a name? Qualitative description revisited. Research in Nursing and Health, 33, 77-84.

Strategy Unit of Cabinet Office. (2002). *Game plan: A strategy for delivering government's sport and physical activity objectives.* London, UK: DCMS/Strategy Unit Report.

The National Archives. (2011). *Data protection act 1998.* Retrieved April 28, 2011, from Legislation Web site: http://www.legislation.gov.uk/ukpga/1998/29/resources

Trankcle, P., and Cushion, C. J. (2006). Rethinking giftedness and talent in sport. *Quest, 58,* 265-282.

Vaeyens, R., Lenoir, M., Williams, A., and Philippaerts, R. (2008). Talent identification and development programs in sport: Current models and future directions. *Sports Medicine, 38,* 703-714.

Van Rossum, J. H. A., Gagné, F. (2005). Talent development in sport. In F. A. Dixon., and S. M. Moon (Eds.), *The handbook of secondary gifted education* (pp. 281-316). Waco, TX: Prufrock Press.

Wall, M., and Côté, J. (2007). Developmental activities that lead to dropout and investment in sport. *Physical Education and Sport Pedagogy, 12,* 77-87.

Wiersma, L., and Sherman, C. (2005). Volunteer youth sport coaches' perspectives of coaching education/certification and parental codes of conduct. *Research Quarterly for Exercise and Sport, 76,* 324-338.

Williams, A., Reilly, T. (2000). Talent identification and development in soccer. *Journal of Sport Science, 18,* 657-667.

Zeisel, J. (1984). *Inquiry by design: Tools for environment-behavior research.* Cambridge, UK: Cambridge University Press.

Date of submission: February 14 2012.

In: Innovative Writings in Sport and Exercise Psychology
Editor: Robert Schinke

ISBN: 978-1-62948-881-3
© 2014 Nova Science Publishers, Inc.

*Chapter 11*

# PSYCHOLOGICAL APPROACHES TO ENHANCING FAIR PLAY

## *John L. Perry*[*1], *Peter J. Clough*[2] *and Lee Crust*[3]
[1]Leeds Trinity University, Horsforth, Leeds, UK
[2]University of Hull, Hull, UK
[3]University of Lincoln, Brayford Pool, Lincoln, UK

### ABSTRACT

This article reviews approaches to studying sportspersonship, moral behavior in sport and broader morality theory to offer practical strategies to enhance fair play. By identifying stages and levels of morality and reviewing research supporting the relationship between goal orientations and moral behavior, we propose five practical strategies. Namely, we suggest that developing a mastery climate, developing a moral community, role taking, reflection and power transfer can be effectively used to progress performers from pre-conventional to a conventional level of morality and ultimately, establish principled morality in sport.

**Keywords:** Fair play, morality, sport, sportspersonship

### INTRODUCTION

Modern sport has many famous examples of good and poor sporting behavior. Positive examples include former England cricket captain Andrew Strauss' withdrawn appeal against Sri Lanka after Angelo Matthews collided with an England fielder (Hopps, 2009). In baseball, pitcher Armando Galarraga accepted an incorrect call from the umpire without dissent that cost him a perfect game (Maynard, 2010) and football player Paolo Di Canio elected to catch the ball to stop play when an opposing goalkeeper lay injured (Haylett, 2000). Conversely,

---

[*] Correspondence concerning this article should be addressed to John L. Perry, Department of Sport, Health and Nutrition, Leeds Trinity University, Brownberrie Lane, Horsforth, Leeds, LS18 5HD. e-mail: j.perry@leedstrinity.ac.uk, tel: 0113 283 7175.

one could point to deviance in sport with many examples. The size of public and media response to such incidents underlines the importance of sportspersonship in the popularity of a sport. For a sport to survive and flourish, it must remain popular. In this paper we provide suggestions for coaches to apply the theoretical aspects of sportspersonship and moral behavior to practice. In short, the purpose is to suggest ways of enhancing fair play in performers with reference to psychological theory.

There is a common colloquial understanding of sportsmanship (referred to hereon as sportspersonship, as is common in sport psychology literature). However, this is not easily defined, particularly as sport is largely distinct from everyday life in terms of morality (Bredemeier and Shields, 1984, 1986, 1987). More likely, people offer common examples of good and poor sporting behaviors when asked to define it. Vallerand, Deshaies, Cuerrier, Briere, and Pelletier (1996) and Vallerand, Briere, Blanchard, and Provencher (1997) provided a five-factor definition of sportspersonship. This included one's full commitment to sport, such as training hard, respect for rules and officials, evidenced by not criticizing a referee, true respect and concern for one's opponent, like not taking advantage of an injured opponent and respect for social conventions such as shaking hands after a performance. Finally, Vallerand et al. (1996; 1997) identified the relative absence of a negative approach as a factor, including losing one's temper or making excuses when defeated. While this definition identifies contributors to sportspersonship, McCutcheon (1999) suggests that the inclusion of one's full commitment is not necessarily the sign of good sportspersonship, using John McEnroe's frequent behaviors on a tennis court as an example. There are however, clear established links between this model of sportspersonship and motivational theories such as achievement goal theory (Nicholls, 1984) and self-determination theory (Deci and Ryan, 1985, 1989). Later, we discuss this relationship and consider how this encourages motivational approaches towards sportspersonship orientations and moral behavior. Below, we consider developmental and social-psychological approaches and based on this research, offer strategies to effectively enhance fair play in sport.

## DEVELOPMENTAL APPROACH

A developmental approach, such as structural developmental, is essentially studying unique stages that an individual passes through naturally in their development rather than through social learning. Much research in child psychology uses the approach to describe how an individual matures as they reach new stages (e.g., Piaget, 1932, 1954). Away from sport, Kohlberg (1969, 1976, 1981, 1984, 1986) pioneered work on moral development from a structural-developmental perspective further used by Haan (1977, 1978, 1983) (Bredemeier and Shields, 1993). Most notably, Kohlberg (1976) proposed a model of moralization (Table 1) that identified six stages at three levels of morality; pre-conventional, conventional and post-conventional.

Pre-conventional morality refers to heteronomous morality and individualism, typically evident in young children when moral reasoning is based on an exchange relationship. For example, a child may act in a moral way to avoid getting into trouble. Conventional morality includes a notion of relationships, interpersonal conformity and an awareness of social systems.

This level requires one to acknowledge that their actions have consequences for others with regard to a society. Post-conventional morality includes more individual rights and universal ethical principles. Such morality is described by Kohlberg (1976) as self-chosen ethical principles where the individual understands a broad perspective of others' rights and will follow their own values.

### Table 1. Kohlberg's model of moralization

| Level and Stage | What is Right | Reasons for Doing Right | Social Perspective of Stage |
|---|---|---|---|
| LEVEL I – PRECONVENTIONAL | | | |
| Stage 1 – Heteronomous Morality | Avoid breaking rules backed by punishment | Avoidance of punishment | *Egocentric.* Doesn't consider the interests of others |
| Stage 2 – Individualism, Instrumental Purpose and Exchange | Following rules only when it is someone's immediate interest to do so | To serve one's own needs or interests | *Concrete individualistic.* Aware that everybody has their own interest to pursue and these conflict |
| LEVEL II – CONVENTIONAL | | | |
| Stage 3 – Mutual Interpersonal Expectations, Relationships and Interpersonal Conformity | Living up to what is expected by people close to you | The need to be a good person in your own eyes and those of others | *Individual in relationships.* Aware of shared feelings, agreements and expectations |
| Stage 4 - Social System and Conscience | Fulfilling the actual duties to which you have agreed | To keep the institution going as a whole | *Differentiates societal point of view.* System defines roles and rules |
| LEVEL III – POST-CONVENTIONAL or PRINCIPLED | | | |
| Stage 5 – Social Contract or Utility and Individual Rights | Being aware that people hold a variety of opinions, that most values and rules are relative to your group | A sense of obligation to law because of one's social contract | *Prior-to-society.* Aware of values and rights prior to social attachments and contracts |
| Stage 6 – Universal Ethical Principles | Following self-chosen ethical principles | The belief as a rational person in the validity of universal moral principles | *Moral point of view.* Recognize the nature of morality or the fact that persons are ends in themselves |

Source: Adapted from Kohlberg, 1976.

A developmental perspective provides us with the notion of age-linked sequential reorganizations of moral attitudes and therefore, it seems logical to consider how individuals can be encouraged to progress through stages and levels of morality. Kohlberg (1976) postulates that progression through moral stages is not defined by internalized rules, but structures of interaction between self and others, specifically identifying environmental influences. Further, he points out that it is the general, everyday quality and consistency of the environment that brings about development, not a single large incident. Therefore, a social perspective is required in order to prescribe positive interactions.

# SOCIAL-PSYCHOLOGICAL APPROACH

A social-psychological approach examines how an individual's thoughts, feelings and behaviors are influenced by the presence of others, such as a society. It enables psychologists to map knowledge of internal processes to observed behaviors. Kavussanu (2008) offers a thorough and insightful review of previous moral behavior research, while Kavussanu and Boardley (2009) distinguish between antisocial and prosocial behavior in sport towards an opponent and towards teammates. This approach follows Bandura (1999) who highlights proactive and inhibitive behaviors. That is, that an individual may act in a morally virtuous way by either refraining from adopting negative behaviors (inhibitive) or by proactively engaging in positive behaviors, such as helping another. It seems logical then, that to proactively engage in behavior that demonstrates the existence of an ethos is a greater level of moral behavior than inhibitive behaviors. For example, a football player refraining from diving to win an undeserved penalty is an example of inhibitive moral behavior and is widely expected. However, informing the official that a penalty should not be awarded for one's team is a form of proactive moral behavior and is widely congratulated. With notable exception (e.g., ice-hockey), it is generally within the interests of a sport to promote virtuous prosocial behaviors and discourage unwanted antisocial behaviors (for a thorough and engaging reflection on why sport thrives in society through prosocial, true competition, as opposed to the more antisocial, "decompetition", see Shields and Bredemeier, 2009).

Previous studies have regularly drawn links between theories of motivation and sporting behavior, positively linking task orientation, where a performer judges success based on self-improvement, with sportspersonship (e.g., Dunn and Causgrove-Dunn, 1999; Gano-Overway, Guivernau, Magyar, Waldron, and Ewing, 2005) and negatively associating task orientation with likelihood to cheat (Stuntz and Weiss, 2003). Vallerand and Losier (1994; 1999) examined the relationship between self-determination and sportspersonship. Self-determination theory (Deci and Ryan, 1985, 1991) posits that individuals strive to satisfy three basic needs; competence, autonomy and relatedness (i.e., engaging socially). Deci and Ryan distinguish between intrinsic (participation is an end in itself e.g., enjoyment) and extrinsic motivation (participation is a means to and end e.g., reward) and describe those with high intrinsic motivation as self-determined. Vallerand and Losier (1994) assessed sportspersonship orientations and self-determination in elite male adolescent ice-hockey players at the beginning and end of a five-month season. The results highlighted a bidirectional relationship in which both concepts influenced each other over time, with the influence of self-determination on sportspersonship greater than the influence of sportspersonship on self-determination.

There is also significant support relating motivational climate with sportspersonship. Ames and Archer (1988) and Ames (1992) originally made a distinction between two forms of motivation climates while studying student behavior in classrooms before Seifriz, Duda and Chi (1992) related this to a sport setting. This distinction was between mastery and performance climates. Later, Newton, Duda, and Yin (2000) elaborated on the original model, including two higher-level dimensions of task-involving mastery and ego-involving performance climates, which each contain three sub-dimensions. The task-involved dimensions are cooperative learning, effort/improvement and importance role, while the ego-involved dimensions are intra-team member rivalry, unequal recognition and punishment for mistakes. Typically, a task-involved climate will encourage performers to identify success by self-improvement. In contrast, an ego-involved climate uses social comparison as a measure of success. A task-involved mastery climate has been positively associated with sportspersonship (Papaioannou, 1997; Miller, Roberts, and Ommundsen, 2004), prosocial behavior (Kavussanu and Spray, 2006, Boardley and Kavussanu, 2009) and negatively associated with antisocial behavior (Boardley and Kavussanu, 2010). Specifically, Boardley and Kavussanu (2010) found that male soccer players higher in task orientation we significantly less likely to display antisocial behavior towards their opponents. Therefore, to encourage personal development and fair play, coaches should aim to develop a task-oriented mastery climate, which is a key strategy that we identify below.

## STRATEGIES FOR DEVELOPING FAIR PLAY

Moral education can be delivered through specific interventions, formal programs or additional consideration during planning, delivery or reflection on existing sessions. Miller, Bredemeier, and Shields (1997) presented a sociomoral education program that they implemented in elementary schools over a 10-week period for at risk physical education pupils. The program (presented in Table 2) draws on Kohlberg's (1976; 1984) stages of moralization, which Shields and Bredemeier (1995) expanded on in physical activity. Rather than presenting the program as a curriculum for coaches to follow, we have used this to consider a range of potential strategies; developing a mastery climate, developing a moral community, role taking, reflection and power transfer.

### Table 2. Moral Action Processes, Sociomoral Education Goals, and Program Intervention Strategies

| Moral action process | Perception and interpretation | Judgment and deciding | Choice | Implementation |
|---|---|---|---|---|
| Program goal | Empathy | Moral reasoning | Task orientation | Self-responsibility |
| Intervention | Cooperative learning | Moral community | Mastery climate | Power transfer |

Source: Miller, Bredemeier and Shields, 1997

## Developing a Mastery Climate

Clearly, there is a link between motivation and observed moral behavior (Boardley and Kavussanu, 2010). Therefore, by addressing motivational determinants, we can encourage desired moral behaviors (i.e., fair play). As task orientation appears to discourage antisocial behavior and encourage prosocial behavior, developing a task-involved mastery motivational climate is a possible way to enhance fair play in sport. Epstein (1988; 1989) promoted the use of the TARGET acronym as a practical way to develop a mastery climate. This identified six environmental characteristics; the nature of tasks, locus of authority, recognition, grouping, evaluation practices and the use of time.

A representation of how these characteristics foster a motivational climate can be found in Table 3. By varying and introducing new tasks, performers are consistently striving for mastery. This places the focus on personal development rather than social comparison. Leadership roles add responsibility to participants, which could include responsibility for fair play.

Recognition should be conducted privately to avoid social comparison and be based on improved mastery of a task. Grouping is a common area for a coach to reflect on.

**Table 3. 'Targeting' a mastery climate**

| Mastery | | Performance |
|---|---|---|
| Challenging and diverse | Tasks | Absence of variety and challenge |
| Students given choices and leadership roles | Authority | No participation by students in decision making process |
| Private and based on individual progress | Recognition | Public and based on social comparison |
| Cooperative learning and peer interaction promoted | Grouping | Groups formed on the basis of ability |
| Based on mastery of tasks and on individual improvement | Evaluation | Based on winning or outperforming others |
| Time requirements adjusted to personal capabilities | Time | Time allocated for learning uniform for all students |

Source: Adapted from Epstein, 1989.

It is important to encourage cooperative learning to provide each individual with the greatest opportunity to develop. When performers are competing for the same prize however (e.g., position on a team or a contract), this can be difficult. It is important to stress to performers in these situations that the best they can do is to improve as much as possible, and cooperative learning, which is a significant part of Miller et al.'s (1997) sociomoral education program, is an effective way to achieve this. Evaluation should be on mastery of skill rather than social comparison. For example, a sprinter running close to a personal best should be evaluated positively regardless of finishing position. To further foster a mastery climate, time should be flexible and adjusted to meet individual task needs. Therefore, training for an individual should only progress once a skill is mastered and not before. By targeting a task-oriented mastery climate, coaches can encourage task orientation and therefore, more prosocial and less antisocial behaviors.

## Developing a Moral Community

The value of community and societies can be significant in shaping the behavior of individuals within them. Power, Higgins, and Kohlberg (1989) refer to a synergy that compels members to adopt group shared norms. This value is noted in Kohlberg's (1976; 1984) model. Referring again to Table 1, the key difference between pre-conventional and conventional levels of morality is the appreciation of a social system. Pre-conventional morality identifies individualism and the conventional level has a more mutual understanding and a desire to keep the institution going. The development of a moral community therefore is a very effective way to encourage progression in moral maturity. Miller et al. (1997) clarify that all people should refrain from doing bad things simply because they are people. This however, is augmented by membership of a group because members are motivated to avoid moral failings due to the profile, reputation and ethos of the group. A moral community is characterized by shared responsibility, trust, respect and care (Miller et al.). A determinant of much of this is brought about by group decision-making and problem-solving. Consequently, coaches may wish to consider how they can incorporate group dilemmas and problem-solving into their practice. For example, a conditioned game requiring a team to combine an amount of passes or for a set amount of team members to reach an individual target to score points for a team can help to develop the community because performers are working together for the same cause. There is enhanced responsibility to the group rather than individual performance.

This is a particularly useful strategy when trying to encourage progression to conventional morality. Further, coaches could encourage groups to work together to solve a problem during practice to build a moral community. For example, by identifying a tactical error in a previous performance, rather than prescribing a solution to players, the coach can ask groups of players to devise their own solutions.

## Role Taking

Considering Kohlberg's (1976) stages of moralization identified in Table 1, role-taking is an effective way to encourage progression at a pre-conventional level. By communicating with another from a variety of roles, including heightened and deficient responsibility (i.e., leading and following), participants can develop a greater awareness of the cognitive perspective of others (Hoffman, 1976). The first progression is awareness that everyone has their own interests, which is necessary for stage two of the model. Piaget's (1932; 1954) cognitive development stages suggest that this would typically occur around the ages of seven or eight.

To progress to conventional morality requires empathy, which is identified by Miller et al. (1997), who studied a similar age group to Piaget's suggested ages. This can be achieved by taking deficient roles such as being on a weaker team or in a weaker or disadvantaged position. When coaching children in particular, putting participants in weaker roles can encourage empathy for teammates and opponents, which is an important step towards fair play.

Consequently, a greater awareness of others' feelings, agreements and expectations develops. Stage four requires enhanced acknowledgement of roles within a social system. Sporting environments in both training and competition provide a distinct social system between and within teams and with officials. A simple way to achieve this could be to swap offensive and defensive players periodically. This can enlighten a performer to the difficulties faced by teammates during play and reduce the potential for one section of a team to place unfair blame on another.

As well as performance roles, there are different social roles adopted, particularly within teams, such as a captain, a highly-committed player, and a joker. Post-conventional or principled morality requires social contract, which goes beyond mere compliance to following self-chosen principles. This level of morality requires significant experience, which can be gained more quickly through role taking, as putting oneself in the place of various people exposes the participant to moral conflict from which they can test and refine their principles as they develop. One way of exposing participants to such moral conflict is to ask them to take the role of an official or coach. In these positions there are instances where one must make a decision that they know will bring about a negative response for some while pleasing others. This is good practice for making decisions based on moral principles.

## Reflection

To play fairly firstly requires an awareness of one's own approach and behavior. This can be most efficiently achieved through reflection. Structured reflection is used frequently in occupations like nursing (Johns, 1994) and teaching (Gibbs, 1988) and has been advocated for use by all practitioners (Murdoch-Eaton, 2002). Such educational approaches are common in sport psychology, as performance profiling and mental skills training regularly identifies existing and desired behaviors through self-evaluation. It is through post-performance reflection that performers can acquire heightened awareness, by moving from autopilot to critical reflection (van-Aswegen, Brink, and Steyn, 2000). From here, coaches are encouraged to include fair play principles in goal setting, particularly at team level. It is important to realize that principled morality is not something that is naturally obtained; it requires deep reflection and behavior modification. In the next section however we propose several other benefits of achieving this level of moral maturity so it is of significant value to the performer. Consequently, coaches should take opportunities to educate performers in fair play by identifying situations of moral conflict when they arise. For example, if a performer chooses to act in particularly positive or negative way, this can be highlighted to others to encourage reflection. It is through exposure to these moral decision situations that arouses internal contradictions in one's reasoning structure. Therefore, exposure to them and reflection on them is crucial for development.

Some coaches may wish to formalize or structure the reflection process, encompassing several or all acts of performance, including fair play. This is a process that could also be adopted in coach education programs, particularly those aimed at coaching children and youth sport. Coaches are encouraged to develop their own reflection templates to meet the reflective ability, time, and need of performers. This may include, for example, reflecting on specific positive and negative points during play, effort and persistence in training, the progress towards set goals, managing concentration, and physical fitness.

## Power Transfer

Ultimately, individuals are much more likely to play fairly if it is in their own interest. If fair play becomes one's own responsibility and that person is accountable for deviations away from fair play, they are more likely to uphold the principles of it. Miller et al. (1997) found that heightened responsibility encouraged a greater perspective of long-term group benefits and even self-sacrifice to achieve this. As identified in Kohlberg's (1976) model, post-conventional (or principled) morality adopts a prior-to-society view. That is, that one is guided by their knowledge of right and wrong towards an individual, regardless of societal norms or values. By transferring power, and therefore responsibility to participants, a coach is enabling each participant to develop their own principles and become self-determined. We can then observe a transition from conventional to principled morality when an individual is prepared to follow these newly-acquired, self-chosen principles above adhering to social norms.

This could be demonstrated by a performer being prepared to stand apart from others to do what they believe is the right. From a practical perspective, examples of power transfer could include allowing performers to make a choice over training practices, encouraging performers to conduct a post-match/event analysis, or providing performers with the option to take pre-match team talks. There are two important points to consider here; Firstly, power transfer is only appropriate when performers are already functioning at a conventional level of morality. Secondly, it is important that the coach identifies and acknowledges instances of self-chosen principled decisions.

Strategies that we have identified here for enhancing fair play are associated with other benefits, such as enhanced intrinsic motivation and reward. While studying work performance, Izadikhah and Jackson (2011) suggest that a mastery approach positively and consistently predicts higher levels of rewarding climates with regard to recognition of effort and enjoyment. Ultimately, reward, including intrinsic rewards, is a key motivator for ones participation in sport. Logically, therefore, such a rewarding climate is one that individuals will strive for.

This may have numerous other advantages such as trust, improved mental wellbeing and non-sporting benefits. Though further research is required in this area, a trusted individual may be looked upon favorably by officials and governing bodies. Izadikhah and Jackson's (2011) study supports benefits of a rewarding climate. There may also be non-sporting benefits, as the moral maturity required to reach a principled level demonstrates a healthy perspective. By restructuring ones moral approach within sport to develop heighted moral maturity, this could have significant benefits in everyday life.

## CONCLUSION

Research around morality in sport and sportspersonship will continue over the coming years. As such, the strategies suggested here are not exhaustive. However, there are several clear themes emerging. Firstly, there is significant research support (e.g., Boardley and Kavussanu, 2010) regarding the predictive ability of goal orientations on positive and negative sport behaviors. Consequently, coaches should strive to foster a task-involved mastery climate. As part of this climate, coaches can develop a moral community incorporating role taking to form empathy. These strategies are sufficient to enable performers to progress to a conventional level of morality. Through reflection and empathy, participants develop their own social system and informal social contracts.

From here, further reflection is necessary to establish the awareness required before an individual can cultivate their own principles. The greatest challenge for a coach in developing a progressive moral community is to avoid simply telling performers what is right and wrong but to empower them to develop a principled level of morality. In time, and with heightened moral maturity, it is these principles that drive social systems and enables the moral community and mastery climate to flourish.

# REFERENCES

Ames, C. (1992). Classrooms: Goals, structures, and student motivation. *Journal of Educational Psychology, 84*, 261–71.

Ames, C., and Archer, J. (1988). Achievement goals in the classroom: Students' learning strategies and motivation processes. *Journal of Educational Psychology, 80,* 260–67.

Bandura, A. (1999). Moral disengagement in the perpetration of inhumanities. *Personality and Social Psychology Review, 3,* 193-209.

Bandura, A. (2002). Selective moral disengagement in the exercise of moral agency. *Journal of Moral Education, 31,* 101-119.

Boardley, I. D., and Kavussanu, M. (2009). The influence of social variables and moral disengagement on prosocial and antisocial behaviors in field hockey and netball. *Journal of Sports Sciences, 27,* 843-854.

Boardley, I. D., and Kavussanu, M. (2010). Effects of goal orientation and perceived value of toughness on antisocial behavior in soccer: The mediating role of moral disengagement, *Journal of Sport and Exercise Psychology, 32,* 176-192.

Bredemeier, J. L., and Shields, D. L. (1984). Divergence in children's moral reasoning about sport and everyday life. *Sociology of Sport Journal, 1,* 348-357.

Bredemeier, B. J., and Shields, D. L. (1985). Values and violence in sports today. The moral reasoning athletes use in their games and in their lives. Psychology Today, 19(10), 22-32.

Bredemeier, B. J., and Shields, D. L. (1986). Game reasoning and interactional morality. *Journal of General Psychology, 147,* 257–275.

Bredemeier, B. J., and Shields, D. L. (1993). Moral psychology in the context of sport. In: R.N. Singer, M. Murphey, and L.K. Tennant (Eds.), *Handbook of research on sport psychology* (pp. 587-599). New York: McMillian.

Deci, E. L., and Ryan, R. M. (1985). The general causality orientations scale: Self-determination in personality, *Journal of Research in Personality, 19,* 109–134.

Deci, E. L., and Ryan, R. M. (1991). A motivational approach to self: Integration in personality. In R. Dienstbier (Ed.), *Nebraska symposium on motivation (vol. 38), Perspectives on motivation* (pp. 237-288). Lincoln, NE: University of Nebraska Press.

Dunn, J. G. H., and Causgrove-Dunn, J. (1999). Goal orientations, perceptions of aggression, and sportspersonship in elite male youth ice hockey players. The Sport Psychologist, 13, 183-200.

Epstein, J. L. (1988). Effective schools or effective students: Dealing with diversity. In R. Haskins, and B. Macrae (Eds.), *Policies for America's public schools: Teacher equity indicators* (pp. 89–126). Norwood: Ablex.

Epstein, J. L. (1989). Family structures and student motivation: A developmental perspective. In: C. Ames, and R. Ames, (Eds.), *Research on motivation in education* (vol. 3) (pp. 259–295). New York, NY: Academic Press.

Gano-Overway, L. A., Guivernau, M., Magyar, M., Waldron, J. J., and Ewing, M. E. (2005). Achievement goal perspectives, perceptions of the motivational climate, and sportspersonship: Individual and team effects. *Psychology of Sport and Exercise, 6,* 215-232.

Gibbs, G. (1988). *Learning by doing: A guide to teaching learning methods.* Oxford: Oxford Polytechnical.

Haan, N. (1977). *Coping and defending: Processes of self-environment organization.* New York: Academic Press.

Haan, N. (1978). Two moralities in action contexts. *Journal of Personality and Social Psychology, 36,* 286-305.

Haan, N. (1983). An interactional morality of everyday life. In N. Haan, R. N. Bellah, P. Rabinow, and W. M. Sullivan (Eds.), *Social science as moral inquiry,* (pp. 218-250) New York: Columbia University Press.

Haylett, T. (2000, December, 16). Di Canio catches mood. *The Telegraph.* Retrieved from http://www.telegraph.co.uk/sport/football/teams/everton/2994775/Di-Canio-catches-mood.html

Hoffman, M. L. (1976). Empathy, role-taking, guilt and development of altruistic motives. In T. Lickona (Ed.), *Moral development and behavior* (pp. 124-143). New York: Holt, Rinehart and Winston.

Hopps, D. (2009, September, 25). England surprise Sri Lanka in Champions Trophy opener. *The Guardian.* Retrieved from http://www.guardian.co.uk/sport/2009/sep/25/england-sri-lanka-champions-trophy.

Izadikhah, Z., and Jackson, C. J. (2011). Investigating the moderating effect of rewarding climate on mastery approach orientation in the prediction of work performance. *British Journal of Psychology, 102,* 204-222.

Johns, C. (1994). Guided reflection. In A. Palmer, S. Burns, and C. Bulman (Eds.). *Reflective practice in nursing* (pp. 110-130). Oxford: Blackwell Science.

Kavussanu, M. (2006). Motivational predictors of prosocial and antisocial behavior in football. *Journal of Sports Sciences, 24,* 575-588.

Kavussanu, M. (2008). Moral behavior in sport: a critical review of the literature, International Review of Sport and Exercise Psychology, 1, 124-138.

Kavussanu, M., and Boardley, I. D. (2009). The prosocial and antisocial behavior in sport scale. Journal of Sport and Exercise Psychology, 31, 97-117.

Kavussanu, M., and Ntoumanis, N. (2003). Participation in sport and moral functioning: the mediating role of ego orientation. In *International Society of Sport Psychology (ISSP) Xth world congress of sport psychology*, Skiathos, Greece, 5, 155–157.

Kavussanu, M., and Roberts, G. C. (2001). Moral functioning in sport: an achievement goal perspective. *Journal of Sport and Exercise Psychology, 23,* 37–54.

Kavussanu, M., Roberts, G. C., and Ntoumanis, N. (2002). Contextual influences on moral functioning of college basketball players. *The Sport Psychologist, 16,* 347–367.

Kavussanu, M., and Spray, C. M. (2006). Contextual influences on moral functioning of male youth footballers. *The Sport Psychologist,* 20, 1-23.

Kohlberg, L. (1969). Stage and sequence: the cognitive developmental approach to socialization. In D. A. Goslin (Ed.), *Handbook of socialization theory* (pp. 347–480). Chicago: Rand McNally.

Kohlberg, L. (1976). Moral stages and moralization. In T. Lickona (Ed.), *Moral development and behavior* (pp. 31-53). New York: Holt, Rinehart and Winston.

Kohlberg, L. (1981). *Essays on moral development, vol. 1: The philosophy of moral development.* New York: Harper and Row.

Kohlberg, L. (1984). *Essays on moral development: vol. 2: The psychology of moral development.* San Francisco: Harper and Row.

Kohlberg, L. (1986). A current statement on some theoretical issues, In S. Modgil, and C. Modgil (Eds.). *Lawrence Kohlberg: Consensus and controversy* (pp. 485–546). Philadelphia: Falmer Press.

Kohlberg, L., and Candee, D. (1984). The relation of moral judgment to moral action. In W. Kurtines, and J. L. Gewirtz (Eds.). *Morality, moral behavior and moral development: Basic issues in theory and research* (pp. 52-73). New York: Wiley Interscience.

Maynard, M. (2010, June, 3) Good sportsmanship and a lot of good will. *New York Times.* Retrieved from http://www.nytimes.com/2010/06/04/sports/baseball/04tigers.html?_r=0

McCutcheon, L. E. (1999). The multidimensional sportspersonship orientations scale has psychometric problems. *Journal of Social Behavior and Personality, 14*, 439-444.

Miller, B. W., Bredemeier, B. J. L., and Shields, D. L. L. (1997). Sociomoral education through physical activity with at-risk children. *Quest, 49*, 114-129.

Miller, B. W., Roberts, G. C., and Ommundsen, Y. (2004). Effect of motivational climate on sportspersonship among competitive youth male and female football players. *Scandinavian Journal of Medicine and Science in Sports, 14*, 193-202.

Miller, B. W., Roberts, G. C., and Ommundsen, Y. (2005). Effect of perceived motivational climate on moral functioning, team moral atmosphere perceptions, and the legitimacy of intentionally injurious acts among competitive youth football players. *Psychology of Sport and Exercise, 6*, 461-477.

Newton, M., Duda, J. L., and Yin, Z. (2000). Examination of the psychometric properties of the perceived motivational climate in sport questionnaire-2 in a sample of female athletes. *Journal of Sport Sciences, 18,* 275-290.

Nicholls, J. G. (1984). Achievement motivation: Conceptions of ability, subjective experience, task choice and performance. *Psychological Review, 91*, 328-346.

Ommundsen, Y., Roberts, G. C., Lemyre, P. N., and Treasure, D. (2003). Perceived motivational climate in male youth soccer: Relations to social-moral functioning, sportspersonship and team norm perceptions. *Psychology of Sport and Exercise, 4*, 397-413.

Papaioannou, A. (1997). Perception of motivational climate beliefs about the causes of success and sportsmanship behaviors of elite Greek basketball athletes. In R. Lidor, and M. Bar-Eli (Eds.), Innovations in sport psychology: Linking theory and practice: proceedings (pp. 534-536). Netanya (Israel), The Zinman College of Physical Education and Sport Sciences, The Wingate Institute for Physical Education and Sport, pt.II.

Piaget, J. (1932). *The moral judgment of a child.* New York: Free Press.

Piaget, J. (1954). *The construction of reality in the child.* New York: Basic Books.

Power, C., Higgins, A., and Kohlberg, L. (1989). *Lawrence Kohlberg's approach to moral education.* New York: Columbia University Press.

Shields, D. L. L., and Bredemeier, B. J. L. (1995). *Character development and physical activity.* Champaign, IL: Human Kinetics.

Shields, D. L., and Bredemeier, B. L. (2009). *True competition: A guide to pursuing excellence in sport and society.* Champaign, IL: Human Kinetics.

Stuntz, C. P., and Weiss, M. R. (2003). Influence of social goal orientations and peers on unsportsmanlike play. *Research Quarterly for Exercise and Sport, 74*, 421-435.

Vallerand, R. J., Briere, N. M., Blanchard, C., and Provencher, P. (1997). Development and validation of the multidimensional sportspersonship orientations scale. Journal of Sport and Exercise Psychology, 19, 197-206.

Vallerand, R. J., Deshaies, P., Cuerrier, J. P., Briere, N. M., and Pellitier, L. G. (1996). Toward a multidimensional definition of sportsmanship. *Journal of Applied Sport Psychology, 8*, 89-101.

Vallerand, R. J., and Losier, G. F. (1994). Self-determined motivation and sportsmanship orientations: an assessment of their temporal relationship. Journal of Sport and Exercise Psychology, 16, 229-245.

Vallerand, R. J., and Losier, G. F. (1999). An integrative analysis of intrinsic and extrinsic motivation in sport. Journal of Applied Sport Psychology, 11, 142-169.

van Aswegen, E. J., Brink, H. I., and Steyn, P. J. (2000). A model for facilitation of critical reflective practice: Part I: Introductory discussion and explanation of the phrases followed to construct the model. Curationis, 23, 117-122.

In: Innovative Writings in Sport and Exercise Psychology
Editor: Robert Schinke

ISBN: 978-1-62948-881-3
© 2014 Nova Science Publishers, Inc.

*Chapter 12*

# SHARED DELIBERATE PRACTICE: A CASE STUDY OF ELITE HANDBALL TEAM TRAINING

## *Ole Lund[*1], Peter Musaeus[2] and Mette Krogh Christensen[1,2]*
[1]Institute of Sports Science and Clinical Biomechanics,
University of Southern Denmark, Campusvej, Odense M, Denmark
[2]Center for Medical Education, INCUBA Science Park – Skejby,
Aarhus University, Brendstrupgaardsvej, Aarhus N, Denmark

### ABSTRACT

In this case study of a Danish elite handball team, we explore team learning processes in order to examine to what extent team members' development of expertise is a shared deliberate practice. By drawing from theoretical frameworks on expertise and deliberate practice (Ericsson, 2006) and team cognition (Salas, Fiore, and Letsky, 2012), we aim to answer what characterizes efficient and successful handball team training. The case study involved participant observation and interviews, and it included the female first team in a Danish handball club Randers HK. The team is amongst the best three teams in Denmark. In particular, the case study found that important factors for shared deliberate practice are concentration, feedback and role modeling. There are four theoretical findings. 1. Deliberate practice in team sport is a shared activity. 2. Both structured tactical training and match training are deliberate practices. 3. Concentration mediates team cognitive skills. 4. Feedback and role modeling mediate team cognitive skills. From an applied perspective, this study points to the value of seeing team sport as necessitating shared deliberate practice. Team players need to train shared understanding and learn how to negotiate the coach's orchestration of the game plan. Specifically, the results may lead experienced coaches in high performance team sports to use experienced athletes to engage in verbal feedback and being explicit role models to less experienced players.

**Keywords:** Deliberate practice; Handball; Expertise; Team Cognition

---

* Email: ole.lund@gmail.com, Mobile: +4521705025.

# INTRODUCTION

Handball[1] is a team game that requires dynamic responses on behalf of team members. Team members need to read each other's and opponents intentions and actions. Even expert performers struggle to learn such skills. This article concerns development of expert handball players' expertise as dynamic skills acquired through deliberate practice in team training. A cornerstone in handball players' expertise is situation awareness defined by Endsley (2006) with reference to skilled practitioners as an "up-to-date understanding of the world around them" (p. 633). Situation awareness is more formally defined as "the perception of the elements on the environment within a volume of time and space, the comprehension of their meaning and the projection of their status in the near future" (Endsley, 1999, cited in Endsley, 2006, p. 634).

The following situation from an elite handball match illustrates the dynamic skills such as situation awareness necessary for expert handball team players: The back court player runs directly towards the chain of defense in an attempt to penetrate it. The pivot realizes her team mate's intentions, tries to block the defender next to her in order to create a gap for the approaching back court player. But the defender avoids the block and runs forward to meet the back court player. This leaves the pivot unguarded. The back court player realizing that her chances of finding a gap in the defense are vanishing picks up the signal from the pivot's raised hands and passes the ball over the approaching defender and into the hands of the pivot. The pivot turns around and scores.

In game situations like the above, an individual handball team member and the team as a whole must make dynamic coordinated responses. They are dynamic because the situation changes moment by moment as opponents take countermeasures and decisions must be fast paced and arisen the moment and rely on the response of several team members. Accordingly, the team must be able to operate as a unit and the expertise of a team goes beyond its individual members (Eccles sand Tennenbaum, 2004). Ericsson and Lehmann (1996, p. 291) hypothesize that "expert performance is an extreme adaptation to task constraints mediated through deliberate practice". The point here is that a maximal adaptation on behalf of expert players is required in the domain-specific constraints inherent in handball (e.g., dynamic team situations coupled with well-defined tactical systems as discussed later). Therefore research is needed to explicate how this adaptive expertise is developed in a team based environment.

Becoming an expert sport team player might also depend on deliberate practice. Ericsson and co-researchers (Ericsson, 2006; Ericsson, 2007; Ericsson, Krampe, and Tesch-Römer, 1993) have argued that the notion of "deliberate practice" describes the qualities demanded of rehearsal practice seen as social activities that results in expert performance:

> Throughout development toward expert performance, the teachers and coaches instruct the individuals to engage in practice activities that maximize improvement. Given the cost of individualized instruction, the teacher designs practice activities that the individual can engage in between meetings with the teacher. We call these practice

---

[1] Handball is a team sport (a team = six outfield players and one keeper) and a ball game played indoors on a court of 40 by 20 meters in games of 2x30 minutes. The overall purpose is to pass (throw) a ball around among one's team and attempt to score more goals than the other team by throwing the ball into the goal of the other team. The game is fast and entails many goals. Also, the game involves a good deal of bodily contact and corporal wrestling.

activities deliberate practice and distinguish them from other activities, such as playful interaction, paid work, and observation of others, that individuals can pursue in the domain (Ericsson, Krampe, and Tesch-Römer, 1993, p. 368).

The question is whether the theory of deliberate practice rooted in a cognitivist framework of expertise sufficiently accounts for team based learning? While Simon and Chase (1973) argued that expert skills acquisition in chess and soccer was fundamentally similar in terms of pattern recognition, Ericsson and Smith (1991) in a literature review concluded that experts after thousands of hours of deliberate practice differ qualitatively in their information processing. Team sports such as soccer and handball are dynamic and require coordinated responses between team players in relation to opponent players as the game unfolds. Team players need the ability to integrate "the operations of the team in a timely way to form a composition of operations that achieves satisfactory performance" (Ecceles and Tennenbaum, 2004, 543).

The aims of this article are twofold: (1) to identify and describe the relevant training situations pertaining to high performance handball team training and (2) to examine how the handball players' development of expertise depends upon shared deliberate practice. By shared deliberate practice we refer both to ways in which deliberate practice is shared between team players and to the idea that deliberate practice should be conceived at team level.

Our argument is that the practice of handball and other team-sports is a matter of social interactions and coordinated actions between the players (Ronglan, 2009) and this type of practice can fruitfully be extended within the theoretical framework of expertise and deliberate practice (Ericsson, 2007). The importance of shared deliberate practice as a form of team based learning is captured by Therese Brisson, Olympic gold winner and six times World Champion in ice hockey:

> An important factor in the development of elite athletes is the training group [...] the less experienced athletes learn from the more skilled, and those who are pushing to get the top challenge the more skilled athletes on a daily basis (Starkes and Ericsson, 2003, p. 293).

## DELIBERATE PRACTICE AND TEAM TRAINING

Research on deliberate practice suggests that extended engagement within a certain practice domain does not in itself necessarily lead to the acquisition of expertise (Ericsson, 2007). The development of expertise requires that training activities are specifically designed to improve the performance of the athlete, and that the athlete deliberately concentrates on improving particular aspects of his/her performance when engaged in training activities.

As a prime example of deliberate practice, Ericsson uses aspiring experts such as violinists' solitary practice in which they work to master specific goals determined by their music teachers at weekly lessons (Ericsson, 2006, p. 693) or chess players playing through published games of the very best chess players in the world (Ericsson, 2006, p. 699). Jenkins (2010, p. 6) argues that the notion of deliberate practice involves the following characteristics: solitary practice that is coach mediated, goal-directed, measurable, and highly structured by the coach. Furthermore deliberate practice requires hard work and sustained concentration and attention in order for the practitioners' current level of performance to be exceeded.

Even though becoming an expert might sometimes require lone training what Ericsson (2007) calls the "solitary and non-social nature" (p. 23) of deliberate practice, he acknowledges that social-cultural factors shape the way deliberate practice is orchestrated within the specific domain. Firstly, deliberate practice-activities are based on the methods of practice that have been developed through time by previous generations in the domain and that this "body of organized knowledge" is "transferred from the current to the next generation through instruction and education" (Ericsson, 2006, p. 692). Secondly, Ericsson (2006) emphasizes that deliberate practice-activities are often structured by coaches, but that the expert athletes "will gradually acquire mechanisms that increase their ability to control, self-monitor, and evaluate their performance ... and thus gain independence from the feedback of their teachers" (p. 696). Furthermore, Ericsson (2006) mentions in passing that there is a form of "team-related deliberate practice" (p. 695), but research needs to be done to clarify whether this form of deliberate practice is the same as or different from as individualized deliberate practice. From what has been reviewed above it could be hypothesized that team handball expertise is not a solitary achievement but hinges on team cognitive skills.

The notion of deliberate practice is commonly used in research that investigates the training of expert athletes. Various researchers have discussed the validity and generality of deliberate practice across different sports disciplines such as darts (Duffy, Baluch, and Ericsson, 2004) wrestling (Hodges and Starkes, 1996), martial arts (Hodges and Deakin, 1998), soccer and field hockey (Helsen, Starkes, and Hodges, 1998), and golf (Jenkins, 2010). Helsen, Starkes, and Hodges (1998) warn that in the context of team sports, the deliberate practice framework need to differentiate between the investment in team training versus individualized training among elite and sub-elite athletes. The notion of shared deliberate practice aims to encompass team training, for instance in competition and match training, in order to account for the development of expertise within sports teams. In a study by Baker, Côte, and Abernethy (2003), it was found that team sport athletes single out competition and match play "as the most helpful form of training for developing perceptual and decision-making skills" (p. 346). This calls for further investigation into how team sports expertise is developed and what characterizes shared deliberate practice.

# METHOD

We adopted the case study as our methodological framework because we want to understand a real-life phenomenon, in this case the peer learning situations in elite handball players' shared practice, in depth and such understanding encompasses important contextual conditions (Yin, 2012). As Flyvbjerg (2006) emphasizes, "The case study produces the type of context-dependent knowledge that research on learning shows to be necessary to allow people to develop from rule-based beginners to virtuoso experts" (p. 221). The case study design was chosen because the handball sport training situation is context dependent and the aim was explorative not testing of quantifiable hypotheses. Our aim has been to be sensitive to and make sense of the athletes' learning experiences, while also examining the events and interactions transpiring between the athletes during practice sessions.

## Case Selection

We selected one of the two best first teams in Danish women's handball. The choice of this particular team in the handball club named Randers HK was based on three criteria. The first, most important, selection criterion was the high performance of the team because we wanted to study examples of best practice, that is a training practice that has consistently shown results superior to other teams in the same performance level. The second selection criterion was the potential presence of peer learning between high-performing handball players (skilled and experienced athletes) and novices (younger and less skilled and less experienced athletes) in the same team. The third selection criterion was availability or accessibility, which is on the one hand the participants' willingness to share their experiences and training situations with us and on the other hand the club managers' acceptance of our presence in numerous training sessions.

## Participants

Since 1996 Randers HK has positioned itself in the top three in the leading Danish handball league for women. In the 2011-12 seasons the club won the Danish league and the team came in second in the previous two years. The team consists of 18 players and is led by one head coach and one assistant coach. In order to focus our case study on team-based peer learning between expert players and novice players we selected four case persons, two experts and two novices[2]. The experts (Mette and Katrine) were between 31 and 33 years old, and they both had more than 10 years of experience in playing handball at the highest international level. The both participated in and/or won Champions League as well as Olympic Games several times. The novices (Sille and Sofie) were between 18 and 19 years old. They had no experiences in playing handball at the highest international level, but were selected to the first team by the head coach because he considered them to be sufficiently talented and hard working to join the training with the more experienced first team players.

## Procedure

The qualitative data were generated from participant observations (Spradley, 1980) of the four case persons' participation in the handball training and interviews (Kvale and Brinkmann, 2009) focusing on the observed training. The observations were made over 13 days of training over the course of one year and were used to contextualize the peer learning situations in focus, prepare an interview guide and to stimulate further descriptions during the interviews. During the training sessions the principal researcher acted as a "passive participant" (Spradley, 1980, p. 59). This means he was present at the training sessions as a bystander, once in a while taking part in informal conversations with the athletes and the

---

[2]The real names of participants have been used. Prior to the study we informed the participants about our interest in providing them anonymity in the presentation of data. However, the participants were interested in disclosing their names in order to make an example of best practice and therefore allowed the publication of their real names. We informed the participants about the consequences in case of lack of anonymity, and consequently we obtained permission to write their real names. In accordance with guidelines laid out by the Danish Data Protection Agency, their consent was obtained with the signing of a statement of consent.

coach before and after the sessions. Field notes were taken at the time, mostly in the form of cues and short sentences. The notes were further developed into more detailed descriptions immediately after each observation being made, and they included both descriptions of transpiring events, conversations, and preliminary theoretical reflections.

We prepared an interview guide taking point of departure in the observed training. The interviews included topics related to the athletes' experiences of good and bad team performances, how good team play was learned during practice and how the players helped and guided each other during practice. Adhering to the alternative method of data management in mixed-method studies suggested by Halcomb and Davidson (2006) the principal researcher audiotaped the interviews, took field notes, completed reflective journalizing and listened to the interviews several times in order to amend and revise the notes. This phase was followed by thematic analysis used to elicit common themes in the interview data and the themes were discussed with a second research team member. The final stage of data management involved a thematic review and re-listening to the audio-recordings to "identify illustrative examples with which to demonstrate the meaning of the themes from the participants' perspective" (Halcomb and Davidson, 2006, p. 42). These examples were transcribed verbatim in order to present the data in papers. The interviews were conducted in Danish. The principal researcher translated the examples provided in this paper into English.

## Analysis of Data

The researchers conducted a theoretical reading of the data (Kvale and Brinkmann, 2009) by applying the theoretical framework to facilitate interpretations of the data and discussions of the findings. The aim was to attempt to triangulate the observations with the interviews with the athletes' own descriptions in order to reach a deeper understanding of how deliberate practice facilitates team learning processes.

The first author collected the data and was therefore thoroughly versed in the case. Familiarity with data was achieved by iterative data collection, review of field notes and listening to whole interviews several times before coding. The analysis was focused on processes of learning within the athletes' practice sessions, such as the structuring of the training, and the way players approach their training and each other. An analytic strategy was for the co-researchers to play the devil's advocate (Kvale and Brinkmann, 2009) by looking for disconfirming data, questioning a particular reading by anyone of the researchers and developing and testing interpretations in dialogues with co-researchers. This study relied both on observations of how players trained and research interviews that were retrospective verbal accounts of how players thought they learned.

As mentioned in the research literature (Ericsson and Simon, 1980), it is a vexed question whether it is valid to deduce from retrospective verbal reports to actual behavior. In this case it is relevant to question whether what a player says she learned through deliberate practice might is in fact how she learned it. In light of this challenge we were careful to deduct uncritically from the observations of skilled practitioners to how they become experts and we used the triangulation of the observations and interviews and the method of playing the devil's advocate and constantly checking findings against the research literature on deliberate practice and team cognition.

As a further argument why interviews as verbal recalls with athletes is a valid means of inquiring into how they learned we will cite the argument by Helsen, Starkes and Hodges (1998) that expert athletes have eased recall because daily training is such an ingrained part of their daily routine.

# RESULTS AND DISCUSSION

The purpose of the study was to identify and describe the relevant training situations pertaining to high performance handball team training, and to examine how the handball players' development of expertise depends upon shared deliberate practice.

The data analysis identified what characterizes shared deliberate practice in a high performance team. First we describe two different types of training situations: structured tactical training and match training. Second we investigate the shared deliberate practice characteristics as they pertain to the team training.

## Structured Tactical Training

In the tactical meetings the coach lays out the tactics that the team must follow in the next game. Often the coach uses video to illustrate the preferred play formation, tactics and habits the opposing team has exhibited in past games. The next step is to explain how the team should respond to these action tendencies of the opposing team. In the structured tactical training the coach makes radical adjustments to the game plan for instance he decides that the game score does not count in order to get the players to work with a few specific tactical systems as part of deliberate practice.

In this type of training the coach often freezes the game so that the players remain in either defensive or offensive formations.

These adjusted game situations are repeated several times in order for the players to adjust their team tasks and team roles. As part of this shared deliberate practice, the coach repeatedly interrupts the training activity and evaluates the players' performances according to how well they align or conform to the tactical system. The coach's evaluation is aimed at both the team and individual players.

These training activities fit Ericsson's description of deliberate practice in so far as they are designed and monitored by the coach, are structured and aimed at explicit well-defined tasks, and aim to improve team and individual performance. The coach aims that deliberate practice target the team's strengths and weaknesses in order to match or rather overmatch the weaknesses of the upcoming opponent team that they are playing next. In these training activities, the coach has considerable influence on defining the critical aspects that the *individual* players have to be aware of and work with in order to improve the team's performance. However, in the research interviews Mette and Katrine stress that tactics should be a *team matter* and not only an individual task, even though the coach addresses tactics as the responsibility of the individual player. Both players warn that the team can sometimes overlook the importance of being critical towards the intended tactics. Mette describes a situation from a match in which a player had a good opportunity to attack and score, but did not seize this opportunity.

Instead she passed the ball as dictated by the coach's tactics and the team did not score. So if the player is too aware of the tactics she might become constrained and incapable of acting according to the dynamic situation of the game. Mette reflects on this problem that renders the player a bit like a "machine" who follows tactical rules without knowing when to apply them by staying alert to what happens in the specific situation:

> You become a bit paralyzed [by the tactics] instead of seeing what actually happens or thinking: How will she [the opponent] respond if I do like that [and not as planned]? That is, to feel one's way. (Mette)

As argued by Ericsson (2006, p. 694), coaches and players have to concentrate on the critical aspects that need improvement. But, as the case study shows, the explicit tactical goals might lead players to narrow their focus of attention. This has detrimental effects on the adaption of the specific game context of the next match. In this way this strategy of concentrating on a specific and critical aspect unintentionally teaches the players to neglect what has been called situation awareness defined by Mohammed, Tesler and Hamilton (2012) as the team members' reflection on the dynamic demands of a concrete situation and the extent to which individual team members' reflection overlap with that of others.

## Match Training

Match training forms a continuum from simulated games (for instance 4 versus 4) to full-fledged training matches against other teams. Half of the team's training was focused on game-like situations in which the players work to refine and adjust their interplay in the team's defensive and offensive lines, rather than training in basic throwing techniques. During match training the coach forms two opposing teams of 4-7 players. The coach also frequently substitutes players and thereby changes the formations of the teams. Furthermore, talented young male players are sometimes invited to participate in the training in order to add variety to the possible team constellations. Mette explains that variety helps the team to deal with unfamiliar challenges and develop team adaptability. Mette and Katrine say that the male players are "stronger and faster" and "make better feints" than their ordinary team mates. When playing against the male players:

> [...] you can't just stay on the crease [the marking line in front of the goal]and believe you can block the guy who comes pounding against you [...].You have to move forward and tackle him hard. (Katrine)

Playing in a variety of demanding match situations stimulates the team members to adjust their style of playing by playing not only "harder" but also "smarter" given that the team members constantly are facing a wide variety of opponents due to the frequent substitutions the coach makes during match training.

Taking the example of golf, Ericsson Prietula and Cokely (2007) argue that once the beginner has learned the basics of the game she does not improve substantially by merely going more rounds, but only by taking multiple shots from the same location and by deliberating on what goes on when playing these shots. Similarly, deliberate practice consists in spending time and space to think and re-think, evaluate and re-evaluate, keep trying the same difficult shots and correct mistakes repeatedly. Thus, whole game training is not a deliberate practice because this often encourages players to "rely on well-entrenched methods rather than exploring alternative methods" (Ericsson, 1993, p. 368). In summary, for match training to be effective, time and space for shared deliberate practice is necessary.

The players in this study emphasize that match training actually offers opportunities for exploring alternative ways of handling a game situation. For instance, Sofie says that match training teaches the players something that cannot be completely learned in highly structured training situations.

> It is in these situations [match training] you are allowed to think for yourself, because a lot of opportunities turn up from players being dragged. And we make gaps for each other, which means that there are more opportunities than if you are just glued in front of one defender [constrained by structured training activities]. (Sofie)

Although Sofie acknowledges the importance of repeating shared movement patterns and team coordinate response during structured tactical training, she tells that players encounter situations during match training that cannot be replicated in the structured training. Katrine emphasizes the importance of match-play without being restricted to following pre-arranged tactics, because these less restricted game-situations force the players to develop shared patterns of movement "out of nothing". This is based on the players' "feel for each other", which can be interpreted as a demanding type of team situation awareness where team players need to make up shared understandings on the spot. This way match training teaches the players to become responsive to the unpredictability of the game.

In summary, studying deliberate practice in a team context reminds us that it is not only the individual player's flexibility and decision-making-skills that are developed during match training, but also the team situation awareness and dynamic decision-making skills.

## What Characterizes Shared Deliberate Practice?

As might be glimpsed in the foregoing, the players found that the quality of the training, whether structured tactical training or match training depends on shared deliberate practice. The analysis found that two key elements in shared deliberate practice are (1) concentration and (2) feedback from coach and role-models. These elements constitute a shared enterprise that supports the following team cognitive skills: team coordination, team situation awareness and shared understanding. First we analyze concentration and feedback as shared deliberate practices. Second we delineate the above team cognitive skills. The argument is that deliberate practice is shared between team players as individuals and at team level, and that team cognitive skills are socially negotiated skills in the sense that they are developed within a specific sport context of team training.

## Concentration

Full concentration is one of the characteristics of deliberate practice (Ericsson 2006, p. 696). The point is that the quality of team training rests on the extent to which all team players are performing in a concentrated way. Katrine and Mette voiced their concerns that their shared practice is sensitive to the degree of concentration and focus with which the training is performed. When the players perform in a way that is not fully focused and concentrated, then they do not put all their efforts into play, which influences the overall training intensity and quality.

The players explained that they can read each other's concentration directly in facial expressions and gestures.

> I believe that is it important with gesturing, eye contact and facial expression. Well, when you look at people you see whether they are [mentally] present or not, whether they are completely focused, and when you say something to them there is a direct contact rather than if you say something to somebody she looks away and stares into the floor. (Katrine)

> I sense that if things are going well people communicate better and you establish eye contact. It is also physical that you touch each other or make a high five […]. This adds more [to the concentration] than if somebody runs next to you but is completely wasted [mentally]. (Sofie)

We also observed that an important mean for players to show that they are highly concentrated is by fighting determinedly for the ball or throwing oneself forcefully over the crease when shooting. The players seem sensitive to and directly affected by the expressed level of concentration in each other's behavior. Consequently, each player's concentration seems to be affected by the relationship between the players in the specific training context.

Our findings suggest that one of the key challenges for the team is to avoid a situation in which team performance is arrested at the level where some of the players perform with reduced concentration and effort. The coach can elevate team concentration during training for instance by punishing the losing team during practice through push-ups etc., but also the players can actively increase the team's concentration. For instance, Katrine tells about the importance for the team of having players such as herself and Mette that can "lead the way" and are capable of motivating others at training. Katrine exemplified how Mette often increases the intensity by repeatedly yelling to the others:

> It's rather funny with Mette. Even though we play on two goals in training [then she yells]: "We must win!", "Come on!", "They should not score now!" and things like that. (Katrine)

Furthermore Katrine exemplified how the experienced players in particular can enhance the overall concentration in training by deliberately exaggerating certain gesticulation for instance when they fight for the ball. This also exemplifies the experienced player has to embrace the other players and compensate for her team mates in order to facilitate her own performance, maintaining high quality training and ultimately increasing her chances of winning games.

Thus, maintaining high quality in training requires a team effort in which the players actively engage themselves, influencing each other in maintaining high levels of concentration, and holding each other accountable in their efforts to become a winning team. This shows that team concentration is not just a mental state inside the individual players' heads, but something that is constituted in the embodied interactions between the players. The experienced players play an important part in maintaining concentration in training by being role models that exhibit high concentration necessary for maintaining high quality training.

## Feedback and Role Modeling

We will discuss feedback (mainly verbal but as mentioned earlier also nonverbal) from the coach and role models. As already mentioned the more experienced players guide and give the other players feedback. The deliberate practice framework emphasizes that aspiring experts' learning is often facilitated by verbal feedback from a coach who makes athletes aware of the aspects that they need to improve, but this framework does not describe what makes the guidance and feedback an efficient learning resource other than its propositional substance. Our study indicates that the style of the relationship between the guiding player and receiving player influences the effectiveness of the verbal feedback. Sille (the younger player) states that her relationship with Mette influences how she perceives Mette's guidance:

> We played a game in which I was substituted for Mette and [then] she guides me in what I have to do and when I have to do it before I enter the court. This way I can really use it [the guidance] and feel confident with what I'm doing. When she tells me to do it, then I have the courage to do it. That is to take a step, go forward and take the good player [in front of me] out. (Sille)

However, Sille experiences Mette's guidance as "an extra hand" that enables her to be confident in her operations.

This is an example of verbal feedback and imitation as a result of the relation that Sille has developed to Mette over the years. Throughout the years she has followed Mette's games on television and she admires Mette's style of playing. She mirrors herself in Mette, because she has the same build and the same defensive position in the team. Thus, Sille sees Mette as a kind of role model.

Mette's guidance highlights critical aspects which she herself might have encountered on the court and which Sille must be aware of in her defensive play. However, the guidance seem to assist Sille's performance, not only because of their content, but also because they are put forward by Mette who – in Sille's eyes – "is so experienced and on top of things, so I trust that what she tells me is correct.

And I haven't experienced it not being correct yet" (Sille). Sille's actions seem to be backed up and supplemented by Mette's richer experience, because her perception of the guidance is influenced by her practical and imagined relationship to Mette. This guidance seems to modify Sille's practical relationship with the particular defensive context, and make her capable of performing timed and confident defensive operations. Since Mette is a role model for Sille her words carry a greater weight.

This could be interpreted an instructional nudge which according to Sutton become a form of "scaffolding that support[s] the embodied rebuilding of action" (Sutton et al. 2011, 93).

The interaction between Mette and Sille show that the social context (including its relational significance) is important to the feedback. For instance reflecting upon imitation Sofie mentions the importance of the experienced player caring for her learning:

Well, she [Katrine] approaches me, positions herself in front of me and has eye-contact with me. She tells me what to do and how to do it and exemplifies how she does it. 'You can do it like this' and she does it and I imitate it, if I can. She does this, not just because I want it, but because she has an interest in teaching me to do it, because she also wishes me to do well. (Sofie)

This indicates that the guidance and feedback given by experienced players are more likely to facilitate learning when the inexperienced player feels that the experienced player is attuned to the inexperienced player's challenges. Katrine's empathy through Katrine's behavior is directly experienced in the form of eye-contact and attempts to model movements for Sofie to imitate. This behavior seems to grant Sofie a sense of belonging in the team and make her feel that "it is okay to make mistakes" and that "no one looks down on you because you make a mistake" (Sofie). As a result, Katrine's behavior stimulates Sofie into risking facing a process of modeling the guidance with her own actions, even though this may very well include failing and stumbling.

In general, Ericsson's notion of expertise as task adaptation through deliberate practice focuses the unidirectional transfer of knowledge, e.g., when a coach passes on his/her guidance and feedback to an athlete (Ericsson et al., 2007). But as exemplified by Mette and Sille both players might have opportunities to learn from each other:

When you need to explain something to others, then you become able to understand it better or become focused on it again. So when I tell Sille: "You have to remember to raise your arms before you move ahead!" ... well, then I become conscious of this myself. (Mette)

In the process of guiding Sille, Mette gets an opportunity to reflect on her own play and movements: "If she did it like this, she would perform better. But hold on! That might also apply for me. It is a bit easier to see what others do wrong" (Mette). In this way, feedback from a role model to a novice is actually a two-way street where guidance is mutual and not a one-way transmission of knowledge from the experienced to the inexperienced player. In other words, when Mette observes Sille's performance, she identifies with Sille's situation and she temporarily perceives the play from Sille's perspective. This enables Mette to give Sille a guidance, which is deliberately and emphatically tailored to Sille's situation. At the same time, Mette herself wins useful experience that influences her corporeal understanding and improvement of her own abilities as a handball player.

## Team Coordination and Team Situation Awareness

During the structured tactical training the players' shared plan and shared situation awareness is highly influenced by the coach's suggestions. This does not mean that team members' team cognition is fully determined by the coach's tactical plan. The tactics must still be mediated by the players' interactions and the dynamic response of the game itself. But the orchestration (Jones and Wallace, 2005) of the situation and the supervision by the coach guides the players' actions and encourage them to perform the tasks advanced by the coach. In this way, structured tactical training serves to reduce complexity and contingency of the game and the players' exposure to alternative options:

It is important that you do the same things [over and over] in order to gain confidence that she [the team mate] is all set when needed because then I can make blind passes or make it hidden [e.g., fake shots]. This means you can add an extra layer on top of what you normally do if you have confidence [in your team mate]. (Mette)

In the interview quotation Mette reflects upon the importance of repetition in tactical training. But thought must be acknowledged that the predesigned and rehearsed play patterns are an essential part of the handball game (similar to American football, but opposed to the more free-flowing game of soccer), reduced exposure in the training situation has a drawback: In structured tactical training the players generally know their team role and the team task, but handball is a dynamic game and require in addition the development of team situation awareness through exposure to the complexity and contingency of both planned and unplanned game situations. This is why structured tactical training is combined with match training.

Parts of the match training consist in playing full-fledged matches, where all the players strive towards the overall goal of winning the game. In the engagement with the others – team mates and opponents – they negotiate and create the flux of the game by pursuing the chances of one's team. In many situations this requires that the players negotiate the task and interpret the situation with the other team players while playing. The players must actively coordinate with their team members in order to guide and support each other's actions of moving or recovering the ball. At the same time, the players coordinate with the opponent team in an attempt to misguide and interrupt their actions of moving or recovering of the ball. This means that the realization of the task of scoring and defending becomes co-constituted by the participating players in the very process of pursuing the task. In other words, in match training the players are encouraged to work with their situation awareness e.g., ability to make sense of each other's actions and co-constitute meaning by tailoring shared patterns of movement in the moment.

## Shared Understanding

As described above Randers HK is amongst the best three teams in Denmark. The players have all practiced handball over many years, and they are shaped by and share the specific practices and norms of the handball culture. However, each player has also developed personal and specific styles of playing. Besides being specialized in certain positions (e.g., goalkeepers, playmakers, pivots, wings, left and right back courts) the players demonstrate distinctive skills, for instance Mette is skilled at anticipating events and subsequently she has excellent timing (particularly in her defensive interventions). Katrine has an ability to claim responsibility in stressed situations (particularly in a taxing offensive) and Sofie is known for her fast speed and acceleration in the offensive play. Intertwined with their individual expert performance the players have developed team cognitive skills that allow them to coordinate their actions. Individual performance depends on a team coordinated response as exemplified by Mette, whose ability to anticipate her opponents' intentions and time her defensive interventions is entirely dependent upon the actions of her team mates:

I get a little more passive if I'm unsure whether they [the team mates] will mark [the opposing player], because when I move as far forward as is often required they [the team mates] have to guard the pivot behind me [...] On the national team, as an example, I [felt] more confident that Tina [pseudonym for a player on the national team], who I had played with for a long time, would cover the pivot because she knew I would do it [move forward]. (Mette)

Thus, one of the main concerns in training the team is to develop a shared understanding (i.e., team cognitive skills such as team coordination and mutual confidence) which enables the players to time their operations during training and games. The case study suggests that shared understanding develop when the participants deliberately train how to engage in shared enterprises such as doing well in highly competitive training sessions or tournament matches. As seen in the foregoing, the shared understanding also depends on the verbal cues and common schemata that team players develop about the game. In saying that these activities are *deliberate* we also imply that players engage in *negotiations* about the meaning of team tasks and the team's shared movement repertoire. This way the team members develop a shared understanding that supports their ability to operate as an expert team. For instance, Katrine emphasizes the importance of the players taking part in the orchestration of the team's interplay and attempting to "make the others perform well". But it is not only a matter of performing well, but also developing a shared understanding of what it takes to train in a team that participates at the highest level. Katrine describes how she as an expert sometimes needs to overact the intensity and seriousness in routine training for instance by yelling and inciting the team "for the sake of the young ones", because they need to be introduced to the shared understanding of how you fill the position as first team player in Randers HK. In other words, expert players need to teach the younger players the tasks and responsibilities of the high performance team member during training as well as games. In addition, Sofie says that a team's adaptability, for instance to difficult opponents, is developed when a player "not only has an eye for her own opportunities in the game, but also the opportunities of the others". This calls for a dynamic expertise that builds on the perceptual skill to pick up on the opportunities of others and enact these within the team. Such an expertise we may call shared understanding is highly dynamic because it entails appreciation and anticipating the movements of one's team mates in relation to the movements of the opposing team, and it entails recognition of the players' ability and necessity to teach and learn from each other. In summary, shared understanding is deliberately practiced in Randers HK by means of mutual apprenticeship among the team members.

## CONCLUSION

We suggested the notion of shared deliberate practice to account for the findings about learning and team training in an elite handball context. This case study is relevant in guiding successful handball training in terms of producing sustained concentration, the importance of reflections and analysis, the continual quest for improvement and the importance of structuring the practice. The theoretical implications for research on deliberate practice are fourfold:

*1. Deliberate practice in team sport is a shared activity.* In his deliberate practice framework Ericsson focuses primarily on the deliberations of the individual athlete and the coach when accounting for how an athlete develops expertise. But this study shows that team cognitive skills and teamwork plays an essential role in accounting for the acquisition of expertise. We have argued that deliberate practice as not fundamentally a solitary and non-social activity. In team practice, developing expertise is about deliberately asserting oneself as a team member whose goals and situation awareness are shared by other team members. In and out of games, players need to see other team members as competitors that can make themselves better as well as mates who can fulfill the objects of the team (namely winning).

*2. Both structured tactical training and match training are deliberate practices.* As a deliberate practice, handball training is structured. Training is comprised of specific exercises that aim to train the players' mutual understanding during training and in games. The exercises are geared not only to the individual player's movement but to entire patterns of movement shared by the players encompassed in gradually incorporated tactics and strategies in the players. From the point of view of Ericsson's concept of deliberate practice, and given the importance of accomplishing a shared understanding of tactics in elite handball, it is therefore surprising that this study shows that only half of the training is devoted to highly structured tactical training. However, if the training is too structured it can hinder the players' development of interactive skills such as exercising adaptability and making mutual decisions on the fly. Therefore the players need to train in game-like situations – regardless whether the players are novices, experienced or a mix as in this case study – in order to learn to deal with the unpredictability of the game.

*3. Concentration mediates team cognitive skills.* Ericsson emphasizes that deliberate practice is characterized by the athletes working with their training in a concentrated way. Similarly, our results underline the importance of handball players training and performing in a highly concentrated way as they strive for excellence. However, on the basis of the study, we argue that concentration is not just a mental state inside the individual player's head, but also something that is constituted in the embodied interactions between the players. The players must remain alert and ready to adjust to the other players and developments in the game, and all the players must be concentrating this way for the training to be efficient. Thus, an important aspect of the team's shared deliberate practice is to be engaged in the team's efforts to build on their shared situation awareness of the task at hand. In this way, concentration is a prerequisite for team situation awareness as well as a result of team training.

*4. Feedback and role modeling mediate team cognitive skills.* The deliberate practice framework underlines the importance of verbal feedback passed on from the coach to the athlete. Similarly, our study shows that the players' learning processes are stimulated by verbal feedback from the coach when he makes the players aware of elements in the game that need to be improved. However, the framework only vaguely describes the interpersonal bearings on the link between feedback and learning. From the results of our study we may argue that the learner's efficient implementation of the guidance depends on the learner's relationship to the guide that gives the verbal feedback. For instance, when an expert player acts as a trusted role model for a younger player the expert's feedback is picked up more detailed and in-depth by the younger player. At the same time, the efficiency of the verbal feedback seems to be closely connected to the guide's sensitivity to the player. Moreover, mutual feedback is a common feature among the players, and we may argue that when a player guides a team mate she becomes more responsive to manners in which she can improve her own performance. Thus, being engaged in an apprenticeship with a team mate, the player puts her own abilities up for negotiation in so far that guiding the team mate from the perspective of her own abilities may help her improve her own performance.

What are the practical implications of the findings? From an applied perspective, this study points to the value of seeing team sport as necessitating shared deliberate practice. Team players need to train shared understanding and learn how to negotiate the coach's orchestration of the game plan. The above mentioned findings warrant inclusion of shared deliberate practice as part of basic coaching courses on team training. Specifically, they may lead coaches in high performance team sports to use experienced athletes to engage in verbal feedback and being explicit role models to less experienced players. Furthermore, the study lends support to recent recommendations regarding supportive features characterizing the positive relationships between the participants in successful athletic talent development environments (Henriksen, 2010). However, this study is limited by the focus on one specific sport, and we must underline the circumscribed transferal of our results to other sports. Future research is warranted in other team sport context than handball to spell out what characterizes shared deliberate practice in these social contexts.

## ACKNOWLEDGMENTS

We would like to thank the team and coaches of Randers HK for kindly giving their time to participate in the study and share their knowledge with us. In particular, we would like to thank Mette for her great courtesy and for making this study possible. We also thank Professor John Sutton, Senior Lecturer Greg Downey and other members of research group in *Sport, Skills and Movement* at the Centre for Cognition and its Disorders at Macquarie University, Sydney for their many helpful comments during the writing of this article. We conducted the study with the aid of a research grant from The Danish Council for Independent Research/Humanities. The study is a part of the larger research project "From Talent to Expert" based at the University of Southern Denmark.

## REFERENCES

Baker, J., Côte, J., and Abernethy, B. (2003). Learning from the experts: Practice activities of expert decision makers in sport. *Research Quarterly for Exercise and Sport, 74*, 342-347.

Duffy, L. J., Baluch, B., and Ericsson, K. A. (2004). Dart performance as a function of facets of practice amongst professional and amateur men and women players. *International Journal of Sport Psychology,35*, 232-245.

Eccles, D. W., and Tennenbaum, G.(2004). Why an expert team is more than a team of experts: Asocial-cognitive conceptualization of team coordination and communication in sport. *Journal of Sport and Exercise Psychology, 26*, 542-560.

Endsley, M. R. (2006). Expertise and situation awareness. In K. A. Ericsson, N. Charness, P. J. Feltovich, and R. R. Hoffman (Eds.), *The Cambridge handbook of expertise and expert performance* (pp. 633–651). Cambridge, UK: Cambridge University Press.

Ericsson, K. A. (2006). The influence of experience and deliberate practice on the development of superior expert performance. In K. A. Ericsson, N. Charness, P. J.

Feltovich, and R. R. Hoffman (Eds.), *The Cambridge handbook of expertise and expert performance* (pp. 685-706). Cambridge, UK: Cambridge University Press.

Ericsson, K. A. (2007). Deliberate practice and the modifiability of body and mind: toward a science of the structure and acquisition of expert and elite performance. *International Journal of Sport Psychology, 38*, 4-34.

Ericsson, K. A., Krampe, R. T., and Tesch-Römer, C. (1993). The role of deliberate practice in the acquisition of expert performance. *Psychological Review, 100*, 363-406.

Ericsson, K. A., and Lehmann, A. C. (1996). Expert and exceptional performance: Maximal adaptation to task constraints. *Annual Review of Psychology, 47*, 273–305.

Ericsson, K. A., Prietula, M. J., and Cokely, E. T. (2007). The making of an expert. *Harvard Business Review*, 1-7.

Ericsson, K. A., and Simon, H. A. (1980). Verbal reports as data. *Psychological Review, 87*, 215–251.

Ericsson, K. A., and Smith, J. (1991). Prospects and limits in the empirical study of expertise: an introduction. In K. A. Ericsson and J. Smith (Eds.), *Toward a general theory of expertise: prospects and limits* (pp. 1-38) Cambridge: Cambridge University Press.

Flyvbjerg, B. (2006). Five misunderstandings about case-study research. *Qualitative Inquiry, 12*, 219-226.

Helsen, W. F., Starkes, J. L., and Hodges, N. J. (1998). Team sports and the theory of deliberate practice. *Journal of Sport and Exercise Psychology,20*, 12-34.

Henriksen, K. (2010). *The ecology of talent development in sport: a multiple case study of successful athletic talent development environments in Scandinavia.* Odense: University of Southern Denmark.

Hodges, N. J., and Deakin, J. (1998). Deliberate practice and expertise in the martial arts: The role of context in motor recall. *Journal of Sport and Exercise Psychology,20*, 260-279.

Hodges, N. J., and Starkes, J. L. (1996). Wrestling with the nature of expertise: A sport specific test of Ericsson, Krampe and Tesch-Römer's (1993) theory of deliberate practice. *International Journal of Sport Psychology,27*, 400-424.

Jenkins, S. (2010). Digging out the dirt: Ben Hogan, deliberate practice and the secret. *Annual Review of Golf Coaching,4*, 1-21.

Jones, R. L., and Wallace, M. (2005). Another bad day at the training ground: coping with ambiguity in the coaching context, *Sport, Education and Society, 10*, 119-134.

Kvale, S., and Brinkmann, S. (2009). *Interviews: Learning the craft of qualitative research interviewing.* Los Angeles: Sage Publications.

Mohammed, S., Tesler, R., and Hamilton, K. (2012). Time and team cognition: Toward greater integration of temporal dynamics. In E. Salas, S.M. Fiore, and M.P. Letsky (Eds.), *Theories of team cognition: Cross-disciplinary perspectives* (pp. 87-116). London: Taylor and Francis/Routledge Academy.

Ronglan, L. T. (2009). Situert læring: om laget som praksisfellesskap. In L. T. Ronglan, A. Halling, and G. Teng (Eds.), *Ballspill over grenser: skandinaviske tilnærminger til læring og utvikling*(pp. 35-47). Oslo: Akilles forlag.

Salas, E., Fiore, S.M., Letsky, M.P. (2012). *Theories of Team Cognition: Cross-disciplinary perspectives.* London: Taylor and Francis/Routledge Academy.

Simon, H. A., and Chase, W. G. (1973). Skill in chess. *American Scientist, 61,* 394–403.

Spradley, J. P. (1980). *Participant observation.* Fort Worth: Harcourt Brace College Publishers.

Starkes, J. L., and Ericsson, K. A. (Eds.) (2003). *Expert performance in sports: Advances in research into sport expertise.* Champaign, IL: Human Kinetics.

Sutton, J., McIlwain, D., Christensen, W., and Geeves, A. (2011). Applying intelligence to the reflexes: Embodied skills and habits between Dreyfus and Descartes. *Journal of the British Society for Phenomenology, 42,* 78-103.

In: Innovative Writings in Sport and Exercise Psychology
Editor: Robert Schinke

ISBN: 978-1-62948-881-3
© 2014 Nova Science Publishers, Inc.

*Chapter 13*

# A LONGITUDINAL QUALITATIVE EXPLORATION OF ELITE KOREAN TENNIS PLAYERS' CAREER TRANSITION EXPERIENCES

## *Sunghee Park*[*1], *David Lavallee*[1] *and David Tod*[2]
[1]School of Sport, University of Stirling, Stirling, UK
[2]Department of Sport and Exercise Science, Aberystwyth University, Aberystwyth, UK

### ABSTRACT

The purpose of this study was to explore elite Korean tennis players' career transition experiences, focusing on psychological components (i.e., self-identity, life skills development, and coping strategies) and socio-cultural influences through the process. A longitudinal qualitative method was employed, and Korean tennis players ($N = 5$; two males and three females; mean age $29.8 \pm 5.54$ years) who were considering retirement participated in the current study. Data were analyzed by interpretative phenomenological analysis and resulted in three super-ordinate themes: (a) sense of self and process of identity shift, (b) available resources during the career transition process, and (c) decision-making processes and consequences of decisions. These results provided practical implications for supporting athletes' career transitions (e.g., developing a balanced self-identity and life skill during their athletic careers, providing proactive intervention) and future research directions (e.g., examining athletes' retirement decision-making process, the need of cross-cultural research).

**Keywords:** Athletic identity, identity foreclosure, IPA, retirement, self-identity, transferable skills

Studies in athletes' career transitions have increased gradually in the past three decades (e.g., Bruner, Munroe-Chandler, and Spink, 2008; Stambulova and Alfermann, 2009;

---

[*] Correspondence concerning this article should be addressed to Sunghee Park, School of Sport, University of Stirling, FK9 4LA, UK. Phone: (44) 1786466489. Fax: (44) 1786466477. E-mail: sunghee.park@stir.ac.uk.

Wylleman, Alfermann, and Lavallee, 2004). Findings from previous studies have indicated that athletic identity (e.g., Lally, 2007), life skills development (e.g., Kerr and Dacyshyn, 2000), and coping strategies (e. g. Alfermann, Stambulova, and Zemaityte, 2004) are closely related to the quality of athletes' career transitions. Researchers (e.g., Lally, 2007; Lavallee and Robinson, 2007) have revealed that athletes with strong athletic identities experienced a higher degree of career transition difficulties and identity crisis during the career transition process, in terms of their narrowly focused lifestyles and identity development. For example, previous literature (e.g., Lally, 2007; Warriner and Lavallee, 2008) has indicated that athletes with a higher degree of athletic identity experienced more negative emotions, including feelings of loss, isolation and fear of an uncertain future, and also took longer to adjust to post-sport life than those who had a more balanced identity. Investigators (e.g., Kerr and Dacyshyn, 2000; Lavallee and Robinson, 2007) have also discovered that the balance in athletes' lifestyles, such as the balance between inside sport and outside sport activities, tends to be associated with individual development, including identity and life skills development and influences the quality of adjustment to post-sport life, in terms of developing a balanced self and social identity and acquiring higher educational achievement. Regarding coping strategies, researchers (e.g., Stephan, Bilard, Ninot, and Delignières, 2003; Taylor and Ogilvie, 1994) revealed that athletes' social support networks and coping resources influence the quality of career transitions.

Through the development of the research area, the concept of transitions in sport has changed from a singular event to a process which occurs to athletes over time, and researchers have tried to focus on athletes' life span development (e.g., Stambulova and Alfermann, 2009; Wylleman et al., 2004). Since athletes' career transition has been considered as a process, researchers (e.g., Lavallee and Robinson, 2007) have suggested the need to examine the process through longitudinal assessments, in terms of examining athletes' changes in psychological and emotional responses (i.e., identity re-formation, coping strategy used). However, in the study area, only a few studies (e.g., Douglas and Carless, 2009; Stephan et al., 2003) have been conducted with longitudinal designs because it is not easy to predict the actual timing of athletes' retirement, and even for the longitudinal studies, most of the data were collected after the actual retirement of athletes (e.g., Stephan et al., 2003). In addition, although researchers (e.g., Cecić Erpič, Wylleman, and Zupančič, 2004) have discussed the importance of athletes' retirement decision-making process in the final stages of their sport careers, the overall process of athletes' career transitions, including both the final stages of athletic careers and post-sport adjustment, have not been examined much in the study area.

Another issue often discussed in the career transition research field recently is the influence of socio-cultural issues and environmental sport contexts in athletes' career transitions, and researchers (e.g., Stambulova and Alfermann, 2009; Stambulova, Alfermann, Statler, and Côte 2009) have emphasized the need to examine socio-cultural and environmental-based variables (e.g., sport systems). Stambulova and Alfermann (2009) stated that the majority of career transition studies have been conducted in the Western nations (i.e., North America, Europe, and Australia), and studies on athletes' career transition are rare in Asian countries.

In the cross-cultural psychology literature, Si and Lee (2007) highlighted that examining cultural similarity and differences could help test the generality and validity of existing knowledge and theories in other cultural contexts and practical implications, such as providing suitable and appropriate support in applied work. In addition, although aforementioned psychological influences (i.e., athletic identity, athletes' life skills development, and coping strategies) have been considered as factors related to the quality of athletes' career transitions, not much evidence has been provided from Korean athletes. Therefore, examining Korean athletes' career transition experiences might be helpful in expanding knowledge of different cultural backgrounds and testing the generality and validity of existing knowledge and theories in other cultural contexts.

To understand Korean tennis players' career transition experiences, it might be helpful to explain Korean sport contexts, in terms of unique Korean semi-professional sport systems. In Korea, there are two different types of elite level tennis players, professional and semi-professional. The professional athletes play international tennis tournaments, such as those on the ATP (Association Tennis Professionals) or WTA (Women's Tennis Association) tours. Two major companies support these players, and only a few Korean athletes (usually fewer than 10 players at the same time) have a chance to become a professional tennis player. Semi-professionals mainly play the domestic league and compete in just a few international tournaments each year. They belong to certain teams (companies) and play for their teams. Some of the semi-professional teams hire athletes as regular employees. In that case, athletes can work at the company after they terminate their sport career, which means they have secure jobs after their retirement from sport.

The semi-professional system in the Korean tennis context is more similar to the professional contexts of most other countries than their semi-professional systems, because during their sporting lifetime semi-professional athletes in Korea only play sport for their team but are not involved in office work.

Other semi-professional teams have a short-term contract with players, and athletes are not considered employees of the company. Players who have a short-term contract with semi-professional tennis teams and professional players need to find a post-sport career when they retire from their sport.

Since researchers (e.g., Lotysz and Short, 2004) revealed that finding a post-sport career is one of the main sources of athletes' career transition difficulties, unique Korean sport contexts might influence athletes' career transition experiences.

The purpose of the current study was to explore elite Korean tennis players' career transition experiences by focusing on psychological factors (e.g., self-identity, psychological status) and socio-cultural influences, including the pre-retirement period and post-sport life adjustment over a period of time (i.e., 2 to 3 months before retirement and within 1 month, 6 months, and 12 months after retirement).

## METHOD

A qualitative longitudinal research design was employed to explore participants' career transition processes in depth. According to Patton (2002), qualitative inquiry generally helps researchers produce rich and detailed information from a small number of participants and collect information about certain cases or situations rather than generalized findings. The participants in the present study were selected purposively based on Smith, Flowers, and Larkin's (2009) sampling strategies.

Smith et al. (2009) suggested that researchers need to select participants with represent perspective on particular phenomena who are fairly homogeneous. In order to select information-rich cases who can offer an insight into a particular experience, the participants for the current study were selected on the basis of two criteria. First, participants had to be either professional or semi-professional tennis players in Korea and second, they should be considering retiring from their sport.

## Participants

The participants in the present study were full-time Korean elite-level athletes, including one female professional tennis player and two male and two female semi-professional tennis players. The players were aged between 24 and 36 ($Mage$ = 29.8, $SD$ = 5.54), had been playing tennis for an average of 20 years ($SD$ = 5), and had spent an average of 10.6 years as professional or semi-professional athletes ($SD$ = 3.78). Participants' profiles are presented in the Table 1, and pseudonyms have been used to protect confidentiality (see Table 1). The participants postponed their retirement for 1 to 3 years, since they had first considered their retirement. Two of them retired from their sport 3 months after their first interviews, and the other three participants postponed their retirement for a year and retired 3 months after their third interviews.

**Table 1. Details of Participants**

| Participants | Gender | Age | Time spent in (semi-) professional tennis career | Reasons for retirement | Higher competitive level while playing | Post-sport career |
|---|---|---|---|---|---|---|
| Alex | Male | 35 | 13 years | Chronic injury/ aging | Semi-professional | Bank assistant |
| Christina | Female | 24 | 6 years | Underperformance | Semi-professional | Bank teller |
| George | Male | 36 | 15 years | Aging/new career | Semi-professional | Bank assistant |
| Isobel | Female | 25 | 7 years | Chronic injury | Semi-professional | Bank teller |
| Meredith | Female | 29 | 13 years | Chronic injury | Professional | Tennis coach |

## Interview Guide

The interview guides were developed based on previous literature on athletes' retirement from sport (Brewer and Cornelius, 2001; Taylor and Ogilvie, 1994) and Patton's (2002) guidelines of question options. The interview guide for the first interview contained several main discussion topics, including demographic questions, individuals' sport careers, athletic identity, reasons for retirement, psychological and emotional experiences, and coping strategies. Later interview guides were based on participants' responses to help researchers to follow the athletes' stories, but major topics (e.g., identity, psychological experiences, and coping strategies) were common to all interviews.

## Procedure

To identify potential participants, in the current study, we utilized purposive sampling. The sampling begins by speaking to a person who knows key informants well and connecting potential participants through referral from various informants (e.g., Clare, 2002; Smith et al., 2009). To select information-rich participants for the current study, we contacted two Korean national tennis team coaches and obtained contact details of athletes who intended to terminate their sport careers. The first author contacted the six potential participants via phone, and five of them agreed to participate in the current study but the sixth decided not to participate because she was not sure whether she was going to retire or not.

All participants were informed about the study, including the purpose, ethical considerations, and the benefits and risks of taking part. Individuals signed consent agreement forms before their first interview. Before the first interview with each participant, we scheduled four interviews with them, including between 2 and 3 months before their retirement, within 1 month, between 5 and 6, and between 11 and 12 months after retirement. However, some changes had to be made with regard to the timing of several participants' retirement (see Table 2). Interviews were conducted either face-to-face or over the telephone owing to geographical limitations. Each participant had at least one face-to-face interview (see Table 2). Although face-to-face interviews were preferred, some previous findings (e.g., Bermack, 1989; Herzog and Rodgers, 1988) indicated no difference in self-disclosure between face-to-face and telephone interviews. The location, date, and time of the interviews were scheduled according to participants' preference.

A total of 23 semi-structured interviews were conducted with the five participants over a period of 20 months. Christina and Meredith, who retired as they had initially planned, participated in four interviews, which were conducted between 2 and 3 months before their retirement, within 1 month, between 5 and 6 months, and between 11 and 12 months after their retirement. The other three participants (i.e., Alex, George, and Isobel) also had their first interviews between 2 and 3 months before their intended retirement, but a few weeks after the interviews, they decided to postpone their retirement from tennis for a year. The second set of interviews with these three athletes was conducted as scheduled, which was 3 months after the first interview, and the interviews were focused on their decisions to postpone their retirement.

The third interviews with the continuing participants took place a year after the first interview, which was again between 2 and 3 months before their retirement. All three athletes who postponed their retirement terminated their sport careers 3 months after the third interviews. All three of them had their fourth interviews within 1 month after retirement, and the final interviews were conducted between 5 and 6 months after their sport career ended.

The time for the first interview with the respondents, which was between 2 and 3 months before their intended retirement from sport, was chosen for the purpose of examining athletes' reactions to their retirement decisions and their attitudes toward retirement in the final stages of their sport careers. More specifically, the purpose of the first interview was identifying participants' reasons for retirement and their psychological experiences of the pre-retirement process, including any change in terms of identity, psychological status and emotional response, and the coping strategies used.

## Table 2. Timetable for interviews

| | The first interview | The second interview | The third interview | The fourth interview | The fifth interview |
|---|---|---|---|---|---|
| Interviews with participants who retired as planned | 1 to 3 months before retirement | Within a month of retirement | Within 5 to 6 months after retirement | Within 11 to 12 months after retirement | |
| **Meredith** | Interview 1 Phone | Interview 2 Face-to-face | Interview 3 Phone | Interview 4 Phone | |
| **Christina** | Interview 1 Phone | Interview 2 Face-to-face | Interview 3 Phone | Interview 4 Phone | |
| Interviews with participants who postponed their retirement | 1 to 3 months before intended retirement | 1 to 2 months after postponement decision | 1 to 3 months before actual retirement | Within a month of retirement | Within 5 to 6 months after retirement |
| **Isobel** | Interview 1 Phone | Interview 2 Face-to-face | Interview 3 Face-to-face | Interview 4 Phone | Interview 5 Phone |
| **George** | Interview 1 Phone | Interview 2 Face-to-face | Interview 3 Face-to-face | Interview 4 Phone | Interview 5 Phone |
| **Alex** | Interview 1 Phone | Interview 2 Face-to-face | Interview 3 Face-to-face | Interview 4 Phone | Interview 5 Phone |

The second round of data collection was conducted within a month of the participants' retirement. Through the second interview, we intended to reveal how athletes perceived or dealt with their sport careers termination soon after they retired, including any identity shift, emotional and psychological experiences, and their use of coping skills.

The third interview was scheduled to take place between 5 and 6 months after participants' sport career ended. In the third interview, we aimed to look at the athletes' life changes and their adjustment to post-sport life, focusing on psychological factors, such as identity shift, emotional and psychological responses, changes in social networks, and coping strategies. The period of time between 5 and 6 months after their actual retirement was chosen on the basis of previous research findings indicating that athletes took 6 months or longer to adjust to their post-sport lives (e.g., Sinclair and Orlick, 1993; Stephan et al., 2003). Additionally, the transtheoretical model (Prochaska and DiClemente, 1984) indicates that when individuals experience life changes, it takes a minimum of 6 months to reach the maintenance stage, which refers to the adaption of new life routines or changes as results of life changes or events. In addition, three participants who postponed their retirement had five interviews each, but they had three interviews before their actual retirement, and their last interview was between 5 and 6 months after retirement. The last interview with two respondents who retired after their first interviews (i.e., Christina and Meredith) was held a year after their retirement. In the final interview, we tried to expand the views expressed in their third interviews, including degree of adjustment and perception of new life experiences.

## Analysis

The total time for the interviews was 1,653 minutes, and they ranged between 35 and 98 minutes, with an average of 72 minutes. Interviews were tape recorded and transcribed verbatim. The total time taken to transcribe the interviews was 80 hours and 28 minutes, and the words totaled 136,333 (in the English version). The original transcribed versions (Korean) were translated into English, and the copies of the original (Korean) and English manuscripts were sent to another expert to check the credibility of the translation work.

To gain an understanding of athletes' career transition experiences, data were analyzed by interpretative phenomenological analysis (IPA). Smith, Jarman, and Osborn (1999) outlined IPA, which is based on phenomenology, hermeneutics, and ideography. IPA researchers focus on the detailed examination of individuals' experiences at a particular moment or during a significant event (Smith et al., 2009).

The process of the analysis for the current study included five different steps based on Smith et al. (2009) suggestions. In line with the principles of IPA, each individual's response was analyzed as a single case, and they were put together in the final stage of the analysis after comparison across cases.

To conduct IPA, researchers are required to immerse themselves in the original data, so the first step of the analysis was reading and re-reading the data while listening to the audio-recording to gain an in-depth understanding of the original data. In the second step, we aimed to explore participants' semantic content and language use in the transcripts. In the second stage, we tried to understand participants' emotional responses, use of language through descriptive notes (describing the context of what participants said), linguistic exploratory notes (specific use of language), and interpreting original data with conceptual coding (explaining interrogative data to conceptual level; Smith et al., 2009). The interpretation (e.g., making sense of findings and offering explanations) in the present data analysis was based on the literature (e.g., Erikson, 1950; Taylor and Ogilvie, 1994). In the third step, we developed emergent themes by reducing the details of the data, including finding interrelationships, connections and patterns between the initial notes, which were from previous stages. In the fourth step, which was the last step for the single case analysis, we aimed to produce super-ordinate themes, which refer to the most representative aspects of the participants' accounts based on the research questions via charting and mapping of the emergent themes. The final step of the analysis was searching for patterns across cases, including finding the most potent themes and connections or differences across the cases.

## Research Credibility

To establish research credibility, we used three kinds of triangulation, *member checking*, *theory triangulation*, and *analyst triangulation* (Patten, 2002). Every time participants had an interview, they had an opportunity to review their own responses as they received a copy of their transcripts and results.

All five participants confirmed that they checked the documents each time. For the interpretation, which is an essential part of IPA, we used theory triangulation, which means using various theoretical frameworks (e.g., Danish, Petitpas, and Hale, 1995; Erikson, 1950; Taylor and Ogilvie, 1994) to analyze the same data. Finally, during the data analysis, three authors had regular meetings to involve ensuring findings were based on the original data. In addition, one of the researchers audited the data trial after the analysis, in order to ensure that the analysis process had been undertaken properly and the interpretation, and results were credible and based on the original data.

## RESULTS

Data analysis resulted in the following three super-ordinate themes: (a) sense of self, others, and the process of identity shift; (b) available resources during the career transition process; and (c) decision-making during the process and consequences of decisions (see Table 3). Each of the super-ordinate themes is presented with sub-themes, which refer to participants' career transition experiences within the contexts.

### Sense of Self, Others, and the Process of Identity Shift

Across the interviews the participants discussed their sense of self, and how their sense of self as an athlete influenced and was influenced by the career transition process. During the career transition process, participants showed identity confusion and identity reformation. These changes in participants' sense of self tended to be influenced by changes in their goals, lifestyles, and social networks during the career transition process.

The sub-themes for the athletes' identity issues were: (a) reciprocal interaction between athletic identity and career transitions, (b) identity confusion and reformation, and (c) interdependent interactions between athletes' sense of self and other people's attitudes.

*Reciprocal interaction between athletic identity and career transitions.* Athletes' sporting experiences influenced on development of their athletic identity, and athletes' sense of self influenced on their decisions in the career transition process. The respondents talked about their lifestyles as athletes, which they perceived as different from non-athletic lifestyles, such as living in a team dormitory and frequent travelling for competitions. Meredith said, "I just played tennis hard…all of my off-court life also focused on tennis. Tennis was in the center of my whole life…I had to travelling to abroad 7 to 8 months in a year, and [I was] always alone". Participants showed a strong athletic identity before their actual retirement, which was a result of their athletic experiences. Some of them tended to have identity foreclosure, which refers state of identity that individuals make commitments to roles without engaging in exploratory behavior (Marcia, Waterman, Matteson, Archer, and Oflofsky, 1993), during their athletic career. Isobel said below during her retirement decision-making process, "I'm thinking I'm a 100% pure athlete…tennis is important…if I can't play tennis well, whole my life became negative. I know it's not good, but I can't control it".

### Table 3. Super-ordinate themes

| Sense of self, others, and process of identity shift |
| --- |
| Sense of self |
| Athletic identity |
| Social identity |
| Comparison |
| Identity confusion |
| Tendency of identity shift |
| Decrease in athletic identity |
| Changes in focus |
| New interest |
| New goals |

| | |
|---|---|
| Changes in priority | |
| New self | |
| Sense of others | |
| Others' influence on sense of self | |
| Others' influence on identity shift | |

**Available resources during the career transition process**
Perceived individual development and resources
Lack of life skill development
Lack of social experiences
Lack of preparation
Lack of organizational support
Lack of support network
Lack of coping skills
Coaches' influence on individual development during athletic career
Parents' influence on individual development during athletic career
Transferable skills
Perceived a high degree of social support
Coping strategies
Social support
Problem-focused coping
Emotional focused coping

**Decision-making during the process and consequences of decisions**
Influential factors in career transition decision
Reasons for retirement
Personal influences
Athletic identity
Readiness for retirement
Emotional influences
Having secure post-sport career
Generativity
Perceived control
Perceived control during athletic career
Perceived control during the decision-making process
Increased control over life after retirement
Psychological experiences during the decision-making process
Difficulties in making decision
Ambiguous of voluntariness of the decision
Psychological consequences of the decision
Positive emotional responses
Negative emotional responses

Respondents also described about how athletic experiences and coaches influenced their social network. Most of the participants had small social networks, within their tennis circle, and they were aware of their lack of social experiences. Christina said, "[My] friends [are] almost all athletes". Meredith also talked about her coach's influence on her social life and the difficulties that she had because of a lack of social experiences:

...my coach banned me to meet my friend and hang around with them, because of that, I think my personality seems to be changed...just this small tennis world I have lived. When I moved to other world, I experienced really uncomfortable feeling.

In the above, Meredith did not simply discuss her coach's influence on her self-development and social life but also interpreted how she felt when she had to be with not-athletic social groups because of a lack of her social experiences. Three out of five respondents in the present study talked about how their coaches encouraged them to focus on their athletic roles and careers than to have other interests outside sport during athletic time. Meredith said, "...I gave up friends and family...I never cared family well because of tennis...only tennis was in the center of my life...whole my life...indirectly my coach did [encouraged me to do that]".

According to Erikson (1968), individuals' self-identity has a strong social aspect and their identity development is embedded in the social environment. Respondents in the present study distinguished the sport world and the non-sport world as two different worlds. Alex said 3 months before his retirement:

> ...from now I have to step into another world. It's a totally different world, I need to adapt to that...I just play tennis for over 20 years...and now there is the world I never have experienced in front of me after retire. Somehow, I'm afraid...I really am afraid of it...

Above quote revealed that athletes perceived sport and non-sport worlds as two different worlds, in terms of differences in lifestyles, values, and focuses between the two contexts. In addition, while Alex was talking about his perception of two different worlds, he also revealed a fear of entering the new world, because the outside sport world is a different world for him from the sport world in which he used to live. When actual retirement happened to athletes, and they started to live post-sport lives, they seemed to get over the fears over time that they had before their retirement. Isobel said, "I am now out here, real world...I feel like I am bit more grown, and I can see how things are going".

The results revealed that sense of athletic self, which is athletic identity, influenced athletes' decisions throughout the process, including the timing of their actual retirement, pre-retirement planning, and post-sport career choice. A strong athletic identity caused a high degree of attachment to sport during their retirement decision-making process, and attachment to sport caused difficulties in making decisions and postponement of actual retirement timing. Isobel talked about her postponement decision at the second interview, "I like my sport...I have been doing this for 10 years. It wasn't easy for me to make the retirement decision... thinking of quitting, it wasn't realistic for me, and I still have attachment to my sport". The results also indicated that athletes' strong athletic identity caused difficulties in making decisions. When Meredith had to face her retirement decision, she expressed strong feeling of existential concerns about meaninglessness in her life because of loss of sporting goals, roles, and athletic self, which had been part of her life for 20 years. She said after her retirement decision, which was 3 months before her retirement:

> My life disappears. I played tennis, I did well, but all those thing are useless...when I terminate my sport life, it seems the end of all those things too, there is no meaning...I just play tennis, only I injured my body and hurt my feelings...

Meredith also expressed her negative emotions through the early stages of career transition process, in terms of difficulties in letting her sport go and facing a new life. She said, "During the retirement process, I had really hard time. I had something is similar to depression. I had even thought something I shouldn't think of. "Why should I live?"…my future was unclear".

Although four out of five respondents finally became office workers, four participants intended to become a coach in the early stages of their retirement process, and these thoughts tended to be related to their strong athletic identity and fears of entering a new life. Meredith, who became a coach, confided how she felt when she thought about having a career outside her sport and admitted that fear of facing a new life was one of the reasons why she decided to remain involved with tennis. She said:

> …I have never tried anything other than tennis…I feel afraid, because I never have done anything by myself…nowadays, I have to do all the things by myself and am afraid of it. So when I was in the decision-making process, I had a fear to face [something] other than tennis.

*Identity confusion and reformation.* Athletes experienced identity reformation during the career transition process, and identity confusion occurred as a result of loss of sporting social sub-groups and roles. The participants showed a strong athletic identity in the early stages of their career transition process. Meredith, for example, talked about her focus 3 months before her retirement, "Even now [after retirement decision was made], I'm just thinking of tennis. 100%. I mean every day of my life". Some of the other participants in the present study showed a decrease in athletic identity in the early stages of their career transition process, such as the decision-making process or latter stages of their sport career. Christina talked about her sense of self after she made her retirement decision, "I feel less like a competitor more likely an amateur who plays tennis for fun".

During participants' identity shifts, participants discussed confusion over their identity. Isobel mentioned her status as "staying in the middle" right after her retirement, and Meredith, who became a coach after her retirement, explained how she felt about her sense of self within 1 month of her actual retirement, "I ended my player's career, and I'm a coach. Now I'm not a player Meredith, but a Lexie's coach. I mean, it's not me". Meredith's comment revealed her confusion as a result of her sport career end, and she did not feel comfortable with her new position or new self, which Erikson (1950) highlighted as a sign of identity crisis or confusion, and the result could be described as "feelings of disoriented and confused", which is related to loss of self and absence of future directions. Athletes' identity confusion resulted from loss of self and also from loss of athletic social groups. Christina reported a loss of contact with friends and experienced difficulties in building new social networks. She seemed to experience identity confusion. She said:

> I never really felt lonely, but now I feel lonely when I'm alone…I feel I have no one around me. I just think "Who am I? What am I doing here?" Yes. I sometimes feel like this when I feel lonely …

Again, the above example indicates the effect of social networks and one's social identity on the sense of self. When she lost her former social networks Christina suddenly started asking herself "Who am I?" and also asking the question "Where do I belong?"

Although respondents showed identity confusion in the initial stages of identity reformation, over time they showed acceptance of new ways of being and a new sense of self. Participants built a new identity based on changes in roles, values, focuses, and lifestyles, and identity reformation was found to be salient after they engaged with new roles and new careers. Meredith said 5 months after her retirement, "...my life also has changed. I became more autonomy. ...I'm thinking I'm a coach much more than the last interview. I feel comfortable with this". The results indicated that participants' identity reformation occurred both naturally over time and as a result of a conscious focus. Alex showed a conscious focus on building a new identity. He said 5 months after retirement:

> I think I see myself as an office worker rather than a tennis man. That makes me feel better. It makes me feel easier to adjust to current life rather than thinking of sport...everything is focusing on this [new career] now...I should let my sport go soon as possible, then it helps me to adjust to my current life better...

*Interdependent interactions between athletes' sense of self and other people's attitudes.* Participants' perceived sense of self interacted with other people's perceptions and attitudes toward their retirement. In other words, through the career transition process, the participants' sense of self tended to correspond with other people's views and attitudes about them, and participants seemed to accept others' changes in attitudes toward their retirement. Christina said 3 months before her retirement, "...all my surroundings know that I'm going to retire, so they often ask me 'When are you going to stop?' ...it's not too bad [to hear this]. I just think that it's time to leave".

Interactions between sense of self and other people's attitude were also found during participants' identity reformation, and the interactions between athletes' and other people's attitudes were interdependence. Isobel talked about how her interactions between others had changed after her retirement; "...they [other people] see me as a bank-teller...and the topic for conversation is now different...now I see them as my customers so I ask them to join my bank as customers".

Another aspect of interactions between perceived self and other people was found in comparison with others. Through the career transition process, all participants compared themselves with others (e.g., active athletes, other former athletes, other coaches, and non-athletes) to evaluate or explain their current situation, status, and feelings. Meredith compared herself with other former players or coaches when explaining her concerns of loss of privilege. She said, "I'm a coach now. It's the same. No differences from other coaches...good sport career can be advantage for me, but I don't really feel any differences from others". Meredith's comparison had a negative outcome (e.g., loss of privilege). In contrast, all four respondents, who were guaranteed secure post-sport careers by their tennis team companies, showed positive outcomes (e.g., enhancing self-satisfaction) by comparing their current situation with other athletes who did not have secure post-sport careers. Alex said below within 1 month of his actual retirement:

> I am in a better position than players from other teams. Other players, when they retire, they have to find second career themselves, in contrast, I have certain thing that I can do after sport career, so I think I am in much better position than others.

To summarize, results indicated that athletic experiences influenced athletes' sense of self, and athletic identity and their career transition had reciprocal interactions. The results of retirement and the process of post-sport life adjustment were that participants experienced identity confusion, but they showed identity reformation between 6 and 11 months after their retirement. Overall, the main finding in identity issues in the present study is that athletic identity influences and is influenced by athletes' career transition.

## AVAILABLE RESOURCES DURING THE CAREER TRANSITION PROCESS

The participants in the present study perceived that their degree of preparation for post-sport life, social support networks, and coping skills influenced their career transitions. These results revealed how individuals' available resources influenced their decisions, as well as the quality of adjustment to post-sport life. Respondents perceived social support as a beneficial resource during the career transition process and used various types of coping strategies (e.g., active coping, acceptance) for many different issues (e.g., need to develop new career skills, building new social networks). Four out of five participants showed maladaptive behavior patterns as results of stress reactions, and these tended to be related to their lack of coping skills. In addition, respondents perceived their coach to be one of the support networks during their career transition.

The sub-themes for available resources were: (a) positive transition outcomes of early preparation, (b) influences of social support, (c) usage of problem-focused coping and emotional-focused coping strategies, (d) maladaptive behavior patterns, and (e) coaches' roles and influences.

*Positive transition outcomes of early preparation.* The earlier those athletes were able to prepare for post-sport life, the more likely they were to experience positive psychological status, emotional responses, and transition outcomes. Respondents spent between 1 and 3 years making a firm retirement decision, since they first consider retirement, they discussed both psychological and vocational preparations, and three of them gained vocational skills during the final stages of their sport careers. The results indicated that pre-retirement planning or preparation for post-sport life is related to post-sport career issues. Respondents showed various negative emotional responses and low degrees of confidence or motivation with regard to their new careers (e.g., fear of facing a new career) during the career transition processes rather than other areas of life adjustment (e.g., financial). The participants attributed their negative emotional reactions to new career adjustment to their lack of life skills and experiences outside sport. Christina, who did not have pre-retirement plans and did not develop vocational skills during her athletic career, had anxieties 3 months before her retirement. She said, "I'm afraid that I have to live by myself out there…I wonder [if] I could handle all these". In contrast, Isobel, who postponed her retirement and tried to develop vocational skills in the final stages of her athletic career, said, "I learned computing skills…it is still better than start work knowing nothing". Christina's and Isobel's comments show that how a degree of athletes' vocational preparation for post-sport lives influenced on their psychological readiness for actual retirement.

Regarding to post-sport career adjustment, most of the participants attributed adjustment difficulties in their new careers to a lack of preparation or vocational skills. George said 5 months after his retirement:

...I know I have to work here [bank office], but I have no knowledge. I have only been playing tennis and don't know about rules for banking, language they use here, and things about loans...I am really in difficult situation...

In addition, the results indicated that participants' degree of preparation influenced work ability, and work ability might have related to their psychological status regarding a new career, such as feelings of achievement or motivation. George, who experienced a high degree of work stress and expressed a low degree of motivation in his new career, said 5 months after his retirement, "Always worry comes first than anything else so I have neither achievement nor progress".

Transferable skills, which are skills acquired in one area that can also be used in other areas (Murphy, 1995), are another aspect of athletes' life skills. Most of the participants were aware of the beneficial influence of their transferable skills from the preparation process and talked about the merits of the skills during the post-sport career adjustment. Isobel said 5 months after her retirement:

...athletes...we have been living as a team for a while, we are polite, we know how to care for others, and know what to do, what we shouldn't do...also I can play tennis...I think it is really beneficial to me [in building new social network]. In addition, my physical strength...I never had been ill or something. It [transferable skills] helps me many different ways.

In contrast, George considered transferable skills as positive resources before his retirement, "I think it [transferable skills] could be beneficial thing for me at the work, such as team spirit and building relationship". However, he changed his perception of his transferable skills and did not accept the beneficial influences of transferable skills after actual retirement. For instance:

I went to play [tennis] with them [colleagues] yesterday...I can build new social network through that activity....but I think all others [things learn from his sport] are negative to me... I mean, like a mental thing...it is different sport and study, it is annoying...

George assumed that playing tennis with others was a positive part of his skills, but he perceived that all other habits he had gained from sport were not helpful for dealing with his current career because of the differences between his sport and office work.

*Influences of social support.* Athletes needed various types of social support (e.g., information, emotion) throughout their career transition process, and the support networks helped athletes to reduce career transition difficulties and encouraged them to deal with different career transition issues (e.g., lack of career skills, adjustment to new lifestyles). Throughout the entire transition process, participants in the current study searched for various types of social support, including information, and emotional, instrumental, and esteem support from close others, such as families, friends, coaches, and teammates. Athletes reported that information and emotion support were beneficial throughout the entire career transition process, and esteem support tended to be beneficial before retirement. Isobel talked about how she searched for information support from former teammates who had been through the same process and used the information to prepare for her post-sport career 3 months before her retirement. She said, "I ask things to a former teammate [retired player] and get information, such as what I have to study, what should I need to prepare...she helps me a lot for preparing work".

Cohen and Wills (1985) discussed two functions of social support in two different models, the main effect model and stress-buffering model. In the main effect model, social support is considered as a social resource that has a positive influence on individuals' cognitions, emotions, and behaviors. The stress buffering model suggests that social support can function as a stress buffer so support is not important if an individual is not experiencing stress.

The results from the present study indicated that respondents' perception of the impact of social support was multi-functional. Four out of five participants perceived that they had a high level of social support networks, and they reported how social support functioned to reduce their career transition stresses. Alex said:

...[the] manager from [the] human resource department told me that they are aware of my contribution [by sport], so they [people in the office] are ready to support me to start a new career. That is really great. I know nothing about the work and have to deal with it, but when I am told that they let me have time to learn some work, that makes me feel much better...

Social support in Alex's case above is more likely to be "stress buffering" because having support from his company helped him to reduce the worries and concerns about his new career which had been a source of stress since he decided to retire. Other respondents described emotional support, which has a similar function to that of a "main effect". Christina said:

...if I was alone I couldn't have done all those [career transition], but he [boyfriend] was with me...when I talk to him about some problems from work he always listens to me carefully, these are all really good for me...

Participants often discussed the importance of co-workers' support after they started their new career, and how supportive networks helped them perform better in their new career. Isobel, who perceived satisfactory support from co-workers, showed less difficulty in adjusting to her new career than the other four participants. She said:

...my manager asked a veteran, who just before gets her childbirth break, to help me for a month. She taught me about a month...so that was grateful thing for me...every time I work, I was guided [by veteran co-worker], so it was really good for me.

In contrast, George, who became a bank assistant after his sport career ended, expressed difficulties in dealing with his new career because of a lack of support from co-workers. He said:

...I have five co-workers, they sometimes teach me, but they are all busy so I feel really sorry to ask them questions...they don't even have enough time for their own work...I feel really sorry (sigh), I have a lot of thoughts and am exhausted.

George also talked about the gap between his perceived social support and his view of the support available, which refers different perceptions about the exchange of resources between provider and recipient (Rosenfeld and Richman, 1997). He said that he was aware how well his significant others had supported him throughout the career transition process, but somehow the support had not brought positive outcomes because of a lack of understanding.

For example, he described the esteem support he received, which had not helped him, 5 months after his retirement:

> ...people say "Even it is hard now, you can do it after time passed". But that is only people who can say that after they overcame it...how much they tell me, if I feel "This is not my thing to do"...I don't know how to overcome it...to be honest, I feel really tough (sigh).

Three out of five participants reported their support networks as being one of the most beneficial resources they had during the career transition process. Isobel said, "...I got more emotional support from my family...such as praying for me and supporting me. That is the biggest thing...that really helps me a lot".

Finally, all five respondents talked about a lack of organizational support for athletes' retirement and stated that national governing bodies should be obliged to support athletes' career transitions. George said, "...it's not possible tennis association to provide these players [retiring athletes] whole things for the future, but they [tennis association] should help them a bit. I believe they should do".

*Usage of problem-focused coping and emotional-focused coping strategies.* Problem-focused coping was effective with career-related issues (e.g., developing vocational skills), and emotional-focused coping was useful for interpersonal issues (e.g., conflict with coaches). Participants attributed work stress or difficulties arising in their new careers to a lack of vocational skill development and experience, and they attempted to develop career skills before they started their new careers or tried to find someone to help them to build their new career experiences through the career transition process. For example, some participants postponed their retirement so they could have time for preparation. George's comment below indicates how he perceived postponement of his retirement as a coping strategy for earning time for preparation. George said:

> I'm going to work at the bank office... so far, I really haven't paid any attention to do that, so if I go to office without knowing anything it'll be tough for me, but if I play tennis 1 more year, I can learn computing [skills] or do some sort of studies.

The outcomes of problem-focused coping in career issues were relatively successful, in terms of managing problems and self-development. For instance, Isobel said, "I could prepare some...like my thoughts...I did some research. It helped me a lot. I think postponement was good for me".

Participants' interpersonal issues were related to conflicts with their coaches or teammates during their decision-making process, loss of social networks, and difficulties in building new social networks. As regards interpersonal issues, athletes employed more emotional-focused coping strategies, such as venting emotion and turning to religion, except for building new social networks. To build new social networks they used problem-focused coping strategies. For example, they perceived playing tennis as a transferable skill and tried to play tennis with co-workers at weekends. Isobel said, "I am getting to know the people because of tennis. When I go to tennis court they really like me, because I am a former player. They all treat me nicely. I can have good social networks because of tennis".

Apart from joining amateur tennis clubs to build a new social network, participants used venting emotion, non-expression, and turning to religion when dealing with conflicts with their coaches, teammates or co-workers, and acceptance and searching for emotional support for the loss of social networks. Meredith discussed using venting emotion with regard to her high degree of negative emotion owing to the loss of her former coach's support. Her coach became her co-worker since Meredith became a coach at the same team after her retirement, and they were still in conflict. Meredith said 11 months after her retirement:

> Nowadays, I cry a lot. If I feel bad I just cry. Am I having depression? I'm not crying because of work or things like that. I'm sometimes weeping to myself, and sometimes crying when I fight with my [former] coach.
> Isobel talked about how she overcame conflict with her coach during the decision-making process, "I have my religion…so I just think of my God's will and just let it be".

Participants also discussed how they managed negative emotions (e.g., loneliness, loss of social support), which resulted from losing former social networks. The process of dealing with these issues was seen as an account-making process perspective, which refers working through the process, including, confiding activity, empathy, compassion, and understanding (Harvey, Weber, and Orbuch, 1990). Christina said:

> I can talk to him [boyfriend] about things that make me unhappy, and then he gives me sympathy…it makes me feel that I have someone to talk to or ring about everything anytime I need. In contrast, when I talk to my family…my mom and dad try to be good, but they don't understand… so when after I spoke to him [boyfriend] I feel much happier.

Christina's remark indicated differences between the social support from her parents and that of her boyfriend, shown in their reactions to her situation, and it seems she obtained a positive result from her account-making, her boyfriend's support, in terms of confiding and receiving empathy.

*Maladaptive behavior patterns.* Athletes who were not able to manage, or were not prepared to, face post-retirement stress were more vulnerable to experiencing maladaptive behavior patterns. Four out of five participants in the present study reported maladaptive reactions to their sport career end. Respondents talked about overeating, smoking, excessive shopping, and alcohol dependence as reactions to difficulties in their new careers or ways to release their work stresses. George said 5 months after his retirement, "I smoke a lot more, because I have too many thoughts and get stressed…I smoke a lot while I am in office. It's because of stress, mental stress". The results indicated that difficulties in their new career or work stress were the most significant stress sources during the athletes' career transition process, and their maladaptive reactions occurred when they could not deal with work stresses. Isobel, who experienced a relatively smoother transition than other participants, and did not show maladaptive reactions, expressed a lower degree of work stress and had stronger support networks within her new career context than the rest of the participants. She said 5 months after her retirement, "…when I first started to work…people next to me help me a lot so, I haven't really had difficulties...now I am quite well adapted... I am just happy with what I have done and no complaints so far".

All four participants who reported maladaptive behavior patterns were aware of the negative influence of maladaptive behaviors, but they confided that they could not stop doing it, because they did not know how to deal with their work stresses. Meredith talked about her recent drinking 11 months after her retirement, "I work every day, I feel tired, but I don't really have ways to release my stress. So I like to drink with people...I do drink to release my stress". Three participants in the present study talked about lack of resources. Christina talked about overeating 5 months after her retirement, "I eat when I have stress". She also mentioned lack of resources 11 months after her retirement:

> I don't have a particular thing to release stress. I get most distressed, because I am still not very good at work, so I try to learn more...I don't try to find something else to release my stress, just try to lean more and try harder.

*Coaches' roles and influences.* Athletes perceived that their coaches were a source of social support, and coaches influenced athletes' decision-making. All the participants expected some kind of support (e.g., information, emotion, and esteem) from their coaches throughout the career transition process. Isobel mentioned her coach's support during her postponement period, which helped her prepare for her post-sport career. She said, "...my head coach let me prepare for my post-sport life...that was also good". In contrast, Meredith expressed unpleasant feelings about changes in the coach-athlete relationship and the loss of her coach's support throughout the career transition process even though she still considered her coach to be one of her close friends. She explained her feeling less than 1 month after her retirement:

> I still think my [former] coach is the best person who knows me...when I try to talk to her she doesn't really listen to me...I guess, she is not my person any more... before [the retirement], she listened to me whatever it was, but not now.

Meredith was the only participant who described a major loss of influence in terms of her coach's attention and support, and she reported conflict with her coach as one of the major transition difficulties experienced throughout the career transition process, because of dependence on her coach during her athletic career. All other participants, however, seemed to be aware of potential changes in coach-athlete relationships. Christina said 3 months before her retirement, "...when I leave the team and rarely visit or contact him...I don't expect that much support [from my coach]".

Participants also discussed their coaches' influence on the timing of their retirement. Three of them perceived a low degree of control over their retirement because of their coaches' involvement in decision-making and reported a gap between the coaches' views and their views on the timing of their retirement. Isobel, who postponed her retirement, expressed unpleasant feelings with regard to her retirement decision-making, "...when he [my coach] tried to stop me from leaving, I felt that he is just being selfish...he just considered his benefits and the team rather than care for my physical condition. I hated it...ones' retirement decision, coaches' impact is huge".

As mentioned earlier, Korean sport has a unique system which involves players being regular employees as semi-professional athletes for commercial companies, playing for the company team without doing office work, and becoming office workers in the same company after their sport career end. Four semi-professional players in the current study belonged to bank teams during their athletic career and took the office positions after their careers ended. Some of the participants perceived that taking a company-related post-sport career was associated with their coaches' decisional power, in terms of the coaches' role in the company, which was higher than the players' position. Christina talked about her coach's potential influence in her new career.

She said within 1 month after her retirement:

> When company sends me to the branch, I have somewhere I want to go, but if he [the coach] doesn't like me, he can send me to other city. If I have good relationships with my head coach, and he supports me, it's said [that] life in office gets easy.
>
> Christina tried to keep a good coach-athlete relationship even after her sport career ended and expected some kind of support from her former coach. Later, 5 months after her retirement, she reported how she felt about her coach's support, "The first day of my office work he [the head coach] came with me [to the office] and introduced me to co-workers…it already supports me a lot".

In summary, the results showed that athletes who had made preparation for post-sport life, and had strong social support networks and coping skills to deal with post-sport life stress experienced smoother career transition than those who had fewer resources during the career transition process. In addition, all participants perceived that their coaches had an influence on their retirement process, and within the Korean semi-professional sports system coaches had roles in athletes' retirement process as employees in the company. Overall, findings on available resource issues in the current study indicated that athletes' available resources moderate the career transition process.

## Decision-making during the Process and Consequences of Decisions

When the athletes faced career transition, they had to make many different decisions, such as whether to retire, the timing of their retirement, how to prepare for their post-sport careers, and selection of a post-sport career. Through the career transition process, athletes in the present study showed a low degree of readiness to face their post-sport life at the first interviews undertaken before their retirement; however, they gained confidence from new experiences outside sport over time. In addition, participants in the present study also talked about changes in their lifestyles after their sport career ended, and they described both positive and negative influences of life changes.

The sub-themes for the decisions and life change issues were: (a) athletes' perceived control over the decision, (b) development of readiness for retirement, and (c) lifestyle changes.

*Athletes' perceived control over the decision.* Athletes perceived that they had freedom of choice, but they had to reach a compromise in their decisions with team coaching staff and consider situational demands (e.g., post-sport career choice). Although three out of five participants in the present study said that an injury put an end to their sport careers, they still reported that they chose to retire voluntarily. Meredith, who retired because of her back injury, discussed her decision: "...voluntarily. I decided it [retirement] by myself. I decided to retire...my team asked [me] to play one another year...so it [retirement] has been delayed".

Data indicated that participants' retirement decision-making was not simple and happened over time (between 1 and 3 years). As mentioned earlier, all participants reported their retirement as a self-choice, but the results showed that they perceived a low degree of control in other areas of transition decisions, such as setting actual retirement timing or making preparations in the final stages of their sport career. Participants discussed two factors influencing their timing of retirement, which were internal (e.g., attachment to sport) and external (e.g., team situation), and four participants said that their postponement of retirement was influenced by team situations, as their teams needed more players to compete next year. Only George reported that although he was influenced by his team situation, his retirement postponement was his choice because of his attachment to sport and a low degree of readiness to face a post-sport career. George said, "...my retirement isn't sudden for me, I have been considering it for the past 2 years already. I have had attachment to sport...I just couldn't decide because I wasn't ready". The findings indicated that voluntariness of retirement decisions was multidimensional and complex and revealed that athletes experienced difficulties and negative emotional responses in making retirement decisions, even those decisions were made voluntarily.

*Development of readiness for retirement.* Athletes showed a low degree of readiness to face their post-sport lives early in the retirement process, but they developed confidence and competence from their experiences during the transition process. In the early stages of respondents' career transition process (i.e., before retirement and within 1 month of retirement), the participants talked about their low degree of readiness to face post-sport life and attributed it to a low amount of preparation and a lack of pre-retirement planning. In addition, participants' low degree of readiness to face their new lives tended to influence their actual departure from sport and caused negative emotions. Alex said that before he made his postponement decision:

I had a fear...after playing tennis for over 20 years without any other experience, now I'm intending to work at office. I felt I know nothing about matters of that kind [new career]. I'm unlearned...I have to face a totally different work over there...the work, I never have tried. I have a lot of fear.

Alex spent another year in his tennis team, and made some preparation, such as learning computing skills and gaining information about his new career. He showed a higher confidence within a month of his retirement, "I am learning one by one, and I feel confidence...I have been only playing tennis, but now I am learning new things, and it makes me feel enjoyable". Although the process of building confidence about their new career was accompanied by setbacks, participants adapted to their new life over time, facing new experiences and learning new skills. Christina talked about it 11 months after her retirement, "I think I feel better as time goes by...when first I started my work I didn't know anything, but now I know how to deal with basic things...I think I have some kind of composure time goes by".

*Lifestyle changes.* Athletes' lifestyle changes occurred as a result of their sport career end, and changes in daily routines, new working environment, and new social networks were sources of transition difficulties. In the three post-retirement interviews, participants talked about changes in lifestyles more at 5 months after retirement than within 1 month or 11 months after retirement. This result seemed to relate to the timing of starting their new careers, or moving out from the team dormitory.

Respondents expressed both positive and negative reactions to their lifestyle changes. Isobel, who expressed positive emotions and higher control over her life after retirement than during her athletic career, said at 5 months after her retirement, "...I moved [out from the team dormitory] middle January. It [life] has completely changed (laugh). My lifestyle...first of all more freedom, I don't have to care about time, because I do not belong to the team anymore". She compared her current life to her player's time and felt she had more freedom and control over her life, because rigid rules and restrictions, which she experienced as an athlete no longer existed in her post-sport life. Christina also reported positive emotions about her sport career end. She said: "This work [new career] is fun and satisfies me...I think I had too much stress there [on the court] so I don't think I have much stress now. I feel much happier after I terminated my sport career".

On the other hand, some players had negative perceptions regarding the changes in their lifestyle. Most of the participants discussed the loss of physical activities and the negative influence of sedentary work environments. Alex said:

> I have prepared both mentally and physically, but the degree of stress I get from work is a lot. Sitting the whole day causes physical pain like neck, spine, and eyes... I think I need more time to adjust to current life, because it is a new life for me.

Another negative perception was related to their social life. During the career transition process, participants showed concerns and worries about changes in their social networks and building new social networks outside sport because of their lack of social experiences. Christina reported difficulties in dealing with her new social groups. She said 5 months after her retirement:

> Even I spend most of my time with these people [colleagues in new career] I don't really have something to talk...when I was with my [former] teammates we always talking about sport, but people in here...this is more stressful for me than work. I sometimes think I'm an alien...I miss my former comrades.

Christina expressed difficulties in building new social networks and regretted the loss of former friends. She tended to get better in terms of building a new network 6 months after the above interview, but still she was not sure about it. She said 11 months after her retirement:

> They [colleagues] do support me, my colleagues are good people. But they all have different personalities, and it is not easy to be good with them all the time...even they are nice to me I still don't know what they really are thinking about me, so it is hard for me to be with them. I just [feel] tired, and it was a bit awkward for me.

To summarize, the results indicated that athletes had to face various decisions during their career transition process, and as a result their sport career end, they experienced lifestyle changes. Participants expressed both positive and negative emotional reactions to these changes, and they seemed to be adjusted to post-sport life and developing confidence over time. Overall, the main finding in the decision and life change area is that the career transition process is accompanied by various decisions and lifestyle changes.

# DISCUSSION

The aim of the present study was to explore Korean elite tennis players' psychological experiences before and after their retirement from sport. The results indicated that (a) athletic identity influences and is influenced by career transition, (b) athletes' available resources moderate the career transition process, and (c) the career transition process is accompanied by critical decisions and lifestyle changes.

## Contributions to Career Transition Research

Several researchers (e.g., Brewer, Van Raalte, and Linder, 1993) have discussed the influence of athletic experience on individuals' identity formation, and others (e.g., Lavallee and Robinson, 2007) have found that athletes' identity is influenced by the termination of their sport careers. Reciprocal interactions between athletes' identity and their career transitions have not, however, been discussed much in the literature, and the present study is the first to provide evidence of circular influences between athletic identity and sport career termination.

The results indicated that athletes' identity, including their sense of self and social identity, was influenced by their athletic experience. When athletes confronted their retirement, the career transition process influenced their sense of self and social networks, and they experienced identity reformation. The findings are in line with Erikson's (1950) claim that individuals' identity develops over time, and identity formation is influenced by life values, lifestyles, and social groups. The results revealed that their sense of athletic self influenced athletes' decisions throughout their career transition process, including the timing of their retirement, pre-retirement planning, and post-sport career choices (e.g., postponement decisions, preparations). It has been reported in previous studies (e.g., Kerr and Dacyshyn, 2000; Lally, 2007) that a strong athletic identity could lead to a high degree of attachment to sport during the career transition process. The current study revealed that a strong athletic identity might influence retirement decision-making, and athletes' attachment to sport might be a source of difficulty in making retirement-related decisions and result in the postponement of actual retirement. The results might indicate that athletes' strong athletic identity could lead to a delay in the career transition process, in terms of difficulties in making decisions. In addition, participants who had strong athletic identities tended not to engage with post-sport life preparation until they had left their sport completely.

Erikson (1950) claimed that identity reformation involved broadening one's self-awareness and a conscious exploration of the self. The findings in the present study indicated that athletes' identity shifts occurred during the later stages of their sports careers, not just after their retirement, and they consciously put effort into changing their identity from an athletic self to a new self. The results paralleled Lally's (2007) findings, which revealed that student-athletes proactively decreased their athletic identity and consciously shifted their focus from their athletic roles to other roles when retirement was imminent. Lally (2007) described student-athletes' proactive shifts in identity as self-protection and assumed that having dual roles (i.e., student and athletes) allowed them to shift their focus (from sport to study) towards the end of their sport careers. The findings from the current study revealed a similar process of identity shift among elite athletes, who did not have student roles, but they tried to identify and engage with non-athletic roles in the latter stages of their sport careers (e.g., developing post-sport career related skills, broadening social networks outside sport). The participants in the current study experienced salient identity reformation and conscious changes in self-awareness, since they started to engage with new careers or roles compared with the earlier stages of their career transitions, which implies that identity reformation is closely related to behavioral changes, changes in lifestyles, roles, and focuses (Erikson, 1950).

During identity reformation, participants in the present study expressed identity confusion as a result of their sport career end, and they expressed uncomfortable feelings with their new positions or new selves, which Erikson (1950) highlighted as a sign of identity crisis or confusion. Some participants expressed feelings of not being anywhere within a month after their retirement, similarly to the sense of "staying in the middle" found in Kerr and Dacyshyn's (2000) study. The longitudinal data in the current study revealed that most participants started to accept their new self as time passed, and they showed some degree of emotional adjustment to their new identity from 5 months after their retirement.

The present results indicated how retiring athletes used social comparison in self-evaluation, and that both positive and negative outcomes emerged from the comparisons. Munroe, Albinson, and Hall (1999) reported that non-selected college athletes used social comparison to reduce the perceived attraction of their sports, but the use of social comparison during the career transition process has not been widely discussed in the literature. In the general psychology literature, Festinger (1954) stated that individuals use comparisons with others to evaluate themselves, and Suls, Martin, and Wheeler (2002) emphasized that individuals' self-evaluation through social comparison is closely related to their self-concept, self-knowledge, and subjective well-being. The current findings indicated that it might be useful to provide information about potential positive and negative outcomes of social comparison to retiring athletes to help them to develop a positive self-concept during their career transition processes.

Folkman and Lazarus (1980) found that people use both problem-focused and emotional-focused coping strategies when they face internal or external conflicts. The results from the present study paralleled Folkman and Lazarus's (1980) findings, and provided evidence of the effectiveness of problem-focused coping in helping athletes to deal with issues during the transition process. The results also supported Pearlin and Schooler's (1978) findings that people tend to use problem-focused coping strategies when they are in work contexts, because vocational stress is often related to problem-managing or problem-solving. Participants tended to use problem-focused coping strategies for career-related issues and discussed its effectiveness. In addition, they used emotional-focused coping strategies for interpersonal issues, and the results indicated that their attempts helped them to deal with emotional changes. The benefits of emotional-focused coping strategies for dealing with interpersonal issues were less apparent than those of problem-focused coping strategies in career-related issues. The current findings advanced knowledge of the effectiveness of available resources, in terms of providing evidence of effective coping strategies in situational-specific contexts during athletes' career transition processes.

Stambulova and Alfermann (2009) emphasized the need for cross-cultural studies in the understanding of athletes' development and career transition, and the findings from the present study indicated that cultural contexts and sport systems could influence athletes' career transition process. The present findings revealed how Korean sport contexts influenced on athletes' process of career transitions. The participants in the present study, even though they chose to retire voluntarily, experienced a low degree of control over their career transition process because of their coaches' involvement, and they attributed their coaches' power over their retirement decision to their post-sport careers, which were provided by their tennis teams. Four out of five participants chose to take office jobs that were provided by their former tennis teams, and they tended to try to keep good coach-athlete relationships. They also tried to follow their coaches' suggestions about the timing of their retirement, because they viewed their coaches as superior officers and coaches had influence on their office work (post-sport careers) since they had decided to take jobs offered by their tennis teams. In addition, all five participants discussed the lack of organizational support and occupational opportunities during the career transition process, and some of them mentioned other nations (i.e., Japan and the USA), which they perceived to offer better occupational opportunities to retired athletes than Korea.

Peterson (2009) emphasized athletes' potential loss of social networks and risk of experiencing isolation and loneliness during their career transition process in terms of athletes' narrow social networks and lack of social experiences during their sport career. Some of the previous research findings (e.g., Kadlcik and Flemr, 2008) also indicated that loss of social networks is one of the consequences of career transitions. The present findings, however, revealed that building new social networks by athletes after retirement could be a source of transition difficulties, in terms of a lack of social experience and delays in social identity reformation. For example, Christina, who seemed to accept her new self-identity as a bank teller 5 months after her retirement, described difficulties in building new social networks and still discussed identity confusion 11 months after her retirement because of her social identity. The results indicated that considering athletes' changes in social contexts in terms of both losses and gains might assist athletes' career transitions.

## FUTURE RESEARCH DIRECTIONS AND PRACTICAL IMPLICATIONS

Although the current study was conducted via longitudinal methods, the data collection was commenced after athletes' retirement decision was made. If future researchers could collect data earlier in the process, such as before athletes make their retirement decision, it might help to explain the overall process of athletes' career transitions, including their career transition decision-making process.

Regarding postponement of retirement, either before or during the data collection, all five participants postponed their retirement for various reasons. Although Isobel and Alex discussed the benefits of postponing their retirement in terms of having extra time to prepare for their post-sport lives, the other three participants said spending another year in the team did not bring any benefits, because they could concentrate neither on sport nor on their retirement preparations. Athletes' retirement timing or postponement of retirement should be examined further in the future. Examining athletes' psychological processes or changes during the athlete retirement decision-making or postponement periods might provide directions for pre-retirement interventions for retiring athletes.

The current findings indicated that coaches played certain roles during athletes' retirement decision-making and influenced athletes' quality of career transitions. In addition, the present study revealed that coach-athlete relationships during athletes' retirement decision-making and career transition process could be sources of athletes' transition difficulties. However, coaches' roles and coach-athlete relationships in the quality of athletes' career transitions have not been widely examined in the study area. In order to understand coaches' influences on athletes' career transitions, future research is needed.

Even though the findings from the present study provided evidence of cultural influences on Korean athletes' career transition process, the study did not focus on comparing cultural similarities or differences with athletes from other cultural backgrounds. Examining athletes with various cultural backgrounds and looking at differences and similarities between cultural or environmental contexts might advance the knowledge on career transition studies and help practitioners to provide suitable and appropriate interventions to retiring athletes.

Several practical implications for assisting athletes' career transition process are presented, based on the current findings, as well as previous findings. As athletes' career transition has been considered as process rather than an event, the current findings revealed that athletes experienced changes in psychological status and emotional reactions throughout the process. The results indicated that providing proactive interventions during their sport careers might help athletes to deal with their career transitions from the earlier stages. For example, the current findings revealed that athletes expressed negative emotions during the early stages of career transition process (e.g., fear of uncertain future, meaninglessness), but most of their negative emotions were influenced by their perceptions of the changes (e.g., entry into new world) rather than the actual contexts (retirement). The results supported Wolff and Lester's (1989) suggestion that it might be helpful to support retiring athletes with cognitive-behavioral therapy, in terms of helping them to reduce maladaptive cognitions (e.g., fear of facing new world) during the transition process.

Athletes' social support networks can be one of the most beneficial resources during their career transitions (e.g., Taylor and Ogilvie, 1994), and the present findings supported this idea. However, the current results indicated that there may be a gap between social support providers' and recipients' views on the available support. Rosenfeld and Richman (1997) observed that social support could be effective when provider and receiver have appropriate interactional exchanges, but otherwise social support may be unhelpful to those in need. George's experience might be interpreted as the result of the failure of interactional exchanges in social support between providers and himself (Rosenfeld and Richman, 1997). The findings indicated that understanding athletes' demands could enhance the positive outcomes from social support, and so could consideration of the interactional exchanges between providers and receivers.

Regarding to transferable skills, although athletes' transferable skills may be beneficial, the benefits of skills are fruitless if athletes are neither aware of the advantage of the skills nor able to transfer them from one domain (sport) to another domain (non-sport). Educating athletes about the use of transferable skills and providing beneficial outcomes of athletes' transferable skills might be good ways to enhance the quality of their career transition, in terms of building their competence outside sport contexts and perceived readiness for retirement.

Some researchers (e.g., Munroe et al., 1999; Fleuriel and Vincent, 2009) have reported athletes' maladaptive reactions to their sport career end (e.g., smoking, alcohol dependence), and participants in the present study also showed maladaptive behavioral patterns (i.e., smoking, alcohol dependence, overeating, and shopping compulsion). Participants said that they were aware of the negative influences of the behaviors, but they could not resist engaging with the behaviors, because they perceived that there were no other ways to release their stress. The results indicated that athletes' maladaptive reactions might be related to their lack of resources during the transition process, and their maladaptive behaviors could be prevented if they found other resources that they could use to release stress during the process.

Finally, as athletes' environment, such as sport systems (e.g., employment types) and socio-cultural influences (e.g., social norms), plays an important role in their quality of career transitions, considering sport systems and environmental influences on athletes' career transition process is essential to assist athletes to deal with their retirement.

## CONCLUSION

The present study is the first study which had been conducted via longitudinal methods with Korean elite-level athletes. The longitudinal data provided insights into athletes' changes in psychological status and emotional reactions, as well as their usage of coping strategies. The findings indicated that athletes experienced changes in psychological status (e.g., identity shift, changes in confidence levels) and emotional reactions not just after retirement but also during the final stages of their sport careers. The results revealed reciprocal interactions between athletes' identities and their career transitions, and their available resources during the process moderated the quality of the process. Athletes confronted various decisions and changes in lifestyle during the process, and these were sources of transition difficulties. In addition, the findings provided evidences of socio-cultural (e.g., sport contexts) influences in athletes' career transition experiences. Several practical implications and future research directions were drawn from the findings.

## REFERENCES

Alfermann, D., Stambulova, N., and Zemaityte, A. (2004). Reactions to sport career termination: A cross-national comparison of German, Lithuanian, and Russian athletes. *Psychology of Sport and Exercise, 5,* 61-75.

Bermack, E. (1989). Effect of telephone and face-to-face communication on rated extent of self disclosure by female collegiate students. *Psychological Reports, 65,* 259–267.

Brewer, B. W., and Cornelius, A. E. (2001). Norms and factorial invariance of the Athletic Identity Measurement Scale (AIMS). *Academic Athletic Journal, 16,* 103-113.

Brewer, B. W., Van Raalte, J. L., and Linder, D. E. (1993). Athletic identity: Hercles' muscles or Achilles heel? *International Journal of Sport Psychology, 24,* 237-254.

Brewer, B. W., Van Raalte, J. L., and Petitpas, A. (2000). Self-identity issues in sport career transitions. In D. Lavallee and P. Wylleman (Eds.), *Career transition in sport: International perspectives* (pp. 29-48). Morgan town: West Virginia University.

Bruner, M. W., Munroe-Chandler, K. J., and Spink, K. S. (2008). Entry into elite sport: A preliminary investigation into the transition experiences of rookie athletes. *Journal of Applied Sport Psychology, 20*, 236-252.

Cecić Erpič, S., Wylleman, P., and Zupančič, M. (2004). The effect of athletic and non-athletic factors on the sports career termination process. *Psychology of Sport and Exercise, 5*, 45-59.

Clare. L. (2002). We'll fight it as long as we can: Coping with the onset of Alzheimer's disease. *Aging and Mental Health, 6,* 139-148.

Cohen, S., and Wills, T. A. (1985). Stress, social support, and the buffering hypothesis. *Psychological Bulletin, 98,* 310-357.

Danish, S. J., Petitpas, A., and Hale, B. D. (1995). Psychological interventions: A life development model. In S. M. Murphy (Eds.), *Sport psychology interventions* (pp. 19-38). Champaign, IL: Human Kinetics.

Douglas, K., and Carless, D. (2009). Abandoning the performance narrative: Two women's stories of transition from professional sport. *Journal of Applied Psychology*, 21, 213-230.

Erikson, E. H. (1950). *Childhood and society.* New York: Norton.

Erikson, E. H. (1968). *Identity: Youth and crisis.* London: Faber.

Festinger, L. (1954). A theory of social comparison processes. *Human Relations, 7,* 117-140.

Fleuriel, S., and Vincent, J. (2009). The quest for a successful career change among elite athletes in France: A case study of a French rugby player. *Leisure Studies, 28,* 173 -188.

Folkman, S., and Lazarus, R. S. (1980). An analysis of coping in a middle-aged community sample. *Journal of Health and Social Behavior, 21,* 219-239.

Harvey, J. H., Weber, A. L., and Orbuch, T. L. (1990). *Interpersonal accounts: A social psychological perspective.* Oxford: Blackwell.

Herzog. A. R., and Rodgers, W. L. (1988). Interviewing older adults; mode comparison using data from face-to-face survey and a telephone resurvey. *Public Opinion Quarterly Volume 52,* 84-99.

Kadlcik, J., and Flemr, L. (2008). Athletic career termination model in the Czech Republic : A qualitative exploration. *International Review for the Sociology of Sport, 43,* 251-269.

Kerr, G., and Dacyshyn, A. (2000). The retirement experiences of elite, female gymnasts. *Journal of Applied Sport Psychology, 12,* 115-133.

Lally, P. (2007). Identity and athletic retirement: A prospective study. *Psychology of Sport and Exercise, 8,* 85-99. doi: 10.1016/j.psychsport.2006.03.003

Lavallee, D., and Robinson, H. K. (2007). In pursuit of an identity: A qualitative exploration of retirement from women's artistic gymnastics. *Psychology of Sport and Exercise, 8,* 119-141.

Lotysz, G. J., and Short, S. E. (2004). "What ever happened to…." The effects of career termination from the National Football League. *Athletic Insight, 6,* 47-66.

Marcia, J. E., Waterman, A. S., Matteson, D. R., Archer, S. L., and Oflofsky, J. L. (1993). *Ego identity: A handbook for psychological research.* New York: Springer-Verlag.

McKenna, J., and Thomas, H. (2007). Enduring injustice: A case study of retirement from professional rugby union. *Sport, Education, and Society, 12,* 19-35.Munroe, K. J.,

Murphy, S. M. (1995). Introduction to sport psychology interventions. In S. M. Murphy (Ed,). *Sport psychology interventions* (pp. 1-16). Champaign, IL: Human Kinetics.

Patton, M. Q. (2002). *Qualitative research and evaluation methods* (3rd ed). California: Sage Publications, Inc.

Pearlin, L., and Schooler, C. (1978). The structure of coping. *Journal of Health and Social Behavior, 19*, 2-21.

Peterson, K. M. (2009).Overtraining, burnout, and retirement. In K. F. Hays (Eds.), *Performance psychology in action* (pp. 225-246). Washington: American psychological association.

Prochaska, J., and DiClemente, C. (1984). *The transtheoretical approach: Crossing traditional boundaries of therapy.* Homewood, Illinois: Dow Jones-Irwin.

Rosenfeld, L. B., Richman, J. M. (1997). Developing effective social support: Team building and the social support process. *Journal of Applied Sport Psychology, 9*, 133-153.

Si, G., and Lee, H. (2007). Cross-cultural issues in sport psychology research. In S. Jowett and D. Lavallee (Eds.), *Social psychology in sport* (pp. 279-288). Champaign, IL: Human Kinetics.

Sinclair, D. A., and Orlick, T. (1993). Positive transition from high-performance sport. *The Sport Psychologist, 7*, 138-150.

Smith, J. A., Flowers, P., and Larkin, M. (2009). *Interpretative phenomenological Analysis.* Thousand Oaks, CA: Sage.

Smith, J. A., Jarman, M., and Osborn, M. (1999). Doing interpretative phenomenological analysis. In M. Murray and K. Chamberlain (Eds.), *Qualitative health psychology: Theories and methods* (pp. 218-240). Thousand Oaks, CA: Sage.

Stambulova, N., and Alfermann, D. (2009). Putting culture into context: Cultural and cross-cultural perspectives in career development and transition research and practice. *International Journal of Sport and Exercise Psychology, 7*, 292-398.

Stambulova, N., Alfermann, D., Statler, T., and Côte, J. (2009). Career development and transitions of athletes. *International Journal of Sport and Exercise Psychology, 7*, 395-412.

Stephan, Y., Bilard, J., Ninot, G., and Delignières, D. (2003). Bodily transition out of elite sport: A one-year study of physical self and global self-esteem among transitional athletes. *International Journal of Sport and Exercise Psychology, 34*, 192-207.

Suls, J., Martin, R., and Wheeler, L. (2002). Social comparison: Why, with whom, and with what effect? *Current Directions in Psychological Science, 11*, 159-163.

Taylor, J., and Ogilvie, B. C. (1994). A conceptual model of adaptation to retirement among athletes. *Journal of Applied Sport Psychology, 6*, 1-20.

Warriner, K., and Lavallee, D. (2008). The retirement experiences of elite gymnasts: Self identity and the physical self. *Journal of Applied Sport Psychology, 20*, 301-317.

Wylleman, P., Alfermann, D., and Lavallee, D. (2004). Career transition in sport: European perspectives. *Psychology of Sport and Exercise, 5*, 7-20.

This research was supported by the Korean Olympic Committee

*Date of re-submission: 24-11-2011.*

In: Innovative Writings in Sport and Exercise Psychology
Editor: Robert Schinke

ISBN: 978-1-62948-881-3
© 2014 Nova Science Publishers, Inc.

*Chapter 14*

# PSYCHOLOGICAL SKILLS TRAINING AND SELF-EFFICACY: THE UNIFORM APPROACH WITH COLLEGE-AGE SWIM EXERCISERS

## *Brittany A. Glynn[1], Jenelle N. Gilbert[2] and Dawn K. Lewis[2]*
[1]University of Ottawa, Ottawa, Canada
[2]California State University, Fresno, CA, US

### ABSTRACT

Thirty-nine college students enrolled in a swimming class participated in a psychological skills training program (PST) called UNIFORM (Gilbert, 2011). The self-efficacy based program examined the relationships between the participants' use of psychological skills, self-efficacy, swim conditioning and techniques. Results demonstrated greater use of the psychological skills of relaxation and self talk. Improvements in swim conditioning and technique, as well as increases in swim conditioning and technique efficacy, and the efficacy to swim in the future were also acknowledged. Imagery, self-talk, goal-setting, emotional control and attentional control were positively associated with swim conditioning and swim technique self-efficacy and future swim self-efficacy. Furthermore, swim conditioning and swim technique self efficacy, as well as future swim self-efficacy, were related to swim performance with results demonstrating swim technique self-efficacy to be the greatest predictor of swim performance. Therefore, PST interventions act as moderators to self-efficacy, while self-efficacy mediates students' performances and subsequent perceptions to swim for exercise in the future. Thus, PST interventions based in self-efficacy may help college-age students improve their swim self-efficacy, conditioning, skills, and efficacy to exercise in the future.

**Keywords:** Psychological Skills Training, Self-Efficacy, Intervention

Although the physical and mental health benefits of exercise have been acknowledged, more than fifty percent of U.S. adults are sedentary (Wang and Beydoun, 2007) and at least fifty percent of people who start an exercise program will drop out within the first six months (Lox, Martin Ginis, and Petruzzello, 2006). Barriers to exercise dissuade adults from maintaining consistent exercise regimens. These barriers may be especially difficult for young college students who have recently transitioned from the structured context of high school (Gyurcsik, Spink, Bray, Chad, and Kwan, 2006; Leslie, Sparling, and Owen, 2001).

College students often face barriers such as lack of motivation, skill, socially active friends, facilities, and time (Gyurcsik et al., 2006; Leslie, Sparling, and Owen, 2001). However, increasing enjoyment, intrinsic motivation, self-esteem, social encounters, performance knowledge, and self-efficacy may help them engage in regular exercise (McAuley, Jerome, Marquez, Elavsky, and Blissmer, 2003; Wilson, Rodgers, Carpenter, Hall, Hardy, and Fraser, 2004). Intervention programs within the college setting may provide opportunities to address the perceived barriers experienced by young adults, while promoting aspects (i.e., performance knowledge and self-efficacy) that increase exercise participation (Leslie et al.). Furthermore, researchers acknowledge that the college experience impacts the development of young adults (Pascarella and Terenzini, 1991) and may subsequently affect their health behavior patterns and long-term lifestyle choices (Leslie et al.). Thus, intervention programs that address the barriers associated with lack of exercise adherence may decrease the number of sedentary college age adults while also increasing the likelihood that they will persist through their perceived barriers in the future (Grubbs and Carter, 2002; Lox, Martin, Ginis, and Petruzzello, 2006).

A common exercise barrier worthy of attention in an intervention program is a lack of exercise self-efficacy. It seems that people are influenced more by how they perceive their performance (success or failure) rather than by the objective outcome of the performance itself (Bandura, 1982; 1997). As noted by Feltz and Payment (2005), "Self-efficacy beliefs are hypothesized to influence the challenges people undertake, the effort they expend in an activity, and their perseverance in the face of difficulties" (p. 25). Thus, individuals who have higher levels of self-efficacy may believe they are better able to overcome barriers to exercise adherence and are more likely to continue exercising in the present, as well as in the future.

Nevertheless, there is a limitation to this predictive relationship: "the influence of the efficacy construct is greatly reduced (or eliminated) as exercise behavior becomes well-learned and habitual" (Lox et al., 2006, p. 53). Therefore, in an exercise intervention program that contains novice and experienced exercisers, the key is to provide challenging activities and intervention strategies to sustain the efficacy construct. Teaching participants how to exercise properly and enhancing their exercise self-efficacy through skill acquisition and improved perceptions of their fitness may minimize the previously mentioned barriers to exercise (Annesi, 2004; Annesi and Whitaker, 2010). This in turn can improve their self-efficacy to use exercise post-intervention.

Psychological skills, such as goal setting and imagery have been associated with improved self-efficacy for performance (Bandura, 1977; Elston and Ginis, 2004; Jones, Mace, Bray, and MacRae, 2002). Relationships between psychological skills (i.e., goal setting) and exercise behaviors, and self-efficacy and exercise behaviors have also been found (Annesi, 2004; Annesi and Whitaker, 2010; Murphy, Bauman, and Chey, 2010; Shores, Moore, and Yin, 2010). Thus, research has primarily examined the bidirectional relationships between self-efficacy and exercise, or psychological skills (goal setting and imagery) and exercise behaviors, or psychological skills and performance with specific populations. However, there is a lack of research examining the relationships between psychological skills, self-efficacy, and exercise performance in relation to male and female college-age exercisers within a psychological skills intervention program. Psychological skills may be used to increase exercise performances, improve self-efficacy and address current health issues (i.e., weight management, sedentary behaviors, obesity) related to a lack of exercise adherence. Therefore, an exercise intervention program for college-age adults which utilizes psychological skills and addresses common exercise barriers, as implemented within intervention strategies, may serve as a useful tool for practitioners when assisting exercisers in reaching successful exercise outcomes.

An intervention framework comprising psychological skills that may increase an individual's exercise self-efficacy and positively affect exercise adherence is the Psychological UNIFORM (Johnson and Gilbert, 2004). UNIFORM is an acronym with each letter representing a different psychological skill or concept (i.e., **U** = Use goal setting, **N** = No mistakes, only learning opportunities, **I** = Imagery, **F** = Fully focused, **O** = Overtly positive, **R** = Relaxation and stress control, **M** = Make routines). The psychological skills and concepts that are included in UNIFORM are based in best practices in the sport psychology literature (Gilbert, 2011) and are commonly used by sport psychology consultants and in sport or life skills programs (Danish, 1997; Danish, Fazio, Nellen, and Owens, 2002; Danish, Forneris, and Wallace, 2005; Goudas and Giannoudis, 2008; Petitpas, Van Raalte, Cornelius, and Presbey, 2004). Furthermore, psychological skills that parallel those found in UNIFORM (e.g., self-talk as found in Overtly positive, goal setting, and imagery) have been attributed to increases in self-efficacy (Bandura, 1977, 1982, 1997; Jones et al., 2002; Shoenfelt and Griffith, 2008).

The psychological skills emphasized in the UNIFORM framework incorporate aspects of the four sources of self-efficacy identified by Bandura (1977, 1982). Interventions that address the four sources (i.e., mastery experiences, vicarious experiences, verbal persuasion, and physiological experiences) may lead to improvements and changes in exercise behaviors for their participants. More specifically, UNIFORM's *No mistakes, only learning opportunities*, may improve self-efficacy by helping one to cognitively restructure a performance failure. If the exercisers believe that the restructured instruction will lead to performance improvement, then they are likely to experience greater self-efficacy. *Imagery*, or cognitive self-modeling, is a vicarious experience (Bandura, 1997; Cumming, 2008; Murru and Ginis, 2010). *Overtly positive*, a form of self-talk, is a form of verbal persuasion and may be used as a motivational tool. Finally, *Relaxation and stress control* are activities directed at minimizing the impact of the person's perception of his/her physiological states on self-efficacy. Because research has demonstrated an association between increases in self-efficacy, which are induced through the sources of self-efficacy as outlined in UNIFORM, and behavior change, further investigation of these relationships within an exercise population is warranted.

An effective approach to study these and related phenomena comprises the case study (e.g., Gucciardi and Gordon, 2009; Horn, Gilbert, Gilbert, and Lewis, 2011; Longbottom and Beals, 2010). Stake (1995) noted that the case study is an important approach when one wants to better understand the particular case in question (i.e., college age exercisers in the current study). Therefore, the purpose of this study was to implement a psychological skills training framework called UNIFORM (Johnson and Gilbert, 2004) with a sample of college exercisers enrolled in a swimming activity class. A second purpose was to investigate the impact of the

UNIFORM program on their use of psychological skills and changes in levels of self-efficacy and swim performance (conditioning and technique).

Three hypotheses were developed for this study. First, the participants would show improvements in swim performance (conditioning and technique), report greater use of the UNIFORM skills/concepts, and experience greater swim and lifetime swimming self-efficacy at mid- and post-intervention in comparison to pre-intervention. Second, the participants' use of UNIFORM skills would be positively associated with swim performance (conditioning and technique), and swim and lifetime swim self-efficacies at mid- and post-intervention. Third, self-efficacy will be positively associated with swim performance.

## METHODS

### Research Design

To examine the effects of the UNIFORM intervention program on the performance and self-efficacy of college-age students enrolled in a 16-week swimming course a within-group repeated measure experimental design was implemented. Examining the effects of the predictor variable (i.e., UNIFORM intervention) upon the criterion variables (i.e., performance and self-efficacy) were measured pre-, mid-, and post-intervention. The participants' within-group pre-intervention scores served as the control for the mid- and post-intervention scores. Because of this it was not necessary to use a separate group of students as a control group. Though it may be considered a study limitation, this decision is supported by Anderson, Miles, Mahoney, and Robinson (2002) who noted that, "it is impractical to offer a service to one group of [students] and deliberately withhold service from another group" (p. 437) when using a case study approach. Further, because of the time involved in implementing UNIFORM, some of the study's measures could have been skewed. More specifically, the UNIFORM group would have received UNIFORM and less swim time, while the control group would receive no UNIFORM but greater swim time. This discrepancy could lead to differences in swim conditioning and swim technique scores and interfere with the relationships being studied. Thus, due to the limitations of using a college level course for this study and in accordance with maintaining curriculum objectives and equal treatment for each student enrolled in the class, a separate control group (i.e., class receiving no UNIFORM exposure) was considered unnecessary.

### Participants

Forty students enrolled in a swimming activity class at a university in the southwest region of the United States were invited to participate in the study. One student chose not to participate. The final sample comprised 39 undergraduate students between the ages of 18 and 48 years ($M = 21.5$; $SD = 5.33$). Because this intervention was conducted in a university classroom, the students' grades were based upon the classroom objectives listed in the course syllabi, which included attendance, participation in class activities, five in-class quizzes pertaining to swimming technique and stroke mechanics, and a class final. Because it is understood that the efficacy construct reduces as the exercise behavior becomes well-learned and habitual (Lox et al., 2006), a college course where the final grade is dependent on progressive improvement at both level of aerobic conditioning and swim stoke proficiency was believed to provide the appropriate challenge to sustain the efficacy construct. Participation in this study was completely voluntary and the variables within this study had no bearing on the students' course grades. Furthermore, the participants could withdraw from this study at anytime without affecting his or her grade in the course. Informed consent was obtained prior to the start of data collection. No participant had any contraindications to beginning a swim exercise program. Demographic surveys were completed by 37 students, 27 of whom indicated that they had been previously exposed to mental skills training. However, this exposure was limited and consisted of high school athletic coaches' pep talks, college lectures or reading popular books. Similar to Thelwell and Greenlees (2003), none of the participants had engaged in consistent mental skills training within an intervention context nor acknowledged application of previously learned sport psychology skills on an ongoing or consistent basis within performance contexts. Thus, it was assumed that this previous exposure minimally impacted the results of the intervention study.

## Procedures

All participants ($N = 39$) participated in the 12-week intervention program where they received UNIFORM psychological skills training twice per week during their scheduled 50-minute university level swim class. The intervention and course material were taught by a second year graduate student enrolled in an applied sport psychology program. The student had comprehensive experience with the UNIFORM program and was a former competitive swimmer.

Two sport psychology professionals with extensive consulting, teaching and research experience oversaw the UNIFORM program, course delivery and research study assuring treatment fidelity. At the time of the study, the sport psychology professionals had been active members of the Association for Applied Sport Psychology for a combined total of 27 years. In addition, lesson plans were developed to achieve consistency in presenting the material to the students.

The first 15 minutes of class were spent discussing swim stroke mechanics and the designated mental skill for that day (i.e., 3-5 minutes of stroke mechanics, 10-12 minutes of UNIFORM). During the 10-12 minutes of UNIFORM instruction, the specific psychological skill designated for that day (e.g., goal setting) was explained. A variety of teaching methods were used including mini lectures, worksheets, partner discussions, and presentations of athlete testimonials regarding their use of sport psychology.

The remainder of the class, approximately 35 minutes, was spent swimming where the students were encouraged to practice their swim techniques and incorporate sport psychology skills as much as possible during this time. For example, during the *Use goal setting* lesson, the students participated in treading water as a class. The class members discussed characteristics of an effective goal, such as making the goal realistic, time specific, and attainable and then decided on a goal together (i.e., a desired amount of time to tread water). Following the treading water activity, the students discussed what went well and what could be improved for future treading activities.

The data collection period was the 16-week semester where participants completed pre-intervention assessments (i.e., demographic survey, TOPS, self-efficacy questionnaires, five swim tests) in Week 1 to 3. The UNIFORM program was taught and applied Week 4 to 16 with mid-tests conducted in Week 9 and 10. Posttest assessments were conducted in Week 15 and 16.

## Instruments

*Test of Performance Strategies.* The Test of Performance Strategies (TOPS; Thomas, Murphy, and Hardy, 1999) was used to assess the students' use of psychological skills at the beginning, middle, and end of the semester (i.e., pre-, mid- and post-intervention). The TOPS is designed to measure athletes' uses of psychological skills in practice and competition settings. It measures the use of six of the eight psychological skills taught through the UNIFORM program (i.e., relaxation, imagery, goal setting, self-talk, emotional control and attentional control). Thus, participants' use of the skills *No mistakes – only learning opportunities* and *Make routines* were not assessed by the TOPS or in this study. Because the participants were college students, not competitive athletes, only the practice items of the TOPS were used. The practice portion of the TOPS consists of eight subscales (i.e., activation, relaxation, imagery, goal setting, self-talk, emotional control, and attentional control) each containing four items for a total of 32 practice items. However, the automaticity and activation subscales were eliminated because they do not correspond with any of the mental skills taught through the UNIFORM program. Also, TOPS practice items using terminology specific to competitive sport practice were modified to reflect performing swim exercise. For example, the item "I use practice time to work on my relaxation technique" was reworded to "I use time during Swim for Fitness to work on my relaxation technique". Participants responded to TOPS items using a 5-point Likert scale ranging from 1 (never) to 5 (always). For this study, the internal consistencies (Cronbach, 1951) for the practice subscales ranged from moderately high (.74) to high (.89) which were similar or more robust than Thomas et al. (1999) whose alpha coefficients ranged from .66 to .81.

*Self-Efficacy questionnaires.* Two self-efficacy questionnaires specific to swim fitness and technique were developed for this study. These included a Swim for Fitness Self-Efficacy (SFSE) questionnaire and the Lifetime Swimming for Fitness Self-Efficacy (LSFSE) questionnaire; both were based on Bezjak and Lee's (1990) Physical Fitness and Self-Efficacy Scale and McAuley's (1991) Exercise-Specific Self-Efficacy Scale. With respect to self-efficacy measures, it is important to remember that self-efficacy is situation-specific to the performance task and efficacy scales should be free from discriminant validation of trait methodology (Bandura, 1977; 1982). Furthermore, Feltz and Chase (1999) stated, "The validity of self-efficacy measures is typically inferred from how well they predict the behaviors hypothesized for the study" (p. 71). Construct validity was achieved via review by a sport psychology professional with expertise in self-efficacy research.

The SFSE examined students' belief in their ability to efficiently swim during class. Students responded to the 12 items via a Likert scale ranging from 0 (Not at all confident) to 10 (Highly confident). Four items assessed the students' self-efficacy for swimming fitness (i.e., conditioning). The remaining eight items assessed students' efficacy to perform their swim techniques. Both subscales had robust internal consistency values, .92 and .98 respectively.

The LSFSE assessed students' self-efficacy to swim for fitness in the future. The 21-item questionnaire investigated common exercise barriers, such as lack of exercise knowledge, lack of time, and social obligations. Students responded via a Likert scale ranging from 0 (Not at all confident) to 10 (Highly confident). The internal consistency for the LSFSE scale was robust ($\alpha = .98$).

*Cooper 12-minute swim test.* The Cooper 12-minute swim test (American Red Cross, 2004; Cooper, 1982) was used to measure cardiovascular fitness. This test is recommended and widely used for measuring improvement and progression in swimming by examining an increase or decrease in distance attained during periodic testing (Huse, Patterson, and Nichols, 2000). Participants' physical fitness levels were assessed by taking into consideration their age, gender, and the total yards swam in 12-minutes.

*Swimming strokes proficiency rubric.* The second performance measure consisted of a scoring rubric published in the American Red Cross (2004) Water Safety Instructor manual. This scoring rubric was used to evaluate proficiencies and mechanics of four competitive swimming strokes (i.e., front crawl, back crawl, breaststroke, and butterfly). To reduce researcher bias, an external evaluator assessed the students' swimming skills. This person was an experienced (i.e., 17 years) American Red Cross Water Safety Instructor (WSI), and also had more than 20 years of experience in teaching swimming and related aquatics activities. The participants' stroke techniques were scored on a scale of 0 (no/absence of skill) to 10 (superior).

## RESULTS

To assess changes in participants' use of UNIFORM skills, self-efficacy, swim conditioning, and swim technique, repeated measures ANOVA with the Bonferroni adjustment for pairwise comparisons were conducted to compare pre-, mid- and post-intervention scores. When the multivariate test, Wilks' Lambda, was significant at $p < .05$, interpretation of within-subjects effects were conducted and are included in this section. Pearson's correlation analyses were conducted to assess associations between UNIFORM, self-efficacy, swim conditioning, and swim technique scores.

### Hypothesis 1

Participants were expected to report improvements in swim conditioning and technique at mid- and post-intervention in comparison to pre-intervention test scores. The participants' level of fitness (i.e., conditioning) was assessed using the Cooper 12-minute swim test (Cooper, 1982). Participants' conditioning, as measured in number of yards swam, significantly improved from pretest ($M = 628.68$, $SD = 162.85$) to mid-test ($M = 668.38$, $SD = 145.42$) and from pretest to posttest ($M = 681.62$, $SD = 138.21$), $F(2, 32) = 17.61$, $p < .00$, $\eta^2 = .35$. Results indicate that participants experienced significant improvement in their aerobic conditioning between the beginning (pre-) to the middle of the semester, as well as between the beginning and end of the semester.

With respect to swim technique, significant differences were found for the four competitive strokes across the semester. Participants' front crawl and breast stroke techniques improved from pre- to mid-test and from pre- to posttest, but not from mid- to posttest (see Table 1 for inferential statistics). Their back crawl and butterfly techniques improved between all assessment points.

It was hypothesized that participants would report greater use of the UNIFORM skills/concepts at mid- and post-intervention in comparison to pre-intervention.

**Table 1. Repeated Measure ANOVA Results of Swim Technique Test Scores Assessment**

| Swim Test | $M$ | $SD$ | $Wilks'\ \lambda$ | $F$ | $df$ | $p$ | $\eta^2$ |
|---|---|---|---|---|---|---|---|
| Front Crawl | | | | | | | |
| Pretest[†^] | 8.84 | 1.53 | | | | | |
| Midtest[†] | 9.34 | 0.98 | | | | | |
| Posttest[^] | 9.60 | 0.63 | .66* | 11.28 | 23 | .00 | .32 |
| | | | | | | | |
| Back Crawl | | | | | | | |
| Pretest[†^] | 8.18 | 1.64 | | | | | |
| Midtest[†!] | 8.82 | 1.24 | | | | | |
| Posttest[^!] | 9.26 | 1.00 | .47* | 22.23 | 23 | .00 | .48 |
| | | | | | | | |
| Breaststroke | | | | | | | |
| Pretest[†^] | 8.18 | 1.70 | | | | | |
| Midtest[†] | 8.60 | 1.61 | | | | | |
| Posttest[^] | 8.74 | 1.56 | .71* | 8.43 | 23 | .00 | .26 |
| | | | | | | | |
| Butterfly | | | | | | | |
| Pretest[†^] | 8.24 | 1.69 | | | | | |
| Midtest[†!] | 8.50 | 1.65 | | | | | |
| Posttest[^!] | 9.12 | 1.32 | .53* | 16.79 | 23 | .00 | .41 |

[†]Significant difference between pre- and midtest scores.
[!]Significant difference between mid- and posttest scores.
[^]Significant difference between pre- and posttest scores.
*Wilks' Lambda ($\lambda$) significant at $p < .05$.

Repeated measures ANOVA showed significant differences between pre-, mid- and post-intervention scores for two of the TOPS subscales, relaxation and self-talk. There was a significant increase in participants' use of relaxation from pre-intervention ($M = 2.75$, $SD = 0.83$) to mid-intervention ($M = 3.20$, $SD = 0.69$) and from pre-intervention to posttest ($M = 3.21$, $SD = 0.66$), $F(2, 22) = 6.95$, $p < .00$, $\eta^2 = .23$. Post-intervention self-talk scores ($M = 3.50$, $SD = 0.70$) were significantly greater than scores at pre-intervention ($M = 2.94$, $SD = 0.86$) and mid-intervention ($M = 2.94$, $SD = 0.86$), $F(2, 26) = 9.88$, $p < .00$, $\eta^2 = .27$. TOPS imagery, goal setting, emotional control and attentional control subscale scores did not show significant changes between the three assessment points.

It was also expected that participants would report enhanced self-efficacy in their swim condition, swim technique and ability to use swimming as a lifetime physical activity at mid- and posttest in comparison to at pretest. Comparison of SFSE scale scores showed participants' self-efficacy in their ability to swim continuously to improve their fitness (i.e., swim conditioning self-efficacy) improved from pre- to posttest (see Table 2 for inferential statistics).

Also, their self-efficacy in their ability to effectively executed the four swim stokes (i.e., swim technique) improved from pre- to mid-test, mid- to posttest, and pre- to posttest. Comparison of LSFSE scores showed participants' self-efficacy to continue swimming as a physical activity in the future improved from mid-test ($M$ = 7.25, $SD$ = 1.71) to posttest ($M$ = 7.90, $SD$ = 1.35), $F(2, 21)$ = 5.37, $p$ = .01, $\eta^2$ = .20.

**Table 2. Repeated Measure ANOVA Results of Swim for Fitness Self-Efficacy (SFSE) and Lifetime Swim for Fitness Self-Efficacy (LSFSE) Scales**

| Swim Test and Time | $M$ | $SD$ | Wilks' $\lambda$ | $F$ | $df$ | $p$ | $\eta^2$ |
|---|---|---|---|---|---|---|---|
| SFSE - Swim Conditioning SE | | | | | | | |
| Pretest^ | 6.56 | 2.49 | | | | | |
| Midtest | 7.29 | 2.14 | | | | | |
| Posttest^ | 7.35 | 1.96 | .77* | 4.84 | 27 | .01 | .15 |
| SFSE - Swim Technique SE | | | | | | | |
| Pretest[†^] | 6.91 | 2.82 | | | | | |
| Midtest[†!] | 7.56 | 2.01 | | | | | |
| Posttest[^!] | 8.46 | 1.81 | .47* | 22.42 | 27 | .00 | .45 |
| LSFSE – Lifetime Swim SE | | | | | | | |
| Pretest | 7.47 | 1.99 | | | | | |
| Midtest[!] | 7.25 | 1.71 | | | | | |
| Posttest[!] | 7.89 | 1.35 | .58* | 5.37 | 21 | .01 | .20 |

[†]Significant difference between pre- and midtest scores.
[!]Significant difference between mid- and posttest scores.
^Significant difference between pre- and posttest scores.
*Wilks' Lambda ($\lambda$) significant at $p$ < .05.

## Hypothesis 2

The second hypothesis of the study aimed at determining the association of UNIFORM's mental skills with self-efficacy and swim performance. First, it was hypothesized that participants' use of mental skills taught through the UNIFORM program would be positively associated with swim performance (conditioning and technique) at mid- and posttest. Pearson correlation of TOPS scales with the Cooper 12-minute swim test distances and the four swim stroke scores at pre-, mid- and post-intervention were conducted. The magnitude of correlation coefficients was interpreted using the guidelines described by Safrit and Wood (1995): ± .80 – 1.00 high magnitude, ± .60 -. 79 moderately high, ± .40 - .59 moderate, ± .20 - .39 low, and ± .00 - 19 no relationship. Analysis of pre-intervention scores revealed several moderate to moderately high correlations of TOPS relaxation and imagery scores with swim performance. That is, at pre-intervention, relaxation was positively correlated with back crawl performance, $r$ = .46, $p$ = .02. Also, imagery was positively correlated with the Cooper 12-minute swim test ($r$ = .42, $p$ = .02), back crawl ($r$ = .65, $p$ = .00), and breaststroke ($r$ = .43, $p$ = .03) performances. However, at mid- and post-intervention, none of the TOPS scale scores were correlated with Cooper 12-minute swim test or the four swim technique scores.

It was also expected that the UNIFORM skills would be positively correlated with the three self-efficacy scores. Pearson correlation analyses of TOPS scale scores with the SFSE and LSFSE scores also showed several significant associations at pre-, mid- and post-intervention. At pre-intervention, imagery had a moderate positive correlation with swim conditioning self-efficacy ($r = .47$, $p = .01$), swim technique self-efficacy ($r = .47$, $p = .01$), and lifetime swim self-efficacy ($r = .41$, $p = .03$). Also, self-talk was positively correlated with swim conditioning self-efficacy ($r = .40$, $p = .03$). At mid-intervention, emotional control held moderate positive associations with swim conditioning self-efficacy ($r = .37$, $p = .04$) and swim technique self-efficacy ($r = .36$, $p = .04$). At post-intervention, five of the mental skills taught through the UNIFORM program were correlated with the three types of self-efficacy. Imagery had a moderate positive correlation with lifetime swim self-efficacy ($r = .47$, $p = .01$). Goal setting was positively correlated with lifetime swim self-efficacy ($r = .57$, $p = .00$). Self-talk was correlated with swim conditioning self-efficacy ($r = .31$, $p = .09$) and lifetime swim self-efficacy ($r = .47$, $p = .01$). Emotional control correlated with swim technique self-efficacy ($r = .40$, $p = .02$). Lastly, attentional control correlated with lifetime swim self-efficacy ($r = .46$, $p = .02$). Interestingly, at post-intervention, four of the seven mental skills taught through the UNIFORM program measured by the TOPS were correlated with participants' self-efficacy to use swimming as a form of exercise in the future.

## Hypothesis 3

The third hypothesis expected self-efficacy to be positively associated with swim performance. Pearson correlation analyses of SFSE scale scores and LSFSE scores with the five swim performance scores showed several significant associations at pre-, mid- and post-intervention. At pre- and mid-intervention,, swim conditioning self-efficacy, swim technique self-efficacy and lifetime swim self-efficacy held significant, positive correlations with all five swim performance scores (see Table 3). Notably, self-efficacy in swim technique was most strongly correlated with swim performance scores (i.e., $r$ ranged from .67 to .86). At post-intervention, self-efficacy in swim conditioning and technique were positively correlated with Cooper 12-minute swim test and back crawl, breaststroke and butterfly technique scores, but not with front crawl technique. At post-intervention, self-efficacy in swim technique continued to hold the strongest correlation with swim performance scores (i.e., $r$ ranged from .63 to .80). Furthermore, self-efficacy in lifetime swim did not correlate with any of the five swim performance measures at posttest. These results indicate that self-efficacy to perform swim strokes effectively is the most influential type of self-efficacy on improvements in swim performances. Given the moderately high to high positive correlations of self-efficacy scores with the swim performance measures and the moderate correlations of TOPS scores with self-efficacy at post-intervention, multiple regression analyses to find the best model to predict swim performances seem reasonable. Five separate stepwise regressions were employed to determine which of the UNIFORM mental skill techniques (i.e., post-intervention TOPS scores) and type of self-efficacy (i.e., posttest SFSE and LSFSE scores) could be used to predict swim performance (conditioning and technique) at post-intervention. Because no *a priori* hypotheses had been made to determine which predictor variables should be entered or their order for entry, the stepwise method was used for the multiple regression analyses. At post-intervention, only swim technique self-efficacy predicted Cooper 12-minute swim performance, adjusted $R^2 = .43$, $F(1, 22) = 18.61$, $p < .00$, back crawl performance, adjusted $R^2 = .53$, $F(1, 19) = 23.08$, $p < .00$, and butterfly performance, adjusted $R^2 = .51$, $F(1, 19) = 21.72$, $p < .00$ (see Table 3). The summation of swim technique self-efficacy and attentional control predicted breaststroke performance, adjusted $R^2 = .65$, $F(1, 18) = 4.74$, $p < .04$. Because none of the predictor variables were correlated with front crawl performance at post-intervention, a predictive model was not found.

**Table 3. Pearson Correlation Coefficients of Self-Efficacy Scores with Swim Performance Test Scores**

| Assessment Point | Swim Test | | Type of Self-Efficacy | | |
|---|---|---|---|---|---|
| | | | Swim Conditioning | Swim Technique | Lifetime Swim |
| Pretest | | | | | |
| | Cooper 12-Minute Swim | $r$ | 0.64 | 0.74 | 0.49 |
| | | $p$ | 0.00 | 0.00 | 0.00 |
| | | $N$ | 32 | 32 | 32 |
| | Front crawl | $r$ | 0.49 | 0.69 | 0.43 |
| | | $p$ | 0.01 | 0.00 | 0.03 |
| | | $N$ | 25 | 25 | 25 |
| | Back crawl | $r$ | 0.69 | 0.83 | 0.69 |
| | | $p$ | 0.00 | 0.00 | 0.00 |
| | | $N$ | 25 | 25 | 25 |
| | Breaststroke | $r$ | 0.73 | 0.85 | 0.53 |
| | | $p$ | 0.00 | 0.00 | 0.01 |
| | | $N$ | 25 | 25 | 25 |
| | Butterfly | $r$ | 0.72 | 0.82 | 0.57 |
| | | $p$ | 0.00 | 0.00 | 0.00 |
| | | $N$ | 25 | 25 | 25 |
| Midtest | | | | | |
| | Cooper 12-Minute Swim | $r$ | 0.68 | 0.69 | 0.39 |
| | | $p$ | 0.00 | 0.00 | 0.02 |
| | | $N$ | 36 | 36 | 34 |
| | Front crawl | $r$ | 0.37 | 0.44 | 0.41 |
| | | $p$ | 0.03 | 0.01 | 0.02 |
| | | $N$ | 35 | 35 | 33 |
| | Back crawl | $r$ | 0.56 | 0.72 | 0.39 |
| | | $p$ | 0.00 | 0.00 | 0.03 |
| | | $N$ | 35 | 35 | 33 |
| | Breaststroke | $r$ | 0.68 | 0.83 | 0.54 |
| | | $p$ | 0.00 | 0.00 | 0.00 |
| | | $N$ | 35 | 35 | 33 |
| | Butterfly | $r$ | 0.73 | 0.80 | 0.55 |
| | | $p$ | 0.00 | 0.00 | 0.00 |
| | | $N$ | 35 | 35 | 33 |
| Posttest | | | | | |
| | Cooper 12-Minute Swim | $r$ | 0.38 | 0.62 | 0.23 |
| | | $p$ | 0.03 | 0.00 | 0.20 |
| | | $N$ | 35 | 35 | 31 |
| | Front crawl | $r$ | 0.02 | 0.28 | 0.10 |
| | | $p$ | 0.92 | 0.12 | 0.62 |
| | | $N$ | 31 | 31 | 27 |
| | Back crawl | $r$ | 0.56 | 0.78 | 0.27 |
| | | $p$ | 0.00 | 0.00 | 0.17 |
| | | $N$ | 31 | 31 | 27 |

**Table 3. (Continued)**

| Assessment Point | Swim Test | | Type of Self-Efficacy | | |
|---|---|---|---|---|---|
| | | | Swim Conditioning | Swim Technique | Lifetime Swim |
| | Breaststroke | $r$ | 0.47 | 0.80 | 0.27 |
| | | $p$ | 0.01 | 0.00 | 0.18 |
| | | $N$ | 31 | 31 | 27 |
| | Butterfly | $r$ | 0.39 | 0.71 | 0.26 |
| | | $p$ | 0.03 | 0.00 | 0.18 |
| | | $N$ | 31 | 31 | 27 |

**Table 4. Stepwise Regression Analysis for the Five Swim Performance Tests at Posttest**

| Swim Test | Predictor Variable(s) | $R$ | Adjusted $R^2$ | $F$ | $df$ | $p$ | $\beta$ |
|---|---|---|---|---|---|---|---|
| Cooper 12-min. | Constant | .68 | .43 | 18.61 | 1, 22 | .00 | 252.92 |
| | Swim Tech SE | | | | | | 51.38 |
| Front Crawl | | - | - | - | - | - | - |
| Back Crawl | Constant | .74 | .53 | 23.08 | 1, 19 | .00 | 4.73 |
| | Swim Tech SE | | | | | | 0.53 |
| Breaststroke | Constant | .83 | .65 | 4.74 | 1, 18 | .04 | 4.50 |
| | Swim Tech SE | | | | | | 0.82 |
| | Attentional Control | | | | | | -0.86 |
| Butterfly | Constant | .73 | .51 | 21.72 | 1, 19 | .00 | 4.72 |
| | Swim Tech SE | | | | | | 0.53 |

A prediction model for front crawl at posttest was not found because none of the predictor variables entered in the stepwise regression correlated with the dependent variable.

# DISCUSSION

The first part of Hypothesis 1 stated that the participants were expected to report improvements in swim conditioning and technique at mid- and post-intervention as compared to their pre-intervention scores. Results indicated that the participants' conditioning and technique improved over the course of the intervention. This was to be expected as the participants were engaged in ongoing aerobic swimming workouts twice a week for 16 total weeks, while also receiving recommendations during these workouts about how to improve their stroke techniques. However, participants did not report significant changes in their swim technique scores of the front crawl from mid- to post-intervention, which may be explained by the course schedule (i.e., the front crawl was emphasized during the first half of the intervention). Thus, it seems logical that this stroke would have significant changes from pre- to mid-intervention but subsequently plateau (mid- to post-intervention) as the participants focused on the other three competitive strokes (back crawl, breaststroke, and butterfly) for the remainder of the course.

The second part of Hypothesis 1 stated that participants were expected to report greater use of the UNIFORM skills at mid- and post-intervention as compared to their pre-intervention scores. Results showed that the participants used relaxation and self-talk (i.e., Overtly positive) more frequently at post-intervention than pre- and mid-intervention. The finding is consistent with the literature where positive self-talk has been associated with increased endurance performances (Hamilton, Scott, and MacDougall, 2007) and such skills are commonly used by elite swimmers (Wang, Huddleston, and Peng, 2003). These significant differences may be attributed to the class activities associated with the UNIFORM skills. For example, teaching the students proper breathing techniques during the first weeks of the course may have inadvertently taught the students *Relaxation and stress control* skills right away. Similarly, the self-talk (*Overtly positive*) activities (i.e., relay races) instructed the participants to encourage their teammates and correct their classmates who were using negative statements. The social aspect of engaging in psychological skills with classmates may have resonated more strongly than the other skills that were individually experienced (i.e., goal-setting, imagery). This coupled with the participants' early exposure to relaxation and the essential *need* to use certain skills (i.e., breathing) as they relate specifically to swim performance may have accounted for the significant differences in their scores.

The lack of significant differences with respect to the other UNIFORM skills/concepts contradicts the literature. For example, goal setting and imagery have been acknowledged for their relationship with swimming performance improvements (Jones et al., 2002; Theodorakis, 1995; Wang, Huddleston, and Peng, 2003), as well as in understanding exercise behaviors and exercise efficacy (Cumming, 2008). The lack of a significant finding may partly be explained by the intervention schedule and its activities. For example, goal setting was the very first UNIFORM skill taught. As the course progressed and more difficult strokes were introduced, the participants' initial goals may not have aligned with aspirations to improve their swim conditioning and technique for each week thereafter. In addition, the intervention activities used to reinforce goal setting (i.e., setting goals for mileage swam and treading water as a group) may not have been appropriate activities to reinforce this skill in application to swimming.

With respect to the lack of significant findings for imagery, environmental limitations (i.e., conducting a guided imagery session poolside) may have impacted the participants' desires to engage in imagery consistently. Specifically, the participants were able to learn the other UNIFORM skills through activities directly in the water while performing swimming activities, but conducting an imagery session directly in the water was not feasible due to safety issues and water temperature. Similar to the goal setting activities, the imagery activity may not have elicited the appropriate retention and use of this skill in application to swimming. Furthermore, these findings highlight the need to design and implement future PST interventions specific to the performance context and performance needs.

The third part of Hypothesis 1 stated that the participants were expected to report enhanced swim self-efficacy at mid-, and post-intervention as compared to their pre-intervention scores. This part of the hypothesis was supported by the results. Increases in swim self-efficacy may be attributed to the participants' exposure to mastery experiences, which are revered as the most influential source of self-efficacy (Bandura, 1997), as well as exposure to vicarious experiences. The participants' sense of accomplishments and vicarious learning may have occurred through class workouts designed to increase aerobic capacity, mastering the technique of the specific stroke being taught, receiving individual instruction to improve their techniques, watching swimming videos to improve their swim mechanics, and witnessing their classmates also improving their swim performance. According to self-efficacy theory, engaging mastery experiences and vicarious learning may have helped the participants overcome their perceived barriers to swimming, while also turning any perceived failures at the beginning of the term (i.e., difficulties in learning a new stroke) into a performance accomplishment (i.e., improved swim technique for specific strokes).

Finally, the fourth part of Hypothesis 1 examined the participants' belief to swim in the future. LSFSE did not significantly increase from pre- to mid-intervention, but significant increases were found from mid- to post-intervention. These findings were expected. The students would not have had enough swimming exposure to experience the sources of self-efficacy leading to observable changes from pre- to mid-intervention. Given enough time to practice swim technique and improve conditioning, coupled with vicarious influences of UNIFORM (i.e., observing classmates of similar ability improving), improvements in self-efficacy occurred as expected from mid- to post-intervention. This supports the literature as exposure to vicarious sources leads to higher levels of self-efficacy when compared to self-efficacy of those not exposed to vicarious sources (Jones et al., 2002).

It was expected from Hypothesis 2 that the participants' use of UNIFORM would be positively associated with swim and lifetime swim self-efficacies. At post-intervention, five of the UNIFORM psychological skills taught (i.e., imagery, self-talk, goal setting, emotional control, and attentional control) correlated with the three types of self-efficacy. These findings are consistent with previous research (Bandura, 1997; Jones et al., 2002; Mills, Munroe, and Hall, 2000-2001; Shoenfelt and Griffith, 2008).

In regards to imagery, previous research indicates a positive relationship between imagery and performance self-efficacy post-intervention (Jones et al., 2002; Mills et al., 2000-2001), as well as imagery and task self-efficacy in relation to exercise performances (Cumming, 2008). Cumming reported that exercise participants employing technique imagery reported higher efficacy for exercise tasks thus increasing the likelihood of exercise behaviors and elevated efficacy beliefs in the future. Therefore, if the participants in the present study believed their performances were successful and increased their self-efficacy for specific swimming tasks, and subsequently associated their success to imagery, they may have developed a relationship with imagery and their belief to swim for fitness in the future (LSFSE).

Self-talk used during the fitness workouts, may have been a form of verbal persuasion. Similar to the participants in Thelwell and Greenlees' (2003) study who used self-talk prior to and at the end of their performances, self-talk (i.e., positive affirmations) may have been employed by the current participants as a way to cope with the perceived difficulties of the swimming class or during their participation in the performance assessments. Although a weak source of self-efficacy (Bandura, 1982, 1997), this form of verbal persuasion may have changed their perceived capabilities to successfully swim for conditioning, thus affecting their levels of SFSE conditioning post-intervention.

Goal setting also had significant relationships to LSFSE at post-intervention. The participants may have created new self-prescribed standards to achieve in their future swimming for fitness endeavors. Particularly, if the participants perceived their ability to swim in the future to be greater than at pre- and mid-intervention, they may have felt efficacious to set new challenges and standards to attain in their future swimming performances.

Additionally, significant relationships were identified between emotional control and attentional control to SFSE (technique) and LFSE post-intervention. While learning new swimming strokes, the participants may have experienced negative emotions and frustrations, particularly while learning specific techniques within challenging stroke mechanics (e.g., butterfly). Although negative emotions have been acknowledged to impede sport performances (Jones, 2003), the participants may have learned to successfully control their emotions while learning new swim techniques which impacted their perceived swim technique efficacy post-intervention. Furthermore, if the participants perceived their swim performances to be improving by focusing on their conditioning and technique, they may have exhibited higher attentional control in relation to swimming for fitness in the future.

Finally, swim conditioning and swim technique self-efficacy (SFSE) as well as lifetime swim self-efficacy (LSFSE) were positively associated with swim performance thus supporting the third hypothesis. In fact, swim technique self-efficacy demonstrated the highest positive association with performance meaning that swim technique self-efficacy was the most influential type of self-efficacy on swim performance improvements. Thus, at post-intervention only swim technique self-efficacy predicted the Cooper 12-minute swim performances, and performance in the back crawl, butterfly, and breaststroke. (There were no predictive relationships with front crawl.) These results fit with self-efficacy theory (Bandura, 1977, 1982, 1997). More specifically, the participants' cognitive beliefs about successfully performing the appropriate technique for each stroke (i.e., butterfly, back crawl, and breaststroke) coupled with successful experiences in improving conditioning and stroke technique would subsequently affect their swim performances in light of mastery experiences.

## CONCLUSION

The purpose of the present study was to use a case study approach to investigate a self-efficacy-based psychological skills training (PST) intervention employed with college-age exercisers. Results showed greater use of the psychological skills of relaxation and self talk. Improvements in swim conditioning and technique, as well as increases in swim conditioning and technique efficacy, and the efficacy to swim in the future were also acknowledged. Psychological skills were positively associated with swim conditioning and swim technique self-efficacy and future swim self-efficacy, which included imagery, self-talk, goal-setting, emotional control, and attentional control. Furthermore, swim conditioning and swim technique self efficacy, as well as future swim self-efficacy, were related to swim performance with results demonstrating swim technique self-efficacy to be the greatest predictor of swim performance.

### Limitations and Directions for Future Research

Although many findings were significant, significant differences were not found in all areas. Limitations of the study may have played a role. More specifically, the participants were college-age students who elected to take the swimming course. Thus, their baseline levels of swimming self-efficacy may have been higher than what would be found in a regular college-age class and the results may not be generalizable to other exercise populations. Furthermore, the intervention had to be incorporated into the class in such a way that the course objectives were not compromised. This meant that only 10-12 minutes were allotted to teach the UNIFORM skills at the beginning of each 50 minute class. If possible, longer class times devoted to teaching and learning the sport psychology skills or even a separate sport psychology class may facilitate participant understanding and provide enhanced opportunity to practice the psychological skills. Though swimming is considered a lifetime activity and is part of the reason a swimming class was chosen for the study, the context in which a swimming class operates (i.e., in a pool, on the pool deck, etc.) may have made learning difficult. Future research could consider using both the activity environment (i.e., swimming pool) supplemented with a classroom environment to teach the UNIFORM skills.

Besides the importance of the intervention environment, the following study highlights the need to design intervention specific activities relevant to the performance context. The participants' lack in using all of the UNIFORM skills/concepts reflects that how an intervention is delivered is just an important as the effectiveness of an intervention. As such, the quality of the activities does matter as well as the ability for these activities to elicit continuous practice and retention of the designated psychological skills. Thus, sport psychology consultants using interventions like UNIFORM may investigate what specific skills are applicable to exercise performance contexts and the specific needs within those contexts. For example, maybe only four of the seven UNIFORM skills will better serve the needs in future exercise performance interventions related to swimming. In addition, because the results within this study demonstrate a strong relationship between self-efficacy and exercise performances, future research may further examine the role of PST interventions (i.e., UNIFORM) as a moderator to enhance self-efficacy, which in turn mediates performances.

Finally, the results within this study are important for understanding the relationships between psychological skills training interventions (PST), exercise performance, and self-efficacy. To date, few studies have examined the interplay between each of these three domains within specific cases of college-level young adult exercisers (Gucciardi and Gordon, 2009; Longbottom and Beals, 2010). Besides utilizing PST interventions to increase self-efficacy, performance interventions (i.e., UNIFORM) may also assist in improving exercise tasks and exercise self-efficacy for both current and future exercise behaviors, which may be a significant tool for practitioners attempting to influence positive behavior change using exercise and physical activity.

# REFERENCES

American Red Cross. (2004). Cooper 12-Minute Swimming Test. *Swimming and Water Safety*. Pennsylvania: The American Red Cross.

Anderson, A. G., Miles, A., Mahoney, C., and Robinson, P. (2002). Evaluating the effectiveness of applied sport psychology practice: Making the case for a case study approach. *The Sport Psychologist, 16*, 432-453.

Annesi, J. (2004). Relationship of perceived health and appearance improvement, and self-motivation, with adherence to exercise in previously sedentary women. *European Journal of Sport Science, 4*(2), 1-13.

Annesi, J., and Whitaker, A. C. (2010). Psychological factors associated with weight loss in obese and severely obese women in a behavioral physical activity intervention. *Health Education and Behavior, 37*, 593-606.

Bandura, A. (1977). Self-efficacy: Toward a unifying theory of behavioral change. *Psychological Review, 84*, 191-215.

Bandura, A. (1982). Self-efficacy mechanism in human agency. *American Psychologist, 37*, 122-147.

Bandura, A. (1997). *Self-efficacy: The exercise of control*. New York: Freeman.

Bezjak, J. E., and Lee, J. W. (1990). Relationships of self-efficacy and locus of control constructs in predicting college students' physical fitness behaviors. *Perceptual and Motor Skills, 71*, 499-508.

Cooper, K. H. (1982). *The aerobics program for total well-being*. New York: Bantam.

Cumming, J. (2008). Investigating the relationship between exercise imagery, leisure-time exercise behavior, and self-efficacy. *Journal of Applied Sport Psychology, 20*, 184-198.

Danish, S. J. (1997). Going for the goal: A life skills program for adolescents. In G. Albee and T. Gullotta (Eds.), *Primary prevention work, Vol. 6. Issues in children's families lives* (pp. 291-312). Thousand Oaks, CA. Sage.

Danish, S. J., Fazio, R., Nellen, V. C., and Owens, S. (2002). Community-based life skills programs: Using sport to teach life skills to adolescents. In J. Van Raalte and B. Brewer, (Eds.), *Exploring sport and exercise psychology* (2nd ed., pp.269-288). Washington, DC: APA Books.

Danish, S., Forneris, T., and Wallace, I. (2005). Sport-based life skills programming in schools. *Journal of Applied School Psychology, 21*, 4-62.

Elston, T. L., and Ginis, K. A. M. (2004). The effects of self-set versus assigned goals on exercise self-efficacy for an unfamiliar task. *Journal of Sport and Exercise Psychology, 26*, 500-504.

Feltz, D. L., and Chase, M. A. (1999). The measurement of self-efficacy and confidence in sport. In J. Duda (Ed.), *Advances in sport and exercise psychology measurement* (pp. 65-90). Morgantown, WV: Fitness Information Technology, Inc.

Feltz, D. L., and Payment, C. A. (2005). Self-efficacy beliefs related to movement and mobility. *Quest, 57*, 24-36.

Gilbert, J. N. (2011). Teaching sport psychology to high school student-athletes: The Psychological UNIFORM and the Game Plan Format. *Journal of Sport Psychology in Action, 2*, 1-9.

Goudas, M., and Giannoudis, G. (2008). A team-based life-skills program in a physical education context. *Learning and Instruction, 18*, 528-536.

Grubbs, L., and Carter, J. (2002). The relationship of perceived benefits and barriers to reported exercise behaviors in college undergraduates. *Family and Community Health, 25*, 76-84.

Gucciardi, D. F., and Gordon, S. (2009). Construing the athlete and exerciser: Research and applied perspectives from personal construct psychology. *Journal of Applied Sport Psychology, 21*, S17-S33.

Gyurcsik, N. C., Spink, K. S., Bray, S. R., Chad, K., and Kwan, M. (2006). An ecologically based examination of barriers to physical activity in students from grade seven through first year university. *Journal of Adolescent Health, 38*, 704-711.

Hamilton, R. A., Scott, D., and MacDougall, M. P. (2007). Assessing the effectiveness of self-talk interventions on endurance performance. *Journal of Applied Sport Psychology, 19*, 226-239.

Horn, C. M., Gilbert, J. N., Gilbert, W. D., and Lewis, D. K. (2011). Psychological skills training with community college athletes: The UNIFORM approach. *The Sport Psychologist, 25,* 321-340.

Johnson, C. A., and Gilbert, J. N. (2004). The psychological UNIFORM: Using mental skills in youth sport. *Strategies, 18,* 5-9.

Jones, M. V. (2003). Controlling emotions in sport. *Sport Psychologist, 17,* 471-486.

Jones, M. V., Mace, R. D., Bray, S. R., and MacRae, A.W. (2002). The impact of motivational imagery on the emotional state and self-efficacy levels of novice climbers. *Journal of Sport Behavior, 25,* 57-73.

Leslie, E., Sparling, P. B., and Owen, N. (2001). University campus setting and the promotion of physical activity in young adults: Lessons from research in Australia and the USA. *Health Education, 101,* 116-125.

Longbottom, J-L., and Beals, K. P. (2010). The role of perfectionism and self-presentation processes in exercise. *Athletic Insight, 12*(1).

Lox, C. L., Martin Ginis, K. A., and Petruzzello, S. J. (2006). *The psychology of exercise: Integrating theory and practice,* (2nd edition). Scottsdale, AZ: Holcomb Hathaway.

McAuley, E. (1991). Efficacy, attributional, and affective responses to exercise participation. *Journal of Sport and Exercise Psychology, 13,* 382-393.

McAuley, E., Jerome, G. J., Marquez, D. X., Elavsky, S., and Blissmer, B. (2003). Exercise self-efficacy in older adults: Social, affective, and behavioral influences. *Annals of Behavioral Medicine, 25,* 1-7.

Mills, K. D., Munroe, K. J., and Hall, C. R. (2000-2001). The relationship between imagery and self-efficacy in competitive athletes. *Imagination, Cognition, and Personality, 20,* 33-39.

Murphy, L. A., Bauman, A. and Chey, T. (2010). Randomized control trial to increase physical activity among insufficiently active women following their participation in a mass event. *Health Education Journal, 69,* 287-296.

Murru, E. C., and Ginis, K. A. M. (2010). Imagining the possibilities: The effects of a possible selves intervention on self-regulatory efficacy and exercise behavior. *Journal of Sport and Exercise Psychology, 32,* 537-554.

Pascarella, E. T., and Terenzini, P. T. (1991). *How college affects students: Findings and insights from twenty years of research.* San Francisco, CA: Jossey-Bass Publishers.

Petitpas, A.J., Van Raalte, J. L., Cornelius, A. E. and Presbey, J. (2004). A life skills development program for high school student athletes. *Journal of Primary Prevention, 24,* 325-334.

Safrit, M. J., and Wood, T. M. (1995). *Introduction to measurement in physical education and exercise science,* 3rd ed. St. Louis, MO: Times Mirror/Mosby.

Shoenfelt, E. L., and Griffith, A. U. (2008). Evaluation of a mental skills program for serving for an intercollegiate volleyball team. *Perceptual and Motor Skills, 107,* 293-306.

Shores, K. A., Moore, J. B., and Yin, Z. (2010). An examination of triple jeopardy in rural youth physical activity participation. *The Journal of Rural Health, 26,* 352-360.

Stake, R. E. (1995). *The art of case study research.* Thousand Oaks, CA: Sage.

Thelwell, R. C., and Greenlees, I. A. (2003). Developing competitive endurance performance using mental skills training. *The Sport Psychologist, 17,* 318-337.

Theodorakis, Y. (1995). Effects of self-efficacy, satisfaction, and personal goals on swimming performance. *The Sport Psychologist, 9,* 245-253.

Thomas, P. R., Murphy, S. M., and Hardy, L. (1999). Test of performance strategies: Development and preliminary validation of a comprehensive measure of athletes' psychological skills. *Journal of Sports Sciences, 17*, 697-711.

Wang, L., Huddleston, S., and Peng, L. (2003). Psychological skill use by Chinese swimmers. *International Sports Journal, 7*, 48-55.

Wang, Y., and Beydoun, M. (2007). The obesity epidemic in the United States- Gender, age, socioeconomic, racial/ethnic, and geographic characteristics: A systematic review and meta-regression analysis. *Epidemiologic Reviews, 29*, 6-28.

Wilson, P. M., Rodgers, W. M., Carpenter, P. J., Hall, C., Hardy, J., and Fraser, S. N. (2004). The relationship between commitment and exercise behavior. *Psychology of Sport and Exercise, 5*, 405-421.

In: Innovative Writings in Sport and Exercise Psychology
Editor: Robert Schinke

ISBN: 978-1-62948-881-3
© 2014 Nova Science Publishers, Inc.

*Chapter 15*

# MOTIVATIONS AND PERCEIVED BENEFITS OF MARATHONING: AN EXPLORATORY STUDY

## *Mary Jo Loughran\*, Deanna Hamilton and Meredith McGinley*
Chatham University, Pittsburgh, PA, US

## ABSTRACT

The relationship between motivations for running a marathon and the benefits derived from its completion has not been systematically explored in the sport psychology literature. This study investigated motivations and perceived benefits of marathon participation in a non-elite population of runners. Ninety-nine runners completed questionnaires examining motivations and perceived benefits of marathon participation immediately after the event. Confirmatory factor analysis of a scale designed for the present study confirmed that the perceived benefits of marathon participation can be categorized as Psychological, Physical, and Relational. As expected, marathoners' motivations for running were predictive of perceived benefits along similar categories. Interestingly, participants also experienced perceived benefits that extended beyond their original motivations for running the marathon. The results of this study add to the body of evidence suggesting that marathon running enhances physical, psychological, and relational health.

In 2010, 503,000 marathon finish times were recorded in 483 timed marathons conducted in the U.S., representing an 8% increase in just one year and the highest total to date (http://www.marathonguide.com, 2012). The same report documented a greater increase in participation among females (10%) than males (6.7%), as well as slower median finish times. These figures suggest that marathon running is an endeavor with broad demographic appeal.

Given the increased popularity of marathons by non-elite runners, an exploration of the benefits derived from participation in the event is merited. Researchers have long known that

---

\* Correspondence concerning this article should be addressed to Mary Jo Loughran, Counseling Psychology Program, Chatham University, Pittsburgh, PA 15232. E-mail: mloughran@chatham.edu.

exercise has a positive effect on mood in clinical (Brosse, Sheets, Lett, and Blumenthal, 2002) and non-clinical populations (Hansen, Stevens, and Coast, 2001; Steinberg, et al., 1998). Pertinent investigations have found that exercise decreases negative mood state (Hansen, et al., 2001), increases positive emotions (Szabo, 2003), and reduces anxiety (Petruzello, Landers, Hatfield, Kubitz, and Salazar, 1991). Although compelling, these reports are not limited in their definition of exercise to an endurance event such as a marathon. The arduous demands of marathon training and completion warrant a separate investigation into the perceived benefits obtained by its participants. However, reports of this kind in the literature are sparse. The present study sought to explore the relationships between the motivations and the perceived benefits of running a marathon. Limited previous research has explored the two topics independently, but few studies have examined the two constructs in relationship to one another. Further, although there is a psychometrically sound instrument to measure motivations of marathoners, no similar scale has been developed to measure the perceived benefits runners experience from participation in the endeavor.

Motivation is a key aspect of the psychosocial profile of the marathon runner (Ogles and Masters, 2003). In comparison with other forms of exercise and recreational activities, marathons are arguably unique in terms of the increased physical and psychological demands placed on participants (Buman, Omli, Giacobbi, and Brewer, 2008). Thus, the motivations of marathon runners would be expected to be different from those of other sport and exercise participants. Explorations of this topic first began appearing in the sport psychology literature in the 1970's, coinciding with a "running boom" in the US. In the first comprehensive attempt to systematically examine motivation in this population, Masters, Ogles, and Jolton (1993) constructed and validated the Motivations of Marathoners Scales (MOMS) using two large samples of marathon runners. The emergent scale consisted of nine subscales: Health Orientation, Weight Concern, Affiliation, Recognition, Competition, Personal Goal Achievement, Psychological Coping, Self-Esteem, and Life Meaning. These nine subscales were further assigned to four broad categories, which include Physical Health Motives, Social Motives, Achievement Motives, and Psychological Motives.

Subsequent studies have utilized the MOMS to further explore motivation among marathoners in relation to demographic characteristics, including gender (Ogles, Masters, and Richardson, 1995), age (Ogles and Masters, 2000), and marathon experience (Masters and Ogles, 1995). Recently, Ogles and Masters (2003) performed cluster analysis on MOMS profiles in a large sample of marathoners to subcategorize typologies of marathoners based on patterns of participation motivation. The following five cluster groups were identified: 1) Running Enthusiasts, 2) Lifestyle Managers, 3) Personal Goal Achievers, 4) Personal Accomplishers, and 5) Competitive Achievers. Havenar and Lochbaum (2007) reported that social and weight control motivations were more prevalent in first time marathoners who dropped out of training as compared to those who finished the race. These published reports serve to substantiate the utility of the MOMS as a psychometrically sound instrument, while at the same time demonstrating the pliable nature of the motivation construct, possibly as a result of the changing demographic characteristics of marathon participants.

In addition to motivation, researchers have attempted to explore other psychosocial factors related to the marathon experience. Although few in number, several studies have attempted to shed light on the benefits or other perceived effects of marathon participation. For example, Ziegler (1991) conducted a post-race exploration of participants' attitudes toward running and perceived benefits of marathoning among competitive and recreational male and female marathoners. Recreational runners of both genders reported experiencing more benefits from running whereas competitive runners reported more positive attitudes toward running. In a qualitative exploration of distance running in women, Leedy (2000) reported that women's perceptions of running contributed to greater empowerment and health benefits in their daily lives, most likely as a consequence of improved self-efficacy and self-worth.

Only one study to date distantly explored the relationship between motivations for marathoning and the perceived effects/benefits of participation. Summers, Machin, and Sargent (1983) explored reasons for beginning to run as well as perceived benefits of running the marathon. The most frequently reported reasons for starting to run were to improve fitness and to lose weight followed by psychological health and goal achievement. Women reported outcomes of marathon completion related to affiliation (meeting new people and training with others) significantly more frequently than did men. Both men and women marathoners reported personal achievement and self-satisfaction as the most common outcomes. In addition, they reported gains in "personal insight" and increases in self-confidence and self-knowledge. These findings, although rather dated, seem to support the argument that runners' motivations may not be entirely predictive of the perceived outcomes of marathon participation. The present study is one of the first to systematically explore the relationship between a marathoner's motivation to participate and the subsequent perceived benefits for having done so.

Prior efforts to explore perceived benefits of marathoning have been hampered by the absence of a validated scale to measure the construct. Therefore, we developed a new scale for the present study intended to measure the psychological, physical, and relationship benefits of marathon training and participation. We expected to find a positive predictive relationship between the subscales within the broad categories of motivations and the perceived benefits of marathoning. That is, we hypothesized that psychological motivations would predict psychological benefits, physical motivations would predict physical benefits, and social motivations would predict social benefits. Given the paucity of research in this area, we had no a priori predictions regarding relationships that would occur between motivations categories and benefits categories.

# METHODS

## Participants

Participants were recruited from the electronic newsletter distributed to registrants of a mid-Atlantic region marathon in the five months prior to the race. A link to a website describing the study was published in the newsletter, along with an invitation to participate. Respondents were contacted via email immediately following the race day. Data were collected during the subsequent two-week period. One hundred fifty-six individuals volunteered to complete the survey. Fifty-seven of the respondents reported having competed in either the half-marathon or the relay event rather than the 26.2 mile event, and these data were excluded from the analysis, leaving a sample size of 99 marathon participants.

The sample consisted of 29 males (28.7%) and 67 females (66.3%), with three participants not responding to the gender query. Age data were collected in aggregate and ranged from 18-21 years to 60 years and older, with a modal range of 41-49 years ($n = 28$). These demographic characteristics were compared to those of the registrant pool for the race. It should be noted that our sample differed from the registrant pool primarily in terms of gender make-up. While our sample had approximately twice as many female participants than males, the inverse proportion of males to females was found in the registrant pool.

**Table 1. Average Finish Time by Gender for All Marathon Participants and Study Participants**

| Gender | Overall Marathon Finishers | Study Participants | Average Finish Time (All Marathon Participants) | Average Finish Time (Study Participants) |
|--------|--------|--------|--------|--------|
| Male | 2584 (63.8%) | 29 (28.7%) | 4:19 | 4:33 |
| Female | 1467 (36.2%) | 67 (66.3%) | 4:43 | 4:39 |

## Procedure

Chatham University Institutional Review Board approval was obtained prior to data collection. Participants completed an electronic consent form as well as the study questionnaires. All identifying information about participants was removed from responses prior to data analysis to preserve the anonymity of participants.

## Measures

The questionnaire packet included the following: 1) a demographic form, 2) the Motivations of Marathoners Scales (MOMS: Masters, Ogles, and Jolton, 1993), 3) a scale developed for this study to assess participants' perceived effects of marathon participation (Perceived Effects of Marathoning Scale), and 4) a series of questions related to finish time and satisfaction with race performance.

*Motivations of Marathoners Scales (MOMS).* The MOMS consists of 56 Likert-scale items comprised of nine subscales. This instrument has been used extensively in marathon research and has well-established psychometric properties (Ogles and Masters, 2000).

Participants were asked to rate their reasons for training and running a marathon on a 7-point Likert-scale ranging from 1 (Not a Reason) to 7 (A Most Important Reason). The MOMS is comprised of nine subscales: General Health Orientation (6 items, *"to improve my health"*, $\alpha = .83$), Weight Concern (4 items, *"to reduce my weight"*, $\alpha = .79$), Affiliation (6 items, *"to meet people"*, $\alpha = .89$), Recognition (6 items, *"to earn respect of peers"*, $\alpha = .92$), Psychological Coping (9 items, *"to improve my mood"*, $\alpha = .90$), Self-Esteem (8 items, *"to feel proud of myself"*, $\alpha = .84$), and Life Meaning (7 items, *"to make my life more purposeful"*, $\alpha = .86$).

*Perceived Effects of Marathoning Scale (PEMS).* The PEMS was developed by the authors for this study to measure the participants' reports of benefits resulting from marathon completion. Items were generated based on the existing literature on the topic, particularly from the findings of Summers, Machin, and Sargent (1983) that identified health, psychological, and affiliation themes in the reported benefits of marathon running and completion. The scale consisted of 30 Likert-scale items instructing participants to rate their responses to statements that began with the stem *"Because I ran this marathon, I now find that I..."*

A confirmatory factor analysis was conducted on the PEMS to verify a three factor structure: Psychological Benefits (10 items, *"am more confident"*, $\alpha = .86$), Physical Benefits (6 items, *"have improved my athleticism"*, $\alpha = .81$), and Relationship Benefits (5 items, *"have stronger relationships"*, $\alpha = .77$). We did not include the five reverse-coded items as these items were strongly related due to their negatively valenced wording, thus strongly "pulling" for their own (and unintended) factor. Several items: "am more competitive", "have achieved greater recognition" and "did something quite worthwhile" did not group with other items (i.e., conceptually or empirically), and therefore were not included in the model. The final 21 item model fit well according to descriptive fit indices, $\chi^2(184) = 249.402$, $p < .01$, CFI = .91, SRMR < .07, RMSEA = .06 (Hu and Bentler, 1999; Kline, 1998). The item loadings on the latent PEMS variables were large and positive (standardized loadings ranged from .44-.81). See Table 2 for a list of the items and corresponding loadings for the three latent PEMS factors.

**Table 2. Standardized Loading Coefficients for the Overall Three-Factor Confirmatory Factor Analysis of the PEMS**

| Item | Psychological | Physical | Relational |
|---|---|---|---|
| Am a happier person | .76 | | |
| Feel like life is more meaningful | .74 | | |
| Have a stronger sense of purpose | .73 | | |
| Like myself as a person better | .68 | | |
| More productive at work | .67 | | |
| Am more confident | .64 | | |
| Will tackle bigger challenges in the future | .56 | | |
| Have made a name for myself | .47 | | |
| Manage my time better | .46 | | |
| Can call myself "marathoner" | .44 | | |
| Am a healthier person | | .81 | |
| Have improved my athleticism | | .67 | |
| Am happier with how my body looks | | .64 | |
| Am less likely to get sick | | .60 | |
| Am happier with my body weight | | 58 | |
| Have achieved an important personal goal | | .51 | |
| Cope with problems better | | | .76 |
| Enjoy people more | | | .70 |
| Have new friendships | | | .64 |
| Have stronger relationships | | | .57 |
| Am more supportive of others | | | .49 |

## RESULTS

*Data analysis plan.* In order to examine the relations between motivations for and perceived effects of marathon running, we examined three sets of predictive models using Structural Equation Modeling (SEM). First, we created composite scores of the three subscales of the PEMS based on the results of the CFA. Next, these three PEMS subscales (Physical Benefits, Social Benefits, and Psychological Benefits) were simultaneously regressed onto the predictors within one of the three broad category scales of the MOMS (Physical Health Motives: Health Orientation and Weight Concern; Social Motives: Affiliation and Recognition; Psychological Motives: Psychological Coping, Self-Esteem and Life Meaning; (See Figures 1-3). Path coefficients between predictors and outcomes were determined to be significant at $p < .05$. Next, we constrained the relations between each of the MOMS predictors and the three PEMS outcomes to be equal to one another.

This was done to examine whether the magnitude of the path coefficients between the single predictor and the three outcomes were equivalent. In order to determine this similarity of strength in path coefficients, a chi-square difference test was then conducted. If the difference in the chi-square between the constrained and unconstrained models was significant (i.e., $p < .05$), the magnitude of these path coefficients would be determined to be significantly distinct from one another. If the chi-square difference test was not significant, then we would have concluded that these path coefficients did not differ across criteria.

*Univariate and bivariate statistics.* Means, standard deviations, and correlations for the main study variables are reported in Table 3. Physical benefits were positively and significantly related to the MOMS 1) Health Orientation, and 2) Psychological Coping. Relational *and* Psychological benefits were positively and significantly related to the MOMS 1) Health Orientation, 2) Affiliation, 3) Psychological Coping, 4) Self-Esteem, and 5) Life Meaning. All three PEMS benefits were positively and significantly intercorrelated. As shown in Table 3,the seven MOMS subscales were generally positively and significantly intercorrelated. However, Recognition was not significantly correlated with both Health Orientation and Psychological Coping Weight Control was not significantly correlated with Affiliation, Psychological Coping, or Life Meaning.

*Physical Health Motives (MOMS) predictors model.* The Physical, Relational, and Psychological PEMS composite subscales were regressed onto the two Physical Health Motives: Health Orientation and Weight Control (Figure 1).

This fully saturated model fit the data perfectly ($\chi^2(0) = 0.00$, $p < .01$, CFI = 1.00, SRMR = 0.00, RMSEA = 0.00). Weight Control was not significantly related to the three PEMS subscales. Health Orientation was significantly and positively related to the three PEMS subscales. Next, the three Health Orientation path coefficients were constrained to be equal to one another. This constrained model fit the data well ($\chi^2(2) = 3.55$, $p = .16$, CFI = .99, SRMR = 0.06, RMSEA = 0.09). The difference in chi-square was not statistically significant ($\Delta\chi^2 (2) = 3.55$, $p > .05$). Thus, Health Orientation was equally predictive of Physical, Relational, and Psychological Benefits of marathon running.

*Social Motives (MOMS) predictors model.* The Physical, Relational, and Psychological PEMS composite subscales were regressed onto the two Social Motives: Affiliation and Recognition (Figure 2). This fully saturated model fit the data perfectly ($\chi^2(0) = 0.00$, $p < .01$, CFI = 1.00, SRMR = 0.00, RMSEA = 0.00).

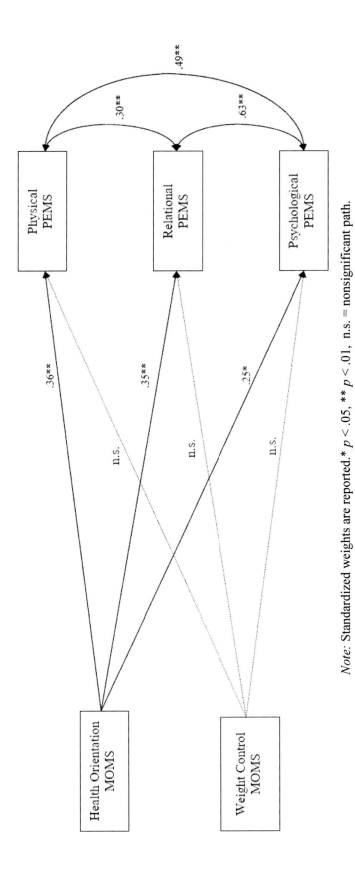

Figure 1. Physical Health Motivations (MOMS) Predicting Physical, Relational and Psychological Benefits (PEMS).

Note: Standardized weights are reported. * $p < .05$, ** $p < .01$, n.s. = nonsignificant path.

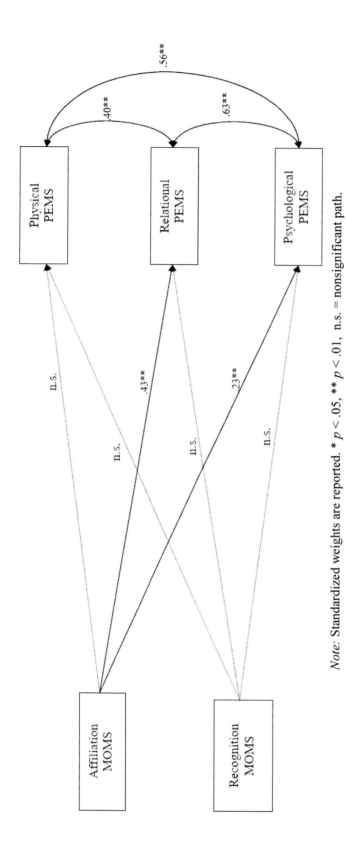

*Note.* Standardized weights are reported. * $p < .05$, ** $p < .01$, n.s. = nonsignificant path.

Figure 2. Psychological Motivations (MOMS) Predicting Physical, Relational and Psychological Benefits (PEMS).

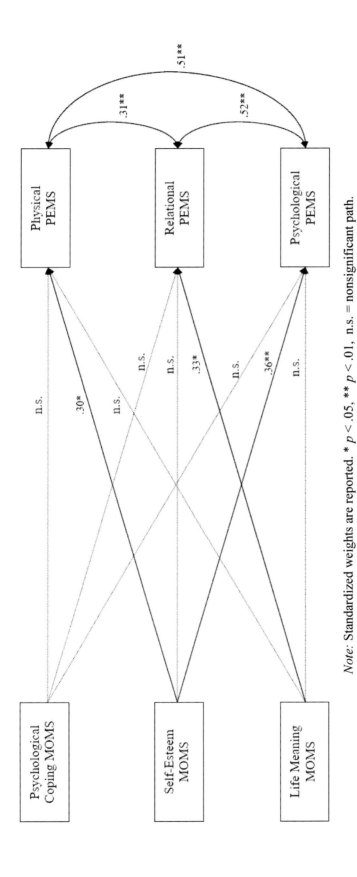

Figure 3. Relational Motivations (MOMS) Predicting Physical, Relational and Psychological Benefits (PEMS).

**Table 3. Means, Standard Deviations, Correlations for the Main Study Variables**

| Variable | 1 | 2 | 3 | 4 | 5 | 6 | 7 | 8 | 9 | 10 |
|---|---|---|---|---|---|---|---|---|---|---|
| MOMS | | | | | | | | | | |
| 1. Health Orientation | -- | | | | | | | | | |
| 2. Weight Control | .33** | -- | | | | | | | | |
| 3. Affiliation | .29** | .07 | -- | | | | | | | |
| 4. Recognition | -.04 | .29** | .45** | -- | | | | | | |
| 5. Psychological Coping | .29** | .01 | .36** | .07 | -- | | | | | |
| 6. Self-Esteem | .28** | .29** | .40** | .58** | .50** | -- | | | | |
| 7. Life Meaning | .28** | .04 | .43** | .40** | .69** | .75** | -- | | | |
| PEMS | | | | | | | | | | |
| 8. Physical | .39** | .18 | .03 | -.04 | .24* | .23* | .17 | -- | | |
| 9. Relational | .32** | .03 | .41** | .10 | .50** | .45** | .57** | .38** | -- | |
| 10. Psychological | .27** | .14 | .30** | .20 | .37** | .54** | .52* | .54** | .65** | -- |
| Mean | 5.91 | 5.16 | 4.69 | 4.04 | 5.01 | 5.39 | 4.81 | 3.89 | 3.68 | 3.64 |
| SD | .73 | 1.05 | 1.22 | 1.25 | 1.08 | .83 | 1.16 | .54 | .59 | .51 |

* $p < .05$, ** $p < .01$.

Recognition was not significantly related to the three PEMS subscales. Affiliation was significantly and positively related to the Relational and Psychological subscales. Next, the three Affiliation path coefficients were constrained to be equal to one another. This constrained model did not fit the data well ($\chi^2(2) = 11.20$, $p < .01$, CFI = .91, SRMR = 0.09, RMSEA = 0.22).

The difference in chi-square was statistically significant ($\Delta\chi^2$ (2) = 11.20, $p < .01$). In order to examine which set of parameters were statistically different from one another, a chi-square difference test was performed for each pairwise set of parameters. The chi-square difference test was statistically significant when comparing the Physical and Relational Benefits paths for Affiliation ($\Delta\chi^2$ (1) = 10.77, $p = .001$). The chi-square difference test was not statistically significant when comparing the Physical and Psychological Benefits paths for Affiliation ($\Delta\chi^2$ (1) = 2.91, $p > .05$). However, this model did not provide good fit given the unacceptable level of the RMSEA ($\chi^2(1) = 2.91$, $p = .09$, CFI = .98, SRMR = 0.04, RMSEA = 0.14), so it was rejected in favor of a model that did not constrain these path coefficients. Finally, the Psychological and Relational Benefits paths for Affiliation were determined to be different according to the chi-square difference test ($\Delta\chi^2$ (1) = 6.37, $p < .05$). Thus, all three Affiliation parameters were concluded to be statistically and significantly different across criteria. The path coefficient for Relational Benefits was larger than the path coefficient for Psychological Benefits, although both were significant and positive. Both of these path coefficients were larger than the non-significant path coefficient for Physical Benefits.

*Psychological Motives (MOMS) predictors model.* The Physical, Relational, and Psychological PEMS composite subscales were regressed onto the three Psychological Motives: Psychological Coping, Self-Esteem, and Life Meaning (Figure 3). This fully saturated model fit the data perfectly ($\chi^2(0) = 0.00$, $p < .01$, CFI = 1.00, SRMR = 0.00, RMSEA = 0.00). Psychological Coping was not significantly related to the three PEMS subscales. Self-Esteem was significantly and positively related to Physical and Psychological Benefits. Life Meaning was significantly and positively related to Relational Benefits. Next, the three Self-Esteem path coefficients were constrained to be equal to one another. This constrained model fit the data well ($\chi^2(2) = 3.14$, $p = .21$, CFI = .99, SRMR = 0.03, RMSEA = 0.08). The difference in chi-square was not statistically significant ($\Delta\chi^2$ (2) = 3.14, $p > .05$). Thus, Self-Esteem was equally predictive of Physical, Relational, and Psychological Benefits of marathon running (all parameters were $p = .025$, standardized $\beta$'s = .27, .25, and .23 respectively). The three Life Meaning paths were then constrained to be equal across criteria. This constrained model did not fit the data well ($\chi^2(2) = 8.38$, $p = .02$, CFI = .95, SRMR = 0.03, RMSEA = 0.18). The difference in chi-square was statistically significant ($\Delta\chi^2$ (2) = 8.38, $p < .05$). In order to examine which set of parameters were statistically different from one another, a chi-square difference test was performed for each pairwise set of parameters. The chi-square difference test was statistically significant when comparing Physical and Psychological Benefits for Life Meaning ($\Delta\chi^2$ (1) = 6.41, $p < .01$). Although neither parameter was significant, the path coefficient for Psychological Benefits was positive, and the path coefficient for Physical Benefits was negative for Life Meaning. The chi-square difference test was statistically significant when comparing Physical and Relational Benefits for Life Meaning ($\Delta\chi^2$ (1) = 7.51, $p < .01$). Similarly, the path coefficient for Relational Benefits was positive and significant, and the path coefficient for Physical Benefits was negative and nonsignificant for Life Meaning. The chi-square difference test was not statistically significant when comparing Psychological and Relational Benefits ($\Delta\chi^2$ (1) = .87,

$p > .05$). Both parameters were positive and marginally significant ($p = .053$, β's = .28 and .25 respectively). Thus, Life Meaning is consistently positively related to Relational Benefits but is not statistically larger than the positive path coefficient, Psychological Benefits. Life meaning was not significantly related to Physical Benefits.

## DISCUSSION

These data provide updated insight based on descriptive information about the self-reported motivations and perceived benefits of marathon participation. Further, the relationship between participants' motivations for running 26.2 miles and the benefits they reaped by doing so were explored. Consistent with existing literature, the participant's motivations for running a marathon in this study were multifaceted and included, among others, psychological, physical, and social components. Likewise, the perceived benefits of marathon completion were similarly categorized as psychological, physical, and relationship-related using the scale developed for use in this study.

As expected, marathoning motivations were predictive of perceived benefits within the same aforementioned general categories. Marathoners endorsing a health orientation motivation were found to perceive physical benefits (e.g., "am less likely to get sick") from marathon completion. Similarly, those motivated by psychological interests of self-esteem and life meaning tended to perceive psychological benefits (e.g., "am more confident"). Within the social category of motivations, affiliation motivation strongly predicted relationship benefits from marathon completion. These results are consistent with the existent literature (Leedy, 2000; Ziegler, 1991) suggesting that running a marathon results in benefits across several domains of human health.

The present study yielded additional predictive value of motivations that extended beyond the one-to-one correspondence described above. In addition to physical health benefits, health orientation also strongly predicted perceived gains in both the relationship and psychological realms, suggesting that running a marathon to improve one's physical health may lead to gains in other areas of life as well. Conversely, in the present study weight control as a marathon motivator proved to be a poor predictor of running benefit, even for physical health. This finding suggests that running a marathon as a weight loss strategy may be rather ill-advised from a cost-benefit analysis perspective. Individuals motivated to run the marathon purely by a wish to lose weight may find that the intense training and associated time commitment required for successful completion of the event is disproportional to any resultant weight loss.

Within the social category of running motivators, several findings emerged. Running with an affiliation motivation proved to be a consistently effective way of improving the marathoner's relationships with others, but also was associated with perceived psychological, albeit not physical, gains. Another finding concerning social motivators was the failure of a recognition motivation to predict perceived benefit in either the physical, psychological, or relational realm. This result suggests that running a marathon solely for the purpose of receiving recognition by others may be an unsatisfying experience for the participant, without any associated gains in physical, psychological, or relationship health. It should be noted that the PEMS may not have had a sufficient enough number of items measuring a recognition factor. This apparent limitation may be addressed in future research using this scale.

The mixed predictive value of the psychological motivators in the present study is worthy of closer examination. Self-esteem motivation was associated with perceived benefits in both physical and psychological realms, but not with relationship benefits. In contrast, marathoners motivated by a desire to find life meaning perceived the opposite, (i.e., enhanced relationship benefits, but not physical or psychological). This apparent contradiction in findings may be better understood in future research with a larger sample size. It may be that a desire to boost one's self-esteem is an internal focus, whereas individuals seeking to find greater life meaning are likely to do so by investing in interactions with others.

Finally, the results of this study failed to find any significantly predictive relationships between a psychological coping motivation and physical, relationship, or psychological perceived benefits of marathoning when examining these variables within a multivariate framework. Although the benefits of regular exercise as a stress reducer and health enhancer are well-documented (King, Hopkins, Caudwell, Stubbs, and Blundell, 2009), it seems that training for and completing a marathon may require the expenditure of more psychological resources than other forms of exercise. Individuals motivated purely by a desire to better manage their stress would likely find greater benefits from less demanding endeavors.

There are several important differences between the current study and the last study to look at marathon motivations and benefits, which was conducted some 28 years ago (Summers et al., 1983). While that study asked participants to list motivating factors and endorse benefits related to marathon training, neither the motivating factors nor post race benefits were measured using a standardized instrument. Also, the current study was able to look directly at the relationship between motivating factors and outcomes via path models in an SEM framework while the 1983 study only described and categorized the motivators and outcomes. In both studies, physical and psychological factors provided motivation for marathon training. However, while goal attainment was an important motivation in the Summers, et al., (1983) study, affiliation (social relationships) was a motivating factor in the current study. The measure developed for this study has several notable features. First, it is the only standardized measure the authors are aware of that focuses on perceived outcomes of marathon participation rather than motivations. Previous research has relied on participant self-report of benefits/outcomes or checklist endorsements of gains but has not employed an instrument designed specifically for post marathon administration. Second, the PEMS has sound psychometric properties. The model had acceptable fit, and was significantly related to theoretically relevant constructs. Third, the PEMS appears to add to the literature exploring the connections between physical health and overall well-being. For example, the findings in the current study demonstrate that training for and completing a marathon may contribute to significant gains in social relationships (regardless of initial motivation) and not just physical well-being.

This study contained several limitations that suggest caution when interpreting its findings. Our modest sample size precluded a more powerful analysis of some potentially influential variables, such as age, gender, and marathon finish time. Future studies should explore the potential mediating effects of these variables on the model. Similarly, future studies may benefit from the inclusion of personality characteristics as a potential contributing factor to an individual's likelihood to benefit in a certain way from running a marathon. For example, the inclusion of an introversion/extroversion measure may shed greater light on the underlying mechanisms connecting running motivations and perceived benefits. To our knowledge, no research reports have explored the potentially influential role played by personality factors in the equation between motivation and benefits of marathoning.

Despite these limitations, our novel findings could positively impact marathoners and potential marathoners. Potential benefits that result from running a marathon include boosts to physical, psychological, and social well-being, independent of one's motivation to participate in the event. Health professionals who seek to encourage their clients to become more or stay active could use the "bonus" effects of marathon participation (potential physical *and* psychological/social gains) to increase the attractiveness of tackling this endeavor.

## REFERENCES

Brosse, A. L., Sheets, E. S., Lett, H. S., and Blumenthal, J. A. (2002). Exercise and the treatment of clinical depression in adults: Recent findings and future directions. *Sports Medicine, 32*, 741-760.

Buman, M. P., Omli, J. W., Giacobbi, P. R., and Brewer, B. W. (2008). Experiences and coping responses of "Hitting the Wall" for recreational marathon runners. *Journal of Applied Sport Psychology, 20*, 282 – 300.

Hansen, C. J., Stevens, L. C., and Coast, R. J. (2001). *Exercise duration and mood state: How much is enough to feel better? Health Psychology, 20*, 267-275.

Havenar, J. and Lochbaum, M. (2007). Differences in participation motives of first-time marathon finishers and pre-race dropouts. *Journal of Sport Behavior, 30*, 270-279.

Hu, L., and Bentler, P. M. (1999). Cutoff criteria for fit indexes in covariance structure analysis: Conventional criteria versus new alternatives. *Structural Equation Modeling, 6*, 1-55.

King, N. A., Hopkins, M., Caudwell, P., Stubbs, R. J., and Blundell, J. E. (2009). Beneficial effects of exercise: Shifting the focus from body weight to other markers of health. *British Journal of Sports Medicine, 43*, 924 – 927.

Kline, R. B. (1998). *Principles and practice of structural equation modeling*. New York, NY, US: Guilford Press.

Leedy, M. G. (2000). Commitment to distance running: Coping mechanism or addiction? *Journal of Sport Behavior, 23*, 255-270.

MarathonGuide.com Staff (2012). USA Marathoning: 2010 Overview. Retrieved from http://www.marathonguide.com/Features/Articles/2010RecapOverview.cfm.

Masters, K. S., Ogles, B. M., and Jolton, J. A. (1993). The development of an instrument to measure motivation for marathon running: The Motivations of Marathoners Scales (MOMS). *Research Quarterly for Exercise and Sport, 64*, 134-143.

Masters, K. S., and Ogles, B. M. (1995). An investigation of the different motivations of marathon runners with varying degrees of experience. *Journal of Sport Behavior, 18*, 69-79.

Ogles, B. M., and Masters, K. S. (2000). Older vs. younger adult male marathon runners: participative motives and training habits. *Journal of Sport Behavior, 23*, 130-143.

Ogles, B. M., and Masters, K. S. (2003). A typology of marathon runners based on cluster analysis of motivations. *Journal of Sport Behavior, 26*, 69-85.

Ogles, B. M., Masters, K. S. and Richardson, S. A. (1995). Obligatory running and gender: An analysis of participative motives and training habits. *International Journal of Sport Psychology, 26*, 233-248.

Petruzzello, S., Landers, D., Hatfield, B., Kubitz, K., and Salazar, W. (1991). A meta-analysis on the anxiety-reducing effects of acute and chronic exercise. *Sports Medicine, 11,* 143-182.

Steinberg, H., Nicholls, B., Sykes, E. A., LeBoutillier, N., Ramlakhan, N., Moss, T., and Dewey, A. (1998). Weekly exercise consistently reinstates positive mood. *European Psychologist, 3*, 271-280.

Summers, J. J., Machin, V. J., and Sargent, G. I. (1983). Psychosocial factors related to marathon running. *Journal of Sport Psychology, 5,* 314-331.

Szabo, A. (2003). The acute effects of humor and exercise on mood and anxiety. *Journal of Leisure Research, 35*, 152-162.

Yoder, Tracy. (2001-2011). Running USA, Statistics. Retrieved from: http://www.runningusa.org/statistics.

Ziegler, S. G. (1991). Perceived benefits of marathon running in males and females. *Sex Roles, 25*(3-4), 119-127.


Submitted March 27, 2012. Resubmitted April 27, 2012.

In: Innovative Writings in Sport and Exercise Psychology
Editor: Robert Schinke

ISBN: 978-1-62948-881-3
© 2014 Nova Science Publishers, Inc.

*Chapter 16*

# AGE AND GENDER-RELATED CHANGES IN EXERCISE MOTIVATION AMONG HIGHLY ACTIVE INDIVIDUALS

## *Matthew A. Stults-Kolehmainen[1], Joseph T. Ciccolo[2], John B. Bartholomew*[*3], *John Seifert[4] and Robert S. Portman[5]*

[1]Yale University Medical School, New Haven, CT and
Northern Illinois University, De Kalb, IL, US
[2]Brown Medical School and the Miriam Hospital, Providence, RI, US
[3]The University of Texas, Austin, TX, US
[4]Montana State University, Bozeman, MT, US
[5]Signal Nutrition, Fair Haven, NJ, US

### ABSTRACT

The purpose of this investigation was to determine differences in exercise motivation across age groups and gender of recreational endurance athletes (N = 2756), ages 18-64. Participants selected their top 3 motives from a list of 10 intrinsic and extrinsic factors, which across all individuals were enjoyment (57.1%), performance (53.3%), and health (51.9%). Performance motivation was endorsed by 79.7% of those aged 18-24 years vs. 37.8% of those aged 55-64 years. Women selected weight maintenance (26.8% vs. 17.4%) and appearance (15.7% vs. 7.0%) to a greater degree than men. Men endorsed improving performance (54.6% vs. 47.1%), living longer (18.5% vs. 9.7%) and feeling better (26.0% vs. 20.3%) as a primary motives more than women. There was a non-significant ($p = 0.049$) age and gender interaction for weight maintenance with gender differences apparent in younger age groups but not in older ages.

**Keywords:** Aging, life span, weight reduction

---

[*] Correspondence to: John B. Bartholomew, Ph.D. The University of Texas at Austin. Department of Kinesiology and Health Education, 1 University Station, D3700, Bellmont Room 710. Austin, TX 78712-1204, USA. E-mail: john.bart@mail.utexas.edu. Office phone: (+1) 512-232-6021; Office fax: (+1) 512-471-0946.

## INTRODUCTION

Approximately 21.9% of adults in the United States participate in light-to-moderate leisure-time physical activity a minimum of five times per week and only 11.1% of adults engage in vigorous leisure-time physical activity at this same frequency (Centers for Disease Control, 2008). According to self-report data from the Behavioral Risk Factor Surveillance System (BRFSS), only 48.8% of US adults meet the minimum level of physical activity necessary for maintaining good health as determined by Healthy People 2010 objectives (Centers for Disease Control, 2008). As measured by accelerometry, minutes of moderate-to-vigorous physical activity (MVPA) drop dramatically from young to old adulthood and differ by gender as well (Troiano et al., 2008). For instance, 20-29 year old men complete an average of 39.7 minutes per day of MVPA while 50-59 year old men engage in MVPA for 26.4 minutes. Younger women in the same age-range complete 23.6 minutes of MVPA and older women of the same age complete 15.4 minutes (Troiano et al., 2008).

Low exercise participation may largely be a function of a lack of motivation for exercise amongst inactive individuals. Indeed, self-motivation is a strong predictor of exercise behavior even when compared to a variety of other psychological constructs (Polman, Pieter, Bercades, and Ntoumanis, 2004; Trost, Owen, Bauman, Sallis and Brown, 2002). Those factors spurring exercise motivation, however, have only recently been systematically mapped. Self-Determination Theory (Deci and Ryan, 1985) is an example of a framework that successfully predicts levels of physical activity (Ryan, Frederick, Lepes, Rubio and Sheldon, 1997). In essence, self-determination is the "capacity or fundamental need to choose and to have choices, rather than reinforcement contingencies, drives, or any other forces or pressures, to be the determinants of one's actions" (Deci and Ryan, 1985). Self-determined individuals, in other words, operate on fully internalized motivations (Vallerand and Perreault, 1999). While an individual may be driven to exercise for enjoyment, a sense of competence, or body related concerns (Frederick and Ryan, 1993), according to Self-Determination Theory her/his motives can be categorized within two types: *intrinsic* or *extrinsic* (Deci and Ryan, 1985). Enjoyment and competence motivations are of an intrinsic nature in which the activity itself is reinforcing. Conversely, body-related motives, such as a desire to lose weight, improving appearance, and fitness, are considered to be highly extrinsic in nature. In these cases, motivation is derived from the secondary outcomes resulting from the activity, which are very important to new exercisers, and consequently extrinsic motives are most predominate when exercise is first adopted. After six to twelve months of consistent exercise, individuals generally move towards a more intrinsic profile (Ingledew, Markland, and Medley, 1998; Mullan and Markland, 1997). Nonetheless, those who maintain an extrinsic orientation over the long term demonstrate lower effort in terms of hours per week of participation, length of workouts, and lower exercise adherence (Brawley and Vallerand, 1984; Frederick and Ryan, 1993; Ryan et al., 1997). Thus, there is evidence that those who can maintain an enduring exercise program (> 6-12 months) have a motivational profile that is different from exercise initiators (Duda, 1989; Ingledew et al., 1998; Ryan et al., 1997).

Unfortunately, research on exercise motivation has largely been limited to inactive individuals with the goal of determining which factors contribute to exercise initiation and short-term exercise maintenance (Biddle and Fox, 1998; Stiggelbout, Hopman-Rock, and van Mechelen, 2008; Teixeira et al., 2006). These investigations typically focus on negative motivators or barriers to exercise, which are highly predictive of sedentary behavior in these populations (Bird et al., 2009). When active people are studied, it is often in the context of either: a) collegiate athletics or b) pathology, such as exercise dependence, overtraining, injury—or it is along a narrow range of motivational factors, such as competency or socialization (De Young and Anderson, 2010; Hamer, Karageorghis, and Vlachopoulos, 2002; Hollembeak and Amorose, 2005; Martens and Webber, 2002; Medic, Mack, Wilson, and Starkes, 2007). Exceptions include studies by Clough, Shepherd, and Maughan (1988) and Barrell, High, Holt, and MacKean (1988), which similarly found that the main motivational factors for marathon and half-marathon runners were well-being, socialization, challenge, status, addiction, and health / fitness. Consequently, the motivations of highly active people who engage in very vigorous activities outside of the collegiate athletics domain are not clearly identified.

With respect to age and gender differences, some information on exercise motivation is available; however, only a few studies have examined large cohorts of individuals across the life span (Allied Dunbar National Fitness Survey, 1992; Ashford, Biddle, and Goudas, 1993; Ashford and Rickhuss, 1992). Little advancement has been made since Biddle (1995) found that less than 6% of studies exploring motivation to exercise included individuals over 50 years of age. Despite a lack of literature in this area, it is likely that age and gender differences in motives to exercise exist. For instance, young children tend to exercise for fun while teenagers primarily participate in activity for social status (Ashford et al., 1993). Young adults are known to be less interested than older adults in exercising for psychological well-being (Ashford et al., 1993), and there is evidence from a large cross-sectional study (N = 4,000) that exercising for health is slightly more common among individuals from younger versus older age groups (16 to 74 years; ADNFS, 1992; Stiggelbout et al., 2008). It is reported in at least one study that no differences in motivation are evident across the lifespan although this study included a relatively small cohort (Davis, Fox, Brewer and Ratusny, 1995). With respect to gender, men endorse motivation for performance reasons to a greater degree than women (Ashford et al., 1993), while women more often report exercising for appearance reasons (Allied Dunbar National Fitness Survey, 1992).

As previously mentioned, few investigations have been devoted to the study of motivation amongst highly active individuals across the lifespan. This is despite a growing literature devoted to the processes of change in motivation across the lifespan, such as the Motivational Theory of Lifespan Development (Heckhausen, Wrosch and Schulz, 2010), which hypothesizes that motives are flexible over the lifetime and are responsive to external and internal pressures. Perhaps by understanding the exercise motives of those who have succeeded in maintaining exercise behavior, efforts can be made to encourage motives that promote long-term adherence to exercise prescriptions. Therefore, the purpose of this study was to determine the motivational profile of a group of apparently healthy adults classified as highly active (i.e., active a minimum of 3 days per week on average). Overall, it is hypothesized that: 1) intrinsic motives, specifically enjoyment, will be reported as the primary sources of motivation, 2) differences in motivation will exist across age groups and between sexes, 3) women will endorse body centric motivations of weight reduction and appearance as primary motivators to a greater degree than men, and 4) motivation for performance reasons will be highest among the youngest age group and will decline with advancing age.

264    Matthew A. Stults-Kolehmainen, Joseph T. Ciccolo, John B. Bartholomew et al.

# METHOD

## Participants

A total of 2756 endurance athletes (triathletes, swimmers, cyclists and runners) from across the entire United States, all active for at least one year, completed an online survey regarding their exercise behavior and goals. The sample included individuals who were 18-64 years, the majority of whom were male (22% female). The participants engaged in a variety of activities on a weekly basis: 90.3% mountain biked, 84.4% completed resistance training, 82.2% swam, 61.0% ran, and 24.9% participated in road cycling. Furthermore, 75.5% of the respondents reported training for a triathlon. All participants exercised 3 to 7 days a week (average of 5.1 days per week) with 53.3% of the participants completing >75 min of exercise per day on average. See Table 1 for participant characteristics.

### Table 1. Participant characteristics

|  | Age group | n | Days of Exercise/ wk | Minutes of Exercise[a] | Training for a triathlon | Mass (lbs.) | BMI |
|---|---|---|---|---|---|---|---|
| Female | 18-24 | 41 | 5.37 | 4.27 | 32% | 129.2 | 21.4 |
|  | 25-34 | 109 | 5.43 | 4.14 | 39% | 138.8 | 22.4 |
|  | 35-44 | 132 | 5.31 | 4.24 | 38% | 136.9 | 22.6 |
|  | 45-54 | 158 | 5.09 | 4.13 | 20% | 138.6 | 22.9 |
|  | 55-64 | 57 | 5.02 | 4.00 | 5% | 140.3 | 23.6 |
| Male | 18-24 | 115 | 5.35 | 4.44 | 36% | 164.7 | 23.2 |
|  | 25-34 | 311 | 5.31 | 4.32 | 45% | 174.2 | 24.4 |
|  | 35-44 | 529 | 4.99 | 4.02 | 29% | 178.7 | 25.1 |
|  | 45-54 | 515 | 4.98 | 4.22 | 12% | 178.8 | 25.3 |
|  | 55-64 | 333 | 4.86 | 4.44 | 7% | 178.5 | 25.2 |

[a] Minutes of exercise refers to the average per session of exercise and is measured categorically. 1 = 30 min, 2 = 45 min, 3 = 60 min, 4 = 75 min, 5 = 90 min, 6 = 120 min, 7 = > 120 min.

## Instrumentation and Procedure

Participants were recruited to complete an online survey by responding to banner advertisements (no longer active) appearing on five nutrition and fitness websites specifically appealing to those interested in endurance activities. These individuals responded to the questions concerning demographics (e.g., gender, age) and exercise behavior. For age, respondents selected an age category in years (18-24, 25-34, 35-44, 45-54, and 55-64). Age groupings were selected to align with the American Community Survey (U.S. Census Bureau, 2010). The years 24 to 25 are the average ages for important social milestones, such as college graduation and marriage (Goldstein and Kenney, 2001) whereas 64 is the approximate age of retirement.

These items were followed by a questionnaire which assessed important personal motives for exercise. More specifically, this questionnaire was comprised of a single question: "What are the *three* most important reasons you exercise regularly?" followed by a list of 10 intrinsic and extrinsic motives. Several validated scales were examined to generate a list of motives for exercise behavior, such as the Exercise Motivation Inventory (Markland and Hardy, 1993), the Reasons for Exercise Inventory (Silberstein, Striegelmoore, Timko, and Rodin, 1988) and the Motivation for Physical Activities Measure (Frederick and Ryan, 1993). A factor analysis conducted by Dacey, Baltzell, and Zaichkowsky (2008) found that exercise motives amongst a group of older adults clustered along 6 dimensions, including: 1) health and fitness, 2) social/emotional benefits, 3) weight management, 4) stress management, 5) enjoyment and 6) appearance. Because our target population was a lifespan cohort of highly active individuals, the motives of health and fitness were divided into separate items. As the literature has well-established that exercise has profound mood enhancing benefits (Lawlor and Hopker, 2001), social and emotional benefits were also separated.

"Emotional benefits" was changed to "mood" to both: a) make the term more specific and b) differentiate it from stress management. Due to the wide age representation of the target population, an item was also devoted to life extension. Moreover, because the target population included a group of highly active individuals, many of whom participate in athletic events, the instrument included an item in regards to performance.

The questionnaire responses following the question posed above were: for health ("I want to be healthy"), for weight management ("I want to maintain my weight"), for performance ("I want to improve my sports performance"), for extending life ("I want to life longer"), for stress management ("I want to reduce my stress"), for appearance ("I want to appear better in my clothes"), for mood ("I want to feel better"), for fitness ("I want to be more fit"), for enjoyment ("I enjoy it"), and for social interactions ("I like the social aspects"). The online survey was constructed in a way to allow only a maximum of three motives to be selected. Participants were not provided with an option to enter a motive not on the list provided by the survey.

## Statistical Analysis

Participants with incomplete responses (n = 456) were initially removed from further inspection leaving a total sample of 2300 individuals. Data for each motive was coded as 0 (not endorsed as an important motive for exercise) or 1 (endorsed as important motive for exercise). Simple cross-tabulations were performed to discern general response trends. For hypotheses 2-4, multiple stepwise binary logistic regression analyses were conducted to determine whether age and gender significantly predicted exercise motives.

Age and gender were entered into step 1 of the analysis and age by gender interaction was entered in step 2. Models for each motive were tested for significance using $\chi^2$, which was calculated from likelihood ratio tests (-2 log likelihood). Odds ratios were calculated for main and interaction effects. Significance level was set at $p < .010$. Analyses were conducted with SPSS version 17.0.

**Table 2. Percentage and number of participants citing each motivator within their top three reasons to exercise, by gender and age group**

| Gender | | Health | Weight Management | Performance | Longer Life | Stress Reduction | Physical Appearance | Feeling Good | Fitness | Enjoyment | Social Aspects |
|---|---|---|---|---|---|---|---|---|---|---|---|
| Female | 18-24 | 41.5% (17) | 29.3% (12) | 73.2% (30) | 9.8% (4) | 14.6% (6) | 14.6% (6) | 17.1% (7) | 34.1% (14) | 56.1% (23) | 9.8% (4) |
| | 25-34 | 47.7% (52) | 27.5% (30) | 58.7% (64) | 3.7% (4) | 22.9% (25) | 17.4% (19) | 16.5% (18) | 36.7% (40) | 54.1% (59) | 14.7% (16) |
| | 35-44 | 42.7% (56) | 29.8% (39) | 53.7% (70) | 6.9% (9) | 23.7% (31) | 19.1% (25) | 16.0% (21) | 37.4% (49) | 61.1% (80) | 9.9% (13) |
| | 45-54 | 60.8% (96) | 25.9% (41) | 34.2% (54) | 13.9% (22) | 21.5% (34) | 9.5% (15) | 22.8% (36) | 44.3% (70) | 57.0% (90) | 10.1% (16) |
| | 55-64 | 57.9% (33) | 21.1% (12) | 31.6% (18) | 17.5% (10) | 10.5% (6) | 17.5% (10) | 33.3% (19) | 38.6% (22) | 59.6% (34) | 12.3% (7) |
| | Total | 51.2% (254) | 27.0% (134) | 47.6% (236) | 9.9% (49) | 20.6% (102) | 15.1% (75) | 20.4% (101) | 39.3% (195) | 57.7% (286) | 11.3% (56) |
| Male | 18-24 | 42.6% (49) | 8.7% (10) | 81.7% (94) | 7.8% (9) | 20.0% (23) | 8.7% (10) | 18.3% (21) | 41.7% (48) | 60.9% (70) | 9.6% (11) |
| | 25-34 | 43.4% (135) | 12.2% (38) | 69.5% (216) | 8.4% (26) | 20.3% (63) | 9.6% (30) | 23.2% (72) | 45.0% (140) | 61.4% (191) | 7.1% (22) |
| | 35-44 | 52.9% (279) | 22.8% (120) | 58.8% (310) | 17.1% (90) | 19.5% (103) | 7.6% (40) | 23.3% (123) | 37.8% (199) | 55.0% (290) | 5.1% (27) |
| | 45-54 | 55.0% (280) | 15.3% (78) | 47.3% (241) | 22.2% (113) | 23.0% (117) | 5.5% (28) | 27.7% (141) | 39.9% (203) | 58.2% (296) | 5.9% (30) |
| | 55-64 | 59.5% (197) | 20.5% (68) | 39.0% (129) | 27.5% (91) | 14.8% (49) | 4.2% (14) | 32.0% (106) | 41.1% (136) | 54.7% (181) | 6.6% (22) |
| | Total | 52.4% (940) | 17.5% (314) | 55.2% (990) | 18.3% (329) | 19.8% (355) | 6.8% (122) | 25.8% (463) | 40.5% (726) | 57.3% (1028) | 6.2% (112) |

**Table 3. Odds ratios\* (OR) and 95% confidence intervals (CI) from 10 stepwise binary logistic regression analyses comparing both genders and all age groups**

| Model | Men | | Women | | 18-24 years | | 25-34 years | | 35-44 years | | 45-54 years | | 55-64 years | |
|---|---|---|---|---|---|---|---|---|---|---|---|---|---|---|
| | OR | 95% CI | OR | 95% CI | OR | 95% CI | OR | 95% CI | OR | 95% CI | OR | 95% CI | OR | 95% CI |
| Health | Ref | | .99 | .81-1.21 | .51 † | .35-.74 | .55† | .42-.73 | .71‡ | .55-.92 | .89 | .69 – 1.15 | Ref | |
| Weight management | Ref | | 1.03 | .52- 2.06 | .37‡ | .18- .74 | .54‡ | .35- .83 | 1.14 | .82- 1.60 | .70 | .49- 1.00 | Ref | |
| Performance | Ref | | .66† | .54- .82 | 6.74† | 4.33- 10.49 | 3.50† | 2.59- 4.63 | 2.30† | 1.78- 2.98 | 1.35 | 1.04- 1.75 | Ref | |
| Extending life | Ref | | .52† | .37- .71 | .27† | .15- .51 | .23† | .15- .36 | .52† | .38- .71 | .76 | .56- 1.02 | Ref | |
| Stress management | Ref | | 1.02 | .79- 1.30 | 1.38 | .84- 2.26 | 1.60 | 1.11-2.32 | 1.55 | 1.10-2.18 | 1.77† | 1.26- 2.48 | Ref | |
| Appearance | Ref | | 2.40† | 1.76- 3.28 | 1.54 | .79- 3.01 | 1.79 | 1.07- 3.00 | 1.58 | .97- 2.58 | .95 | .56- 1.60 | Ref | |
| Mood | Ref | | .76 | .59- .97 | .47‡ | .30- .75 | .59† | .43-.81 | .60† | .45- .79 | .78 | .59- 1.02 | Ref | |
| Fitness | Ref | | .95 | .77- 1.16 | .97 | .66-1.41 | 1.10 | .83- 1.46 | .88 | .68- 1.14 | 1.01 | .79-1.31 | Ref | |
| Enjoyment | Ref | | 1.00 | .82- 1.22 | 1.19 | .81- 1.73 | 1.18 | .89- 1.57 | 1.03 | .80- 1.33 | 1.11 | .86- 1.42 | Ref | |
| Social interactions | Ref | | 1.89† | 1.34- 2.65 | 1.21 | .63- 2.34 | 1.14 | .68- 1.89 | .77 | .47- 1.27 | .86 | .52- 1.39 | Ref | |

\* Odds ratios close to 1.0 indicate no group differences; Ref. = Reference group; † = significant at $p < .001$ level; ‡ = significant at $p < .01$ level.

## RESULTS

All ten motives received varying degrees of endorsement as primary (i.e., three most important) motives for exercise; however, the motivators with the highest percentage across all age groups were enjoyment (56.9%), performance (53.0%), and health (52.2%). Furthermore, these motives varied across age groups. Table 2 reports the endorsement of each motivator by both age group and gender. Performance motivation was endorsed by 79.7% for those aged 18-24 years compared to 37.8% for those 55-64 years, with other age groups incrementally declining with advancing age. Living longer was one of three important motivators for only 8.2% of the youngest group, but 26.1% of the oldest.

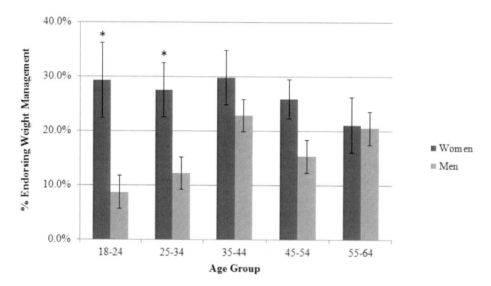

Figure 1. Percent of respondents endorsing weight management as a motive for exercise. Error bars represent standard errors. There was no main effect of gender. Interaction of age and gender was not significant at the $p < .01$ level ($p = .049$).* Youngest two age groups were significantly different from the reference group (ages 55-64; $p < .05$).

Improving fitness was more important than performance for only the oldest age-group. Women selected weight maintenance (26.8% vs. 17.4%) and appearance as important motives (15.7% vs. 7.0%) to a greater degree than men. Women also endorsed social interaction as a motive across all age-groups except for the youngest category. Men endorsed improving sports performance (54.6% vs. 47.1%), living longer (18.5% vs. 9.7%), and feeling better (26.0% vs. 20.3%) as one of their top three most important motivators. Less discernable trends were identified for stress reduction as a motive for exercise.

Stepwise binary logistic regression models for each motive were significant at the $p < .001$ level except for stress reduction ($p = .031$), fitness ($p > .100$), and enjoyment ($p > .100$). Age was a significant predictor of an individual's selection of the following as a motive to exercise: health ($\chi^2 = 28.78$, df = 4, $p < .001$), sports performance ($\chi^2 = 147.35$, df = 4, $p < .001$), living longer ($\chi^2 = 67.24$, df = 4, $p < .001$), and mood ($\chi^2 = 20.45$, df = 4, $p < .001$). Except for performance, these motives were endorsed to a greater extent by older age groups. The youngest age group was more likely (OR = 6.74, CI = 4.33- 10.49, $p < .001$) than the oldest age group to endorse performance as a motive for exercise. Gender was a significant predictor of an individual's selection of: performance ($\chi^2 = 14.75$, df = 1, $p < .001$), living longer ($\chi^2 = 18.01$, df = 1, $p < .001$), appearance ($\chi^2 = 28.81$, df = 1, $p < .001$), and social motives ($\chi^2 = 12.60$, df = 1, $p < .001$). The first two of these motives were endorsed to a greater degree by men while the opposite was true for appearance and social motives. See Table 3 for odds ratios (OR) and confidence intervals for gender and each age category. Logistic regression revealed a non-significant gender by age interaction for motivation to exercise to maintain weight ($\chi^2 = 9.55$, df = 4, $p = .049$). Specifically, odds ratios were non-significant for the youngest (OR = 4.21, 95% CI = 1.32- 13.46, $p = .015$) and second-youngest age groups (OR = 2.65, 95% CI = 1.10- 6.36, $p = .030$). While not significant, odds ratios point to an increased endorsement of this motive with the oldest age group. See Figure 1.

# DISCUSSION

The purpose of the study was to examine motivational profiles of highly active individuals across gender and ages. The top three motivators across all gender and age groups were enjoyment, performance, and health; however, these motives varied by age group and gender, thus confirming hypotheses. According to these data, performance motivation varies substantially between emerging adulthood and the 55-64 age range. Those in the youngest age category were 6.7 times more likely to endorse performance as a primary motive compared to those in the oldest age category (see Table 3).

As expected, it appears that the motivation to exercise for health and to extend life was most endorsed by older age groups. In this sample, the youngest two age groups were 73% and 77% less likely to endorse extending life as a motivation to exercise. In regards to gender, highly active women have a more body centric motivational profile than men; in other words, they endorse motives that indicate a greater emphasis on appearance and body mass, thus supporting this hypothesis as well. In fact, women were 2.4 times more likely than men to endorse appearance as a motive for exercise (see Table 2).

Logistic regression revealed that there was not a gender by age interaction in weight management motivation at the p < .01 level ($p = .049$). A trend was observed whereas young women endorsed weight maintenance motivation more than men, whereas those in the oldest age group were equally likely to endorse this motive regardless of gender. See Figure 1.

## Enjoyment

The current finding that participants primarily engage in exercise for enjoyment corroborates previous research reported on both exercise and physical activity motivation (Dacey et al., 2008, Ingledew et al., 1998; Stiggelbout et al., 2008). However, to the best knowledge of the current authors, this is the first study to identify the importance of this motive amongst *highly active* individuals. An extensive survey of 15,000 triathletes conducted by the USA Triathlon (2009) indicated that enjoyment was the primary motive for exercise amongst highly active exercisers (USA Triathlon, 2009). This group was also highly motivated by challenge (95% endorsement) and the pursuit of greater fitness (87% endorsement).

Despite the apparent importance of enjoyment in spurring motivation for exercise, little work has investigated the factors that enhance this construct. For instance, in a group of 123 highly active cyclists and fitness exercisers exercising on average 5.3 days per week, Frederick-Recascino and Schuster-Smith (2003) found that interest/enjoyment motivation and days per week of exercise were highly related to competitive drive of the athlete. On the other hand, an over-emphasis on competition, particularly from external sources, may undermine motivation. Therefore, as Ntoumanis and Biddle (1999) suggest, an environment promoting mastery of exercise as a goal in and of itself may be more conducive for enjoyment. Interestingly, Davis et al. (1995) also determined that the personality factors of extraversion and neuroticism are positively related to and highly predictive of enjoyment motivation for exercise. A structural equation model supported the direct influence of self-determination perceptions on enjoyment for exercise (Markland, 1999). Unfortunately, this model only explained a small amount of the variance in perceived enjoyment. In another study, Ashford et al. (1993) determined that the primary predictor of exercise enjoyment was socio-psychological well-being, which accounted for 8.5% of the variance in enjoyment. Certainly, enjoyment is influenced by a myriad of other variables that also vary by age and gender.

## Age Group Differences

The current results are both supported and contradicted by previous studies examining age-related differences in exercise motivation. Unlike results from the ADNFS Study (1992), which demonstrated that exercise for health was more important for younger age groups than older ones, these data demonstrate that health motivation for exercise is a stronger motivator for older individuals. Thus, the current results reflect the more intuitive and empirically supported notion that the emphasis on physical health grows in importance in stages of life where the quality of physical health is more uncertain (Heckhausen et al., 2010). As the current study was cross-sectional, we were unable to observe any changes or processes associated with aging.

The results of this study, which indicate that motives for exercise vary throughout the life span, may be reflective of the individual's life stage and its associated needs, expectations, perspectives, developmental deadlines, opportunities and societal norms. All of these, in turn, influence salient goals and desired outcomes (Havinghurst, 1952). The younger individual is driven to achieve developmental gains and to establish oneself as a competent individual, areas facilitated by sport and exercise participation (Heckhausen, 1997; Ogilvie, Rose, and Heppen, 2001). With this in mind, it's unsurprising that performance and fitness motives are highly endorsed by this age group. As the young person ages, however, they begin to experience a life in flux, resulting in conflicting goals. As a primary example, the drive to attract a mate may take precedence over fitness-related endeavors or, conversely, may influence one's decision to remain in sport (Nurmi, 1992; Sheldon and Kasser, 2001). Indeed, this pressure becomes magnified because the potential to experience seminal events—such as committing to a partner and having children, or graduating from college and establishing finances—emerges, peaks, and declines within certain development periods (Heckhausen et al., 2010). Leaving home and graduating from school creates needs for identity and social affiliation, and certainly social motives were endorsed by many younger adults in this cohort (Nurmi, 1992; Sheldon and Kasser, 2001). Some milestones, on the other hand, such as establishing a career, limit opportunities to be physically active, which wear on one's proclivity to strive for and attain fitness goals (Wiese and Freund, 2000). This likely explains why adults in their third and fourth decade of life discontinue exercise (Mihalik, Oleary, McGuire, and Dottavio, 1989).

While the stages of life may delimit how one approaches exercise, the process of aging—with its effects on the body and, thus, one's perceived ability—may play an equally important role. The third decade of life is generally when one's ability to perform physically reaches its peak and, consequently, energy expended towards such goals peaks in this time frame. During the transition into middle age the rate of experiencing developmental gains diminishes, particularly for one's physical ability. Not only are physical setbacks commonly experienced, but one begins to notice the first physical declines (Cross and Markus, 1991). This may weaken the reinforcement of exercise. Perceptions of a slowing metabolism and a growing waistline may explain why the current data found that men place more emphasis on weight management at middle to older age (Tiggemann, 2004). At this time, a focus on health-related goals in order to prevent a loss of control capacity emerges (Cross and Markus, 1991; Heckhausen, 1997; Nurmi, 1992). Consequently, goal disengagement with performance-based objectives increases as a function of assigning less importance to these goals (Rothermund and Brandtstadter, 2003). This occurs with an associated shift in the actual pursuit of goals that are judged to be more attainable.

In older age these processes accelerate and one must face their mortality, resulting in further re-prioritization of one's time and energy. Older adults are more driven to prevent loss of social, mental and physical functioning (Ebner, Freund, and Baltes, 2006; Heckhausen, 1997; Ogilvie et al., 2001). Motives to exercise may be influenced by a greater need for quality of life and maintenance of independence. These maturational considerations may explain why mental well-being, extending life, and health motives for exercise participation are more important in older age groups. Interestingly, a special situation surrounds retirement, in which opportunities for leisure time exercise may increase (Hirvensalo and Lintunen, 2011). The interaction of these factors may result in maintained exercise participation while the individual still has capacity to exercise.

The above discussion may explain why exercise behavior declines over the lifespan, as an individual may simply be either motivated or amotivated, but it does not necessarily explain why motivations may shift amongst those who continue to exercise. This last point touches on the limitations encountered when utilizing developmental perspectives to explain motivation for exercise behavior. While such theories recognize and attempt to explain the multifarious nature and variability of motivation across the life span it should be noted, however, that motivations vary also within age-groups. In other words, individual motivations frequently do not align with the typical pattern for a given developmental period. Indeed, there is no consensus as to what constitutes a developmental period (Heckhausen et al., 2010) nor did we inquire about developmental benchmarks in this study. We also did not inquire about the particular competitive level or various aspects of the environment which might influence exercise motives.

These factors, along with other aspects of an individual's context and situation are more emphasized in hierarchical models of Self-Determination Theory from Vallerand and Perreault (1999). Whether across development periods (Heckhausen; 2010) or various contexts, however, these frameworks are broad and unspecific to any given health behavior. Hence, an exercise-specific meta-theory of lifespan motivation across contexts would be an instrumental tool in understanding changing motivations across developmental periods. Despite the aforementioned limitations, when taken together, the constellation of physical, emotional, and cognitive changes observed across the lifespan are furthermore likely to influence the specific type, format, and setting of exercise an individual selects.

## Gender Differences

In terms of gender, these data support previous findings that men and women have different motives for exercise (Ashford et al., 1993, ADNFS, 1992). As noted above, men exercise to a greater degree for performance reasons, while women exercise more than men because of extrinsic factors such as appearance and weight control. The findings in this study concur with a multitude of other studies that find that women exercise more than men for management of body mass (ADNFS, 1992; Markland and Hardy, 1993; McDonald and Thompson, 1992, Silberstein et al., 1988). This well-observed trend may be reflective of gender roles, social norms and expectations related to gender (Cash, Novy, and Grant, 1994). In particular, the drive for attractiveness and achieving high mate value may be a primary motive for women to exercise (Buss, 1988; Jonason, 2007). Interestingly, a trend was observed (Figure 1) in that the gender difference for weight management as a motive was not detectable in older age groups, concurring with results from Davis et al. (1995). This trend may be a result of a complex interplay between changing needs, goals, and health situation. Davis et al. (1995) speculate that men may exercise more for weight loss in older ages because of a greater awareness of the associations between health outcomes and obesity. It is important to note that these data do not directly support the main effects found by Davis and colleagues (1995), who concluded that motivation patterns were largely similar in regularly active individuals across age and gender.

## Limitations

This study is limited in several respects. First, we did not inquire about important influences on motivation, such as status in regards to professional contracts or participation in collegiate sports, contexts in which individuals would feel that they *have* to exercise (Hollembeak and Amorose, 2005; Martens and Webber, 2002; Medic et al., 2007). Given the large number of respondents and lifespan representation it is not likely that professional status had an undue influence on results. Likewise, there may be important demographic distinctions that are indiscernible because we did not collect information on geographic location or ethnicity (see Resnick, Vogel, and Luisi, 2006). Presumably, based on the fact that the current sample was mainly comprised of competitive endurance athletes and triathletes this cohort was likely of a higher income status and Caucasian majority (USA Triathlon, 2009). Because the websites from which participants were recruited were unlimited to a specific geographic location, it is likely that these individuals were from all regions of North America; however, it must be noted that certain areas (e.g., the American West and South) likely have a large representation in this cohort (USA Triathlon, 2009). Future investigations should compare highly active individuals to exercise initiators and/or inactive individuals. Further research should also be conducted to compare motivational profiles of highly active, but non-competitive individuals (such as group exercise participants and regular fitness club members) to highly active collegiate and/or professional athletes (Davis and Cowles, 1989). Finally, tracking individuals over time would provide better information in regards to the influence of aging versus the social impact of the age-related cohort (Klein and Becker, 2008).

Perhaps the greatest limitation of this study rests with the motivation instrument we utilized. Although individuals in this study only had to endorse three motives, it is likely that highly active individuals have more than three motives to exercise. Likert-scale instruments, such as the Exercise Motivation Inventory (Markland and Hardy, 1993), in which *each* motivation is evaluated by participants may provide a more psychometrically valid approach to a similar study. On the other hand, such instruments require substantially more response time than the instrument currently used. Should this extra time then inhibit certain individuals from participation, an advantage to the present approach versus using a Likert-based instrument is that a greater quantity of responses may be collected. This type of approach is supported by studies comparing Likert scales to these alternative measures (Svensson, 2001).

Aside from the consideration of psychometrics, making sense of the complex nature of exercise motivation would be substantially aided with the future use of a strong theoretical framework (Biddle and Nigg, 2000; Plonczynski, 2000), such as Motivational Theory of Life Span Development (Heckhausen et al., 2010) or Self-Determination Theory (Deci and Ryan, 1985; Vallerand, 2007). A recent investigation by Brunet and Sabiston (2011) with a convenience sample found that intrinsic motivation was related to more physical activity in three different age groups of adults. Extrinsic motivation, specifically external regulation, only influenced physical activity in young adults, however. The influence of extrinsic motivators, the whole of which are a central concept in self-determination theory, were not the focus of the current study but should accordingly be given more weight in future research. Indeed, awards, monetary incentives and other extrinsic factors may ultimately undermine exercise behavior (Frederick and Ryan, 1995). Some motives defy strict classification along the continuum of self-determination, such as sports performance, which was endorsed as a top-three motivator for exercise in the current study. For instance, the meaning of performance may differ based on age and gender. Performance may be understood as a proxy for competitive standing or status (external standards and rewards, accomplishment or achievement) amongst younger individuals, whereas it may be understood as an intrinsic factor reflective of personal challenge (internal standards and rewards or feelings of personal mastery) amongst others. Therefore, performance can be seen as both an intrinsic and extrinsic motivator; consequently, this factor has been parsed in some research (Ashford et al., 1993). Because of this complexity, it may be more parsimonious to interpret the performance motive in light of simpler value-expectancy theories of motivation (Eccles and Harold, 1991). According to this perspective, an individual would be motivated to exercise if they not only desired enhanced performance but found that exercise had a high probability of manifesting success in this endeavor. Despite this utility, value-expectancy theories do not account as well as the meta-theories above for motivational variability both across demographics and within environmental, contextual and social situations.

## Application

From an application viewpoint, understanding the unique age and gender-related motivational profiles of highly active individuals may be an invaluable tool when prescribing exercise programs for this group of people. While the current data would support the notion that all programs should strive to magnify enjoyment (Hillsdon, Thorogood, Anstiss and Morris, 1995), it is important to recognize that individuals exercise for a variety of reasons, and these motives are related to gender and age. This has broad implications for the format of exercise programs and communication between trainers and clients. For instance, men in older age groups value weight management more than their younger counterparts, and care about sport performance less. This may dictate then that trainers conduct longer training sessions with lower intensity, perhaps in line with ACSM recommendations for weight control (Donnelly, Blair, Jakicic, Manore, Rankin, and Smith, 2009).

Lastly, in order to effectively use this research to promote exercise compliance and adherence in this population, it is not sufficient to simply identify the motivational factors of highly active individuals. Rather, the motivational factors that are predominate at their life stage (e.g., performance, attractiveness) should be related to their psychological needs (e.g., competence or relatedness) at this stage (Pahmeier, 2008). Such an emphasis may meet the call for greater individualization of exercising counseling and programming (Garber, Blissmer, Deschenes, Franklin, Lamonte, Lee, Nieman, and Swain, 2011).

It is also premature at this time to make inferences about how this information maybe be utilized to spur irregular exercisers into a more active lifestyle. The current data captured motivational profiles at a slice of time; hence, no inferences about causation or processes of change are warranted. Consequently, it is unknown whether motivation for exercise changes as one becomes more active or whether the individual changes behavior in response to changing motivations and movement along the continuum of self-direction. Longitudinal data is just emerging in this realm of inquiry and indicates that those who progress forward in their exercise behavior have little change or perhaps a decline in extrinsic motivation (Buckworth, Lee, Regan, Schneider, and DiClemente, 2007). How very active individuals change over time is also not known. However, even highly active individuals likely vary in both motivation and exercise behavior across a span of a year or longer. Consequently, the motives of the highly active individuals in this study do not necessarily indicate an *optimal* profile of motivation. Accordingly, it would be incorrect to presuppose that programs targeting specific inactive demographic groups should be constructed in a way to promote motives of their more active counterparts. For instance, it would be questionable to direct younger inactive women to primarily focus on enhancing extrinsic factors, such as weight control, in order to propel them to activity levels of more active women. Until sufficient experimental and longitudinal data are available it is unknown how to most effectively use this information to promote high levels of exercise behavior.

Central to this issue, however, is the need for programs that enhance the motivational profile of inactive individuals of various ages and both genders. Despite immediate psychological benefits, unaccustomed exercise is frequently associated with feelings of displeasure over a period of several days to weeks (e.g., fatigue, soreness, boredom, frustration about a lack of noticeable change in body composition); therefore, a person must have sufficient motivation to sustain this complex behavior (Lox, Ginis and Petruzzello, 2006). It is possible that emphasizing extrinsic factors may be the most effective means to motivate a person to initiate exercise, but the best way to encourage adherence is to emphasize enjoyment. Such efforts may promote long-term adherence, although this has yet to be tested (Buckworth and Dishman, 2007). The technique of motivational interviewing, on the other hand, advocates the engagement of intrinsic motivation at program initiation (Harland, White, Drinkwater, Chinn, Farr, and Howell, 1999). Promising methods combine aspects of multiple behavior change theories, such as modeling by successful long-term exercisers, but to date these programs are neither time efficient nor economical. Unfortunately, motivation-based programming was not within the scope of the current study, but should have focus in future research.

## CONCLUSION

In conclusion, the motivational profile of individuals varies as a function of gender and age group. This sample was provided a list of 10 possible exercise motives. Across both genders and all age categories, the pre-dominant motives for exercise were enjoyment, performance, and health, with younger age groups endorsing performance motivation more than older age groups. It appears that, regardless of age, women have a more extrinsic motivational profile than men with a greater emphasis on appearance. However, gender differences in weight management as a motivational source dissipate by the latter fifties with women endorsing this motive less as they age and men endorsing it to a greater degree. Future researchers should formulate investigations within the context of major theoretical frameworks such as Self-Determination Theory (Deci and Ryan, 1985) and the Motivational Theory of Lifespan Development (Heckhausen et al., 2010). Finally, from an application viewpoint, differences in motivation should be considered when designing exercise prescriptions or when consulting for exercise adherence.

## ACKNOWLEDGMENTS

Charles (Chuck) Abolt provided assistance with numerous facets of the preparation of this manuscript.

## REFERENCES

Allied Dunbar National Fitness Survey. (1992). *Allied Dunbar National Fitness Survey main findings.* London, United Kingdom: Sports Council and Health Education Authority.

Ashford, B., Biddle, S., and Goudas, M. (1993). Participation in community sports centers: Motives and predictors of enjoyment. *Journal of Sports Sciences, 11*, 249-256.

Ashford, B., and Rickhuss, J. (1992). Life-span differences in motivation for participating in community sport and recreation. *Journal of Sports Sciences, 10*, 626.

Barrell, G., High, S., Holt, D., and MacKean, J. (1988). *Motives for starting running and for competing in full and half marathon events.* Paper presented at the Sport, Health, Psychology and Exercise Symposium Proceedings, London.

Biddle, S. J. H. (1995). Exercise motivation across the life span. In S. J. H. Biddle (Ed.), *European Perspective on Exercise and Sport Psychology* (pp. 3-35). Champaign, IL: Human Kinetics.

Biddle, S. J. H., and Fox, K. R. (1998). Motivation for physical activity and weight management. *International Journal of Obesity, 22*, S39-S47.

Biddle, S. J. H., and Nigg, C. R. (2000). Theories of exercise behavior. *International Journal of Sport Psychology, 31*, 290-304.

Bird, S., Radermacher, H., Feldman, S., Sims, J., Kurowski, W., Browning, C., and Thomas, S. (2009). Factors influencing the physical activity levels of older people from culturally-diverse communities: An Australian experience. *Aging and Society, 29*, 1275-1294.

Brawley, L. R., and Vallerand, R. J. (1984). *Enhancing intrinsic motivation for fitness activities: Its systematic increase in the fitness environment.* Unpublished manuscript.

Brunet, J., and Sabiston, C. M. (2011). Exploring motivation for physical activity across the adult lifespan. *Psychology of Sport and Exercise, 12*, 99-105.

Buckworth, J., and Dishman, R. K. (2007). Exercise adherence. In G. Tenenbaum and R. C. Eklund (Eds.), *Handbook of sport psychology* (3rd ed., pp. 509-535). New York: John Wiley and Sons, Inc.

Buckworth, J., Lee, R. E., Regan, G., Schneider, L. K., and DiClemente, C. C. (2007). Decomposing intrinsic and extrinsic motivation for exercise: Application to stage of motivational readiness. *Psychology of Sport and Exercise, 8*, 441-461.

Buss, D. M. (1988). The evolution of human intrasexual competition: Tactics of mate attraction. *Journal of Personality and Social Psychology, 54*, 616-628.

Cash, T. F., Novy, P. L., and Grant, J. R. (1994). Why do women exercise? Factor analysis and further validation of the reasons for exercise inventory. *Perceptual and Motor Skills, 78*, 539-544.

Centers for Disease Control. (2008). Prevalence of self-reported physically active adults-United States, 2007. *Morbidity and Mortality Weekly Report, 57*, 1297-1300.

Clough, P. J., Shephard, J., and Maughan, R. J. (1988). *Motivations for running.* Paper presented at the Sport, Health, Psychology and Exercise Symposium Proceedings, London.

Cross, S., and Markus, H. (1991). Possible selves across the life span. *Human Development, 34*, 230-255.

Dacey, M., Baltzell, A., and Zaichkowsky, L. (2008). Older adults' intrinsic and extrinsic motivation toward physical activity. *American Journal of Health Behavior, 32*, 570-582.

Davis, C., and Cowles, M. (1989). A comparison of weight and diet concerns and personality-factors among female athletes and non-athletes. *Journal of Psychosomatic Research, 33*, 527-536.

Davis, C., Fox, J., Brewer, H., and Ratusny, D. (1995). Motivations to exercise as a function of personality-characteristics, age, and gender. *Personality and Individual Differences, 19*, 165-174.

De Young, K. P., and Anderson, D. A. (2010). Prevalence and correlates of exercise motivated by negative affect. *International Journal of Eating Disorders, 43*, 50-58.

Deci, E. L., and Ryan, R. M. (1985). *Intrinsic motivation and self-determination in human behavior.* New York, NY: Plenum Press.

Donnelly, J. E., Blair, S. N., Jakicic, J. M., Manore, M. M., Rankin, J. W. and Smith B. K. (2009). Appropriate physical activity intervention strategies for weight loss and prevention of weight regain for adults. *Medicine and Science in Sports and Exercise, 41*, 459-471.

Duda, J. L. (1989). Goal perspectives and behavior in sport and exercise settings. In C. Ames and M. L. Maehr (Eds.), *Advances in motivation and achievement* (Vol. 6, pp. 81-115). Greenwich, CT: JAI Press.

Ebner, N. C., Freund, A. M., and Baltes, P. B. (2006). Developmental changes in personal goal orientation from young to late adulthood: From striving for gains to maintenance and prevention of losses. *Psychology and Aging, 21*, 664-678.

Eccles, J. S., and Harold, R. D. (1991). Gender differences in sport involvement: Applying the Eccles' expectancy-value model. *Journal of Applied Sport Psychology, 3*, 7-35.

Frederick, C. M., and Ryan, R. M. (1993). Differences in motivation for sport and exercise and their relationships with participation and mental health. *Journal of Sport Behavior, 16*, 125-145.

Frederick, C. M., and Ryan, R. M. (1995). Self-determination in sport- A review using cognitive evaluation theory. *International Journal of Sport Psychology, 26*, 5-23.

Frederick-Recascino, C. M., and Schuster-Smith, H. (2003). Competition and intrinsic motivation in physical activity: A comparison of two groups. *Journal of Sport Behavior, 26*, 240-254.

Garber, C. E., Blissmer, B., Deschenes, M. R., Franklin, B. A., Lamonte, M. J., Lee, I., Nieman, D. C., and Swain, D. P. (2011). Quantity and Quality of Exercise for Developing and Maintaining Cardiorespiratory, Musculoskeletal, and Neuromotor Fitness in Apparently Healthy Adults: Guidance for Prescribing Exercise. *Medicine and Science in Sports and Exercise, 43*, 1334-1359.

Goldstein, J.R. and C.T. Kenney (2001). Marriage Delayed or Marriage Forgone? New Cohort Forecasts of First Marriage for U.S. Women. *American Sociological Review* 66, 506-519.

Hamer, M., Karageorghis, C. I., and Vlachopoulos, S. A. P. (2002). Motives for exercise participation as predictors of exercise dependence among endurance athletes. *Journal of Sports Medicine and Physical Fitness, 42*, 233-238.

Harland, J., White, M., Drinkwater, C., Chinn, D., Farr, L, and Howell, D. (1999). The Newcastle exercise project: a randomised controlled trial of methods to promote physical activity in primary care. *British Medical Journal, 319*, 828-831.

Havinghurst, R. J. (1952). *Developmental tasks and education.* New York, NY: McKay Company.

Heckhausen, J. (1997). Developmental regulation across adulthood: Primary and secondary control of age-related challenges. *Developmental Psychology, 33*, 176-187.

Heckhausen, J., Wrosch, C., and Schulz, R. (2010). A motivational theory of life-span development. *Psychological Review, 117*, 32-60.Hillsdon, M., Thorogood, M., Anstiss, T., and Morris, J. (1995). Randomized controlled trials of physical-activity promotion in free-living populations – A review. *Journal of Epidemiology and Community Health, 49*, 448-453.

Hirvensalo, M., and Lintunen, T. Life-course perspective for physical activity and sports participation. *European Review of Aging and Physical Activity, 8*, 13-22.

Hollembeak, J., and Amorose, A. J. (2005). Perceived coaching behaviors and college athletes' intrinsic motivation: A test of self-determination theory. *Journal of Applied Sport Psychology, 17*, 20-36.

Ingledew, D. K., Markland, D., and Medley, A. R. (1998). Exercise motives and stages of change. *Journal of Health Psychology, 3*, 477 - 489.

Jonason, P. K. (2007). An evolutionary psychology perspective on sex differences in exercise behaviors and motivations. *Journal of Social Psychology, 147*, 5-14.

Klein, T., and Becker, S. (2008). Is there really a decline in sports activity during the course of life? An analysis of age- and cohort-related differences in sports activity. *Zeitschrift Fur Soziologie, 37*, 226-245.

Lawlor, D. A., and Hopker, S. W. (2001). The effectiveness of exercise as an intervention in the management of depression: systematic review and meta-regression analysis of randomised controlled trials. *British Medical Journal, 322*, 763-767.

Lox, C. L., Ginis, K. A. M., and Petruzzello, S. J. (2006). *The Psychology of Exercise: Integrating Theory and Practice.* Scottsdale, AZ: Holcomb Hathaway.

Markland, D. (1999). *Internally informational versus internally controlling exercise motives and exercise enjoyment: The mediating role of self-determination.* Paper presented at the Proceedings of the 4th Annual Congress of the European College of Sport Science, Rome. University Institute of Motor Sciences.

Markland, D., and Hardy, L. (1993). The exercise motivations inventory - preliminary development and validity of a measure of individuals' reasons for participation in regular physical exercise. *Personality and Individual Differences, 15*, 289-296.

Martens, M. P., and Webber, S. N. (2002). Psychometric properties of the sport motivation scale: An evaluation with college varsity athletes from the US. *Journal of Sport and Exercise Psychology, 24*, 254-270.

McDonald, K., and Thompson, J. K. (1992). Eating disturbance, body-image dissatisfaction, and reasons for exercising - gender differences and correlational findings. *International Journal of Eating Disorders, 11*, 289-292.

Medic, N., Mack, D. E., Wilson, P. M., and Starkes, J. L. (2007). The effects of athletic scholarship of motivation in sport. *Journal of Sport Behavior, 30*, 292-306.

Mihalik, B. J., Oleary, J. T., McGuire, F. A., and Dottavio, F. D. (1989). Sports involvement across the life-span - Expansion and contraction of sports activities. *Research Quarterly for Exercise and Sport, 60*, 396-398.

Mullan, E., and Markland, D. (1997). Variations in self-determination across the stages of change for exercise in adults. *Motivation and Emotion, 21*, 349-362.

Ntoumanis, N., and Biddle, S. J. H. (1999). A review of motivational climate in physical activity. *Journal of Sports Sciences, 17*, 643-665.

Nurmi, J. E. (1992). Age-differences in adult goals, concerns, and their temporal extensions - a life course approach to future-oriented motivation. *International Journal of Behavioral Development, 15*, 487-508.

Ogilvie, D. M., Rose, K. M., and Heppen, J. B. (2001). A comparison of personal project motives in three age groups. *Basic and Applied Social Psychology, 23*, 207-215.

Pahmeier, I. (2008). Sport activities from the lifespan perspective. *Zeitschrift Fur Gerontologie Und Geriatrie, 41*, 168-176.

Plonczynski, D. J. (2000). Measurement of motivation for exercise. *Health Education Research, 15*, 695-705.

Polman, P., Pieter, W., Bercades, L. T., and Ntoumanis, N. (2004). Relationship between psychological and biological factors and physical activity and exercise behavior in Filipino students. *International Journal of Sport and Exercise Psychology, 2*, 81-97.

Resnick, B., Vogel, A., and Luisi, D. (2006). Motivating minority older adults to exercise. *Cultural Diversity and Ethnic Minority Psychology, 12*, 17-29.

Rothermund, K., and Brandstadter, J. (2003). Coping with deficits and losses in later life: From compensatory action to accommodation. *Psychology and Aging, 18*, 896-905.

Ryan, R. M., Frederick, C. M., Lepes, D., Rubio, N., and Sheldon, K. M. (1997). Intrinsic motivation and exercise adherence. *International Journal of Sport Psychology, 28*, 335-354.

Sheldon, K. A., and Kasser, T. (2001). Getting older, getting better? Personal strivings and psychological maturity across the life span. *Developmental Psychology, 37*, 491-501.

Silberstein, L. R., Striegelmoore, R. H., Timko, C., and Rodin, J. (1988). Behavioral and psychological implications of body dissatisfaction: Do men and women differ? *Sex Roles, 19*, 219-232.

Stiggelbout, M., Hopman-Rock, M., and van Mechelen, W. (2008). Entry correlates and motivations of older adults participating in organized exercise programs. *Journal of Aging and Physical Activity, 16*, 342-354.

Svensson, E. (2001). Construction of a single global scale for multi-item assessments of the same variable. *Statistics in Medicine, 20*, 3831-3846.

Teixeira, P. J., Going, S. B., Houtkooper, L. B., Cussler, E. C., Metcalfe, L. L., Blew, R. M., and Lohman, T. G. (2006). Exercise motivation, eating, and body image variables as predictors of weight control. *Medicine and Science in Sports and Exercise, 38*, 179-188.

Tiggemann, M. (2004). Body image across the adult life span: Stability and change. *Body Image, 1*, 29-41.

Troiano, R. P., Berrigan, D., Dodd, K. W., Masse, L. C., Tilert, T., and McDowell, M. (2008). Physical activity in the United States measured by accelerometer. *Medicine and Science in Sports and Exercise, 40*, 181-188.

Trost, S. G., Owen, N., Bauman, A. E., Sallis, J. F., and Brown, W. (2002). Correlates of adults' participation in physical activity: review and update. *Medicine and Science in Sports and Exercise, 34*, 1996-2001.

U.S. Census Bureau (2010). *American Community Survey 2010.* Retrieved from http://factfinder2.census.gov.

USA Triathlon. (2009). *The mind of the athlete report.* Retrieved from http://www.usatriathlon.org/about-multisport/demographics.aspx.

Vallerand, R. J., and Perreault, S. (1999). Intrinsic and extrinsic motivation in sport: Toward a hierarchical model. In R. Lidor and M. Bar-Eli (Eds.), *Sport psychology: Linking theory and practice.* Morgantown, WV: Fitness Information Technology, Inc.

Vallerand, R. J. (2007). Intrinsic and extrinsic motivation in sport and physical activity: A review and a look at the future. In G. Tenenbaum and R. C. Eklund (Eds.), *Handbook of sport psychology* (pp. 59-83). Hoboken, NJ: John Wiley and Sons.

Wiese, B. S., and Freund, A. M. (2000). The interplay of work and family in young and middle adulthood. In J. Heckhausen (Ed.), *Motivational psychology of human development: Developing motivation and motivating development* (Vol. 131, pp. 233-249). New York, NY: Elsevier Science.

In: Innovative Writings in Sport and Exercise Psychology
Editor: Robert Schinke

ISBN: 978-1-62948-881-3
© 2014 Nova Science Publishers, Inc.

*Chapter 17*

# EXAMINING THE SUPERSTITIONS OF SPORT FANS: TYPES OF SUPERSTITIONS, PERCEPTIONS OF IMPACT, AND RELATIONSHIP WITH TEAM IDENTIFICATION

*Daniel L. Wann[1]\*, Frederick G. Grieve[2], Ryan K. Zapalac[3], Christian End[4], Jason R. Lanter[5], Dale G. Pease[6], Brandy Fellows[7], Kelly Oliver[7] and Allison Wallace[7]*

[1]Murray State University, Murray, Kentucky, US
[2]Western Kentucky University, Bowling Green, Kentucky, US
[3]Sam Houston State University, Huntsville, Texas, US
[4]Xavier University, Cincinnati, Ohio, US
[5]Kutztown State University, Kutztown, Pennsylvania, US
[6]University of Houston, Houston, Texas, US
[7]Murray State University, Murray, Kentucky, US

## ABSTRACT

The current work examined the superstitious behaviors of sport fans. A sample of 1661 college students completed a questionnaire packet assessing demographics, team identification, sport fandom, superstitions, perceptions of superstition impact and importance, and why they engaged in the superstitions. A total of 675 persons reported at least one superstition. Higher levels of sport fandom and higher levels of team identification correlated with a greater number of superstitions listed. Further, persons with higher levels of team identification reported greater perceptions of the impact and importance of their superstitions. The categorization of the superstitions revealed that

---

\* Portions of this research were presented at the annual meeting of the Association for Applied Sport Psychology, Salt Lake City (2009). Address correspondence to Daniel L. Wann, Department of Psychology, Murray State University, Murray, KY 42071 (270-809-2860) or to dwann@murraystate.edu via Internet.

apparel superstitions were most prominent. Other prominent superstitions included vocalizations, consumption of food/drink (nonalcoholic), watching or not watching the action, and good luck charms/superstitious rituals.

In the past two decades, much has been learned about sport fandom due to the combined efforts of sport psychology professionals, sport sociologists and sport marketing/management professionals. Indeed, we now have a better understanding of many important aspects of the fan experience including biased perceptions of other fans, teams, and players (Markman and Hirt, 2002), aggression and hostility (Dimmock and Grove, 2005), emotional responses (Madrigal, 2003), and factors related to attendance (Laverie and Arnett, 2000), to name but a few. However, voids in our understanding of fans and spectators still remain. In the present investigation, we focused on one such void, namely, the superstitions of fans.

Superstitions are behaviors involving actions believed to lead to or cause a specified (usually desirable) outcome (Womack, 1992). Individuals engage in these behaviors because they believe there is a causal relationship between their action(s) and certain outcomes. With respect to sport fans, superstitious behavior would involve actions thought to assist a team (e.g., wearing a "lucky" shirt or sitting in a "lucky" seat will increase the team's chances of winning). It is important to differentiate between *superstitious rituals* and *routine* behaviors. Although superstitious rituals and routines are similar concepts, they are distinct. As noted, superstitious rituals and behaviors are believed to lead to or cause a specified outcome. Routines, on the other hand, involve a set or series of actions that lack a "special, magical significance" that is attributed to superstitious behaviors (Schippers and Van Lange, 2006, p. 2533). Superstitious rituals, more so than routines, are designed to decrease the anxiety that people feel in relation to a given event (Keinan, 2002). For example, consider a sport fan who wears a specific shirt each time he attends one of his favorite team's games (e.g., a team replica jersey). This action may simply be a routine or may in fact be superstitious in nature. If he simply wears this shirt out of habit and does not believe there is any potential benefit to his team by wearing the shirt then his actions are merely routine in nature. On the other hand, if he believes that this is his "lucky shirt" and he feels that when he wears the shirt his team performs better (i.e., there is a causal relationship between wearing the shirt and team success), then his actions involve a superstitious ritual; such a belief will decrease the anxiety he feels in regards to his team's performance.

Little is known about the superstitious rituals of fans (although studies have targeted athlete superstitions, e.g., Brevers, Dan, Noel, and Nils, 2011). We could find only two empirical pieces investigating these behaviors. One, an Associated Press poll (Superstition Study, 2007) examining slightly over 1000 adults, found that 13% of respondents indicated that they engaged in superstitious behaviors to try to assist their favorite sport teams. The second empirical discussion of fan superstition comes from Kelley and Tian (2004). In their study of fans' journal entries, the authors found that instances of superstitious behavior. For instance, one participant reported that if his/her team was performing well he/she would "remain in that same position" (page 40). Others discussed the importance of wearing certain items of clothing believed to bring their team good luck. Although these reports indicate that some fans engage in superstitions, they were descriptive in nature and many questions remain unanswered. For instance, potential predictors of superstition were not examined. Further, the studies did not investigate whether certain types of superstitious behavior were more common than others.

The current investigation was designed to examine the superstitions of sport fans. The initial purpose was to examine the number of superstitions listed by fans, both at the arena and at other places (e.g., home or office). Secondly, we were interested in potential predictors of the superstitions listed. We examined two predictors: level of team identification and level of sport fandom. Team identification concerns the extent to which a fan feels a psychological connection with a team (Wann, Melnick, Russell, and Pease, 2001). Team identification is a powerful predictor of a variety of fan behaviors (Wann, 2006a). For instance, Wann and Zaichkowsky (2009) recently found level of team identification predicted beliefs in sport curses. Furthermore, research on athletes suggests that increases in sport involvement correspond with increase in superstitious beliefs (Neil, Anderson, and Sheppard, 1981) and athlete identity is a significant predictor of superstitious behavior (Brevers et al., 2011; Todd and Brown, 2003). Taken together, these findings support our hypothesis that there would be a positive relationship between level of identification with a favorite sport team and the number of superstitions reported related to that team. With respect to sport fandom (i.e., the extent to which an individual follows a team, sport, or athlete, see Wann et al., 2001), predictions were less clear given that it is often team identification, and not mere sport fandom *per se*, that predicts fan behaviors (Wann, 2006b). However, because fandom predicts beliefs in sport team curses (Wann and Zaichkowsky, 2009), we included this variable as a predictor within the framework of a research question asking, "To what extent does level of sport fandom predict amount of superstition among fans?"

We were also interested in fans' perceptions of the importance and impact of their superstitions. We examined the extent to which engaging in the superstitious act was important to the fan and the extent that he or she believed that the superstitious act had a direct impact on the outcome of a sporting event. In terms of potential predictors of importance and involvement, once again we examined the impact of team identification and sport fandom. Using the logic outlined above, we hypothesized that persons with higher levels of team identification would place a greater amount of importance on their superstitions and that they would report that these acts have greater levels of impact on game outcomes. Also, similar to the aforementioned discussion of sport fandom, the impact of this variable was examined via a research question asking, "To what extent does level of sport fandom predict amount of importance and perceptions of impact of fan superstitions?"

There were two additional focus points of the current investigation that did not involve hypotheses (due to a lack of previous research or theory to serve as a basis for predictions). First, we were interested in which types of superstitions were most common (e.g., lucky charms, apparel). Although researchers had classified forms of athlete superstition (Buhrmann, Brown, and Zaugg, 1982), to our knowledge such an analysis had yet to be done on fan superstitions (the specific categories examined in the current investigation were determined after examining the participants' responses, see Results section below). Second, we investigated potential superstition differences among types of sports. Specifically, we tested for sport differences in the number of superstitions listed as well as differences in perceptions of importance and impact.

## METHOD

### Participants

The original sample consisted of 1880 college students from seven universities in the Unites States. The participants received extra course credit in exchange for their participation. A total of 219 of these persons failed to accurately complete one or more sections of the questionnaire packet (e.g., they failed to list a favorite team, did not clearly specify the sport in question, left key items blank, etc.).

Therefore, these individuals were removed from the data set, resulting in a final sample of 1661 participants (904 male; 754 female; 3 not reporting gender). These respondents had a mean age of 22.65 years ($SD = 7.59$; range = 18 to 73).

### Materials and Procedure

Prior to data collection, approval was received from each university's Institutional Review Board (IRB). Data were collected over a four-year period during each month of the year (thus, across all sport seasons). Upon entering the testing session and providing their consent, participants (tested in groups) were handed a questionnaire packet containing five sections. The first section requested demographic information assessing gender and age.

The second section of the protocol contained the five-item Sport Fandom Questionnaire (SFQ; Wann, 2002). This reliable and valid Likert-scale instrument assesses sport fandom, that is, the extent to which an individual follows a team, sport, or athlete (Wann, 2002, reported test-retest correlation = .94 for two testing sessions separated by 4 weeks). A sample item on the SFQ reads, "I consider myself to be a sport fan." Response options to the SFQ ranged from 1 (*low fandom*) to 8 (*high fandom*). The third section contained the Sport Spectator Identification Scale (SSIS; Wann and Branscombe, 1993). This scale assesses the extent to which a fan feels a psychological connection to a team and has strong reliability and validity (Wann and Branscombe, 1993, reported a test-retest correlation of .60 for two testing sessions separated by one year). A sample item reads, "How important to you is it that the (Target Team) wins?" The SSIS contains seven Likert-scale items with response options ranging from 1 (*low identification*) to 8 (*high identification*). Participants listed their favorite sport team and targeted this team when completing the SSIS. They were to include the name of the team and the sport involved.

The fourth and fifth sections assessed the participants' sport fan superstitious rituals. Section four assessed behavior at the event (e.g., at the arena or stadium) while section five assessed behavior at other places (e.g., at home or in the car). The items and instructions contained in these sections were identical with the exception of the situation in question. At the top of each one-page section, participants listed the team they had targeted on the previous page (i.e., the team for which they had completed the SSIS). For section four, participants then read, "We are interested in superstitions that sports fans engage in for their favorite sport team *at the arena or event*. There are spaces below in which you should describe your superstitions or rituals in great detail, including what exactly the superstition or ritual entails, when it is performed, and how it is performed. Please be as descriptive as possible. Then, after each superstition, please answer the questions that follow." For section five, the phrase "*at the arena or event*" was replaced with "*at places other than the arena* (e.g., home, office, car)." Each section then had a blank space labeled "Superstition 1:" in which participants described their first superstition (both at the event and away from the event). They then answered three questions about the superstition they had just described. The first question was, "How important is it to you to perform this superstition for each event or game?" Participants circled a Likert-scale response ranging from 1 (*not important*) to 8 (*very important*). The second question was, "How much of an impact do you believe this superstition has on the outcome of the game or event?" Participants were instructed to circle a Likert-scale response ranging from 1 (*no impact at all*) to 8 (*very large impact*). Finally, they responded to an open-ended question asking, "Why do you do this?" Both section four and section five also contained a section labeled "Superstition 2" which was followed by the same three items. Thus, participants could list up to four total superstitious rituals and answered the same three questions for each superstition listed.

After completing and returning their questionnaire packet (approximately 15 to 30 minutes), participants were debriefed and excused from the testing session.

# RESULTS

We were interested in the superstitious rituals of sport fans, that is, sport fan behaviors they believe have an impact on the outcome of a competition (as opposed to nonsuperstitious routines). Consequently, we selected those participants who listed a minimum of one superstitious ritual that meet at least one of two criteria. First, we selected participants who reported a minimum response of 2 to the item assessing their perceptions of the impact of the target behavior. Thus, these persons reported a belief that their actions had at least a minimal influence on the outcome. Second, we selected participants whose response to the "why" item indicated that they engaged in the behavior because of a belief that it would help the team. This included responses such as "for good luck," "to help the team," "it helps us win," and so forth. This resulted in a sample of 675 participants (40.6%) reporting a minimum of one superstition (i.e., a minimum of one behavior they believed had at least a minimal influence on their team's performance).

This left a sample of 986 participants (59.4%) who did not list at least one superstition. Of those persons listing a superstition, 544 listed one "at the arena" superstition, 214 listed a second "at the arena" superstition, 363 listed one superstition "at other places", and 128 listed a second superstition "at other places." Thus, the 675 persons listing a minimum of one superstition reported a total of 1,249 superstitious behaviors (i.e., actions with a "why" response indicating a luck related factor or an impact score greater than 1).

## Number of Superstitions Listed

Participants could list up to four superstitions (i.e., two at the event and two away from the event). To examine the relationship between the number of superstitions listed and levels of sport fandom (i.e., SFQ scores, Cronbach's alpha = .93) and degree of team identification (i.e., SSIS scores, alpha = .90), a pair of one-way analyses of variance (ANOVAs) were computed with number of superstitions listed (0 to 4) serving as the grouping variable and level of team identification and fandom serving as the dependent variables. The ANOVA computed on sport fandom was significant, $F(4, 1656) = 49.11$, $p < .001$, $\eta^2 = .11$. Post hoc tests (Newman-Keuls) revealed that the zero superstitions group ($n = 986$, $M = 21.91$, $SD = 10.67$) reported significantly lower SFQ scores than those in the other four groups (one superstition listed $n = 311$, $M = 28.00$, $SD = 9.00$; two superstitions listed $n = 223$, $M = 29.38$, $SD = 8.66$; three superstitions listed $n = 72$, $M = 29.07$, $SD = 8.60$; four superstitions listed $n = 69$, $M = 30.32$, $SD = 8.53$). Those in the other four conditions did not significantly differ in level of sport fandom. The ANOVA computed on team identification was also significant, $F(4, 1656) = 58.56$, $p < .001$, $\eta^2 = .12$. Simple effects tests revealed that the zero superstitions group ($M = 33.54$, $SD = 13.34$) reported significantly lower SSIS scores than those in the other four groups, who did not differ in level of team identification (one superstition listed $M = 41.26$, $SD = 10.18$; two superstitions listed $M = 43.58$, $SD = 8.98$; three superstitions listed $M = 42.83$, $SD = 10.50$; four superstitions listed $M = 44.77$, $SD = 9.07$). We then computed a regression analysis in which SFQ and SSIS scores served as predictor variables and number of superstitions listed was the dependent variable (zero order correlations between the variables were: SFQ and SSIS = .746; SFQ and number of superstitions listed = .291; SSIS and number of superstitions listed = .317; all $ps < .001$). The combined effect of the two predictor variables on number of superstitions was significant, $F(2, 1658) = 99.30$, $p < .001$ ($R = 0.327$; $R^2 = 0.107$; adjusted $R^2 = 0.106$). With respect to independent contributions to number of superstitions listed, as hypothesized team identification accounted for a significant proportion of the unique variance ($t = 6.47$, $p < .001$; $B = 0.019$; $SE\ B = 0.003$; $Beta = 0.225$). In addition, sport fandom also accounted for a significant proportion of the variance ($t = 3.52$, $p < .001$; $B = 0.013$; $SE\ B = 0.004$; $Beta = 0.122$).

## Perceptions of the Importance and Impact of the Superstitions

We then examined participants' perceptions of the importance and impact of their superstitions (all analyses in this section were conducted on those responses which were superstitious in nature). Means and standard deviations appear in Table 1. As depicted in the table, each of the scores was significantly above the midpoint on the 1-8 scale (i.e., 4.5, all $ts > 2.35$, all $ps < .02$), suggesting that participants believed that their superstitions were both important to them and they believed the behavior had an impact on the outcome of competitions.

**Table 1. Means and Standard Deviations for Perceptions of Importance and Impact of Participants' Superstitions at the Arena and Superstitions at Other Places**

| | Importance | | Impact | | |
|---|---|---|---|---|---|
| *Superstition Location* | *M* | *SD* | *M* | *SD* | *n* |
| At the Arena Superstition 1 | 6.30 | 1.66 | 4.92 | 2.07 | 544 |
| At the Arena Superstition 2 | 6.37 | 1.73 | 5.01 | 2.12 | 214 |
| Other Places Superstition 1 | 6.26 | 1.58 | 4.80 | 2.12 | 363 |
| Other Places Superstition 2 | 6.34 | 1.58 | 4.95 | 2.18 | 128 |

*Note*: All means were significantly greater than the mid-point (4.5) on the 1-8 scale, all $ts > 2.35$, all $ps < .02$.

We next examined the relationship between sport fandom and team identification and participants' perceptions of the importance and impact of their superstitions. A series of eight regression equations were computed in which sport fandom and team identification served as predictor variables and the importance and impact of each superstition (up to four) were utilized as the dependent variables. Correlations for these analyses appear in Table 2.

**Table 2. Correlations between Sport Fandom (SFQ) and Team Identification (SSIS) and the Importance and Impact of Participants' Superstitions at the Arena and Superstitions at Other Places**

| At the Arena Superstition Number 1 ($n = 544$) | | | | |
|---|---|---|---|---|
| | 1 | 2 | 3 | 4 |
| Sport Fandom (1) | -- | | | |
| Team Identification (2) | .657*** | -- | | |
| Importance of Superstition (3) | .351*** | .553*** | -- | |
| Impact of Superstition (4) | .267*** | .395*** | .502*** | -- |
| At the Arena Superstition Number 2 ($n = 214$) | | | | |
| | 1 | 2 | 3 | 4 |
| Sport Fandom (1) | -- | | | |
| Team Identification (2) | .659*** | -- | | |
| Importance of Superstition (3) | .272*** | .453*** | -- | |
| Impact of Superstition (4) | .314*** | .390*** | .537*** | -- |
| At Other Places Superstition Number 1 ($n = 363$) | | | | |
| | 1 | 2 | 3 | 4 |
| Sport Fandom (1) | -- | | | |
| Team Identification (2) | .731*** | -- | | |
| Importance of Superstition (3) | .355*** | .497*** | -- | |
| Impact of Superstition (4) | .250*** | .317*** | .512*** | -- |
| At Other Places Superstition Number 2 ($n = 128$) | | | | |
| | 1 | 2 | 3 | 4 |
| Sport Fandom (1) | -- | | | |
| Team Identification (2) | .710*** | -- | | |
| Importance of Superstition (3) | .392*** | .443*** | -- | |
| Impact of Superstition (4) | .218* | .296** | .577*** | -- |

Note: $* = p < .05$; $** = p < .01$; $*** = p < .001$.

The first pair of regressions examined the importance and impact of participants' first superstition listed at the arena. With respect to perceptions of importance, the combined effect of the two predictor variables was significant, $F(2, 542) = 119.50$, $p < .001$ ($R = 0.554$; $R^2 = 0.306$; adjusted $R^2 = 0.304$). With respect to independent contributions to perceptions of importance, as hypothesized team identification accounted for a significant proportion of the unique variance ($t = 11.94$, $p < .001$; $B = 0.097$; $SE\ B = 0.008$; $Beta = 0.567$). Sport fandom did not ($t = -0.45$, $p = .653$; $B = -0.004$; $SE\ B = 0.009$; $Beta = -0.021$). As for perceptions of impact, the combined effect of the two predictor variables was again significant, $F(2, 542) = 49.88$, $p < .001$ ($R = 0.395$; $R^2 = 0.156$; adjusted $R^2 = 0.153$). With respect to independent contributions to perceptions of impact, as predicted, team identification accounted for a significant proportion of the unique variance ($t = 7.36$, $p < .001$; $B = 0.082$; $SE\ B = 0.011$;

*Beta* = 0.386). Sport fandom, on the other hand, did not ($t$ = 0.24, $p$ = .808; $B$ = 0.003; *SE B* = 0.013; *Beta* = 0.013).

The second pair of regressions examined the importance and impact of participants' second superstition listed at the arena. With respect to perceptions of importance, the combined effect of the two predictor variables was significant, $F(2, 211)$ = 27.52, $p$ < .001 ($R$ = 0.455; $R^2$ = 0.207; adjusted $R^2$ = 0.199). With respect to independent contributions to perceptions of importance, as hypothesized, team identification accounted for a significant proportion of the unique variance ($t$ = 5.94, $p$ < .001; $B$ = 0.085; *SE B* = 0.014; *Beta* = 0.485), while sport fandom did not ($t$ = -0.58, $p$ = .564; $B$ = -0.010; *SE B* = 0.016; *Beta* = -0.047). As for perceptions of impact, the combined effect of the two predictor variables was again significant, $F(2, 211)$ = 19.80, $p$ < .001 ($R$ = 0.398; $R^2$ = 0.158; adjusted $R^2$ = 0.150). With respect to independent contributions to perceptions of impact, as predicted, team identification accounted for a significant proportion of the unique variance ($t$ = 3.86, $p$ < .001; $B$ = 0.070; *SE B* = 0.018; *Beta* = 0.324), while sport fandom did not ($t$ = 1.19, $p$ = .234; $B$ = 0.025; *SE B* = 0.021; *Beta* = 0.100).

The third pair examined the importance and impact of participants' first superstition listed at places other than the arena. With respect to perceptions of importance, the combined effect of the two predictor variables was significant, $F(2, 360)$ = 59.06, $p$ < .001 ($R$ = 0.497; $R^2$ = 0.247; adjusted $R^2$ = 0.243). With respect to independent contributions to perceptions of importance, as hypothesized, team identification accounted for a significant proportion of the unique variance ($t$ = 7.60, $p$ < .001; $B$ = 0.085; *SE B* = 0.011; *Beta* = 0.509), while sport fandom did not ($t$ = -0.25, $p$ = .805; $B$ = -0.003; *SE B* = 0.012; *Beta* = -0.017). As for perceptions of impact, the combined effect of the two predictor variables was again significant, $F(2, 360)$ = 20.24, $p$ < .001 ($R$ = 0.318; $R^2$ = 0.101; adjusted $R^2$ = 0.096). With respect to independent contributions to perceptions of impact, as predicted, team identification accounted for a significant proportion of the unique variance ($t$ = 3.92, $p$ < .001; $B$ = 0.064; *SE B* = 0.016; *Beta* = 0.287), while sport fandom did not ($t$ = 0.56, $p$ = .579; $B$ = 0.010; *SE B* = 0.018; *Beta* = 0.041).

The fourth set of regressions examined the importance and impact of participants' second superstition listed at places other than the arena. With respect to perceptions of importance, the combined effect of the two predictor variables was significant, $F(2, 125)$ = 16.45, $p$ < .001 ($R$ = 0.456; $R^2$ = 0.208; adjusted $R^2$ = 0.196). For independent contributions to perceptions of importance, as hypothesized, team identification accounted for a significant proportion of the unique variance ($t$ = 2.93, $p$ < .01; $B$ = 0.055; *SE B* = 0.019; *Beta* = 0.331), while sport fandom did not ($t$ = 1.39, $p$ = .167; $B$ = 0.027; *SE B* = 0.019; *Beta* = 0.157). As for perceptions of impact, the combined effect of the two predictor variables was again significant, $F(2, 125)$ = 6.01, $p$ < .01 ($R$ = 0.296; $R^2$ = 0.088; adjusted $R^2$ = 0.073). With respect to independent contributions to perceptions of impact, as predicted, team identification accounted for a significant proportion of the unique variance ($t$ = 2.35, $p$ < .03; $B$ = 0.065; *SE B* = 0.028; *Beta* = 0.285), while sport fandom did not ($t$ = 0.13, $p$ = .897; $B$ = 0.004; *SE B* = 0.029; *Beta* = 0.016).

## Specific Types (Categories) of Superstitions

The superstitions listed were placed into categories by pairs of raters (these analyses were again restricted to those responses that were superstitious in nature). All raters ($N = 6$) had extensive training in social scientific research and, in particular, had published in the area of sport fandom. Agreement between raters was greater than 98% (all disagreements were settled through discussion). A total of 64 different categories emerged. Many categories contained only one or two entries. Those categories with less than 1% of responses either at the arena or at other places were placed into an "other" group. This resulted in a total of 24 categories (plus the "other" category) in which at least 1% of the sample listed the category at one (or both) of the locations. The categories and examples of each can be found in Table 3. Percentages are listed in Table 4. Superstitions involving apparel were the most prominent type as 41% of at the arena superstitions and 28% of at other places superstitions fell into this category. For superstitions at the arena, vocalizations (e.g., yelling, singing) were second most common (10%) while superstitions involving the consumption of food, drink (nonalcoholic), candy, or gum were third (6%). For superstitions at other places, watching or not watching the action was second most common (9%), followed by three superstitions listed third with 5%: good luck charms and rituals; consumption of food, drink (nonalcoholic), candy, or gum; and vocalizations.

### Table 3. Superstition categories and examples

Apparel (wearing or not wearing clothing)
1.                 "Wear lucky jersey I bought when … they beat the NY Mets by 6 runs."
2.                 "Wear the jersey. If Pats are losing at halftime, take it off."

Body (body, hair, beard, writings, makeup, tattoos, paint)
1.                 "Wear war paint."
2.                 "I shave my back before every game."

Stay in/change seat (stand or stay in seat when winning, change seat if losing)
1.                 "Don't get up if winning/playing well."
2.                 "I I'm sitting in a certain spot and the Astros are playing well I stay there."

TV channel (stay on same channel if winning, change if losing)
1.                 "Don't change channel on TV."
2.                 "Change the TV as soon as they start losing."

Religion (prayer, religious signs, religious objects, religious readings)
1.                 "Praying for the team's victory at the Notre Dame basilica."
2.                 "Make the sign of the holy cross."

Listen to music (listening to songs, music)
1.                 "I listen to the same song before every game."
2.                 "Playing the school song as the team runs out of the locker room."

## Table 3. (Continued)

Alcohol (drink or don't drink alcoholic beverages)

1.      "I must drink lite beer."
2.      "Drinking a whole can or bottle of beer when my team scores."

Other good luck charm/superstitious rituala (other good luck objects or actions not in other categories)

1.      "Bring lucky foam tomahawk."
2.      "I rub the Tiger statue before the game."

Select lucky seat (select specific/lucky seat)

1.      "I never sit on the home side, I always sit behind the team's bench."
2.      "During games, spouse and self must sit in winning spots (playoff games only)."

Food and nonalcoholic drink (consumption of food, nonalcoholic beverages, candy, or gum)

1.      "When we go we each have a specific food that we must eat during the game."
2.      "If I eat grapefruit for breakfast, they win."

Arrival time (arrive early or at a specific time)

1.      "Get there one hour before the game starts."
2.      "I like to arrive very early at the stadium, well before the game.

Interact with players (interact with players, converse with players, wish them good luck)

1.      "Wish good luck to each member of the team before the contest."
2.      "Wish my friends good luck an odd number of times, not even, just odd."

Stand/sit at specific times (standup and sit down at specific times during event, do the "wave")

1.      "Stand during the last out of the bottom of the ninth inning – standing should occur only after there are two strikes on the batter."
2.      "We stay standing until the first time the Mavs score."

Watch/don't watch entire game (must or can't watch entire game )

1.      "Must watch the game straight through…never get up for commercials, food, etc."
2.      "Have to keep watching once you start (only exception is bathroom break)."

Vocalizations (talking, not talking, sayings, heckling, cheering, chanting, singing, booing)

1.      "Yelling at the playing and what to do."
2.      "If it's my team I don't speak when they are at the free throw line."

Displays (display sign, poster, towel, blanket, sticker, flag, comforter, roster)

1.      "Terrible towel."
2.      "I have to display some kind of decal or signage throughout the team's season."

Watch in a group (must watch with others, be in a group, be with family)

1.      "I cannot watch the game alone."
2.      "Get with friends."

Pregame activities (tailgating, pregame festivities, parties, camping out for tickets/seats)
1. "Pregame rally to cheer for team."
2. "Must go to bonfire and watch outhouse fall."

Internet/radio (must or can't listen on radio/Internet, change station if losing)
1. "Always listen to every game on the radio. Even if the game's on TV we listen to the radio and just mute the TV."
2. "I get on my computer and listen to them play."

Body movement/gestures (move specific body part(s), touch own body, crossing fingers, pace)
1. "Raise Owl hand sign in air when taking free throws."
2. "At the most extreme times. I'll cross my fingers."

Close eyes/can't watch (must close eyes during specific parts of contest)
1. "I close my eyes on big free throws."
2. "When the opposing team is on base I don't watch the pitch because I think I will jinx our
   pitcher and the other team will score runs."

Watch/don't watch in specific place (must/can't watch in certain room, with/without certain people)
1. "I have to watch the game at home."
2. "I watch the game at the sports bar."

Thoughts/cognition (don't think about specific things (e.g., losing), never lose hope)
1. "I think about the worst."
2. ""Never think 'double play' when my team is batting."

Sexual act (engaging in some form of sexual behavior)
1. "I have sex with nothing on but a jersey and one blue and one yellow sock on."
2. "Force my girlfriend to call me Roger Clemens in the act of making love."

## Table 4. Percentages of Most Frequently Listed At the Arena and At Other Places Superstitions for Participants with a Least One Superstition

| Superstition | % At the Arena | % At other Places |
|---|---|---|
| Apparel | 41% | 28% |
| Body | 3% | 1% |
| Stay in/change seat | 1% | 4% |
| TV channel | 0% | 3% |
| Religion | 3% | 2% |
| Listen to music | 0% | 1% |
| Alcohol | 3% | 3% |
| Other good luck charm/rituala | 2% | 5% |
| Select lucky seat | 3% | 3% |

## Table 4. (Continued)

| Superstition | % At the Arena | % At other Places |
|---|---|---|
| Food and nonalcoholic drink | 6% | 5% |
| Arrival time | 1% | 0% |
| Interact with players | 1% | 2% |
| Stand/sit at specific times | 2% | 0% |
| Watch/don't watch entire game | 3% | 9% |
| Vocalizations | 10% | 5% |
| Displays | 1% | 3% |
| Watch in a group | 2% | 1% |
| Pregame activities | 2% | 1% |
| Internet/radio | 0% | 3% |
| Body movement/gestures | 4% | 2% |
| Close eyes/can't watch | 2% | 1% |
| Watch/don't watch in specific place | 0% | 2% |
| Thoughts/cognition | 0% | 1% |
| Sexual act | 0% | 1% |
| Other (categories with < 1% listed) | 10% | 14% |

*Notes*: aIncludes good luck charms not included in other categories (e.g., apparel, lucky seat). A list of superstitions incorporated into the "other" category is available from the first author upon request.

## Comparisons between Types of Sports

The next series of analyses involved comparisons of fans of different sports. Participants with at least one superstition listed teams (or individual sport athletes) from 39 different sports (i.e., teams/athletes from 39 different sports were targets for the SSIS, a complete list is available from the first author). Five sports were most common: Professional Baseball (23.6%), Professional Football (NFL; 20.3%), College Football (17.0%), College Men's Basketball (12.4%), and Professional Men's Basketball (10.1%). No other sport was target more than 3% of the time. Thus, we choose to make comparisons between these five sports. The first analysis involved a one-way ANOVA in which sport type served as the grouping variable and SSIS scores were the dependent variable (see Table 5). This analysis revealed a significant sport type effect, $F(4, 558) = 5.86$, $p < .001$, $\eta^2 = .04$. Post hoc tests (Newman-Keuls) revealed that identification scores for college football and college men's basketball were higher than the other three sports ($p < .05$). No other comparisons were significant. The second analysis involved a one-way ANOVA examining the total number of superstitions listed (this analysis also involved only persons with at least one superstitious behavior).

# Examining the Superstitions of Sport Fans

**Table 5. Means and Standard Deviations for Team Identification (SSIS), Perceptions of Importance, and Perceptions of Impact by Target Sport**

| Measures | Target Sport | | | | |
| --- | --- | --- | --- | --- | --- |
| | Pro Baseball | Pro Football | College Football | College Men's Basketball | Pro Men's Basketball |
| Team identification | 41.25 | 41.34 | 45.52 | 44.74 | 40.72 |
| | (9.61) | (10.52) | (8.77) | (8.33) | (9.63) |
| Number of Superstitions | 1.88 | 1.91 | 1.65 | 2.08 | 1.84 |
| | (1.04) | (1.02) | (0.76) | (1.06) | (0.96) |
| At the Arena Importance 1 | 6.18 | 5.95 | 6.89 | 6.27 | 6.14 |
| | (1.51) | (1.93) | (1.48) | (1.51) | (1.76) |
| At the Arena Impact 1 | 4.80 | 4.98 | 5.13 | 4.98 | 4.88 |
| | (1.92) | (2.08) | (2.25) | (2.06) | (2.22) |
| At the Arena Importance 2 | 6.59 | 5.52 | 6.56 | 6.68 | 6.26 |
| | (1.20) | (2.09) | (1.87) | (1.43) | (1.59) |
| At the Arena Impact 2 | 4.80 | 4.69 | 5.19 | 5.24 | 5.11 |
| | (1.78) | (2.08) | (2.53) | (2.30) | (2.03) |
| At Other Places Importance 1 | 6.10 | 6.14 | 6.49 | 6.33 | 6.33 |
| | (1.50) | (1.70) | (1.54) | (1.55) | (1.49) |
| At Other Places Impact 1 | 4.51 | 4.79 | 4.86 | 4.91 | 5.03 |
| | (2.06) | (2.06) | (2.25) | (2.07) | (2.37) |
| At Other Places Importance 2 | 6.03 | 6.26 | 7.09 | 6.60 | 6.94 |
| | (1.64) | (1.71) | (1.14) | (1.54) | (1.00) |
| At Other Places Impact 2 | 5.00 | 4.97 | 3.91 | 5.10 | 5.56 |
| | (1.99) | (2.24) | (2.63) | (2.43) | (1.93) |

*Notes*: Standard deviations appear in parentheses below each mean.

Sport type again served as the grouping variable while number of superstitions listed was the dependent variable (means and standard deviations appear in Table 5). This analysis revealed a significant sport type main effect, $F(4, 558) = 2.52$, $p < .05$, $\eta^2 = .02$. Post hoc tests (Newman-Keuls) revealed that college men's basketball fans reported a greater number of superstitions than college football fans ($p < .05$). No other comparisons were significant.

The next series of analyses involved eight one-way ANOVAs in which sport type served as the grouping variable while importance and impact of the superstition were the dependent variables. A separate analysis was run for the importance and impact of each of the four possible superstitions (i.e., up to two at the arena and up to two at other places) resulting in a total of eight ANOVAs. Because of the differences in identification noted above, SSIS scores were used as a covariate (this was particularly important given the strong relationship between identification scores and perceptions of importance and impact described above). Means and standard deviations appear in Table 5. Only two of the analyses reached significance. First, with respect to perceptions of importance of the first superstition listed at the arena, participants targeting a professional football team reported lower perceptions of importance than persons targeting the other sports, $F(4, 439) = 2.59$, $p < .05$, $\eta^2 = .02$. Post hoc tests (Newman-Keuls) revealed that perceptions of importance of the first superstition listed at the arena were higher among college football fans than the other four sports ($p < .05$). No other comparisons were significant. Second, with respect to perceptions of importance of the second superstition listed at the arena, participants targeting a professional football team again reported lower scores, $F(4, 171) = 2.83$, $p < .05$, $\eta^2 = .05$. Post hoc tests (Newman-Keuls) revealed that perceptions of importance of the second superstition listed at the arena were greater for college men's basketball fans than for professional football fans ($p < .05$). No other comparisons were significant.

## Examination of Qualitative Responses

One of the key advantages of qualitative research is the richness and detail found in the participants' responses. We share some of these responses below. However, it warrants mention that some of the superstitions described below seem rather far-fetched. This may lead one to wonder whether the participant truly believed the action could impact the outcome of the event. Yet an examination of the "Why" responses provided strong validity for the superstitious nature of the information offered. For example, one person wrote "After each touchdown, I stand up and sit down." One could question whether this fan really believes this behavior increases his team's chances for victory. However, his impact score was 8 (the highest score possible) and when asked why he engaged in this behavior he wrote, "I think next touchdown will happen if I do this." A University of Louisville football fan explained his food superstition ("I must have nachos and a bag of peanuts only to be followed by a hot dog") by stating "on notable occasions it has affected the outcome." These types of "Why" responses were extremely common and included statements such as "The team always seems to win when I do this" and "We caused the loss of 10 games in the 1992-1993 season." These statements underscore the superstitious nature of the participants' actions – they truly believed in a cause-effect relationship.

*Apparel superstitions.* We read about a number of apparel items people wore for good luck, including hats, jerseys, underwear, socks, jackets, and ties. A Houston Aeros hockey fan wrote, "Before every game I put my socks in the freezer for two hours and then wear them to the game." Perhaps just as interesting was his reason for this behavior as he wrote, "This is what they do to the game pucks. I feel it gives us a slight advantage." For a Rice University Baseball fan, it was not just what he wore that mattered but, rather, how he got dressed. He had to "get dressed in a certain order" because "we won the first time I did it." One amusing set of apparel superstitions was reported by a University of Kentucky basketball fan. This person reported four apparel superstitions: cap, shirt, shoes, and underwear. What was interesting was that for the cap, shirt, and shoes the participant reported impact scores of 4, 5, and 5 (on the 1-8 scale). However, the underwear received a score of 8, suggesting that this was the most important part of the ensemble. For a Texas Christian University baseball fan, it was not simply wearing the hat that mattered but, instead, touching it. This fan wrote, "I hex the opposing pitcher by rubbing the bill of my cap with my fingers" because "It helps our team win." Similarly, a Kansas City Chiefs fan reported "taking my cap off and putting it back on 8 times before every snap in the fourth quarter" because "It seems like if I do this with sincerity, the football gods smile on my beloved Chiefs." Perhaps the most scientific response was offered by a St. Louis Cardinals fan reporting he would "always have to get out my lucky baseball glove and wear my lucky St. Louis Cardinals hat/shirt" because "The team record this year when I wear the hat and glove is 45-19." Interestingly, some fans preferred to wear the opponent's apparel. Such was the case on a Texas A&M Football fan who indicated, "I wear a UT (University of Texas) shirt when the Aggies play the Longhorns." The fan's reason was to "jinx UT." And for some fans, not wearing their team's apparel is the key to victory. One Houston Astros fan wrote, "When in the playoffs and World Series, I couldn't wear the shirt during the game. The one time I did they were losing so I took it off and before it was over my head they hit a home run."

For one Cincinnati Cyclones fan, it was not wearing his lucky t-shirt that matter but, instead, displaying it on his wall. This fan wrote, "I hang my autographed tee-shirt on my wall during the season. If the Cyclones have a bad season, I wash it after the last game. If the Cyclones have a good season I take the shirt down and put it back in my closet." When asked why, the fan responded, "The superstition makes me feel as if I can help the team out." For a University of Kentucky Men's Basketball fan, his entire family supports his superstition involving apparel. This fan stated, "My family and I (and our friends) get together at someone's house for every Kentucky game that is on TV. A superstition that we have is everyone must wear something Kentucky. If someone shows up without something Kentucky on, then they are banned from the house and can not watch the game until they have something Kentucky on."

*Body Movement Superstitions.* Superstitions involving body movements were also quite common, such as the Houston Texans fan who wrote, "I hold my breath before offensive snap." A Boston Celtics fan "helped" her team by writing "#33 on my hand" in honor of former Celtic great Larry Bird. A Houston Astros fan stated, "However many times I clapped the time before something good happens, I will clap that same number the next time." A memorable female Rice University Men's Basketball fan stated that, "If the game is on TV I blow a kiss at the screen before a free throw." A baseball fan wrote that, while watching his team on television, he felt compelled to "do push-ups during commercials." For one high school football fan, it was not her body movements that matter but, rather, the movements of the cheerleaders. Specifically, this individual wrote, "If one of the cheerleaders falls, the team won't do well."

*Personal hygiene superstitions.* Personal hygiene (or lack there of) was the focus of some superstitions. One Houston Astros fan wrote that *she* preferred "not showering for a week before a playoff game." Another Houston Astros fan wrote "Don't go potty until the 7th inning." A supporter of the US National Soccer team wrote that during the tournament her "legs are not to be shaved." Apparel superstitions can also become a matter of personal hygiene when the fan refuses to change during a streak. For instance, a New York Yankees fan wrote, "I wear the same work socks until the Yankees lose, then I change them." This fan's description of the origin of this superstition was also interesting as he stated, "They went on a streak when I didn't do laundry and wore the same socks so I stuck with it." The importance of personal hygiene was apparent in the apparel superstition described by a female fan of the St. Louis Cardinals who wrote, "I have a pair of Cardinal underwear that I have worn to every game I've went to in the past 3 years and they have never lost." (Importantly, she added "Yes, I wash them.")

*Bad luck people superstitions.* Other fans described how certain people were bad luck and, consequently, not allowed to watch games. For instance, a Dallas Cowboys fan wrote, "I can never go to the game with my wife. I feel she is bad luck" because "They lose when she is there." This fan's superstition extends to watching the game on TV as well because "They always seem to lose when she watches with me." A New England Patriots fan did not simply condemn one person for being bad luck but, rather, an entire gender. This person wrote that, "Mom, or any other woman (sister, girlfriend), is allowed to watch one series. The result is inevitable, the other team scores or forces a damn turnover. Therefore, no women! They are bad luck." Another Patriots fan shared a similar belief, "My mom is bad luck, she is not allowed to watch the game. If a girlfriend is there, she can't talk. If the team loses, she is bad luck." A Philadelphia Eagles fan felt he was the bad luck person and, as a result, refused to attend any games. This person wrote, "The three Eagles games I've been to in my life they've lost, so I'm scared to go." One Houston Astros fan wrote about how he had to determine the identity of the bad luck individual. This respondent said, "My family believes that when my mom comes to a game, the Astros lose. We often go together but at times my brothers and I go with my dad and sometimes mom comes too." When asked why, all was revealed: "Just following patterns. We used to think the whole family was a curse. We never saw them win in person but my mom missed a game and they won." But it was not just women who were perceived to bring bad luck. One football fan wrote, "I won't watch a Rams game in the same room as my father. He seems to bring bad luck." For a University of Kentucky Men's Basketball fan, it was the in-laws who brought bad luck: "When I go to my in-laws, they lose."

*Good luck charm and superstitious rituals.* There were also a number of unique good luck charms and superstitious rituals. Some of these were standards, such as the Florida State University football fan who would "carry a four-leaf clover in my pocket to each game." Others were a bit more inventive. One Texas A&M Football fan wrote, "If the Aggies are down, I light incense next to my Buddha statue in my back yard" to "pull off the win through my good karma." A St. Louis Cardinals fan wrote that, "When watching the game on TV we always wave a Kleenex in the air when the Cardinals are batting." A Notre Dame football fan mixed religion with a good luck charm for his superstition, writing that he places "the Notre Dame leprechaun in front of the cross on the mantle" because "It helps them win." Another unique ritual was offered by a St Louis Cardinals fan who would "Rub a pack of baseball cards on the family cat for luck." A University of Tennessee football fan wrote, "After every UT touchdown or field goal, I push the button on my mascot to play Rocky Top" (the team's song) "So they will score again." And for a Cincinnati Reds fan, simply having a lucky object was not enough. This person wrote, "I have an Austin Kearns bobble head on my desk *that I talk to* during games."

*Food, drink, and candy superstitions.* Food, drink, and candy were often reported as good luck items. However, for some it was not *what* was consumed, but *how* it was consumed. One such person, a Rice University football fan, wrote that he would "chew bubble gum on the right side of his mouth." One Dallas Stars fan's food ritual was amazingly detailed. He wrote, "At old arena, every game I got in the Hebrew National Hot Dog line first. There, I bought a hot dog and a bottle of water. Then I got in the popcorn chicken line. I'd eat all but 3-4 bites of my hot dog in line, wrapped the rest up for my seat. At the first intermission, I got chocolate yogurt with M&Ms. At the new arena, I replaced both the hot dog and popcorn chicken with a chicken tender basket." Although this may simply seem like a fan's meal preference, his response to the "why" question revealed otherwise, as he stated that he engaged in this ritual because, "I want the Stars to win...and I'm doing my part." For a Minnesota Vikings fan, food could also be bad luck as he wrote that he "Cannot order pizza during the game." Finally, a Notre Dame football fan had an interesting combination of two superstitions. His first superstition was "I recite Psalms 23 before the game and before each quarter" while his second superstition was "Drink at least three beers between each quarter."

*Additional memorable superstitions.* Two final superstitions also warrant mention. A participant supporting the University of Houston Women's Basketball Team believed that she would jinx the team if she revealed her superstitions. She replied, "If I tell my 'game day rituals,' the team will almost undoubtedly lose." Thus, essentially, her superstition involved not revealing her superstitions. Finally, a Dallas Cowboys football fan wrote that "When *listening on radio*, I don't let anybody talk when they are close to a touchdown or gaining yards. I feel it might interrupt the players' concentration."

## DISCUSSION

In the current investigation, we were interested in documenting the superstitious rituals of sport fans. Slightly over 40% of our college-aged participants reported at least one superstition related to their team. This proportion is higher than previous estimates that had found totals in the mid-teens (Superstition Study, 2007). Of course, due to demographic differences in the two samples (e.g., the current sample was limited to college students), comparisons across studies should be done with caution. It was hypothesized that level of team identification would be related to the number of superstitions listed and the analyses reported above confirmed this expectation. Interestingly, although team identification and the number of superstitions listed were positively correlated, additional analyses found no difference in level of identification among persons listing one through four superstitions. Rather, the key difference was in whether or not the individual listed any superstitions. This suggests that, although highly identified fans are more likely to report sport fan superstitions than less identified fans, the relationship levels off after the first superstition. We examined the relationship between sport fandom and number of superstitions as well (within the framework of a research question). The results mirrored those involving team identification, as sport fandom and number listed were positively related. The key difference was between those with no reported superstitions and those with any superstition. A regression analysis employing both team identification and sport fandom as predictors of the number of superstitions listed revealed that each variable accounted for a significant proportion of the unique variance. Thus, being a great sport fan and having high levels of identification are each individually related to the number of superstitions reported.

When analyzed across five sports, college men's basketball fans listed the greatest number of superstitions. These fans also had particularly high levels of team identification. Given that team identification and number of superstitions are correlated, one may be tempted to conclude that the higher number of superstitions listed by college basketball fans was simply a reflection of their high levels of identification (relative to many of the other sports examined). While this conclusion remains plausible, it is interesting to note that the sport with the highest levels of identification, college football, had the *fewest* number of superstitions listed. This result suggests that there may indeed be sport differences in amount of superstitions that are not simply accounted for by team identification.

We were also interested in perceptions of the impact and importance of the superstitions. All means were significantly greater than the scale mid-point, revealing that the superstitions were important to the participants who often believed they had a direct impact on the team's performance and outcome of the event. Regression analyses examining predictors of perceptions of importance and impact (i.e., team identification and sport fandom) were incredibly consistent. In each case, team identification was a significant unique predictor of impact/importance while fandom was not. Combining the analyses of number of superstitions listed and perceptions of the importance/impact paints an interesting picture. Persons reporting at least one superstition have higher levels of both team identification and sport fandom. However, only team identification predicts the importance attached to the superstitions and perceptions of their impact; sport fandom does not. Thus, although being a highly involved fan may predict the adoption of superstitions, one's psychological connection needs to be greater for one to believe the superstition is important and can impact the team's performance.

When analyzed across sport types, few differences in perceptions of importance and impact were found. In fact, only two significant findings emerged and the effect sizes for the significant results were quite small (and thus, interpretations should be done with caution). However, the two significant findings were consistent, as lower perceptions of importance for superstitions at the arena were reported by persons targeting professional football. College football fans reported the fewest number of superstitions while professional football fans attached lower levels of importance to their superstitions occurring at the arena. Although it may be tempting to conclude that football fans seem to be less superstitious than fans of other sports, such an inference is premature. Additional data that replicate the current findings are needed.

The categorization analyses revealed that superstitions involving apparel were most common, both at the arena and at other places. Other common superstitions occurring at the arena included vocalizations and the consumption of food and nonalcoholic beverages. Watching or not watching the action was common at other venues, as were good luck charms/superstitious rituals, consumption of food and nonalcoholic drinks, and vocalizations. Comparing frequencies of superstitions across locale (at the arena versus at other locations) reveals that apparel superstitions were more common at the arena, as were vocalizations. Good luck charms/rituals were more prominent at other places, as were superstitions involving staying in or changing a seat and watching or not watching the entire game. It warrants mention that, with the exception of superstitions involving apparel, even the most common superstitions were listed by no more than 10% of the sample.

The data reported above indicate that superstitions are quite common among fans, particularly those with high levels of team identification. General research on superstition reveals that such behaviors are utilized in an attempt to give persons a sense of control (Keinan, 2002; Schippers and Van Lange, 2006). Spectators clearly believe they can influence games involving their teams (Wann, Dolan, McGeorge, and Allison, 1994). Superstitious behaviors provide fans with a method of attempting to assist their team (Kelley and Tian, 2004). With respect to athletes, research suggests that superstitions can actually facilitate performance. For instance, Damisch, Stoberock, and Mussweiler (2010) demonstrated that activating good-luck superstitions and charms improved putting performance in golf. Further, they found that these beneficial results were due to increased perceptions of self-efficacy when superstitions were present. These findings suggest that persons may continue to use superstitions because they ultimately lead to the reward of better performance (via increased efficacy). For fans, this suggests that their use of superstitions provides them with a sense of control and influence over the game (a game in which they are not an active participant). If the chosen superstition is "successful" (i.e., if the team succeeds subsequent to the fan's use of the superstition), the fan will likely feel as if he or she successfully assisted the team. Because of the role played by self-efficacy in the superstitions of athletes (Damisch et al., 2010), future investigators should examine how self-efficacy impacts the superstitious actions of fans. It may be that superstitions are most prominent among fans that have high levels of self-efficacy with respect to their ability to impact the game. Because perceptions of influence and team identification are positively correlated (Wann et al., 1994), such a possibility has merit. Using team identification and self-efficacy as predictors of superstitious behavior would allow researchers to identify which variable (or both) has the greatest impact on the tendencies for fans behave superstitiously.

Other researchers have examined situational variables that facilitate the use of superstitions. One such variable that has received considerable attention concerns stressful and uncertain environments. Investigators have found that persons are more likely to rely on superstitions when they are placed in uncertain or stressful situations (Keinan, 2002). Schippers and Van Lange (2006) found that athletes were more committed to their superstitious rituals when facing an equal or superior opponent. One might expect fans to report a similar pattern of effects and indicate greater commitment to their superstitions right before or during an important competition (Brevers et al., 2011). Given that our data were acquired in a non-competitive state in a university classroom, assessing fan superstitions levels right before an important game may actually reveal *greater* perceptions of superstition importance and impact than reported here.

It is clear that both personal and situational variables impact superstition. Future research endeavors should attempt to develop a model of fan superstition that incorporates both types of variables. Many personal variables could be included in the model, such as team identification and self-efficacy, as noted above. Other personal variables that play a role in superstitious behavior that could be added to the model include desire for control (Burger and Cooper, 1979) and locus of control (Schippers and Van Lange, 2006). Important potential situational variables include the stress of the environment and the importance of the game. One particularly interesting situational factor could be the number of games played in a specific sport. The regular season in NFL football (16 games), NBA basketball (81 games), and MLB baseball (162 games) differ widely. Perhaps fans following teams in sports with longer seasons are more likely to develop superstitions because of the greater opportunity afforded by the longer season (i.e., greater opportunities for positive consequences to follow superstitious actions and, thus, greater likelihood that the superstition is formed). By developing such a models that include both personal and situation variables, researchers could determine which variables play the greatest role and the extent to which they interact (see Keinan, 2002).

Two other areas of additional research warrant mention. First, future endeavors should focus on the process of superstition development among fans. The present work illuminated current superstitions, but did not shed light on how fan superstitions form. Participants could be asked to explicitly explain the development of their superstition and longitudinal research methods would be beneficial as well (e.g., track behaviors fans with a new interest in a team to detect the development of superstitions). Second, researchers could use the superstitions detailed here to develop a quantitative measure of superstitious behavior among fans. That is, they could use the categories identified in the current research (as well as the category descriptors) to develop a questionnaire specifically assessing superstitious tendencies among fans.

## Applied Implications

The data detailed above has implications for both sport marketers and consultants working with athletes. Sport marketers are charged with increasing ticket and merchandise sales and are often searching for innovative ways to reach their sales goals (Wann et al., 2001). Incorporating strategies related to fan superstition may be one such novel approach. That is, superstitions may be one other avenue to target consumers for increased revenues and attendance and, thus, could be potentially leveraged by sport marketers. As mentioned earlier, the impact of sport fan superstitions lies in the identification that one has with the brand. Thus, the highly identified sport fan may be seeking ways to better "help" their team, a concept that could tie back to product sales. Given that apparel superstitions are the most cited superstition in the current study, these findings could assist marketers involved in designing marketing campaigns. As Kwon, Trail, and Lee (2008) note, sport brands must look to many different methods to help foster team identification in their consumers. Targeting superstitions and utilizing them as a part of a campaign could have a reciprocal effect of also helping foster identification while simultaneously boosting merchandise sales. In essence, the tactic could build an increased sense of community and affiliation (Pritchard, Stinson, and Patton, 2010), leading to increased identification. For example, the Houston Texans of the National Football League often run a "Battle Red" promotional day in which the team wears a red "alternate" uniform and fans wear red apparel (Kuharsky, 2009). The team's performance on these promotional days has been better than average (7-4 as of January 2011). The franchise could link these perceptions of the uniform "helping" the team to their actual performance, providing the Texans with a promotional strategy that involves fan superstitions. The result is an increase in sales of game-specific apparel (in this case, "Battle Red" apparel), which directly impacts the team's profitability (Sessions, 2004). Such a tactic has also been used effectively in other professional leagues including the National Basketball Association (Feschuk, 2009), the National Hockey League (National Hockey League, 2011), and Major League Baseball (Major League Baseball, 2011), which all produce special edition St. Patrick's Day apparel that undoubtedly capitalizes on a "luck" merchandising angle. Care must be taken in designing these approaches, however, as they can sometimes be interpreted in a manner different from their original intent. Such an example involved the Toronto Raptors of the National Basketball Association producing a St. Patrick's Day jersey that possessed a shamrock, which is often associated with their rival, the Boston Celtics (Feschuk, 2009). As a result, the superstition of wearing someone else's logo could take the impressions (and resulting product sales) in an unwanted direction. Future research may want to examine the impact of superstitions on product sales (or the lack thereof) and the specific implications of these superstitions on the implementation of a marketing campaign.

Further, the findings from the current study have significant implications for sport psychology professionals looking to assist athletes with performance enhancement strategies. As numerous studies have noted (e.g., Wadey and Hanton, 2008), attentional focus is a skill that is critical to effective performance. As a result, being able to focus on performance relevant stimuli can assist the athlete in the competitive environment (Weinberg and Gould, 2011). The aforementioned superstitions that spectators and fans utilize to "assist" their team may carry into the stands. As such, this could present one or more distractions that the athlete needs to be psychologically prepared for. While some of the superstitions listed are fairly benign (e.g., wearing "lucky" apparel), other superstitions could result in significant distractions (e.g., shouting, bringing in "props" for luck, etc.) for the unprepared athlete. A thorough survey of these spectator and fan superstitions provides the professional providing sport psychology services a more clear expectation of what to prepare athletes for in the competitive environment. Additionally, these superstitions are not stimuli currently witnessed in the practice environment, thus preparation for these stimuli could carry over into consultative sessions. The results of that additional preparation could mean the difference for the athlete looking to have an effective attentional focus package to implement in performance settings.

Furthermore, athletes often interact with fans, and having an understanding of why fans exhibit certain, perhaps strange, behaviors can lead to less anxiety or nervousness from the athlete. As with superstitious behavior itself, such an understanding can decrease the uncertainty associated with the experience (Brooks, 2009). And, if such an encounter takes place during or near a sporting contest, a decrease in anxiety can facilitate performance (Barnard, Broman-Fulks, Michael, Webb, and Zawilinski, 2010). Additionally, athletes can be influenced by spectator actions via the spectator effect, whereby performance is increased when spectators are present (Walsh and Gill, 2008). It is possible that this effect may be enhanced when spectators have lower levels of anxiety and can lend positive support to the athletes.

Third, sport psychology consultants may be able to gain insight into the athlete experience through a greater understanding of fans and spectators. The affective, cognitive, and behavioral reactions of fans and spectators often mirror that of athletes (Wann et al., 2001). Further, the impact of athletic identity (Brewer, Van Raalte, and Linder, 1993) and team identification can be similar. By learning about the common behaviors of fans, such as superstitious rituals, sport practitioners may be able to infer valuable knowledge about athletes. Given that apparel superstitions are quite common for both fans (given the data reported here) and players (Bleak and Frederick, 1998), this line of reasoning appears to have validity.

In conclusion, a few limitations of the current project warrant mention. First, the sample tested in the current investigation was quite homogenous, consisting of young college students. Future efforts should expand on the current results by testing more diverse populations, such as younger and older fans as well as non-college students. Further, only five specific sports were examined. Additional work is needed to investigate the superstitious behavior of fans of other sports, particularly individual sports (all five of those studied here were team sports). And lastly, as noted above, because this was only an initial investigation of fan superstitions, future research is needed to replicate the effects detailed here to substantiate their generalizability.

## REFERENCES

Barnard, K. E., Broman-Fulks, J. J., Michael, K. D., Webb, R. W., and Zawilinski, L. L. (2010). The effects of physiological arousal on cognitive and psychomotor performance among individuals with high and low anxiety sensitivity. *Anxiety, Stress, and Coping, 24*, 201-216.

Bleak, J. L., and Frederick, C. M. (1998). Superstitious behavior in sport: Levels of effectiveness and determinants of use in three collegiate sports. *Journal of Sport Behavior, 21*, 1-18.

Brevers, D., Dan, B., Noel, X, and Nils, F. (2011). Sport superstition: Mediation of psychological tension on non-professional sportsmen's superstitious rituals. *Journal of Sport Behavior, 34*, 3-24.

Brewer, B. W., Van Raalte, J. L., and Linder, D. E. (1993). Athletic identity: Hercules' muscles or Achilles' heel? *International Journal of Sport Psychology, 24*, 237-254.

Brooks, M. (2009). Born believers: How your brain creates God. *New Scientist Magazine, 201*, 30-33.

Buhrmann, H. G., Brown, B., and Zaugg, M. K. (1982). Superstitious beliefs and behavior: A comparison of male and female basketball players. *Journal of Sport Behavior, 5*, 175-185.

Burger, J. M., and Cooper, H. M. (1979). The desirability of control. *Motivation and Emotion, 3*, 381-393.

Damisch, L., Stoberock, B., and Mussweiler, T. (2010). Keep your fingers crossed!: How superstition improves performance. *Psychological Science, 21*, 1014-1020.

Dimmock, J. A., and Grove, J. R. (2005). Relationship of fan identification to determinants of aggression. *Journal of Applied Sport Psychology, 17*, 37-47.

Feschuk, D. (2009, March 16). Green gear has Raptors feeling like league joke. *Toronto Star*, p. S06.

Keinan, G. (2002). The effects of stress and desire for control on superstitious behavior. *Personality and Social Psychology Bulletin, 28*, 102-108.

Kelley, S. W., and Tian, K. (2004). Fanatical consumption: An investigation of the behavior of sports fans through textual data. In L. R. Kahle and C. Riley (Eds.), *Sports marketing and the psychology of marketing communication* (pp. 27-65). Mahwah, NJ: Erlbaum

Kuharsky, P. (2009, September 25). Like it or not, Battle Red Day gets results [Web log post]. Retrieved from http://espn.go.com/blog/afcsouth/post/_/id/3796/battle-red-day-like-it-or-not-results-are-good.

Kwon, H. H., Trail, G. T., and Lee, D. (2008). The effects of vicarious achievement and team identification onBIRGing and CORFing. *Sport Marketing Quarterly, 17*(4), 209-217.

Laverie, D. A., and Arnett, D. B. (2000). Factors influencing fan attendance: The influence of identity salience and satisfaction. *Journal of Leisure Research, 32*, 225-246.

Madrigal, R. (2003). Investigating an evolving leisure experience: Antecedents and consequences of spectator affect during a live sporting event. *Journal of Leisure Research, 35*, 23-48.

Major League Baseball. (2011). Celebrate St. Patrick's Day: Gear up and go green with your team! Retrieved March 14, 2011 from http://shop.mlb.com/family/index.jsp? categoryId=3040011andcp=3040011

Markman, K. D., and Hirt, E. R. (2002). Social prediction and the "allegiance bias". *Social Cognition, 20,* 58-86.

National Hockey League. (2011). St. Patrick's Day gear now available! Retrieved March 14, 2011 from http://shop.nhl.com/family/index.jsp?categoryId=11226115andab=CMS_HP_ US_Include_StPatsGear_022411

Neil, G., Anderson, B., and Sheppard, W. (1981). Superstitions among male and female athletes of various levels of involvement. *Journal of Sport Behavior, 4,* 137-148.

Pritchard, M. P., Stinson, J., and Patton, E. (2010). Affinity and affiliation: The dual-carriage way to team identification. *Sport Marketing Quarterly, 19,* 67-77.

Schippers, M. C., and Van Lange, P. A. M. (2006). The psychological benefits of superstitious rituals in top sport: A study among top sportpersons. *Journal of Applied Social Psychology, 36,* 2532-2553.

Sessions, S. (2004, December 26). 'Battle Red' brand beats the blues for Texans. *Houston Business Journal.* Retrieved from http://www.bizjournals.com/houston/stories/2004/ 12/27/editorial3.html.

Superstition Study. (2007). Washington DC: Ipsos Public Affairs.

Todd, M., and Brown, C. (2003). Characteristics associated with superstitious behavior in track and field athletes: Are there NCAA divisional differences? *Journal of Sport Behavior, 26,* 168-187.

Wadey, R., and Hanton, S. (2008). Basic psychological skills usage and competitive anxiety responses: Perceived underlying mechanisms. *Research Quarterly For Exercise and Sport, 79,* 363-373.

Walsh, J., and Gill, G. (2008). Effect of spectators on the performance of a physiotherapy exercise. *Physiotherapy, 94,* 163-168.

Wann, D. L. (2002). Preliminary validation of a measure for assessing identification as a sport fan: The Sport Fandom Questionnaire. *International Journal of Sport Management, 3,* 103-115.

Wann, D. L. (2006a). The causes and consequences of sport team identification. In A. A. Raney and J. Bryant (Eds.,) *Handbook of sports and media* (pp. 331-352). Mahwah, NJ: Erlbaum.

Wann, D. L. (2006b). Understanding the positive social psychological benefits of sport team identification: The Team Identification – Social Psychological Health Model. *Group Dynamics: Theory, Research, and Practice, 10,* 272-296.

Wann, D. L., and Branscombe, N. R. (1993). Sports fans: Measuring degree of identification with the team. *International Journal of Sport Psychology, 24,* 1-17.

Wann, D. L., Dolan, T. J., McGeorge, K. K., and Allison, J. A. (1994). Relationships between spectator identification and spectators' perceptions of influence, spectators' emotions, and competition outcome. *Journal of Sport and Exercise Psychology, 16,* 347-364.

Wann, D. L., Melnick, M. J., Russell, G. W., and Pease, D. G. (2001). *Sport fans: The psychology and social impact of spectators.* New York: Routledge Press.

Wann, D. L., and Zaichkowsky, L. (2009). Sport Team Identification and Belief in Team Curses: The Case of the Boston Red Sox and the Curse of the Bambino. *Journal of Sport Behavior, 32,* 489-502.

Weinberg, R. S., and Gould, D. (2011). *Foundations of sport and exercise psychology* (5th ed.). Champaign, IL: Human Kinetics.

Womack, M. (1992). Why athletes need ritual: A study of magic among professional athletes. In W. J. Morgan (Ed.), *Sport and the humanities: A collection of original essay.* (pp. 191–202). Knoxville, TN: Bureau of Educational Research and Service.

In: Innovative Writings in Sport and Exercise Psychology
Editor: Robert Schinke
ISBN: 978-1-62948-881-3
© 2014 Nova Science Publishers, Inc.

*Chapter 18*

# "EVERYTHING WAS DIFFERENT": A QUALITATIVE STUDY OF US PROFESSIONAL BASKETBALL PLAYERS' EXPERIENCES OVERSEAS

### *Rainer J. Meisterjahn*[*] *and Craig A. Wrisberg*
Cardinal Stritch University, Milwaukee, WI, US
University of Tennessee, Knoxville, TN, US

## ABSTRACT

Research on international labor migration in professional sports (e.g., Magee & Sugden, 2002) suggests that the experiences of athletes in foreign cultures are often diverse and entail numerous pressures. In order to examine such experiences in greater depth, existential phenomenological interviews (Thomas & Pollio, 2002) were conducted with ten current and former professional basketball players, ages 24 to 55, from the US. Thematic analysis of the interview transcripts produced eight major themes that clearly characterized participants' experiences: Learning the Local Mentality, Experiencing Isolation, Connecting with Others, Exploring the Physical Environment, Dealing with the Business, Adjusting to Team Resources, Managing Team Dynamics, and Playing the Game. Taken together, the results suggest that while playing overseas required participants to manage a variety of cultural and sport-related stressors, it also afforded them opportunities for personal and professional development.

**Keywords:** FIBA, NBA, international labor migration, geographic relocation

## INTRODUCTION

Globalization is a phenomenon that has received considerable attention in the sport studies literature (Maguire, 2005). Characteristics of sport globalization include the growth

---

[*] Corresponding Author: Rainer J. Meisterjahn, Ph.D. 1630 North Hawley Road, Milwaukee, WI 53208, Email: rmeiste1@utk.edu, Phone: 865-323-8570.

and development of worldwide sport organizations, internationally implemented rules, and the establishment of global competitions (Maguire, 2005). One important aspect of sport globalization is labor migration, which involves the movement of professional athletes within and between countries and continents (e.g., Magee & Sugden, 2002).

The existing research suggests that athletes are motivated to play their sport in another culture for a variety of reasons (Magee & Sugden, 2002). The results of several case studies incorporating semi-structured interviews with athletes in the sports of cricket, association football, and rugby union revealed that participants' primary motivation was to advance professionally to the highest level of their respective sports (e.g., Stead & Maguire, 2000a, 2000b). Other research involving structured interviews with athletes has revealed additional sources of motivation, including the possibility of further developing sport-specific skills (Stead & Maguire, 2000b), earning the most money possible, fulfilling a dream to play professionally, playing and living in a desired foreign location, and experiencing new cultures (Magee & Sugden, 2002). The results of one study (Magee & Sugden, 2002) also revealed that athletes who brought relatives or significant others with them chose the location because they felt integration into the local culture would be relatively smooth for their family members (e.g., their children would experience little difficulty adjusting to the local school system).

Less research attention has been devoted to examining the lived experiences of athletes who play their sport professionally in foreign countries, which was the primary issue addressed in the present study. Previous research does suggest that professional sport participation in a foreign culture is not without its challenges (Schinke, Yukelson, Bartolacci, Battochia, & Johnstone, 2012). For example, some literature has indicated that professional athletes' lives are often characterized by a lack of stability, adjustment issues, and assorted other pressures, both professionally and personally (e.g., Cronson & Mitchell, 1987). A disconcerting phenomenon reported by professional soccer players in one study was the frequent change of geographical location they must deal with (Magee & Sugden, 2002), though historically job relocation has been considered a common phenomenon in professional sports to which players (and their families) must adapt (Roderick, 2012). Regardless, Poli (2010) has observed that for some athletes "career paths fragmented between a multitude of countries are more and more frequent" (p. 1004), and in certain situations players can be released from a team, such as when the team's owner feels the player's performance does not meet expectations (Falcous & Maguire, 2005).

Research also suggests that athletes can face various issues of alienation when playing in a foreign culture (Maguire & Pearton, 2000b). For example, those who lack familiarity or proficiency with the local language and customs can experience difficulty developing a supportive social network (Cronson & Mitchell, 1987). For some, the stress of playing overseas can be magnified if the player has the additional responsibility of a family or significant other. Family members may be unwilling or unable to move with the athlete (e.g., due to financial reasons) or, if they do, may encounter stressors of their own after relocating (e.g., professional job opportunities may be limited for the athlete's spouse or partner). Whenever such problems arise, the athlete is usually the one to bear the "blame" since it was his decision to leave the home country in the first place (Roderick, 2012).

Finally, athletes playing in a foreign culture must manage the usual stressors associated with professional sport participation, where the "business of winning" takes precedence over the well-being of individuals. Moreover, some research suggests that the negative impact of sport-specific stressors such as long, exhausting training sessions (e.g., Noblet & Gifford, 2002) or demanding coaches (Duchesne, Bloom, & Sabiston 2011) can be exacerbated by the uncertainties of a foreign culture.

One sport that has seen perhaps the greatest migration of athletes from the US is professional basketball. By the mid-1990s over 400 Americans were competing in Europe's professional men's basketball leagues (Maguire & Pearton, 2000a), with many more playing in leagues outside of Europe. Over the past five years, over 6,700 Americans have played professionally overseas ("Americans Overseas," 2013). Possible explanations for migration in such large numbers include the abundance of basketball talent produced at both the high school and college levels in the US (Falcous & Maguire, 2005) combined with the limited opportunities to play in the dominant professional league, the National Basketball Association (NBA). As a result, many players must seek out opportunities to play overseas in order to earn income and possibly extend their careers. Some who do so--such as C.J. Watson of the Brooklyn Nets--eventually sign with an NBA team ("C. J. Watson Bio," 2012). However, it should be noted that there are also NBA players who have moved overseas because they received more lucrative financial offers from foreign teams. For example, Josh Childress enjoyed a very successful career with the NBA's Atlanta Hawks before signing a contract worth $20 million with the Euroleague club Olympiacos Piraeus (Thamel, 2008).

Given the relatively large number of US basketball players participating in foreign leagues and the limited research conducted to date on these players' experiences, the purpose of the present study was to examine this form of labor migration from a cultural sport psychology (CSP) perspective (Schinke, Hanrahan, & Catina, 2009). The primary rationale for selecting a CSP lens for conducting this research was its emphasis on the role of self-awareness in identifying and controlling for researchers' values, biases, and identity (Ryba & Schinke, 2009) and the assumption that sport contexts are also cultural contexts which occur naturally and in which each individual contributes his or her own unique cultural identity to any particular experience (Schinke & Moore, 2011). Thus, the research question addressed in the present study was "What are the salient aspects of the first-person, lived experiences of US basketball players playing professionally in a foreign culture?"

Recent scholars have argued that an athlete's identityy and life experiences are to a large extent reciprocally related (Ryba & Wright, 2010). In light of this relationship, it might be expected that US basketball players' personal and professional experiences overseas (the coach-athlete dynamic being one example) would include varying aspects of both acculturation and enculturation. Acculturation is a process of cultural change during which the individual moves *toward* the cultural practices and/or beliefs of the dominant societal group (Marín, 1992). It has been described as a multi-way process that is fluid of all identities and experiences within the sport context (see Schinke, McGannon, Parham, & Lane, 2012). Enculturation is presumed to occur whenever individuals adopt or embrace the cultural practices of their own racial or ethnic groups (Berry, 1993). In one sense, acculturation and enculturation might be viewed as the opposite ends of a continuum, with any particular individual displaying different degrees of both processes in response to different cultural phenomena (Schinke et al., 2009). For example, a player might demonstrate increased acculturation by learning the local language and enjoying the local food while maintaining a high degree of enculturation with respect to the style of clothing he wears or by maintaining a strict adherence to the religious beliefs of his or her native culture.

Previous studies investigating labor migration in professional sports have primarily focused on selected aspects of athletes' experience, most prominently their reasons for migrating (e.g., Magee & Sugden, 2002). Some studies have also shed light on some of the personal challenges (e.g., family issues) athletes encounter (e.g., Schinke, Yukelson, et al., 2012). However, while the majority of these studies have provided valuable insights into the phenomenon of labor migration, additional research on the more nuanced aspects of sport participants' lived experiences in other cultures is needed. As Roderick (2012) has argued, "[Previous] literature has been undertaken largely from a top-down, macro-perspective, which unavoidably limits the subjectivity of migrating athletes who must negotiate practical micro issues…" (p. 321).

From a CSP perspective, it might be expected that participants' experience of labor migration would be framed by a dynamic interaction between their respective cultural identities and a number of unique aspects of the cultural context, including relationships with coaches, teammates, fans, and local citizens. Moreover, it might be assumed that players' experience would be characterized by a dynamic and ongoing process of acculturation and enculturation in response to unique aspects of the foreign culture as well as the demands of playing basketball within that context.

In order to obtain an unfiltered understanding of US basketball players' experience overseas, an existential phenomenological interview approach (Thomas & Pollio, 2002) was employed in the present study. Existential phenomenology, a term originally coined by Merleau-Ponty (1945/1962), moves beyond the "why" question traditionally examined in studies of human phenomena to the "what" question, which seeks to reveal the nature of those phenomena (Valle, King, & Halling, 1989). More specifically, the goal of existential phenomenology is to obtain rigorous descriptions of people's lived experience of a phenomenon rather than to construct abstract explanations from a third-person point of view (Pollio, Henley, & Thompson 1997). In order to effectively capture a person's experience the researcher establishes a free-flowing dialogue with the participant (Pollio et al., 1997).

Throughout the interview, the participant is assumed to be the expert. Hence, the researcher's focus remains solely on the words of the participant. Due to the two-way process of communication in phenomenological interviewing and the primary importance of the participant's contribution to that process, the term *co-participant* (Lather, 1991) is used to describe the interviewees in phenomenological research. Consistent with the CSP perspective, an existential phenomenological interview respects the notion that the athlete is "indissolubly linked to his or her world" (Dale, 1996, p. 309). Accordingly, athlete and world co-exist, and, at all times, the individual is presumed to be acting upon the world or vice versa. Given the unique and unfamiliar world(s) US basketball players might be expected to face when playing in a foreign culture, existential phenomenology interviewing was considered to be the most promising vehicle for obtaining deeper insights into their overseas experiences.

## METHOD

### Co-Participants

The co-participants in this study were 10 current and former US professional basketball players with a mean age of 32.3 years. In order to protect their identity, each was assigned a pseudonym. On average, the co-participants had spent 6.2 seasons overseas and played in more than three different countries (mean = 3.2). Nine players had participated at the highest level of competition in at least one of the countries where they played while the remaining co-participant had played in the second division or lower in the sole country where he had competed. Three of the co-participants had gained playing experience in Greece, Spain, and/or Italy, which have traditionally been the countries containing the most competitive professional basketball leagues in Europe. However, other countries in which co-participants had played included Argentina, Australia, Belgium, Chile, China, England, Finland, France, Germany, Holland, Iceland, Indonesia, Italy, Lebanon, Mexico, New Zealand, Norway, Poland, Portugal, Saudi Arabia, Turkey, United Arab Emirates, and Venezuela.

## Procedure

The procedure used in this study was based on Thomas and Pollio's (2002) recommendations for conducting existential phenomenological research. In order to gain an initial awareness of his own biases and expectations, the first author, who subsequently conducted all the interviews in this study and is hereafter referred to as "the interviewer," participated in a bracketing interview. In the interview, he stated what he believed would be the primary components of US basketball players' experiences in a foreign culture (e.g., that co-participants experienced a more team-oriented approach overseas compared to the US). The bracketing interview was particularly valuable and necessary in light of the interviewer's extensive experiences both overseas (i.e., growing up in Germany) and in basketball (e.g., as a player and coach). After participating in the interview, the interviewer obtained the assistance of a group of phenomenological researchers who read the interview transcript aloud during one meeting and identified meaning units (i.e., "the potential meanings and possible interrelationships among meanings of a phrase or group of phrases"; Dale, 1996, p. 316) in order to develop key themes. Specifically, the research group's purpose was to help facilitate bracketing of the researcher's assumptions and, thus, offer "a broader perspective than that of the individual" (Dale, 1996, p. 316). The interviewer took written notes of the bracketing interview themes and referred to them throughout all subsequent interviews with co-participants. These "reminders" served to focus his attention on co-participants' responses and avoid injecting his personal expectations.

After obtaining human subjects approval from the Institutional Review Board, the primary researcher contacted players in Germany and the Southeastern region of the US either directly via email or face-to-face, or through their coach. Specifically, he sought out players he knew personally as well as players who competed for a coach he knew or who competed in a local US summer league. Potential co-participants were informed of the purpose, procedures, and requirements of the study. Those athletes possessing playing experience on the international club level and willing to discuss their experience were invited to participate. Interviews were scheduled at a time and place that was convenient and comfortable to each individual. Consistent with previous recommendations for conducting qualitative research the final number of co-participants was determined by data saturation (Guest, Bunce, & Johnson, 2006). Specifically, no further interviews were conducted when the information being obtained became redundant.

Most co-participants were interviewed at their homes or in an office setting. Nine players were interviewed face-to-face while the other was interviewed via phone. All interviews were audio-recorded. Informed consent and demographic information were obtained prior to each interview, which commenced with the following question: "When you think about your experience of being a professional basketball player overseas, what are some things that stand out to you?" Additional follow-up questions were occasionally posed using the respective co-participant's phrasing (e.g., "You said initially it was hard to adjust to the different culture. What are some things you did to eventually adjust to it?"). By doing this, the interviewer allowed co-participants to determine the flow of dialogue while also helping them "focus on unfolding themes and details" (Thomas & Pollio, 2002, p. 26).

Immediately following each interview, the interviewer recorded field notes consisting of observations of co-participants' demeanor and body language, flow of the dialogue, and other relevant details. All co-participants appeared to provide transparent accounts of their experiences. Hence, the field notes were primarily used to determine whether players' responses might have been impacted by unexpected or unusual occurrences surrounding the interview (e.g., temporary interruptions such as a cell phone call), which did not appear to be the case.

## Data Analysis

Each interview was transcribed verbatim by one of the researchers or a university student with transcription skills. The transcript was then read multiple times for clarity and returned to the co-participant for verification of accuracy and, if necessary, alteration (Thomas & Pollio, 2002). Of the 10 co-participants, seven provided feedback indicating their transcript was accurate. One of those seven co-participants asked that a reference he had made to a former teammate be removed. The researchers were unable to reach the remaining three co-participants with their request for feedback. Four of the transcripts were examined with the assistance of the phenomenological research group in order to obtain a diverse perspective of co-participants' responses, while the remaining six transcripts were analyzed solely by the researchers. The utilization of such a group is "somewhat unique to the phenomenological interview method" and "allows the researcher to remain at the level of the experience of the participant" (Dale, 1996, p. 316).

The research group consisted of individuals (i.e., university students and faculty) from various disciplines (e.g., sport psychology, education, and nursing), who had experience in phenomenological research and gathered weekly to lend assistance to one another in the analysis of interview transcripts. While transcripts were being read aloud, group members, during frequent pauses, pointed out meaning units that they deemed notable and eventually helped the primary researcher develop themes based on frequently occurring meaning units (Thomas & Pollio, 2002). It is important to note that by identifying themes across interviews, the phenomenological researcher does not intend to seek generalizability; rather, the researcher recognizes "ways in which one experience resembles another" (Dale, 1996, p. 317).

Finally, the authors developed a conceptual framework that appeared to capture the themes and their relationships to each other. The researchers then shared this information with the research group and, after some discussion and fine-tuning, achieved consensus on a final thematic structure. Next the researchers presented the thematic structure to the co-participants (via email) and asked them to determine whether it accurately reflected their experiences (Thomas & Pollio, 2002). Five of the co-participants responded to the request and all indicated that the structure was an accurate representation. Interestingly, two of those five co-participants were amongst the three who had previously failed to provide feedback on the accuracy of their transcripts, perhaps due to time constraints.

# RESULTS

The thematic structure that emerged from the interviews with co-participants in this study consisted of both salient (i.e., *figural*) and contextual (i.e., *ground*) components. Figural components are those that individuals were consciously aware of when experiencing a phenomenon (e.g., playing basketball) while ground components represent the context in which co-participants' experiences occurred (e.g., overseas) (Merleau-Ponty, 1945/1962).

Put another way, "figure and ground co-create each other in human experience" (Thomas & Pollio, 2002, p. 18), meaning neither one can exist in the same form in the absence of the other. In addition, something may emerge as figural in one situation and recede into the (back) ground in another situation where something else may become figural. For example, an individual may be acutely aware of the taste of a new food at a foreign restaurant one moment and then, suddenly, hone in on and feel overwhelmed by the novelty of his unfamiliar surroundings (e.g., people and objects around him) while temporarily "forgetting" about his meal.

Of the eight figural themes (see Table 2) that were identified, four pertained to co-participants' personal life overseas (*Learning the Local Mentality*, *Experiencing Isolation*, *Connecting with Others*, and *Exploring the Physical Environment*) and four centered in their experiences of professional basketball life (*Dealing with the Business*, *Adjusting to Team Resources*, *Managing Club Dynamics*, and *Playing the Game*). All of these themes occurred within the context of two grounds: *Overseas World* and *Development*. In the following sections, a discussion of the figural themes preceded by a brief explanation of each of the grounds is presented. In addition, quotes (accompanied by the respective co-participant's pseudonym) are offered as examples of the meaning units on which the themes were based.

# GROUNDS

*Overseas world.* The ground of *Overseas World* refers to the various countries and cultures co-participants spent time in as professional basketball players and represented one aspect of the context in which the eight figural themes emerged.

The following quote, for example, illustrates a number of differences one co-participant encountered upon entering the foreign world. "Yeah when I first came over here...everything seemed different, just walking down the street, going into stores, trying to communicate with, with people..." (Rick).

This sense of feeling overwhelmed by the novelty of a new environment was shared by all the co-participants and speaks to the inherent challenges these players faced beyond the basketball court during their time overseas.

*Development.* This ground refers to the personal and professional development co-participants experienced during their time overseas.

Arguably, in order to be able to grow and mature, a person needs to be able to assess his/her development over time. This implies a process of constant comparison of one's present and past life.

Co-participants in the current study frequently drew comparisons between their previous life in the US and their experiences overseas. One described his experience of personal development as follows:

> ...in Australia I think it was a bit, it was a bit of an adjustment...all of a sudden you're in this country, you don't know anybody...I don't know, you just like learn a lot...who you are, kind of how you interact with people... (Mark)

Another co-participant shared that some of his American teammates on his overseas club team gave him "different pointers like, uh, ways of setting a ball screen or what to do when certain people are guarding you a certain way," (Wesley) thus helping him to develop as a player. Some co-participants discussed their motivation to develop basketball-wise in terms of working their way up to stronger leagues. One player explained, "Italy or Spain, I always wanted to go to one of those countries and play because it's a little higher level" (Eric).

## FIGURAL THEMES

*Learning the local mentality.* This theme refers to co-participants' gradual development of an understanding of the local lifestyle and value system in the overseas culture. Several co-participants emphasized the sharp contrast they saw in how locals in a foreign culture and people in the US viewed the role of work. More specifically, they learned that overseas the family frequently took precedence over one's work, or, in some cases, the two were integrated (i.e., traditional family businesses). As one player stated, "...overseas they cut their hours ...they get off from two to five so they can go home and be with their family. Then they go back from six to nine...It ain't always just work" (Jalen). These co-participants, in several cases, expressed an appreciation for the balance between work and family that the locals (e.g., in Germany) enjoyed.

Co-participants also discussed the active lifestyle they often witnessed in foreign cultures, which contrasted with their perception of the more sedentary lifestyle of many people in the US. One athlete explained, "I've noticed that [in Germany] there's a lot of bike riding going on and walking and using public transportation ...it's a healthier lifestyle..." (Freddy). Overall, players' remarks indicated that the lifestyle of people overseas was generally more health-oriented than that of people in the US. Similar to the work-family balance co-participants described, they also communicated their approval of the active lifestyle choices displayed by some host cultures (e.g., Holland) they had lived in.

Some co-participants talked about the interpersonal dynamics they witnessed among locals and the attitudes local people seemed to hold towards outsiders. One athlete discussed locals' melancholic mindset and their initial hesitancy in opening up towards others compared to his experience in the US:

...the American way of thinking is, is very positive, very open-minded about new ideas, uh, and being optimistic. Then there is another side of it of opening up very quickly but sort of, uh, keeping it, uh, like...the, uh, tip of the iceberg. And, uh, in, in Germany it's...rather pessimistic, melancholic...the way people think. (Othella)

This player added that once one is able form connections with the locals, however, ensuing friendships are typically very genuine despite Germans' initial hesitancy and rather reserved approach. A few co-participants spoke more specifically to differences they recognized in how locals approached their social life, particularly with regard to partying and going out. For example, one player discussed the "social schedule" locals operated on and explained, "...one difference too was... they don't leave to go to the bar or club 'til one o'clock or something in the morning...that was an adjustment for me..." (Brandon). Some of the co-participants shared that they learned to embrace such local customs, which helped them feel more comfortable in the host culture.

*Experiencing isolation.* Perhaps not surprisingly, those co-participants who found it difficult to cultivate relationships with locals also reported feeling isolated and lonely. Several of the players discussed being homesick, particularly during their early experiences in a foreign country, which contributed significantly to their sense of loneliness. One athlete described his early struggles during his first experience overseas by saying, "You're a long way from home...you're there on your own. You know in Turkey, my first year overseas, I didn't think I was going to make it" (Lamar). Expanding on these adjustment issues, almost all of the co-participants pointed to the language barriers they faced in non-English speaking countries as a significant challenge. The inability to communicate with locals, whether to socialize or make simple inquiries about product labels at the grocery store, seemed to contribute to co-participants' feelings of loneliness. One athlete explained, "...you don't want to go out anywhere 'cause you don't speak the language...so you kind of tend to just stay by yourself and it gets lonely" (Jalen).

*Connecting with others.* This theme refers to the connections co-participants attempted to make with others in the US, from a distance, or in the host culture in an effort to enhance their level of emotional comfort or become more socially integrated, respectively. Co-participants emphasized the challenge of being away from home and reported that they kept in touch with their families and friends by communicating via phone and internet as well as by visiting occasionally. As one athlete, who had played overseas for 13 seasons, explained:

...the first couple of years it was, it was difficult...now I think it's a lot easier for players to come over cause you got the internet, you got movies in English...when I was here in, in France my first year, I had no VCR, I had no cable, and no internet. Phone calls were about 50 to 70 cents a minute... (Eric)

Several co-participants discussed the importance of meeting people and establishing friendships locally rather than relying solely on family and friends back in the US to meet their social needs. In some cases, players were able to get acquainted with locals, which enhanced their experience in the host culture. One player stated, "...I usually tried to make it a point to become friends with several people in the community because... without them I would have no idea what's going on in their community" (Jalen). However, most players reported building friendships primarily with their group of teammates, both American and local.

A few co-participants indicated that they were living overseas with their families and had made the host country their temporary home. Some were joined by their wives and were raising their children in the host country. One co-participant explained that Germany "feels like home because…obviously now I'm married with two kids so I mean this…has been…my family's home for you know the past six, seven years" (Rick). That meant that his kids were integrated in the local school system and his wife had formed meaningful relationships with other parents in the host community. Additionally, some co-participants discussed their willingness and ability to learn the local language, which served to strengthen connections with the local culture and people. One player explained, "If you're willing to learn and, uh, speak to people in their first language then they see that you're…making an effort because most of the Germans do speak English…" (Eric). Thus, attempts to master the local language not only helped co-participants handle practical challenges (e.g., finding their way around the grocery store) more effectively but also served to demonstrate to locals their willingness to become a part of the community.

*Exploring the physical environment.* This theme refers to co-participants' leisure time, which was often spent traveling, sightseeing, going to restaurants, or exploring other leisure opportunities locally. Several co-participants talked about opportunities to travel within and between countries and cities, sometimes enjoying sight-seeing in the process. One player stated, "…you go sight-seeing to different countries and different land sights in the city if you want…just traveling a bunch of different countries…different cities…I'd never been to Rome, so it was really cool to go there" (Wesley). Those co-participants who shared this attitude expressed a sense of excitement for the opportunities to explore the world that they were given while playing professionally in foreign lands. Additionally, most co-participants talked about local leisure activities such as exploring clubs and trying out restaurants. One player listed various places he had discovered in his environment overseas. "[I] went to local bars, went to local restaurants, spent time at the local parks, local hospitals…and kept myself busy like that a lot of the time" (Jalen). Overall, several players alluded to the value in seeking out local leisure opportunities to combat boredom and gain comfort while away from the familiar surroundings of the US.

*Dealing with the business.* This theme refers to the business elements of being a professional basketball player that co-participants confronted in the foreign clubs they played for. Most players discussed significant issues with contractual agreements they had either experienced firsthand or heard about from other American players. One co-participant, for example, stated, "…it is a business over there but it was just such…a dishonest business and, and shady…anybody could get cut at any time no matter what your contract said…" (Brandon). Several co-participants alluded to the contractual and financial insecurity, which they described as a common occurrence in many overseas leagues (e.g., Holland, Australia). Some players added that they had to get used to short contracts (i.e., teams would typically only sign them for one to two years) and face the challenge of finding a new team at the end of their agreement with the club they played for. Upon signing a contract with a foreign team, players reported often experiencing immense pressure to perform at their highest level at all times. Failure to perform up to expectations could lead to immediate contract termination by the club. One athlete commented on the stress he encountered as a result of such performance expectations:

...they pay you to perform. So my first couple of months I wasn't really performing to what they thought I should. So they brought me in and was like..."you got one more game to show us what you got or we're going to find somebody else"...that's when I knew it was a business. (Jalen)

Despite the harsh realities of the business many players encountered, they also identified some crucial benefits their clubs offered them. For example, an advantage of being a professional basketball player overseas was that teams provided players with accommodation such as housing and transportation (i.e., players are often provided with a private car throughout their tenure with a team). The quality of this accommodation, however, seemed to vary from team to team. One co-participant who had been in a variety of situations emphasized the importance of making good choices when given different housing options by the club. He explained, "...some of the places will give you an option between...stay[ing] in an apartment, a house, or a hotel... I've been in some good apartments and I've been in some okay apartments but...I normally pick the hotel route..." (Jared). Overall, reported experiences regarding the business side of playing basketball overseas varied considerably from player to player and country to country, which strengthens Jared's point about being selective.

*Adjusting to team resources.* This theme refers to the resources teams provided their players with. These resources seemed to be directly (e.g., athletic training and strength and conditioning services) and indirectly (e.g., team travel arrangements to away-games) linked to player performance. Several players talked about the availability of coaches, doctors, and trainers on their foreign teams and the different levels of satisfaction they experienced with each depending on the quantity and quality of staff. As one player stated:

> The better the professional team, the more stuff you're going to have. The less professional, the less you're going to have. Like my first year I went in, I don't even know we had a trainer...Then I've been on teams where we had two trainers. (Jalen)

Some co-participants commented on the low quality of the facilities they trained and played in overseas compared to ones they remembered from their college days in the US. One player who had been retired for some time explained, "When I came to Germany back in 1977, um, they were playing mostly in like school gyms and I had just come from a, from a program where we played in front of 12 to 20 thousand people" (Othella). Another currently active player shared a similar perspective when he stated, "...a lot of the gyms over here are, uh, like high school gyms or, or even worse..." (Eric). Accordingly, players had to adjust to the playing conditions in order to be able to perform well. A significant issue some players encountered in this context was the long drives to away-games, as illustrated in the following comments:

> ...one of the things to, to get used to was, um, the low budget on the team...man, we took some small buses and, and sometimes two, two or three mini vans where you know you got six or eight guys all lined up in this row...for this three-hour drive... (Brandon)

The relatively primitive travel accommodations represented a sharp contrast to the more convenient flight arrangements and charter bus trips most players were accustomed to from their playing days in US colleges. One co-participant (Rick) specifically indicated that the long bus trips had a significant impact on players' performance since the away-team typically arrived at the competition site fatigued and with tight muscles while the home team was rested and ready to play.

*Managing club dynamics.* This theme addresses the variety of interpersonal dynamics co-participants encountered in the respective clubs they played for. The theme also refers to the delicacy with which the players had to manage these interrelations. Co-participants' perceptions of the coaches they played for and the way coaches treated them varied widely. One player commented on the differences in coaching styles he experienced overseas, "[there is] the hard 'Yugo-style' where you practice twice a day hard every day…some coaches like the laid back mentality where you just go once a day and you just perform on Saturday…" (Freddy). Another co-participant addressed the importance of being able to relate to at least one of the coaches on the coaching staff and the challenges that sometimes arose when there was just a head coach and no assistants due to a club's limited budget:

> …A lot of their clubs over here you have the head coach and that's it…when you're on a basketball team there's always players that maybe don't get along with the coach…but when you have three or four coaches…you'll probably always have one or two coaches…that you can bond with… (Rick)

Co-participants' dynamics with teammates were highly complex, as alluded to by several co-participants. A few players discussed the separation they felt between themselves and their local teammates, particularly during the early stages of a season when everyone was still somewhat unfamiliar. One co-participant who was one of the few full-time professional athletes on his team explained:

> …a lot of teams only have two or three professional players…so because they're the only people getting money and…they're the best players…they're more responsible for, for the success of the team. And it kind of puts a separation…between those players and, and the rest of…the team… (Rick)

In some cases, this sense of separation was a result of the player's perception that local teammates' thought that Americans on the team were "selfish" and unwilling to share the basketball (Brandon). In other cases, however, co-participants explained that they had formed positive relationships with American and local teammates and not only performed well together on the court but spend quality time with each other off the court as well.

Additionally, most of the co-participants discussed their encounters with local fans in very positive terms. One player explained that he and his teammates would mingle with the fans and share a beer at the bar after home games (Brandon). Another athlete who remained overseas after retiring from his professional playing career described the local fans with a sense of fondness:

> …the thing that amazed me was after I stopped playing…how we as a team touched many people's lives. And even now, I stopped playing in 1987…I still have people approach me and talk about how they enjoyed that time…[during] those 10 years where I played. (Othella)

A few co-participants described the dynamics they encountered with club management. However, their experiences seemed to vary. One player who was very pleased with management also realized his situation might be unique. He explained, "...some clubs you have no interactions with the office... Here it's a little different...the club seems to be more of a family... [which] I don't think happens very often in this business" (Freddy). Another player's perception of the way the club he competed for was managed was less positive. He repeatedly pointed to conflicts with various members of the organization and in one case stated, "[My organization] was very poorly run... and...there was really a lack of leadership in any area because...anytime anything went wrong people...were blaming...each other but not necessarily to their face" (Brandon).

*Playing the game.* This theme refers to how the game of basketball is approached and played overseas. In order to achieve success overseas co-participants felt they had to understand what their club expected of them on the court and what they needed to do to meet those expectations.

In many cases players were asked to assume a role that they perhaps were not accustomed to playing when they were in college in the US. One co-participant, who had enjoyed success in a supporting role on his college team, which had won a national championship, was thrust into a situation where he was expected to play a primary role on his foreign team. He explained, "...in my second year in Germany...we had about 34, 35 games and I played every minute of every game except for the last game where I fouled out a couple of minutes before the end..." (Othella).

Overall, co-participants found it challenging to adjust their games so as to thrive in the roles their clubs placed them in, though they were typically able to make the transition successfully.

Several of the co-participants compared the level of competition overseas to the level they had experienced in college. In some cases, players perceived the quality of foreign competition to be a "downgrade." In contrast, one player stated that he had encountered a high level of competition playing overseas and reported, "[The Spanish league] had top players...day in and day out [you had to] practice hard...compete at practice...10, 11 guys could be...playing" (Lamar). In either case, players felt a responsibility to adapt to a new level of play compared to the level they had competed on previously in the US.

Some co-participants also commented on how the style of play overseas differed from that in the US and required some adjustments. One player explained, "...the game itself is different. You have to slow yourself down overseas. It's real, real fundamentally sound overseas..." (Jared). For the most part, these players expressed an appreciation for the style of play they were exposed to in other countries and acknowledged their positive development as professional players.

For these co-participants part of adapting to the game of professional basketball overseas included learning FIBA rules. Some of these rules were considerably different from US college rules, which presented a significant challenge. One player referred to differences in the goal-tending and traveling rules and said, "...the rules are...different...being able to hit the ball...when the ball is...in the cylinder. And also, [the] traveling [rule] over there is a lot different..." (Wesley). Another athlete elaborated on the traveling rule by saying, "For Americans, that first step, we are allowed to take one long step and a dribble...or we are allowed to fake right and go left with that dribble. Overseas...it's called a travel every single time" (Jalen). Having to learn to play by these new rules added to the aforementioned adjustments players had to make so as to be able to meet the performance demands of their foreign teams.

Several players commented on their own experience of preparing to compete for these teams. As was alluded to by some players, in FIBA-affiliated professional leagues it is not uncommon for teams to make frequent roster changes by releasing players and bringing in new ones. In many cases, these changes take place in season, which can be a challenge for those players who start with a new team without the benefit of having gone through training camp. One co-participant explained, "[Starting with a team in the middle of the season] was different...you have to get used to it, learn the plays and stuff...it was better in Turkey 'cause I was right there from the beginning..." (Lamar).

## DISCUSSION

The purpose of the present study was to investigate the overseas experiences of US professional basketball players using an existential phenomenological interview approach (Thomas & Pollio, 2002). This research utilized a CSP framework (Schinke et al., 2009), which emphasizes the importance of exploring cultural identity and context, both in sport psychology research and practice, in order to fully understand athletes' experience.

Similar to the results of previous studies (e.g., Magee & Sugden, 2002), co-participants in the present research discussed a variety of reasons for migrating, including some that were out of their control (e.g., teams not renewing their contracts). Also consistent with previous research (e.g., Stead & Maguire, 2000a, 2000b), several co-participants pointed to their motivation to work their way up to higher levels of play while overseas to be their chief motivation for migration. Arguably, in order to achieve this objective, development as a basketball player was deemed crucial for these athletes. Not surprisingly, therefore, most co-participants reported experiencing growth during their time playing overseas. More interestingly, though, several specifically emphasized the growth they experienced in the way of personal development at least as much as their growth as basketball players. In order to enjoy that level of personal growth, these players eventually realized they needed to be able to adapt to their new, strange environments. As one player explained, " The problem is a lot of Americans usually isolate themselves...but...you have to integrate yourself into that city or that country's culture to become a part if you want to make it work and have a good time" (Eric).

Thus, the present results indicate that co-participants' experience of acculturation (Marín, 1992) (e.g., by partaking in local customs such as going out with local teammates late at night or learning the language) contributed to the level of acceptance and comfort they enjoyed in the host culture. More specifically, those US players who made a conscious effort to adopt behaviors to fit in with their local teammates found their efforts rewarded by a response from those teammates that included an increased curiosity and openness toward American culture. Most of the co-participants also alluded to experiences of enculturation (Berry, 1993). More specifically, these players tended to seek out US teammates with whom they shared a similar cultural background, eat at local American restaurants, and watch American movies. Taken together, the results suggested that co-participants' adoption of acculturative and enculturative practices was dynamic in nature and occurred on a continuum (Schinke et al., 2009).

Even those players that had confronted considerable personal and professional stressors and challenges seemed to feel that they were able to benefit and grow from their circumstances. Perhaps it was these challenges that encouraged players to improve and develop themselves both on and off the court. These findings appear inconsistent with some previous literature, which primarily emphasized the obstacles encountered by professional athletes in foreign countries (e.g., Cronson & Mitchell, 1987). While the players in the current study experienced various challenges, many also seemed to seek out opportunities. Thus, the present results suggest that a pro-active approach to playing basketball overseas by seeking new experiences on and off the court can offer players the enhanced possibility of professional and personal development.

It is important to note that interrelationships, both between and within co-participants, existed among the eight themes that represented co-participants' figural experiences. For example, negative dynamics with teammates on the court might have contributed to one player's sense of isolation in his personal life while prompting another to remedy the situation by seeking out connections and improving communication. Regardless of the quality of co-participants' experiences, the quote "everything was different" (Rick) speaks to the overwhelming sense of unfamiliarity players encountered in their "new worlds" as they negotiated their cultural identities through processes of acculturation (Marín, 1992) and enculturation (Berry, 1993). Nonetheless, to varying degrees, all co-participants developed a sense of comfort over time and came to appreciate the cultures they lived in.

However, in light of the encountered differences overseas, co-participants also mentioned a number of stressors, such as relocation and the lack of a social support system (e.g., Schinke, Yukelson, et al., 2012). The challenge of making friends and social connections overseas was usually magnified by language barriers and unfamiliarity with the local customs and culture. Consistent with Holliday's (2010) findings, some of the players in the current study felt a sense of not belonging in the host country, particularly during their early experiences overseas. Similar to athletes in previous studies (e.g., Weedon, 2011) some co-participants perceived an uncomfortable pressure from the host culture to acculturate and "fit in," despite the absence of structural mechanisms to assist with this process. However, being away from family and friends in the US also forced several co-participants to develop a sense of independence (Noblet & Gifford, 2002) and, perhaps, overcome what has been described as a state of being "fixed in perpetual adolescence" (Cronson & Mitchell, 1987, p. 22).

In addition to discussing aspects of their personal lives, co-participants in the present research addressed several aspects of their experiences that related to their lives as professional athletes. Many of these accounts included reports of challenges and stressors similar to those discussed in previous research (e.g., Feltz, Lirgg, & Albrecht, 1992). For example, players described stressful encounters due to their failure to meet specific performance demands of the team. More specifically, on-court performance that, despite the player's best efforts, might be deemed unsatisfactory by coaches or management could threaten the player's job security and create high levels of stress. Some co-participants attributed this form of stress to the "cutthroat business" they were dealing with. Another potential stressor appeared to be the nature of team practices. Earlier research identified long training sessions as a major source of stress for many athletes (Noblet & Gifford, 2002). Consistent with this research, some of the present players mentioned the physical and mental demands posed by their coaches, such as "Eastern-European methods" of physical drilling (e.g., practicing hard twice a day every day) and punishment (e.g., running sprints following a loss). Other co-participants indicated that their coaches treated them with respect and understood when to push players and when to allow them to rest and relax.

While all of the players discussed various cultural aspects of their time overseas, those who had been in the foreign culture the longest provided the more detailed accounts. Moreover, several emphasized the developmental process they had encountered over time, which had allowed them to expand their identities, particularly through off-court experiences, such as socializing with local people. In a similar vein, Orlick (2008) has suggested that in order to maintain physical, mental, and emotional health athletes should make an effort to find joy in non-performance domains. For several of the present co-participants their willingness to adopt and enjoy a more balanced lifestyle that was not solely devoted to professional endeavors seemed to characterize their social-psychological development.

## PRACTICAL IMPLICATIONS

The findings of the current study appear to have several practical implications for sport performers and practitioners. Experts in CSP have pointed to self-reflexivity as a crucial strategy for effective sport psychology research and consultation in multicultural sport contexts (see Schinke, McGannon, et al., 2012). Self-reflexivity has been described as the process of confronting one's own cultural background, personal interests, and biases with the purpose of expressing one's social position without marginalizing other individuals' culture and identity (McGannon & Johnson, 2009). Thus, in order to enhance both US players' basketball performance and experience in the host culture, overseas coaches, agents, sport psychology consultants, and the players themselves are encouraged to engage in this process. While it is important to acknowledge that these parties are interdependent to various degrees, the examples below represent recommendations for specific interactions based on the present findings.

Overseas coaches could help US players feel welcome and enhance their adjustment overseas by simply showing interest in the players' personal lives and inquiring about cultural customs and beliefs (e.g., the player's conceptualization of team). In addition, coaches could possibly diminish players' stress by outlining performance expectations within the context of the international style of play early on and clarifying players' roles, particularly if the player's new role is different from one the player assumed during his/her college experience.

Player agents could provide assistance by making players aware of variations in the availability of crucial resources (e.g., athletic training services), which US athletes might otherwise take for granted. They could also alert players to potential contractual issues, such as contract breaches by the club. Lastly, player agents could provide a helpful service by connecting players, particularly inexperienced ones who have never been outside of the US, with an overseas support network (e.g., veteran international players from the US).

Sport psychology consultants could assist players in seeing the potential for professional and personal growth overseas and encourage them to take a pro-active approach to their new situation (e.g., by interacting with local teammates and community members off the court rather than isolating themselves). Additionally, consultants could help athletes prepare for performance demands of competition overseas by visualizing themselves in their expected role (e.g., primary scorer) and becoming familiar with the unique aspects of the international game (e.g., reading books and obtaining video files detailing FIBA rules).

Finally, the present findings suggest that players could optimize their overseas experience by setting goals for personal growth and positively engaging with the local culture (e.g., learning the local language by interacting with foreign teammates every day) and maintaining a focus on controllable factors (e.g., concentrating on the "essentials" such as the availability of basic practice facilities rather than the "luxuries" like state-of-the-art arenas), particularly when playing for a low-budget team. In summary, coaches, agents, consultants, and players are equally encouraged to engage in self-reflective practices, examining their own cultural beliefs while also attempting to understand others' beliefs so as to enhance each party's cultural experience.

## Future Directions

The current study appears to offer a potentially fruitful conceptual foundation for future cross-cultural research in professional sports. While the themes that emerged from analysis of the interviews may contain many of the generic aspects of professional athletes' experiences in a foreign culture, additional research (e.g., with US athletes competing in other sports overseas), however, is needed to support this possibility. In addition, it would be interesting to determine the usefulness of this framework in examining US coaches' experiences in foreign cultures. It is reasonable to presume that coaches would face similar acculturative and enculturative challenges as the athletes interviewed for this study. However, it is also possible that additional aspects of coaches' experiences (e.g., the challenge of blending local and foreign players in order to build team cohesion) might be discovered using in-depth interviews. Future research might also examine the overseas experiences of female athletes, including basketball players competing at the club level overseas. Finally, it would be beneficial to determine whether the experiences of college and professional basketball players from other countries who move to the US are similar to those of the current sample of US players.

## LIMITATIONS

While the heterogeneous sample (e.g., some players were retired and some were still playing) perhaps made for a more interesting and diverse study, it is possible that a more homogenous co-participant pool would have led to different results. Co-participants who were still active at the time of this study were interviewed during the off-season. Thus, it is conceivable that their basketball-specific experiences might have been less figural for them than if they had been interviewed in season. Additionally, all of the present co-participants had garnered extensive playing experience in college prior to pursuing a professional career overseas. Hence, it is possible that younger players with less previous experience might encounter more significant adjustment issues than did the present co-participants.

## CONCLUSION

Previous literature has discussed both the challenges (e.g., Schinke, Yukelson, et al., 2012) and opportunities (e.g., Elliott & Weedon, 2010) athletes encounter during their migration experience, though attention to the latter has been limited. However, little research has investigated the relationship between these two factors, particularly from the first-person, lived perspective of the athlete. Hence, the most unique contribution of this study is the finding that co-participants emphasized extensively how the mastery of a variety of cultural challenges allowed them to develop on a personal and athletic level. The overseas experiences of these players appeared to involve an ongoing negotiation of their respective identities as athletes and people. While their adaptation to a foreign culture appeared to occur in two domains, personal and professional, these domains also seemed to be inextricably intertwined. Regardless of the extent to which co-participants sought out opportunities to grow, most perceived their overall experience to be positive in spite of, and sometimes because of, the various overseas challenges they encountered.

## REFERENCES

Americans Overseas (2013, January 1). *USBasket*. Retrieved from http://www.usbasket.com

Berry, J. W. (1993). Ethnic identity in plural societies. In M. E. Bernal & G. P. Knight (Eds.), *Ethnic identity: Formation and transmission among Hispanics and other minorities* (pp. 271-296). Albany, NY: State University of New York Press.

C. J. Watson Bio (2012). *National Basketball Association*. Retrieved from http://www.nba.com

Cronson, H., & Mitchell, G. (1987). Athletes and their families: Adapting to the stresses of professional sports. *The Physician and Sportsmedicine, 15* (5), 121-127.

Dale, G. A. (1996). Existential phenomenology: Emphasizing the experience of the athlete in sport psychology research. *The Sport Psychologist, 10*, 307-321.

Duchesne, C., Bloom, G. A., & Sabiston, C. M. (2011). Intercollegiate coaches' experiences with elite international athletes in an American sport context. *International Journal of Coaching Science, 5* (2), 1-20.

Elliott, R. & Weedon, G. (2010). Foreign players in the English Premier Academy League: 'Feet-drain' or 'feet-exchange'? *International Review for the Sociology of Sport, 46* (1), 61-75.

Falcous, M., & Maguire, J. (2005). Globetrotters and local heroes? Labor migration, basketball, and local identities. *Sociology of Sport Journal, 22*, 137-157.

Feltz, D., Lirgg, C., & Albrecht, R. (1992). Psychological implications of competitive running in elite young distance runners: A longitudinal analysis. *The Sport Psychologist, 6*, 128-138.

Guest, G., Bunce, A., & Johnson, L. (2006). How many interviews are enough?: An experiment with data saturation and variability. *Field Methods, 18*(1), 59.

Holliday, A. (2010). Complexity and cultural identity. *Language and Intercultural Communication, 10*, 165-177.

Lather, P. (1991). *Getting smart: Feminist research and pedagogy with/in the postmodern*. New York, NY: Routledge.

Magee, J., & Sugden, J. (2002). "The world at their feet:" Professional football and international labor migration. *Journal of Sport and Social Issues, 26*, 421-437.

Maguire, J. (Ed.) (2005). *Power and global sport: Zones of prestige, emulation, and resistance.* New York: Routledge.

Maguire, J., & Pearton, R. (2000a). Global sport and the migration patterns of France 1998 World Cup finals players: Some preliminary observations. *Soccer and Society, 1,* 175-189.

Maguire, J., & Pearton, R. (2000b). The impact of elite labor migration on the identification, selection and development of European soccer players. *Journal of Sports Sciences, 18,* 759-769.

Marín, G. (1992). Issues in the measurement of acculturation among Hispanics. In K. F. Geisinger (Ed.), *Psychological testing of Hispanics* (pp. 235-251). Washington, DC: American Psychological Association.

McGannon, K. R., & Johnson, C. R. (2009). Strategies for reflective cultural sport psychology research. In R. J. Schinke & S. J. Hanrahan (Eds.), *Cultural sport psychology* (pp. 57-75). Champaign, IL: Human Kinetics Inc.

Merleau-Ponty, M. (1945/1962). *The phenomenology of perception* (C. Smith, trans.). London: Routledge and Kegan Paul.

Noblet, A. J., & Gifford, S. M. (2002). The sources of stress experienced by professional Australian footballers. *Journal of Applied Sport Psychology, 14,* 1-13.

Orlick, T. (2008). *In pursuit of excellence* (4th ed.). Champaign, IL: Human Kinetics.

Poli, R. (2010). Understanding globalization through football: The new international division of labour, migratory channels and transnational trade circuits. *International Review for the Sociology of Sport, 45* (4), 491-506.

Pollio, H. R., Henley, T. B., & Thompson, C. J. (1997). *The phenomenology of everyday life.* New York, NY: Cambridge University Press.

Roderick, M. J. (2012). An unpaid labor of love: Professional footballers, family life, and the problem of job relocation. *Journal of Sport and Social Issues, 36* (3), 317-338.

Ryba, T. V., & Schinke, R. J. (2009). Methodology as a ritualized eurocentrism: Introduction to the special issue. *International Journal of Sport and Exercise Psychology, 7,* 263-274.

Ryba, T. V., & Wright, H. K. (2010). Sport psychology and the cultural turn: Notes toward cultural practice. In T. V. Ryba, R. J. Schinke, & G. Tenebaum (Eds.). *The cultural turn in sport psychology* (pp. 3-27). Morgantown, WV: Fitness Information Technology.

Schinke, R. J., & Moore, Z. E. (2011). Culturally informed sport psychology: Introduction to the special issue. *Journal of Clinical Sport Psychology, 5,* 283-294.

Schinke, R. J., Hanrahan, S. J., & Catina, P. (2009). Introduction to cultural sport psychology. In R. J. Schinke & S. J. Hanrahan (Eds.), *Cultural sport psychology* (pp. 1-12). Champaign, IL: Human Kinetics.

Schinke, R. J., McGannon, K. R., Parham, W. D., & Lane, A. M. (2012). Toward cultural praxis and cultural sensitivity: Strategies for self-reflexive sport psychology practice. *Quest, 64,* 34-46.

Schinke, R. J., Yukelson, D., Bartolacci, G., Battochio, R. C., & Johnstone, K. (2012). The challenges encountered by immigrated elite athletes. *Journal of Sport Psychology in Action, 2* (1), 10-20.

Stead, D. & Maguire, J. (2000b). Rite de passage or passage to riches? The motivation and objectives of Nordic/Scandinavian players in English league soccer. *Journal of Sport and Social Issues*, 24, 36-60.

Stead, D., & Maguire, J. (2000a). No boundaries to ambition—soccer labour migration and the case of Nordic/Scandinavian players in England. In J. Bangsbo (Ed.), *Soccer and science in an interdisciplinary perspective* (pp. 35-55). Copenhagen, Denmark: University of Copenhagen Press.

Thamel, P. (2008, October 11). Big, fat Greek contract makes Europe irresistible. *New York Times*. Retrieved from http://www.nytimes.com

Thomas, S. P., & Pollio, H. R. (2002). *Listening to patients: A phenomenological approach.* New York: Springer.

Valle, R., King, M., & Halling, S. (1989). An introduction to existential phenomenological thought in psychology. In R. V. Halling & A. S. Halling (Eds.), *Existential phenomenological perspectives in psychology* (pp. 3-16). New York: Plenum Press.

Weedon, G. (2011). 'Glocal boys': Exploring experiences of acculturation amongst immigrant youth footballers in Premier League academies. *International Review for the Sociology of Sport, 47* (2), 200-216.

*Submitted May 27, 2012*
*Submitted with First Revisions December 18, 2012*
*Submitted with Final Revisions January 15, 2013*

# INDEX

## A

access, 6, 21, 108
accessibility, 183
accommodation(s), 279, 315
accounting, 23, 150, 193
accreditation, 151
acculturation, 307, 308, 318, 319, 323, 324
acid, 121
acquisition group, 45
acquisition phase, 41, 45
ACTH, 118, 120, 121, 123
activity level, 94, 96, 97, 100, 101, 102, 274
acute stress, 34
adaptability, 186, 192, 193
adaptation, 106, 128, 180, 190, 195, 224, 322
adjustment, 67, 94, 198, 199, 202, 208, 209, 210, 219, 231, 306, 312, 313, 320, 321
administrators, 112
adolescents, 5, 53, 64, 149, 241
adrenal gland, 120
adrenaline, 120
adulthood, 5, 262, 269, 277, 279
adults, 44, 94, 103, 105, 223, 225, 226, 227, 242, 258, 262, 263, 265, 270, 271, 273, 276, 277, 278, 279, 282
advancement, 32, 263
advertisements, 264
aerobic capacity, 237
aggression, 132, 174, 282, 302
AIMS, viii, 93, 95, 96, 97, 98, 99, 100, 101, 102, 222
alcohol abuse, 53
alcohol dependence, 213, 222
alertness, 45
alienation, 306
amenorrhea, 121, 128
American culture, 318
American Heart Association, 105

American Psychological Association, 115, 323
American Red Cross, 231, 240
anemia, 124
anger, 52, 53, 61, 62, 64, 124
ANOVA, 100, 101, 139, 231, 232, 233, 286, 292
antisocial behavior, 168, 169, 170, 174, 175
anxiety, 2, 3, 52, 87, 94, 104, 124, 246, 259, 282, 301, 302, 303
APA, 115, 241
appraisals, viii, 71, 76, 84, 85, 86, 87
aptitude, 148
Argentina, 309
arousal, 44
Asian countries, 198
aspiration, 154
assessment, ix, 2, 4, 7, 14, 117, 132, 138, 149, 177, 232
assessment tools, 4, 149
athletic identity, viii, 93, 94, 95, 96, 97, 99, 100, 101, 102, 104, 105, 106, 198, 199, 200, 204, 206, 207, 208, 218, 301
Athletic Identity Measurement Scale, viii, 93, 95, 97, 102, 106, 222
athleticism, 249
atmosphere, 110, 176
ATP, 199
attachment, 75, 133, 140, 144, 206, 216, 218
attitudes, 15, 69, 73, 81, 144, 167, 201, 204, 208, 246, 312
authority, 169
automaticity, 230
autonomic nervous system, 118, 119
autonomy, 16, 21, 28, 31, 32, 35, 52, 168, 208
avoidance, 4, 5, 9, 10, 11, 13, 17
awareness, xi, 31, 51, 55, 73, 75, 87, 115, 142, 166, 171, 172, 173, 180, 186, 187, 190, 191, 193, 194, 219, 272, 309

# Index

## B

background information, 98
bad day, 195
badminton, vii, 37, 38, 39, 41, 42, 43, 44, 45, 46, 47, 48, 49
banking, 210
barriers, 26, 32, 226, 227, 231, 238, 241, 263
base, viii, 35, 107, 239, 291
basic needs, 168
basketball players, viii, 175, 302, 305, 307, 308, 309, 311, 318, 321
beer, 290, 316
behavior modification, 172
behavioral change, 219, 241
behavioral sciences, 15
behaviors, xiii, 41, 53, 94, 95, 96, 102, 134, 166, 168, 169, 172, 173, 176, 211, 214, 222, 226, 227, 230, 237, 238, 240, 241, 277, 278, 281, 282, 283, 285, 298, 300, 301, 318
Belgium, 309
benchmarks, 271
benefits, xi, xii, 26, 37, 40, 48, 51, 94, 103, 109, 114, 141, 172, 173, 201, 214, 219, 220, 221, 225, 241, 245, 246, 247, 248, 250, 256, 257, 258, 259, 265, 274, 303, 315
benign, 301
beverages, 290, 298
bias, 23, 55, 231, 303
binding globulin, 121, 129
biofeedback, 42, 44, 48
biofeedback training, 44
bipolar disorder, 52
blame, 171, 306
blood, 120, 122, 123, 127, 129
blood pressure, 122, 127, 129
BMI, 264
board members, 21
body composition, 94, 103, 274
body dissatisfaction, 279
body fat, 128
body image, 106, 279
body weight, 249, 258
boredom, 274, 314
brain, 60, 120, 302
brand loyalty, 141
breakdown, 59
breathing, 237
brothers, 59, 296
burnout, ix, 20, 21, 30, 34, 35, 117, 118, 119, 120, 122, 124, 126, 127, 128, 224
business environment, 108, 109
businesses, 312

## C

campaigns, 300
cardiovascular disease, 94, 103
career development, 224
case studies, 306
case study, xi, 54, 179, 182, 183, 186, 192, 193, 195, 223, 227, 228, 239, 240, 242
categorization, xiii, 132, 281, 298
category a, 289
category d, 62, 300
causal relationship, 2, 3, 104, 282
causality, 174
causation, 274
CDC, 95, 97, 102, 105
cell phones, 113
Census, 264, 279
central nervous system, 123
certification, 21, 22, 32, 162
CFI, 249, 250, 255
Chad, 226, 241
challenges, 32, 53, 60, 62, 104, 112, 186, 188, 190, 226, 238, 249, 277, 306, 308, 311, 314, 316, 319, 321, 322, 323
charm, 290, 291, 296
chicken, 296
child athletes, 149, 157, 159, 160, 162
childhood, 161
children, x, 44, 68, 147, 148, 149, 152, 154, 156, 159, 161, 166, 171, 172, 174, 176, 241, 263, 270, 306, 314
Chile, 309
China, 309
Christianity, 67
chronic diseases, 94, 103
chronic fatigue, 68
clarity, 33, 310
classes, 45, 108
classification, 273
classroom, 5, 110, 112, 114, 174, 228, 240, 299
classroom environment, 240
clients, 109, 111, 113, 258, 274
climate(s), xi, 90, 165, 168, 169, 170, 173, 174, 175, 176, 278
clinical depression, 258
clothing, 282, 289, 307
cluster analysis, 246, 258
clusters, 153
codes, 162
coding, 23, 153, 184, 203
cognition, xi, 179, 184, 190, 195, 291, 292
cognitive development, 143, 171, 175
cognitive dissonance, 140, 143

# Index 327

cognitive perspective, 171
cognitive skills, xi, 179, 182, 187, 191, 192, 193
cognitive-behavioral therapy, 221
collaboration, 5
college athletics, viii, 67, 93
college campuses, 68
college students, xii, xiii, 52, 53, 67, 95, 116, 225, 226, 230, 241, 281, 284, 297, 301
colleges, 52, 315
combined effect, 286, 287, 288
commercial(s), 215, 290, 295
common symptoms, 126
communication, viii, 31, 32, 71, 72, 73, 75, 76, 77, 79, 81, 82, 83, 84, 85, 86, 87, 88, 90, 109, 112, 113, 194, 222, 274, 302, 308, 319
communication skills, 72, 88, 109
community(ies), x, xi, 1, 4, 26, 28, 29, 30, 105, 110, 113, 115, 135, 165, 169, 170, 171, 173, 223, 242, 275, 276, 300, 313, 314, 320
compassion, 213
compensation, 109
compensatory effect, 123
competition, x, 6, 13, 15, 22, 27, 39, 49, 66, 88, 98, 103, 118, 123, 127, 144, 147, 148, 156, 157, 159, 161, 168, 171, 176, 182, 230, 270, 276, 285, 299, 303, 309, 316, 317, 320
competitive sport, 94, 95, 103, 106, 156, 230
competitiveness, 102
competitors, 27, 60, 193
compilation, vii
complementarity, 86
complexity, 190, 191, 273
compliance, 39, 133, 143, 144, 172, 274
composition, 181
compounds, 120
comprehension, 79, 180
compulsion, 4, 222
computer, 80, 81, 291
computing, 209, 212, 216
conceptual model, 106, 224
conceptualization, 194, 320
concordance, 73
conditioning, xii, 38, 149, 160, 225, 228, 229, 230, 231, 233, 234, 236, 237, 238, 239, 315
confidentiality, 113, 152, 200
configuration, 64
conflict, 60, 61, 75, 159, 167, 172, 212, 213, 214
conformity, 166
congress, 175, 278
connectivity, 113
conscientiousness, 2
consensus, 71, 148, 176, 271, 310
consent, 22, 99, 183, 201, 229, 248, 284, 310

construction, 16, 176
consulting, ix, 107, 108, 109, 110, 111, 112, 113, 114, 115, 229, 275
consumers, 141, 300
consumption, xiii, 132, 141, 143, 144, 282, 289, 290, 298, 302
content analysis, 19, 30, 89
contextual interference, 42, 44, 47, 48
contingency, 4, 136, 190, 191
contradiction, 257
control condition, 39
control group, 39, 40, 43, 228
controlled trials, 277, 278
convergence, 150
conversations, 72, 75, 76, 86, 87, 183
conviction, 63
cooperation, 5, 97, 109
cooperative learning, 168, 170
coordination, 187, 192, 194
coping strategies, xii, 197, 198, 199, 200, 201, 202, 209, 212, 219, 222
correlation(s), 7, 8, 9, 11, 80, 81, 98, 99, 100, 138, 139, 140, 231, 233, 234, 250, 284, 286
correlation coefficient, 80, 233
cortex, ix, 117, 120
cortisol, 118, 120, 121, 122, 129
cost, 133, 165, 180, 256
cost-benefit analysis, 256
counseling, 52, 69, 113, 114, 116, 274
counseling psychology, 113, 114
creep, 61
criticism, 61, 65
cross-sectional study, 263
CST, 138
cues, 42, 43, 184, 192
cultural beliefs, 321
cultural identities, 308, 319
cultural influence, xii, 197, 199, 221, 222
cultural practices, 307
culture, 76, 79, 106, 108, 191, 224, 306, 307, 308, 309, 310, 312, 313, 314, 318, 319, 320, 321, 322
curricula, 13
curriculum, 5, 108, 112, 114, 169, 228
customer relations, 143
customers, 208
cyclical process, 152
cycling, 5, 119, 123, 264
cytokines, 118, 122, 123, 128
Czech Republic, 223

## D

damages, 123

328 Index

dance, 17, 97
danger, 150
data analysis, 34, 67, 99, 152, 153, 158, 185, 203, 248
data collection, 21, 22, 23, 33, 150, 152, 153, 184, 202, 220, 229, 230, 248, 284
data set, 137, 284
database, 68, 69
deaths, 52
decision makers, 194
decision-making process, xii, 83, 197, 198, 204, 205, 206, 207, 212, 213, 220
decoding, 73
deficit, 52
demographic characteristics, 6, 246, 248
demographic data, 15
Denmark, vii, ix, xi, 117, 179, 191, 194, 195, 324
Department of Education, 71, 89
dependent variable, 9, 10, 138, 236, 286, 287, 292, 293
depression, xi, 2, 14, 17, 51, 52, 53, 54, 55, 56, 59, 60, 61, 62, 63, 64, 65, 66, 68, 69, 94, 103, 104, 118, 124, 207, 213, 278
depressive symptoms, 53, 54, 68
depth, viii, ix, xi, 51, 53, 66, 75, 107, 110, 152, 157, 182, 193, 199, 203, 305, 321
detachment, 118
detectable, 272
detection, 148, 159, 162
developmental process, ix, 117, 148, 320
diabetes, 94, 103
dialogues, 184
dichotomy, 160
diet, 276
differential diagnosis, 121
directors, 32
disclosure, 73, 201, 222
discomfort, 140
discrimination, 144
diseases, 94, 123, 124
disorder, 52
dissatisfaction, 278
dissonance, 140
distress, 60, 69
distribution, 80
diversity, vii, 33, 105, 174
doctors, 315
dominance, 30
donors, 110
drawing, xi, 127, 159, 179
dream, 306
drugs, 63
dynamic factors, 21

## E

ecology, 195
editors, 150
education, 33, 79, 88, 109, 114, 149, 151, 158, 159, 161, 162, 169, 170, 172, 174, 176, 182, 277, 310
educational background, 115
elementary school, 169
elite sports, viii, 71
Emancipator, 75
emotion, 210, 212, 213, 214
emotional exhaustion, 59
emotional experience, 200
emotional health, 320
emotional reactions, 209, 217, 221, 222
emotional responses, 198, 203, 205, 209, 216, 282
emotional stability, 2, 16
emotional state, 52, 80, 242
emotional well-being, 7
empathy, 75, 109, 171, 173, 190, 213
employees, 32, 199, 215
employers, 114
employment, 124, 222
empowerment, 32, 247
encouragement, 136
enculturation, 307, 308, 318, 319
endocrine system, 120
endorsements, 257
endurance, xiii, 118, 120, 121, 123, 129, 149, 237, 241, 242, 246, 261, 264, 272, 277
energy, 4, 119, 120, 124, 126, 128, 135, 140, 141, 271
England, 88, 143, 165, 175, 309, 324
environment(s), 44, 48, 108, 109, 110, 114, 118, 154, 157, 163, 167, 171, 175, 180, 194, 195, 216, 222, 240, 270, 271, 276, 299, 301, 311, 314, 318
environmental characteristics, 169
environmental factors, 42
environmental influences, 167, 222
epidemic, 243
equality, 29
equipment, 44
equity, 174
estrogen, 121
ethics, 90, 151
ethnic groups, 307
ethnicity, 272
etiology, ix, 117, 118, 119
etiquette, 114
Europe, 198, 307, 309, 324
European Union, 127
everyday life, 68, 166, 173, 174, 175, 323

evidence, x, xii, 3, 29, 33, 45, 114, 147, 148, 149, 157, 159, 161, 199, 218, 219, 221, 245, 262, 263
evolution, 118, 276
examinations, 124
exchange relationship, ix, 107, 108, 109, 114, 166
excitation, 44
execution, 43, 83
exercise participation, 226, 242, 262, 270, 271, 277
exercise performance, 227, 238, 240
exercise programs, 274, 279
exertion, 118, 123, 127
experimental design, 33, 228
expertise, xi, 87, 88, 91, 159, 179, 180, 181, 182, 185, 190, 192, 193, 194, 195, 196, 230
exposure, viii, 53, 107, 110, 112, 113, 149, 172, 190, 191, 228, 229, 237, 238
extraction, 23
extraversion, 2, 3, 270
extrinsic motivation, 168, 177, 274, 275, 276, 279

## F

Facebook, 113
face-to-face interaction, 108
facial expression, 188
factor analysis, xii, 2, 71, 80, 81, 90, 245, 249, 265
fairness, 17
faith, 159
families, 210, 241, 306, 313, 314, 322
family life, 323
family members, 31, 66, 132, 306
family support, 295
fat, 123, 324
fatty acids, 120
fear(s), 65, 116, 198, 206, 207, 209, 216, 221
feelings, 21, 28, 32, 47, 54, 59, 60, 61, 62, 64, 72, 74, 75, 76, 80, 81, 118, 133, 167, 168, 171, 198, 206, 207, 208, 210, 214, 219, 273, 274, 313
fibers, 123
fidelity, 229
Filipino, 278
financial, 29, 133, 209, 306, 307, 314
financial support, 29
Finland, vii, ix, 117, 119, 121, 124, 309
fitness, 149, 161, 226, 230, 231, 232, 238, 239, 247, 262, 263, 264, 265, 268, 269, 270, 273, 276
five-factor model, 2, 17
flexibility, 26, 187
flight, 43, 315
fluid, 307
food, xiii, 282, 289, 290, 294, 296, 298, 307, 311

football, 5, 12, 14, 54, 97, 131, 151, 154, 156, 157, 165, 168, 175, 176, 191, 223, 292, 293, 294, 295, 296, 297, 298, 299, 300, 306, 323
force, 4, 34, 187
formal education, 79, 149, 157, 159
formation, 20, 134, 185, 198, 218
foundations, 48, 150
France, 223, 309, 313, 323
franchise, 300
freedom, 142, 215, 217
freedom of choice, 215
funding, 29, 149

## G

gender differences, xiii, 9, 12, 52, 100, 102, 141, 142, 261, 263, 275, 278
gender role, 12, 272
gene expression, 129
generalizability, 302, 310
Germany, 309, 312, 313, 314, 315, 317
gestures, 188, 291, 292
gifted, 108, 148, 162
giftedness, 161, 162
global competition, 306
global scale, 279
globalization, 305, 323
glucocorticoids, 121
glucose, 120, 123
glucose regulation, 129
glycogen, 123
goal attainment, 84, 87, 257
goal setting, 47, 104, 172, 226, 227, 229, 230, 232, 237, 238
goal-setting, xii, 225, 237, 239
God, 213, 302
Godin Leisure Time Exercise Questionnaire, viii, 93, 97
governance, 29, 31, 32
grades, 3, 5, 228
graduate education, viii, 107
graduate program, 110, 114, 115
graduate students, ix, 107, 108, 110, 114, 115
grass, 154
Greece, 175, 309
grounding, 148
group identification, 144
group identity, 144
group membership, 134, 135
grouping, 23, 169, 285, 292, 293
growth, 75, 113, 115, 118, 120, 121, 129, 149, 159, 161, 305, 318, 320, 321
growth hormone, 118, 120, 121

guardian, 175
guessing, 57
guidance, 66, 189, 190, 193
guidelines, 94, 104, 115, 149, 183, 200, 233
guilt, 175
gymnastics, 54, 223
gymnasts, 17, 223, 224
gyms, 315

## H

hair, 289
happiness, 53, 132
harmony, 4, 6
healing, 124
health, viii, xii, xiii, 52, 53, 66, 67, 68, 90, 93, 94,
    95, 96, 103, 106, 123, 124, 127, 128, 224, 226,
    227, 245, 247, 248, 256, 257, 258, 261, 262, 263,
    265, 268, 269, 270, 271, 272, 275, 312
health care, 90
health condition, 127
health psychology, 128, 224
heart rate, 118, 121, 122, 123, 129
height, 149, 157
helplessness, 62
hermeneutics, 203
heterogeneity, 22
high school, 4, 5, 13, 15, 226, 229, 241, 242, 295,
    307, 315
higher education, 68, 198
hiring, 115
Hispanics, 322, 323
homes, 310
homogeneity, 9
Hops, 12, 14
hormone(s), 118, 120, 121, 127, 128
hormone levels, 120
host, 312, 313, 314, 318, 319, 320
hostility, 124, 282
hotel, 315
housing, 315
human, 20, 30, 34, 35, 53, 58, 75, 128, 129, 161,
    211, 241, 256, 276, 279, 308, 309, 311
human agency, 241
human behavior, 34, 161, 276
human development, 279
human experience, 53, 58, 311
human health, 256
human subjects, 309
husband, 28
hygiene, 295
hyperactivity, 52
hypersensitivity, 122

hypnosis, 38, 41, 46, 49
hypogonadism, 121
hypothalamus, ix, 117, 120, 123, 128
hypothesis, 102, 128, 135, 140, 223, 233, 234, 237,
    239, 269, 283

## I

Iceland, 309
ideal, 79, 156
identity foreclosure, 197, 204
idiosyncratic, 123
illusion, 87
image, 48, 108, 111, 124, 278, 279
imagery, vii, 37, 38, 39, 40, 44, 46, 47, 49, 226, 227,
    230, 232, 233, 234, 237, 238, 239, 241, 242
imitation, 158, 189
immune function, 128
immune system, 122
immunoglobulin, 118, 122
improvements, 40, 42, 76, 227, 228, 231, 234, 236,
    237, 238, 239
in vivo, 153
incidence, 52
income, 272, 307
increased competition, 52
independence, 63, 182, 271, 319
independent variable, 9, 137
individual development, 198, 205
individual differences, 122
individual rights, 167
individualism, 166, 171
individualization, 274
individualized instruction, 180
Indonesia, 309
industry, 111, 141
ineffectiveness, 118
inertia, 124
infection, 118, 119, 122, 126
inferences, 274
inflammation, 123
information processing, 181
informed consent, 22, 98, 152
inhibition, 119
initiation, 262, 275
injury(ies), 17, 55, 60, 61, 62, 63, 64, 66, 115, 200,
    215, 263
insecurity, 314
insomnia, 126
instinct, 157, 159
institutions, 104, 114
instructional feedback, vii, 37, 44
insulin, 94, 118, 120

insulin sensitivity, 94
integration, 195, 306
intelligence, 2, 196
intentionality, 90
interaction effect(s), 101, 138, 265
interaction process, 73
interdependence, 85, 208
interface, 90
interference, 44, 48, 49, 52
internal consistency, 7, 97, 136, 231
internal processes, 168
internalization, 4, 53, 133, 144
internationalization, 88
interpersonal communication, 88
interpersonal factors, 19
interpersonal relationships, 65, 108
interrelations, 316
intervention, xii, 20, 39, 41, 43, 44, 48, 53, 88, 124,
    197, 226, 227, 228, 229, 230, 231, 232, 233, 234,
    236, 237, 238, 239, 240, 242, 276, 278
intervention strategies, 226, 227, 276
intrinsic motivation, 90, 158, 168, 173, 226, 273,
    275, 276, 277
intrinsic rewards, 173
introversion, 257
investment(s), 21, 29, 32, 33, 133, 162, 182
invitation to participate, 247
isolation, 198, 220, 313, 319
Israel, vii, 37, 176
issues, 18, 20, 29, 55, 61, 63, 64, 65, 66, 67, 87, 94,
    95, 98, 103, 104, 152, 158, 160, 176, 198, 204,
    209, 210, 212, 213, 215, 219, 223, 224, 227, 237,
    306, 308, 313, 314, 320, 321
Italy, 309, 312

## J

Japan, 220
job performance, 16, 143
job satisfaction, 16
justification, 106, 140

## K

Korea, 199, 200, 220

## L

labeling, 150
lack of control, 61, 64
lactic acid, 121
language barrier, 313, 319

languages, 133
later life, 279
laws, 81, 296
lead, x, xi, 1, 4, 40, 44, 53, 60, 61, 94, 115, 118, 120,
    123, 142, 147, 148, 149, 162, 179, 181, 186, 188,
    194, 218, 227, 228, 256, 282, 294, 299, 301, 314
leadership, 72, 74, 75, 88, 90, 115, 170, 317
leadership style, 72, 74, 75, 90
learners, vii, 37, 43, 47
learning, vii, xi, 6, 37, 38, 41, 43, 44, 45, 46, 47, 48,
    49, 72, 76, 77, 79, 83, 88, 89, 108, 110, 111, 114,
    115, 148, 151, 159, 161, 169, 170, 174, 175, 179,
    181, 182, 183, 184, 189, 190, 192, 193, 216, 227,
    230, 237, 238, 240, 301, 307, 317, 318, 321
learning environment, 148
learning process, vii, xi, 37, 179, 184, 193
Lebanon, 309
legal issues, 115
legislation, 162
legs, 295
leisure, 241, 262, 271, 302, 314
leisure time, 271, 314
lens, 307
lesson plan, 229
life changes, 26, 202, 215
life course, 278
life experiences, 202, 307
lifestyle changes, 215, 216, 217, 218
lifetime, 52, 199, 228, 232, 234, 238, 239, 240, 263
light, 21, 98, 114, 120, 158, 184, 239, 246, 257, 262,
    273, 296, 300, 307, 308, 309, 319
Likert scale, 97, 230, 231, 273
lipids, 94
liver, 123, 160
loans, 210
local community, 26
locus, 16, 169, 241, 299
loneliness, 59, 60, 213, 220, 313
longitudinal study, 104
loss of appetite, 119
love, 26, 58, 291, 323
loyalty, 135, 143
Luxemburg, 127
lymphocytes, 122

## M

magnitude, 133, 233, 250
major depression, 67
major issues, 28
Major League Baseball, 300, 303
majority, 26, 30, 53, 86, 103, 198, 264, 272, 308
majority group, 134

malnutrition, 119
man, 111, 208, 315
management, 6, 88, 184, 265, 267, 272, 278, 282, 317, 319
manipulation, 151
MANOVA, 9, 10, 137, 138
mantle, 296
mapping, 81, 203
marketability, 108, 109, 115
marketing, ix, 107, 108, 110, 113, 116, 132, 282, 300, 302
marriage, 264
married couples, 89
martial art, 182, 195
Marx, 2, 17
masculinity, 106
mass, 242, 269, 272
matrix, 80, 81
matter, vii, 63, 156, 181, 185, 192, 240, 295, 314
maturation process, 149
measurement(s), x, 35, 53, 90, 95, 120, 121, 124, 143, 147, 148, 150, 153, 158, 160, 241, 242, 323
media, 134, 166, 303
median, 245
medical, ix, 117, 124, 127
medical history, 127
medication, 68
medicine, 67, 117
membership, 134, 143, 171
memory, 42
mental age, 154
mental energy, 60
mental health, xi, 5, 16, 51, 52, 53, 54, 225, 277
mental illness, 53
mental image, 40, 49
mental imagery, 40, 49
mental state, 124, 188, 193
mentor, 114, 115
mentoring, 88
mentorship, 25, 109
merchandise, 300
Merleau-Ponty, 308, 311, 323
messages, 73, 98
messenger RNA, 123
meta-analysis, 3, 16, 144, 259
metabolism, 118, 271
methodology, x, 71, 76, 79, 80, 88, 90, 104, 147, 150, 153, 230
Mexico, 309
Microsoft, 7
middle class, 151
migration, viii, 305, 306, 307, 308, 318, 322, 323, 324

military, 121, 129
minorities, 322
misconceptions, 54
misuse, 68, 149
modelling, 48
models, xi, 18, 20, 30, 148, 156, 158, 161, 162, 179, 187, 189, 194, 211, 250, 271, 299
moderate activity, 98
moderators, xii, 225
Montana, xiii
mood change, 119
mood states, 2, 118, 123, 124, 128
mood swings, 65
moral behavior, x, 165, 166, 168, 169, 176
moral development, 166, 176
moral judgment, 176
moral reasoning, 166, 174
morality, x, 165, 166, 167, 171, 172, 173, 174, 175
mortality, 271
motivation, xiii, 19, 21, 23, 31, 33, 34, 75, 91, 105, 124, 161, 168, 169, 174, 176, 177, 209, 210, 226, 240, 246, 247, 256, 257, 258, 261, 262, 263, 268, 269, 270, 271, 272, 273, 274, 275, 276, 277, 278, 279, 306, 312, 318, 324
motor behavior, 49
motor skills, 48, 49, 156
motor task, 41, 49
multidimensional, 102, 106, 133, 148, 176, 177, 216
multiple factors, 123
multiple regression analyses, 234
multiplication, 77
multivariate analysis, 9, 17, 137
muscle strength, 120
muscles, 104, 222, 302, 316
music, 59, 68, 181, 289, 291
mutuality, 72, 74, 75, 85, 86, 87

## N

narratives, 61
National Basketball Association, 300, 307, 322
National Institute of Mental Health, 52, 68
natural killer cell, 122
negative emotions, 198, 206, 213, 216, 221, 239
negative influences, 215, 222
negative mood, 123, 246
negative outcomes, 94, 219
neglect, 186
negotiating, 52, 66
negotiation, 194, 322
nervousness, 301
networking, 109, 110, 114, 115
neuroendocrine system, 119, 120

# Index

neuromuscular loading, ix, 117
neurons, 120, 121
neutral, 79
New England, 296
New Zealand, 309
next generation, 182
non-athletes, viii, x, 1, 2, 5, 10, 11, 13, 14, 69, 93,
94, 96, 100, 101, 102, 103, 208, 276
non-clinical population, 246
normal distribution, 80
North America, vii, 20, 145, 162, 198, 272
Norway, vii, ix, 1, 4, 5, 13, 71, 79, 309
novelty seeking, 4, 9, 12
nursing, 172, 175, 310
nutrition, 264

## O

obesity, 227, 243, 272
observed behavior, 168
obstacles, 150, 319
occupational health, 119
officials, x, 19, 20, 21, 22, 23, 24, 25, 26, 27, 28, 29,
30, 31, 32, 33, 34, 61, 94, 166, 171, 173
omission, 33
openness, 318
operations, 28, 181, 189, 192
opportunities, viii, ix, 26, 28, 29, 31, 32, 107, 108,
109, 110, 111, 112, 114, 141, 151, 159, 172, 187,
190, 192, 220, 226, 227, 230, 270, 271, 299, 305,
306, 307, 314, 319, 322
optimal performance, 14, 32
orchestration, xi, 179, 190, 192, 194
organ, 118, 119
organizational guidelines, 13
organize, 47, 66, 77
osteoporosis, 94, 121
overlap, 186
overtraining, ix, 117, 118, 119, 120, 121, 122, 123,
124, 126, 127, 128, 129, 263
oxygen, 119, 120, 122, 123, 160

## P

Pacific, 97
pain, 16, 57, 61, 62, 63, 217
paints, 298
parallel, 227
parasympathetic activity, 122
parents, 21, 136, 161, 213, 314
participant observation, xi, 33, 179, 183
path model, 257

pathology, 263
pattern recognition, 181
pedagogy, 322
peer relationship, 35
peer review, 56
perceived control, 215
perceived health, 240
perceived outcome, 247, 257
percentile, 30
perfectionism, 61, 65, 242
performance appraisal, viii, 71, 72, 76, 79, 83, 84,
85, 86, 87
performers, xi, 69, 165, 166, 169, 170, 171, 172,
173, 180, 320
permission, 97, 183
perpetration, 174
perseverance, 226
personal accounts, 32
personal autonomy, 31
personal development, 169, 170, 312, 318, 319
personal goals, 242
personal hygiene, 295
personal identity, ix, 131, 133, 135, 138, 140, 142
personal life, 311, 319
personality, ix, 1, 2, 4, 5, 7, 9, 10, 11, 12, 13, 14, 15,
16, 17, 66, 73, 111, 112, 144, 161, 174, 205, 257,
270, 276
personality characteristics, 4, 11, 14, 257
personality dimensions, ix, 1, 4, 12, 13, 14
personality factors, 2, 258, 270
personality measures, 11, 13
personality research, 1, 4
personality traits, 2, 11, 14
persuasion, 227, 238
phagocytosis, 122
phenomenology, 53, 66, 67, 68, 150, 203, 308, 322,
323
physical activity, viii, 12, 15, 23, 69, 93, 94, 95, 96,
97, 98, 99, 100, 101, 102, 103, 104, 105, 106,
121, 122, 162, 169, 176, 232, 233, 240, 241, 242,
262, 269, 273, 276, 277, 278, 279
physical education, 26, 40, 43, 44, 45, 89, 169, 241,
242
physical environment, 314
physical exercise, 118, 119, 120, 121, 122, 123, 127,
278
physical fitness, 149, 162, 172, 231, 241
physical health, 103, 256, 257, 270
physical well-being, 257
physiological, 161
physiological arousal, 302
pilot study, 116
pitch, 111, 115, 291

playing, viii, 60, 62, 65, 111, 115, 154, 156, 157, 181, 183, 184, 185, 186, 189, 191, 200, 210, 212, 215, 216, 289, 290, 305, 306, 307, 308, 309, 311, 314, 315, 316, 317, 318, 319, 321
Poland, 309
policy, 151
policy makers, 151
politics, 29, 32
poor performance, 60, 61
population, xii, 10, 13, 33, 52, 53, 54, 66, 94, 95, 96, 97, 102, 227, 245, 246, 265, 274
Portugal, 309
positive attitudes, 247
positive behaviors, 168
positive correlation, 98, 135, 139, 234
positive emotions, 217, 246
positive feedback, 43
positive interactions, 110, 167
positive mental health, 52
positive mood, 2, 259
positive relationship, ix, 11, 95, 96, 102, 104, 107, 108, 109, 111, 144, 145, 194, 238, 283, 316
positivism, 109
praxis, 323
prayer, 67, 289
precursor cells, 123
predictor variables, 234, 236, 286, 287, 288
pregnancy, 66
preparation, 34, 37, 38, 98, 103, 124, 205, 209, 210, 212, 215, 216, 218, 275, 301
prestige, 323
prevention, 68, 120, 123, 124, 241, 277
principles, 167, 172, 173, 203
private schools, 5
probability, 273
problem-focused coping, 209, 212, 219
problem-solving, 134, 171, 219
professional development, viii, 88, 305, 312
professionalism, 109, 110, 111, 113
professionals, ix, 38, 107, 108, 109, 110, 111, 113, 199, 229, 258, 282, 301
profit, 5, 13, 34
profitability, 300
programming, 94, 104, 241, 274, 275
pro-inflammatory, 123
project, viii, xii, 81, 109, 194, 277, 278, 301
prolactin, 120, 121
prosocial behavior, 144, 168, 169
protection, 162, 219
protective role, 103
protein synthesis, 120
PST, xii, 225, 237, 239, 240
psychiatric disorders, 52

psychological association, 224
psychological development, 149, 160, 320
psychological distress, 67
psychological health, 247
psychological processes, 221
psychological resources, 257
psychological well-being, 141, 144, 145, 263, 270
psychologist, 111, 116
psychometric properties, 7, 176, 248, 257
psychopathology, 69
psychosocial factors, 246
psychotherapy, 52, 54
puberty, 157, 158
public health, 94, 105
public schools, 174
publishing, 111
punishment, 167, 168, 319

## Q

qualitative research, 33, 34, 35, 53, 54, 67, 68, 69, 76, 88, 150, 161, 162, 195, 294, 309
quality of life, 271
query, 247
questioning, 60, 75, 76, 84, 184
questionnaire, xiii, 5, 6, 15, 22, 39, 74, 89, 90, 98, 118, 123, 124, 126, 127, 136, 137, 176, 230, 231, 248, 264, 265, 281, 284, 285, 300
quizzes, 228

## R

race, 98, 246, 247, 248, 257, 258
racing, 58, 161
radio, 140, 291, 292, 297
rating scale, 7
reactions, 122, 132, 201, 213, 217, 222, 301
reading, 23, 184, 203, 229, 320
reality, 73, 75, 87, 112, 176
reasoning, 169, 172, 174, 301
recall, 185, 195
receptors, 122
reciprocal interactions, 208, 222
reciprocity, 75
recognition, 29, 53, 168, 169, 173, 192, 249, 256
recommendations, xi, 31, 51, 194, 236, 274, 309, 320
recovery, 68, 118, 119, 120, 121, 122, 123, 124, 126, 127, 128
recreation, 105, 123, 275
recreational, xiii, 41, 46, 111, 131, 143, 246, 258, 261
recruiting, 31, 132, 151

referees, 30, 34, 35
reflective practice, 177, 321
reflexes, 196
reflexivity, 320
regeneration, 128
regression, 42, 99, 100, 234, 236, 243, 265, 267, 268, 269, 278, 286, 287, 297
regression analysis, 99, 100, 243, 278, 286, 297
regression equation, 287
regression model, 268
rehabilitation, 61, 62, 66
reinforcement, 262, 271
reinforcement contingencies, 262
rejection, 65, 124
relatives, 306
relaxation, xii, 39, 42, 44, 225, 230, 232, 233, 237, 239
relevance, 152
reliability, 6, 13, 16, 98, 133, 137, 161, 162, 284
religion, 212, 213, 296
religious beliefs, 307
reproduction, 121
reputation, 109, 110, 171
reputation enhancement, 109
requirements, 34, 48, 170, 309
researchers, 2, 3, 20, 21, 43, 54, 80, 150, 151, 180, 182, 184, 198, 199, 200, 203, 218, 220, 222, 226, 246, 275, 283, 299, 300, 307, 309, 310
resilience, 2
resistance, 127, 264, 323
resources, xii, 20, 53, 54, 148, 149, 157, 162, 197, 198, 204, 205, 209, 210, 212, 214, 215, 218, 219, 221, 222, 315, 320
response, 7, 13, 20, 22, 23, 25, 28, 33, 44, 61, 118, 121, 122, 123, 127, 128, 136, 137, 139, 143, 166, 172, 180, 187, 190, 191, 201, 203, 265, 273, 274, 284, 285, 295, 297, 307, 308, 318
response format, 7
response time, 273
restaurants, 314, 318
restrictions, 59, 217
restructuring, 26, 173
retirement, xii, 26, 52, 55, 63, 94, 95, 96, 104, 105, 106, 197, 198, 199, 200, 201, 202, 204, 205, 206, 207, 208, 209, 210, 212, 213, 214, 215, 216, 217, 218, 219, 220, 221, 222, 223, 224, 264, 271
retribution, 65
rewards, 273
rights, 167
risk(s), xi, 51, 53, 69, 94, 103, 105, 112, 169, 176, 201, 220
risk factors, 53, 69
RMSEA, 249, 250, 255

role conflict, 52, 68
root(s), 80, 154
routines, 47, 49, 202, 216, 227, 230, 282, 285
rowing, 79
rugby, 20, 34, 150, 151, 152, 154, 155, 156, 157, 223, 306
rules, 26, 27, 151, 166, 167, 186, 210, 217, 306, 317, 320

## S

sadness, 59, 67
safety, 53, 237
saturation, 23, 151, 152, 309, 322
Saudi Arabia, 309
Scandinavia, 195
schemata, 192
scholarship, xiii, 63, 278
school, 4, 5, 6, 12, 13, 14, 17, 22, 43, 44, 59, 61, 79, 112, 121, 157, 158, 174, 241, 270, 289, 306, 314, 315
science, 175, 195, 242, 324
scope, 21, 275
secretion, 118, 120, 122, 123
security, 319
sedentary behavior, 227, 263
sedentary lifestyle, 312
self-awareness, 218, 307
self-concept, 17, 95, 106, 131, 133, 140, 219
self-confidence, 2, 39, 119, 247
self-doubt, xi, 51, 56, 60, 61, 64
self-efficacy, ix, xii, 16, 107, 108, 109, 110, 111, 116, 225, 226, 227, 228, 230, 231, 232, 233, 234, 237, 238, 239, 240, 241, 242, 247, 299
self-esteem, x, 1, 3, 4, 7, 9, 11, 12, 14, 15, 16, 66, 118, 134, 143, 145, 224, 226, 256, 257
self-evaluations, 16
self-identity, xii, 94, 140, 197, 199, 206, 220
self-image, 108, 111, 112
self-improvement, 168, 169
self-interest, 26
self-knowledge, 219, 247
self-presentation, 145, 242
self-reflection, 55
self-report data, 262
self-reports, 69
self-worth, 247
semen, 120, 128
seminars, 28
semi-structured interviews, x, 147, 201, 306
sensations, 42
sensitivity, 126, 127, 193, 302, 323
servers, 47, 48

services, 69, 109, 112, 113, 115, 301, 315, 320
sex, 12, 15, 105, 115, 121, 129, 278, 291
sex differences, 12, 278
sex role, 15
sexual behavior, 291
shape, 21, 182
showing, 48, 85, 134, 135, 156, 320
siblings, 136
significance level, 7
signs, 62, 120, 126, 289
silver, 133
single test, 126
skeletal muscle, 128, 129
skewness, 7
skill acquisition, 49, 226
skills training, xii, 3, 111, 172, 225, 227, 229, 239, 240, 242
skin, 122
sleep disorders, 124
sleep disturbance, 118, 119, 126
smoking, 213, 222
soccer, 2, 16, 90, 97, 111, 132, 162, 163, 169, 174, 176, 181, 182, 191, 306, 323, 324
social acceptance, 4
social activities, 53, 180
social benefits, 247
social capital, 113, 116
social category, 256
social circle, 60
social comparison, 169, 170, 219, 223
social construct, 151
social constructivism, 151
social context, 189, 194, 220
social contract, 167, 172, 173
social desirability, 13, 23
social development, 161
social environment, 206
social group, 206, 207, 217, 218
social identity, 133, 134, 143, 144, 198, 207, 218, 220
social identity theory, 144
social influence, 140, 143
social interactions, 181, 265
social learning, 166
social life, 205, 206, 217, 313
social network, 108, 116, 202, 204, 205, 207, 209, 210, 212, 213, 216, 217, 218, 219, 220, 306
social norms, 108, 141, 173, 222, 272
social obligations, 231
social relations, 3, 59, 108, 257
social relationships, 3, 59, 108, 257
social roles, 171
social situations, 273

social status, 263
social support, 198, 205, 209, 210, 211, 212, 213, 214, 215, 221, 223, 224, 319
social support network, 198, 209, 211, 215, 221
social theory, 108, 115
socialization, ix, 52, 131, 132, 133, 134, 135, 139, 141, 142, 143, 175, 263
socializing agent, 135, 138, 141, 142
society, 28, 88, 167, 168, 173, 176, 223
sociology, 116
software, 98
solidarity, 109
solution, 71, 80, 81, 171
South Africa, 120
South Korea, vii, xi
Spain, 309, 312
specialization, 16, 149, 160
speech, 111
spending, 25, 186, 220
spin, 38
spine, 217
sport psychologists, 33, 66, 116
sportspersonship, x, 165, 166, 168, 173, 174, 175, 176, 177
Sri Lanka, 165, 175
stability, 2, 306
staffing, 20
standard deviation, 7, 80, 137, 250, 286, 293, 294
standard error, 268
state(s), 2, 4, 42, 44, 49, 69, 72, 83, 85, 86, 118, 123, 124, 128, 140, 145, 149, 151, 189, 204, 227, 246, 258, 299, 319, 321
statistics, 68, 90, 99, 232, 233, 250, 259
stereotypes, 17, 54
steroids, 123
stimulation, 118, 120, 121
stock, 133
strategy use, 49, 198
stress, ix, 20, 30, 34, 51, 52, 53, 62, 111, 117, 118, 119, 120, 121, 123, 126, 127, 128, 170, 185, 209, 210, 211, 212, 213, 214, 215, 217, 219, 222, 227, 237, 257, 265, 268, 299, 302, 306, 314, 319, 320, 323
stress fracture, 121
stress reactions, 209
stressful events, 34
stressful life events, 64
stressors, viii, xi, 20, 51, 52, 53, 118, 123, 305, 306, 319
stroke, 228, 229, 231, 232, 233, 236, 237, 239
structural changes, 28
structural equation modeling, 258

structure, 15, 23, 26, 31, 32, 54, 56, 58, 67, 77, 90, 96, 106, 155, 160, 172, 195, 224, 249, 258, 311
structuring, 184, 192
student motivation, 174
style, 75, 134, 152, 186, 189, 307, 316, 317, 320
subjective experience, 176
subjective meanings, 79
subjective well-being, 219
subjectivity, 76, 79, 80, 308
substance abuse, 52
substitutes, 186
substitutions, 186
suicidal ideation, 52, 53
suicide, 52, 68
supervision, 34, 115, 116, 190
supervisor, 115
suppression, 120
surveillance, 97, 105
susceptibility, 103
sympathy, 213
symptoms, ix, 52, 53, 54, 65, 67, 68, 69, 117, 118, 119, 120, 123, 126
syndrome, 118, 120, 121, 124, 126, 127, 128
synthesis, 69

## T

tactics, 75, 185, 186, 187, 190, 193
Taiwan, 106
talent, x, 16, 147, 148, 149, 154, 156, 157, 158, 160, 161, 162, 194, 195, 307
target, 27, 31, 39, 40, 41, 86, 151, 171, 185, 265, 285, 292, 300
target behavior, 285
target population, 265
target zone, 39
teachers, 42, 180, 181, 182
team members, xi, 171, 179, 180, 186, 190, 191, 192, 193
team sports, xi, 3, 5, 10, 12, 49, 90, 179, 182, 194, 301
teams, ix, xi, 79, 124, 131, 136, 140, 141, 143, 144, 145, 148, 151, 171, 175, 179, 182, 183, 186, 191, 199, 208, 215, 216, 220, 282, 292, 298, 299, 307, 314, 315, 316, 318
techniques, ix, xii, 3, 20, 27, 33, 35, 46, 48, 55, 67, 75, 90, 107, 108, 150, 153, 186, 225, 229, 231, 232, 234, 236, 237, 239
technology(ies), 113, 116
teens, 297
telephone, 201, 222, 223
temperament, 4, 5, 7, 9, 10, 12, 13, 15, 16
temperature, 45, 237

tempo, x, 147, 148
tenants, 111
tennis, vii, xi, 37, 38, 39, 40, 41, 42, 43, 44, 45, 46, 47, 48, 49, 97, 166, 197, 199, 200, 201, 204, 205, 206, 207, 208, 210, 212, 213, 216, 218, 220
tension, 2, 52, 124, 302
tenure, 315
test scores, 231
testing, 9, 17, 33, 39, 41, 46, 81, 104, 182, 184, 199, 231, 284, 285, 301, 323
testis, 128
testosterone, 118, 120, 121
test-retest reliability, 97, 98
therapist, 72
therapy, 224
third dimension, 133
thoughts, 41, 47, 62, 72, 74, 76, 82, 140, 168, 207, 211, 212, 213
threats, 153
throws, 291
thyroid, 124
time commitment, 58, 256
time constraints, 26, 311
time frame, 30, 271
time periods, 33
TNF-α, 122
top-down, 308
training programs, 38, 46, 47, 108
traits, ix, 14, 15, 16, 109, 110, 149
transcendence, 5
transcription, 23, 152, 310
transcripts, viii, 23, 56, 152, 203, 305, 310, 311
translation, 150, 203
transmission, 190, 322
transparency, 28, 29, 153
transportation, 312, 315
treatment, ix, xi, 28, 29, 51, 67, 117, 228, 229, 258
trial, 41, 45, 111, 149, 203, 242, 277
triangulation, 150, 184, 203
tribalism, 136, 137
tumor necrosis factor, 122
Turkey, 309, 313, 318
turnover, 296
tutoring, 152
type 2 diabetes, 94

## U

UK, x, xi, 115, 147, 149, 151, 160, 161, 162, 163, 165, 194, 195, 197
underlying mechanisms, 257, 303
unhappiness, 132
uniform, 170, 300

338 Index

United Kingdom, vii, 147, 275
United States (USA), vii, xi, xii, xiii, 105, 107, 127,
132, 220, 242, 228, 243, 258, 259, 261, 262, 264,
269, 272, 276, 279
universe, 76
universities, 52, 284
unstructured interviews, xi, 51

## V

validation, 16, 18, 89, 104, 144, 177, 230, 243, 276,
303
variables, 4, 6, 7, 8, 9, 10, 13, 18, 45, 46, 88, 90, 97,
134, 151, 174, 198, 228, 229, 235, 249, 250, 257,
270, 279, 286, 287, 288, 299
variations, 46, 132, 320
varimax rotation, 80
vein, 320
velocity, 40, 46, 149, 157
Venezuela, 309
venue, 25
verbal persuasion, 227, 238
videos, 42, 237
videotape, 39, 41, 43, 48
violence, 12, 174
vision, 157
visualization, 39
vocalizations, xiii, 282, 289, 298
volleyball, 2, 35, 97, 242
vulnerability, 118

## W

waking, 122
walking, 311, 312

war, 289
watches, 296
water, 54, 59, 61, 62, 63, 229, 237, 296
wear, 113, 271, 294, 295, 300
weeping, 213
weight control, 246, 256, 272, 274, 279
weight gain, 65
weight loss, 240, 256, 272, 276
weight management, 227, 265, 268, 269, 271, 272,
274, 275, 276
weight reduction, 261, 263
welfare, 162
well-being, 4, 7, 11, 14, 16, 21, 241, 257, 258, 263,
271, 306
white blood cells, 122
wholesale, 33
windows, 149, 159
withdrawal, 122, 152
work environment, 217
workers, 118, 119, 207, 211, 213, 215
working class, 151
working hours, 124
working population, 119
work-related stress, 119
World Health Organization (WHO), 6, 7, 8, 9, 14
worldwide, 306
worry, 210
wrestling, 79, 97, 180, 182

## Y

Yale University, xiii
young adults, 17, 64, 67, 226, 242, 273
young people, 52
young women, 121, 269